Authorized Self-Study Guide
Cisco Voice over IP (CVoice)

Kevin Wallace

Cisco Press

800 East 96th Street
Indianapolis, IN 46240 USA

Cisco Voice over IP (CVoice)

Kevin Wallace

Published by:
Cisco Press
800 East 96th Street
Indianapolis, IN 46240 USA

Printed in the United States of America 1 2 3 4 5 6 7 8 9 0

First Printing August 2006

Library of Congress Cataloging-in-Publication Number: 2005936929

ISBN: 1-58705-262-8

Warning and Disclaimer

This book is designed to provide information about the Cisco Voice over IP (CVoice) certification topics. Every effort has been made to make this book as complete and as accurate as possible, but no warranty or fitness is implied.

The information is provided on an "as is" basis. The authors, Cisco Press, and Cisco Systems, Inc. shall have neither liability nor responsibility to any person or entity with respect to any loss or damages arising from the information contained in this book or from the use of the discs or programs that may accompany it.

The opinions expressed in this book belong to the author and are not necessarily those of Cisco Systems, Inc.

Trademark Acknowledgments

All terms mentioned in this book that are known to be trademarks or service marks have been appropriately capitalized. Cisco Press or Cisco Systems, Inc. cannot attest to the accuracy of this information. Use of a term in this book should not be regarded as affecting the validity of any trademark or service mark.

Feedback Information

At Cisco Press, our goal is to create in-depth technical books of the highest quality and value. Each book is crafted with care and precision, undergoing rigorous development that involves the unique expertise of members from the professional technical community.

Readers' feedback is a natural continuation of this process. If you have any comments regarding how we could improve the quality of this book, or otherwise alter it to better suit your needs, you can contact us through e-mail at feedback@ciscopress.com. Please make sure to include the book title and ISBN in your message.

We greatly appreciate your assistance.

Corporate and Government Sales

Cisco Press offers excellent discounts on this book when ordered in quantity for bulk purchases or special sales.

For more information please contact: U.S. Corporate and Government Sales 1-800-382-3419
corpsales@pearsontechgroup.com

For sales outside the U.S. please contact: International Sales international@pearsoned.com

Publisher	**Paul Boger**
Cisco Representative	**Anthony Wolfenden**
Cisco Press Program Manager	**Jeff Brady**
Executive Editor	**Brett Bartow**
Managing Editor	**Patrick Kanouse**
Development Editor	**Dayna Isley**
Project Editor	**Seth Kerney**
Copy Editor	**Emily Rader**
Technical Editors	**Michelle Plumb**
	Larry Roberts
	Anthony Sequeira
Editorial Assistant	**Vanessa Evans**
Book and Cover Designer	**Louisa Adair**
Composition	**Carlisle Publishing Services**
Indexer	**Tim Wright**

CISCO SYSTEMS

Corporate Headquarters
Cisco Systems, Inc.
170 West Tasman Drive
San Jose, CA 95134-1706
USA
www.cisco.com
Tel: 408 526-4000
      800 553-NETS (6387)
Fax: 408 526-4100

European Headquarters
Cisco Systems International BV
Haarlerbergpark
Haarlerbergweg 13-19
1101 CH Amsterdam
The Netherlands
www-europe.cisco.com
Tel: 31 0 20 357 1000
Fax: 31 0 20 357 1100

Americas Headquarters
Cisco Systems, Inc.
170 West Tasman Drive
San Jose, CA 95134-1706
USA
www.cisco.com
Tel: 408 526-7660
Fax: 408 527-0883

Asia Pacific Headquarters
Cisco Systems, Inc.
Capital Tower
168 Robinson Road
#22-01 to #29-01
Singapore 068912
www.cisco.com
Tel: +65 6317 7777
Fax: +65 6317 7799

Cisco Systems has more than 200 offices in the following countries and regions. Addresses, phone numbers, and fax numbers are listed on the
Cisco.com Web site at www.cisco.com/go/offices.

Argentina • Australia • Austria • Belgium • Brazil • Bulgaria • Canada • Chile • China PRC • Colombia • Costa Rica • Croatia • Czech Republic
Denmark • Dubai, UAE • Finland • France • Germany • Greece • Hong Kong SAR • Hungary • India • Indonesia • Ireland • Israel • Italy
Japan • Korea • Luxembourg • Malaysia • Mexico • The Netherlands • New Zealand • Norway • Peru • Philippines • Poland • Portugal
Puerto Rico • Romania • Russia • Saudi Arabia • Scotland • Singapore • Slovakia • Slovenia • South Africa • Spain • Sweden
Switzerland • Taiwan • Thailand • Turkey • Ukraine • United Kingdom • United States • Venezuela • Vietnam • Zimbabwe

About the Author

Kevin Wallace, CCIE No. 7945, CCSI, CCVP, CCNP, CCDP, MCSE 4, CNE 4/5, is a full-time instructor for Thomson NETg. With 17 years of Cisco internetworking experience, Kevin has been a network design specialist for The Walt Disney World Resort and a network manager for Eastern Kentucky University. Kevin holds a bachelor of science degree in electrical engineering from the University of Kentucky. Among Kevin's other publication credits are *Voice over IP First-Step, CCDA/CCDP Flash Cards and Exam Practice Pack* (coauthored with Anthony Sequeira), *CCIE Routing and Switching Flash Cards and Exam Practice Pack* (coauthored with Anthony Sequeira), and *Cisco IP Telephony Flash Cards and Exam Practice Pack,* all of which are available from Cisco Press. Additionally, Kevin authored the *Cisco Enterprise Voice over Data Design (EVoDD)* 3.3 course, was a contributing author for the *Cisco IP Telephony Troubleshooting (IPTT)* 2.0 course, and has written for Cisco's *Packet* magazine. Kevin also holds the IP Telephony Design Specialist, IP Telephony Operations Specialist, and IP Telephony Support Specialist CQS certifications.

About the Technical Reviewers

Michelle Plumb is a full-time certified Cisco instructor for Thomson NETg focusing on the Cisco IP telephony track. Michelle has more than 15 years in the field as an IT and telephony specialist and maintains a high level of Cisco and Microsoft certifications, including CCVP, Cisco IP Telephony Support Specialist, Cisco IP Telephony Operations Specialist, Unity, and MCSE NT40/2000. Michelle has been a technical reviewer for numerous books related to the Cisco CCNP and Cisco IP Telephony course material track.

Anthony Sequeira (CCIE-R/S No. 15626) possesses high-level certifications from both Cisco and Microsoft. For the past 15 years, he has written and lectured to massive audiences about the latest in networking technologies. Anthony is currently a Cisco Certified Systems Instructor with Thomson NETg. Anthony currently lives with his wife and daughter in Tampa, Florida.

Dedication

This book is dedicated to Viv, my wife and my life for 12 amazing years—the best is still to come.

Acknowledgments

I'd like to thank Brett Bartow with Cisco Press for offering me the privilege of working on this book. Also, thanks to all my CVoice students over the past several years who continually cause me to look at this information in new ways.

A big thank you also goes out to the team of instructors at Thomson NETg. I've never met any instructors more genuinely concerned with helping their students be successful. Of course, that attitude is a direct reflection of our leadership, provided by Tom Warrick and Michael Watkins.

I'm also indebted to the technical editors for this book. Michelle, Anthony, and Larry, I've had the privilege of teaching courses with each of you, and I have tremendous respect for your opinions and insights. Additionally, thanks to my niece, Shayla Brinegar, for her review and feedback on the traffic engineering portion of this book.

On a personal note, undertaking a project of this magnitude would have been unthinkable without the support of my family. My wife Vivian is my biggest cheerleader, while my daughter, Sabrina, and I constantly debate about who loves the other more. Well Sabrina, it's officially in print, I love you more, infinity, period, end of discussion. Meanwhile, my daughter Stacie inspires me with her love of writing. I can't wait to coauthor a book with you someday! I'm so blessed to have you as my family. And, of course, I thank my Heavenly Father for His favor and mercy in my life.

Contents at a Glance

Table of Contents

Icons Used in This Book

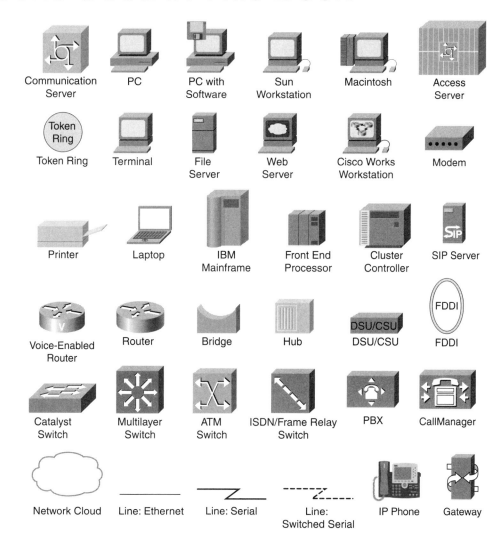

Communication Server

PC

PC with Software

Sun Workstation

Macintosh

Access Server

Token Ring

Terminal

File Server

Web Server

Cisco Works Workstation

Modem

Printer

Laptop

IBM Mainframe

Front End Processor

Cluster Controller

SIP Server

Voice-Enabled Router

Router

Bridge

Hub

DSU/CSU

FDDI

Catalyst Switch

Multilayer Switch

ATM Switch

ISDN/Frame Relay Switch

PBX

CallManager

Network Cloud

Line: Ethernet

Line: Serial

Line: Switched Serial

IP Phone

Gateway

Command Syntax Conventions

The conventions used to present command syntax in this book are the same conventions used in the IOS Command Reference. The Command Reference describes these conventions as follows:

- **Boldface** indicates commands and keywords that are entered literally as shown. In actual configuration examples and output (not general command syntax), boldface indicates commands that are manually input by the user (such as a **show** command).
- *Italics* indicate arguments for which you supply actual values.
- Vertical bars | separate alternative, mutually exclusive elements.
- Square brackets [ ] indicate optional elements.
- Braces { } indicate a required choice.
- Braces within brackets [{ }] indicate a required choice within an optional element.

Foreword

Cisco Voice over IP (CVoice), Second Edition is an excellent self-study resource for the CCVP CVoice exam. Whether you are studying to become CCVP certified or are simply seeking to gain a better understanding of basic IP Telephony operation, router configuration, and integration with an existing PSTN network, you will benefit from the information presented in this book.

Cisco Press Self-Study Guide titles are designed to help educate, develop, and grow the community of Cisco networking professionals. As an early-stage exam preparation product, this book presents a detailed and comprehensive introduction to the technologies used to implement and support data and voice integration solutions. Developed in conjunction with the Cisco certifications team, Cisco Press books are the only self-study books authorized by Cisco Systems.

Most networking professionals use a variety of learning methods to gain necessary skills. Cisco Press self-study titles are a prime source of content for some individuals and can also serve as an excellent supplement to other forms of learning. Training classes, whether delivered in a classroom or on the Internet, are a great way to quickly acquire new understanding. Hands-on practice is essential for anyone seeking to build, or hone, new skills. Authorized Cisco training classes, labs, and simulations are available exclusively from Cisco Learning Solutions Partners worldwide. Please visit www.cisco.com/go/training to learn more about Cisco Learning Solutions Partners.

I hope and expect that you'll find this guide to be an essential part of your exam preparation and a valuable addition to your personal library.

Don Field
Director, Certifications
Cisco System, Inc.
August 2006

Introduction

With the rapid adoption of Voice over IP (VoIP), many telephony and data network technicians, engineers, and designers are now working to become proficient in VoIP. Professional certifications, such as Cisco's Cisco Certified Voice Professional (CCVP) certification, offer validation of an employee's or a consultant's competency in specific technical areas.

Goals and Methods

The primary objective of this book is to help the reader pass the CVoice exam (642-432), which is a required exam for the CCVP certification and for Cisco's IP Telephony Support Specialist and Rich Media Communications Specialist certifications.

Unlike most Cisco certification exams, the CVoice exam attracts two primary categories of candidates: those with a telephony background and those with a data networking background. Therefore, the first two chapters of this book provide a review of traditional telephony technology, along with a brief introduction to VoIP components. These first two chapters especially benefit readers who have a data background but lack a strong telephony background.

After getting you up to speed on basic telephony components, this book covers the CVoice exam objectives, not by "teaching to the exam," but rather by explaining exam-relevant (and real-world applicable) concepts in a logical sequence of topics. Additionally, this book reinforces learning through the following features:

- Chapter review questions
- Practice items
- Real-world content not covered in the CVoice course
- Hands-on lab exercises tailored to home lab environments

Who Should Read This Book?

This book is primarily targeted toward candidates of the CVoice exam. However, because CVoice is one of Cisco's foundational VoIP courses, this book also serves as a VoIP primer to noncertification readers.

Many Cisco resellers actively encourage their employees to attain Cisco certifications and attract new employees already possessing Cisco certifications, for higher discounts when purchasing Cisco products. Additionally, having attained a certification communicates to your employer or customer that you are serious about your craft and have not simply "hung out a shingle" declaring yourself knowledgeable about VoIP. Rather, you have proven your competency through a rigorous series of exams.

How This Book Is Organized

Although the chapters in this book could be read sequentially, the organization allows you to focus your reading on specific topics of interest. For example, if you already posess a strong telephony background, you could skim through the first couple of chapters, which offer a review of fundamental telephony concepts, and concentrate your study on the remaining chapters. Specifically, the chapters in this book cover the following topics:

Chapter 1, "Introduction to Voice Technologies"—This chapter introduces you to traditional telephony networks and telephony concepts. Additionally, the building blocks of packet telephony networks are addressed.

Chapter 2, "Analog and Digital Voice Connections"—This chapter expounds on much of the content in Chapter 1 (for example, analog and digital connections) by examing the interworkings of telephony operations at an electrical level. Also, this chapter discusses strategies for overcoming specific challenges in a VoIP network (for example, the transmission of fax and modem tones).

Chapter 3, "Voice Interface Configuration"—This chapter discusses how to attach a Cisco voice-enabled router to existing telephony devices, such as a PBX or an analog phone. This chapter also covers the syntax required to configure analog and digital voice ports.

Chapter 4, "Voice Dial Peer Configuration"—This chapter shows you how to add call routing intelligence to a Cisco voice-enabled router through the use of "dial peers." Since dialed digits might need manipulation under certain circumstances (for example, adding a 9, a 1, and an area code when sending a call out over the public switched telephone network [PSTN]), this chapter discusses multiple digit manipulation techniques.

Chapter 5, "VoIP Fundamentals"—After the preceeding chapters lay a strong foundation for how to construct a basic VoIP network, this chapter discusses potential challenges and design considerations associated with sending voice across an IP-based network. For example, the bandwidth required to successfully transmit voice varies based on such factors as voice sample size, Layer 2 encapsulation, and voice coding/decoding algorithm (that is, "CODEC").

Chapter 6, "VoIP Signaling and Call Control Protocols"—As VoIP networks grow larger, designers must understand the characteristics of call control protocols that set up calls between VoIP devices. Specifically, this chapter covers the theory and configuration of the H.323, SIP, and MGCP call control protocols.

Chapter 7, "Improving and Maintaining Voice Quality"—Simply adding VoIP packets to an existing data network can result in unacceptable voice quality from an end user's perspective. Therefore, this chapter addresses the quality challenges associated with a VoIP design and discusses various Cisco quality of service (QoS) mechanisms to help mitigate these challenges. While the configuration of QoS mechanisms is a study in and of itself, this chapter introduces the reader to a feature called AutoQoS, which can help administrations apply a robust QoS configuration to both router and switch platforms, with a minimum amount of configuration.

This book concludes with two appendixes and a glossary. Appendix A, "Answers to Chapter Review Questions," provides the answers to the review questions that appear in each chapter. Appendix B, "Cisco VoIP Applications," describes several implementations of VoIP networks. The glossary defines important terms you encounter throughout the book.

After reading this chapter, you should be able to perform the following tasks:

- Identify the components, process, and features of traditional telephony networks that provide end-to-end call functionality
- Describe two methods of call control used on voice and data networks and provide one protocol example for each
- List five components or capabilities that are required in order to provide integrated voice and data services in campus LAN, enterprise, and service provider environments

CHAPTER 1

Introduction to Voice Technologies

Voice over IP (VoIP) is experiencing explosive growth. Many corporate environments have migrated, are actively migrating, or are researching the process of migrating to VoIP. Some long-distance providers are using VoIP to carry voice traffic, particularly on international calls. Companies, such as Vonage, offer VoIP service as a replacement for traditional telephony service in the home.

Migration is a process that involves gradually phasing out old components and replacing them with new ones. Many terms have been used to describe the technologies and applications for transporting voice in a converged packet network environment. When designing a converged network, it is necessary to clearly define all requirements and understand the various options that are available.

An important first step in designing a converged network is to understand the traditional telephony network and how it interfaces with voice components. You must know, from the start, how legacy voice equipment is connected and its possible migration paths.

The next step toward a good design is being knowledgeable about the components available for VoIP networks. You should be aware of the difference between voice and data flows within the network and the tools for controlling voice calls. Network requirements vary according to the size of the location. Knowing the difference between campus, enterprise, and service provider environments is crucial for choosing the right components and technologies.

This chapter provides an overview of the basic telephony functions and devices, including private branch exchanges (PBXs), switching functions, call signaling, and multiplexing techniques. It also reviews the basic components of the VoIP network and identifies the different requirements in campus, enterprise, and service provider environments. Together, these concepts and techniques provide a solid introduction to the VoIP arena.

Fundamentals of Telephony Networks

In traditional telephony networks, many components and processes are transparent to the customer. As you move from traditional telephony networks to converged voice and data networks, you must manage new components and processes to ensure seamless end-to-end call handling. To maintain acceptable service levels, you need to understand which devices you must now support and the processes that are necessary to ensure end-to-end call functionality.

Basic Components of Telephony Networks

A number of components must be in place for an end-to-end call to succeed. These components are listed here and shown in Figure 1-1:

- Edge devices
- Local loops
- Private or central office (CO) switches
- Trunks

The next sections describe each of the basic components in more detail.

Edge Devices

The two types of edge devices used in a telephony network include:

- **Analog telephones**—Analog telephones are most common in home, small office/home office (SOHO), and small business environments. A direct connection to the public switched telephone network (PSTN) is usually made by using analog telephones. Proprietary analog telephones are occasionally used in conjunction with a PBX. These telephones provide additional functions such as speakerphone, volume control, PBX message-waiting indicator, call on hold, and personalized ringing.

- **Digital telephones**—Digital telephones contain hardware to convert analog voice into a digitized stream. Larger corporate environments with PBXs generally use digital telephones. Digital telephones are typically proprietary, meaning that they work with the PBX or key system of that vendor only.

Local Loops

A local loop is the interface to the telephone company network. Typically, it is a single pair of wires that carry a single conversation. A home or small business may have multiple local loops. You learn more about local loops in Chapter 2, "Analog and Digital Voice Connections."

Figure 1-1   *Basic Components of a Telephony Network*

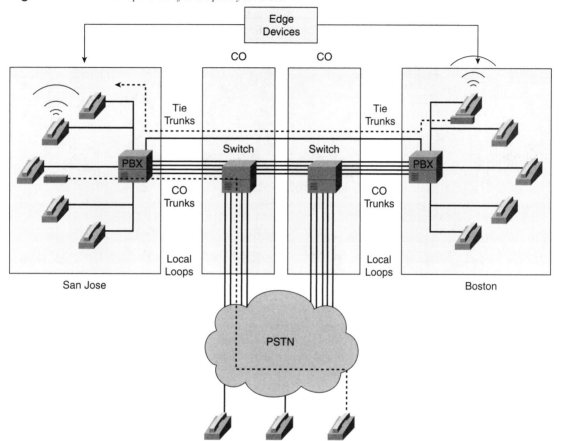

Private or CO Switches

The CO switch terminates the local loop and handles signaling, digit collection, call routing, call setup, and call teardown. You learn more about these switches in the upcoming section "CO Switches and Switching Systems."

A PBX switch is a privately owned switch located at the customer site. A PBX typically interfaces with other components to provide additional services, such as voice mail. You learn more about PBXs in the section "Privately Owned Switches" later in this chapter.

Trunks

The primary function of a trunk is to provide the path between two switches. There are several common trunk types, as shown in Figure 1-2, including the following:

- **Tie trunk**—A dedicated circuit that connects PBXs directly
- **CO trunk**—A direct connection between a local CO and a PBX
- **Interoffice trunk**—A circuit that connects two local telephone company COs

---

NOTE   The telephone installed in your home is considered an edge device because it terminates the service provided by your local telephone company. The local loop is the pair of wires that come to your house and provide residential telephone service. Trunks are the interconnections between telephone switches. They can be between private switches or telephone company switches.

Figure 1-2   *Trunk Types*

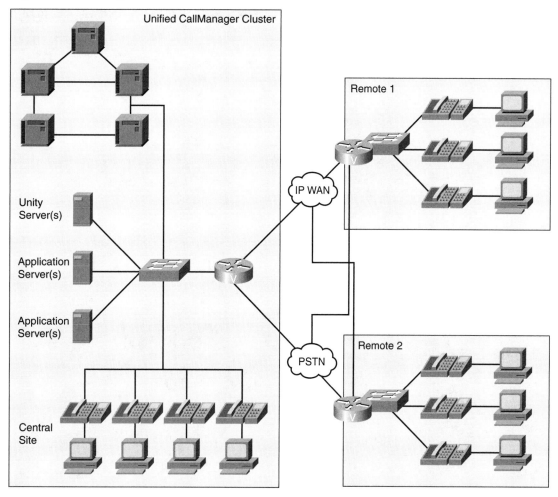

CO Switches and Switching Systems

Figure 1-3 shows a typical CO switch environment. The CO switch terminates the local loop and makes the initial call-routing decision.

Figure 1-3   *CO Switches*

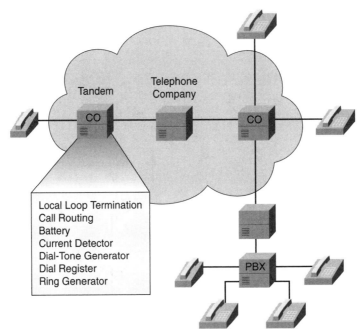

The call-routing function forwards the call to one of the following:

- Another end-user telephone, if it is connected to the same CO
- Another CO switch
- A tandem switch (that is, an intermediary switch between the source and destination switch)

The CO switch makes the telephone work with the following components:

- **Battery**—The battery is the source of power to both the circuit and the telephone. It determines the status of the circuit. When the handset is lifted to let current flow, the telephone company provides the source that powers the circuit and the telephone. Because the telephone company powers the telephone from the CO, electrical power outages should not affect the basic telephone, also known as a *POTS* (plain old telephone service) phone.

- **Current detector**—The current detector monitors the status of a circuit by detecting whether it is open or closed. Table 1-1 describes current flow in a typical telephone.

- **Dial-tone generator**—When the digit register is ready, the dial-tone generator produces a dial tone to acknowledge the request for service.

- **Dial register**—The digit register receives the dialed digits.

- **Ring generator**—When the switch detects a call for a specific subscriber, the ring generator alerts the called party by sending a ring signal to that subscriber.

NOTE   Some telephones on the market offer additional features that require a supplementary power source that the subscriber supplies; for example, cordless telephones. Some cordless telephones may lose functionality during a power outage.

Table 1-1   *Current Flow in a Typical Telephone*

Handset	Circuit	Current Flow
On cradle	On hook/open circuit	No
Off cradle	Off hook/closed circuit	Yes

When configuring a PBX connection to a CO switch, the signaling should match that of the CO switch. This configuration ensures that the switch and the PBX can detect on hook, off hook, and dialed digits coming from either direction.

Switching systems provide three primary functions:

- Call setup, routing, and teardown
- Call supervision
- Customer ID and telephone numbers

CO switches switch calls between locally terminated telephones. If a call recipient is not locally connected, the CO switch decides where to send the call based on its own call routing information, which is stored in a *call-routing table*. The call then travels over a trunk to another CO or to an intermediate switch that may belong to an inter-exchange carrier (IXC). Although intermediate switches do not provide dial tone, they act as hubs to connect other switches and provide interswitch call routing.

PSTN calls are traditionally circuit-switched, which guarantees end-to-end path and resources. Therefore, as the PSTN sends a call from one switch to another, the same resource is associated with the call until the call is terminated.

NOTE   CO switches provide local service to residential telephones. The CO switch provides dial
tone, indicating that the switch is ready to receive digits. When you dial your phone, the CO
switch receives the digits, then routes your call. The call routing may involve more than one
switch as the call progresses through the network.

Privately Owned Switches

In a corporate environment, where large numbers of staff need access to each other and the
outside, individual telephone lines are not economically viable. A PBX is a smaller,
privately owned version of the CO switches used by telephone companies, as illustrated in
Figure 1-4.

Figure 1-4   *PBX*

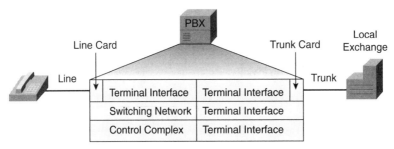

Most businesses have a PBX telephone system, a key telephone system, or a Centrex
service. Large offices with more than 50 telephones or handsets choose a PBX to connect
users, both in-house and to the PSTN.

PBXs come in a variety of sizes, from 20 to 20,000 stations. The selection of a PBX is
important to most companies, because a PBX has a typical life span of seven to ten years.

All PBXs offer a standard, basic set of calling features. Optional software provides
additional capabilities.

A PBX connects to telephone handsets using line cards and to the local exchange using
trunk cards.

A PBX has three major components:

- **Terminal interface**—The terminal interface provides the connection between
  terminals and PBX features that reside in the control complex. Terminals can include
  telephone handsets, trunks, and lines. Common PBX features include dial tone and
  ringing.

- **Switching network**—The switching network provides the transmission path between two or more terminals in a conversation. For example, two telephones within an office communicate over the switching network.

- **Control complex**—The control complex provides the logic, memory, and processing for call setup, call supervision, and call disconnection.

PBX Installations

PBX switches are installed in large business campuses to relieve the public telephone company switches from having to switch local calls. When you call a coworker locally in your office campus, the PBX switches the call locally instead of having to rely on the public CO switch. The existence of PBX switches also limits the number of trunks needed to connect to the telephone company's CO switch. With a PBX installed, not every office desktop telephone needs its own trunk to the CO switch. Rather, the trunks are shared among all users.

Small organizations and branch offices often use a key telephone system, as shown in Figure 1-5, because a PBX offers functionality and extra features that they may not require. A key system offers small businesses distributed answering from any telephone, unlike the central answering position required for a PBX. Notice in Figure 1-5 that telephones interconnect to a key system via *connector blocks*, while trunks coming in from the local exchange interconnect to the key system via *termination blocks*.

Figure 1-5 *Key Telephone System*

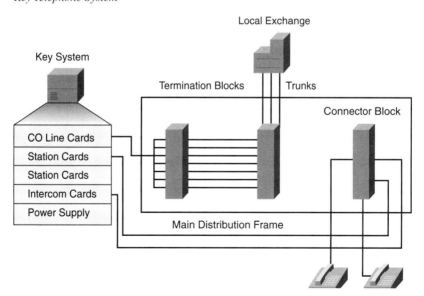

Today, key telephone systems are either analog or digital and are microprocessor based. Key systems are typically used in offices with 30 to 40 users, but can be scaled to support over 100 users.

A key system has three major components:

- **Key service unit**—A key service unit (KSU) holds the system switching components, power supply, intercom, line and station cards, and the system logic.

- **System software**—System software provides the operating system and calling-feature software.

- **Telephones (instruments or handsets)**—Telephones allow the user to choose a free line and dial out, usually by pressing a button on the telephone.

Larger companies use proprietary telephone networks with PBXs. In a key telephone system, each telephone has multiple lines that allow users to access outside lines to their CO. When a call comes into the company, a line or a key lights up on the telephone and indicates that a particular line is in use. Users can call another extension or let another person know where to pick up a call by using an intercom function, such as an overhead paging system or speakerphone.

Key telephone system functionality has evolved over time to include a class called *hybrid telephone systems*. The hybrid system adds many features that were previously available only in PBXs. There is no single definition of the functions and features that are classified as a hybrid system because all vendors provide a mix that they believe gives them a competitive advantage.

The main difference between a key telephone system and a hybrid telephone system is whether a single-line telephone can access a single CO local loop or trunk only (key telephone system) or whether the single-line telephone can access a pool of CO local loops or trunks (hybrid telephone system).

Call Signaling

Call signaling, in its most basic form, is the ability of a device to communicate a need for service to a network. The call-signaling process requires the network to detect a request for service and termination of service, send addressing information, and provide progress reports to the initiating party. This functionality corresponds to the three call-signaling types:

- Supervisory signaling
- Address signaling
- Informational signaling

A basic call setup, as illustrated in Figure 1-6, includes supervisory, address, and information signaling components. The supervisory signaling is used, for example, to detect that a phone went off hook. Address signaling occurs when a caller dials digits, and information signaling is represented by the dial tone heard by the caller.

Figure 1-6   *Basic Call Setup*

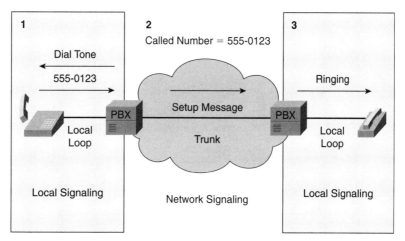

This call setup can be broken down into three major steps. These steps include:

1. **Local signaling: originating side**—The user signals the switch by going off hook and sending dialed digits through the local loop.

2. **Network signaling**—The switch makes a routing decision and signals the next, or terminating, switch through the use of setup messages sent across a trunk.

3. **Local signaling: terminating side**—The terminating switch signals the call recipient by sending ringing voltage through the local loop to the recipient telephone.

Supervisory Signaling

A subscriber and telephone company notify each other of call status with audible tones and an exchange of electrical current. This exchange of information is called *supervisory signaling*, as shown in Figure 1-7.

Figure 1-7 *Supervisory Signaling*

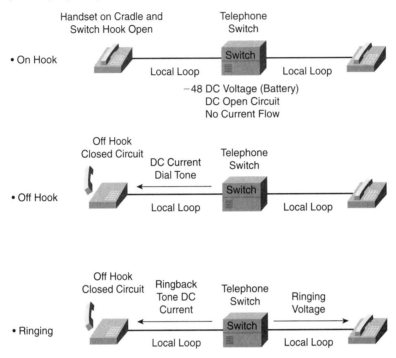

There are three different types of supervisory signaling:

- **On hook**—When the handset rests on the cradle, the circuit is on hook. The switch prevents current from flowing through the telephone. Regardless of the signaling type, a circuit goes on hook when the handset is placed on the telephone cradle, and the switch hook is toggled to an open state. This prevents the current from flowing through the telephone. Only the ringer is active when the telephone is in this position.

- **Off hook**—When the handset is removed from the telephone cradle, the circuit is off hook. The switch hook toggles to a closed state, causing circuit current to flow through the electrical loop. The current notifies the telephone company equipment that someone is requesting to place a telephone call. When the telephone network senses the off-hook connection by the flow of current, it provides a signal in the form of a dial tone to indicate that it is ready.

- **Ringing**—When a subscriber makes a call, the telephone sends voltage to the ringer to notify the other subscriber of an inbound call. The telephone company also sends a ringback tone to the caller, alerting the caller that it is sending ringing voltage to the recipient telephone. Although the ringback tone sounds similar to ringing, it is a call-progress tone and not part of supervisory signaling.

NOTE   The ringing pattern in the United States is 2 seconds of ringing tone followed by 4 seconds of silence. Europe uses a double ring followed by 2 seconds of silence.

Address Signaling

There are two types of telephones, as shown in Figure 1-8: a push-button (tone) telephone and a rotary-dial telephone.

Figure 1-8   *Address Signaling*

These telephones use two different types of address signaling to notify the telephone company where a subscriber is calling:

- **Dual-tone multifrequency (DTMF)**—Each button on the keypad of a touch-tone pad or push-button telephone is associated with a pair of high and low frequencies. On the keypad, each row of keys is identified by a low-frequency tone and each column is associated with a high-frequency tone. The combination of both tones notifies the telephone company of the number being called, thus the term *dual-tone multifrequency (DTMF)*.

- **Pulse**—The large numeric dial-wheel on a rotary-dial telephone spins to send digits to place a call. These digits must be produced at a specific rate and within a certain level of tolerance. Each pulse consists of a "break" and a "make," which are achieved by opening and closing the local loop circuit. The *break segment* is the time during which the circuit is open. The *make segment* is the time during which the circuit is closed. The break-and-make cycle must correspond to a ratio of 60 percent break to 40 percent make.

A governor inside the dial controls the rate at which the digits are pulsed. For example, when a subscriber calls someone by dialing a digit on the rotary dial, a spring winds. When the dial is released, the spring rotates the dial back to its original position. While the spring rotates the dial back to its original position, a cam-driven switch opens and closes the connection to the telephone company. The number of consecutive opens and closes, or breaks and makes, represents the dialed digit.

Information Signaling

Tone combinations indicate call progress and are used to notify subscribers of call status. Each combination of tones represents a different event in the call process. These events, whose frequencies and patterns are listed in Table 1-2, include the following:

- **Dial tone**—Indicates that the telephone company is ready to receive digits from the user telephone.

- **Busy**—Indicates that a call cannot be completed because the telephone at the remote end is already in use.

- **Ringback (line or PBX)**—Indicates that the telephone company is attempting to complete a call on behalf of a subscriber.

- **Congestion**—Indicates that congestion in the long-distance telephone network is preventing a telephone call from being processed.

- **Reorder tone**—Indicates that all the local telephone circuits are busy, thus preventing a telephone call from being processed.

- **Receiver off hook**—Indicates that a receiver has been off hook for an extended period of time without placing a call.

- **No such number**—Indicates that a subscriber has placed a call to a nonexistent number.

NOTE   A call placed from your residential telephone uses all three types of call signaling. When you lift the handset, a switch in your telephone closes to start current flow and notifies the telephone company that you want to make a call (supervisory signaling). The telephone company then sends dial tone to indicate that it is ready to receive your dialed digits (informational signaling). You then dial your digits by pressing numbers on the keypad (address signaling).

Table 1-2 *Information Signaling Tone Combinations*

Tone	Frequency (Hz)	On Time (sec)	Off Time (sec)
Dial	350 + 440	Continuous	Continuous
Busy	480 + 620	0.5	0.5
Ringback, line	440 + 480	2	4
Ringback, PBX	440 + 480	1	3
Congestion (toll)	480 + 620	0.2	0.3
Reorder (local)	480 + 620	0.3	0.2
Receiver off hook	1400 + 2060 + 2450 + 2600	0.1	0.1
No such number	200 to 400	Continuous	Continuous

Digital versus Analog Connections

Supervisory, address, and informational signaling must be carried across both analog and digital connections. Depending on your connection to the network, you must configure specific signaling to match the type of signaling required by the service provider. Figure 1-9 illustrates digital and analog connections coexisting in the same network.

Figure 1-9 *Address Signaling*

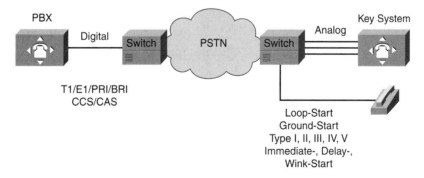

Digital PBX connections to the network are common in many countries. They may be T1 or E1 lines carrying channel associated signaling (CAS) or PRI lines using common channel signaling (CCS).

CAS is a signaling method that allows passing on-hook or off-hook status by setting bits that are associated with each specific voice channel. These bits are carried in band for T1 and out of band for E1.

An ISDN connection uses the D channel as the common channel to carry signaling messages for all other channels. CCS carries the signaling out of band, meaning that the signaling and the voice path do not share the same channel.

Analog interfaces require configuration of a specific signaling type to match the provider requirement. For interfaces that connect to the PSTN or to a telephone or similar edge device, the signaling is configured for either *loop start* or *ground start*, the functions of which are discussed in Chapter 2. For analog trunk interfaces that connect two PBXs to each other (that is, E&M interfaces), or a PBX to a CO switch, the signaling is either wink-start, immediate-start, or delay-start, with the signaling type set to 1, 2, 3, 4, or 5.

Multiplexing

A two-wire analog local loop typically carries one call at a time. To make better use of wiring facilities, different multiplexing techniques have been implemented to enable two-wire or four-wire connections to carry multiple conversations at the same time.

Time-division multiplexing (TDM) is used extensively in telephony networks to carry multiple conversations concurrently across a four-wire path, as shown in Figure 1-10. TDM involves simultaneously transmitting multiple separate voice signals over one communications medium by quickly interleaving pieces of each signal, one after another. Information from each data channel is allocated bandwidth based on preassigned timeslots, regardless of whether there is data to transmit.

Figure 1-10 *Time-Division Multiplexing*

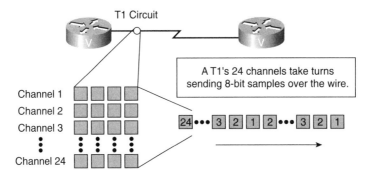

Frequency-division multiplexing (FDM), as illustrated in Figure 1-11, involves carrying multiple voice signals by allocating an individual frequency range to each call. FDM is typically used in analog connections, although its functionality is similar to that of TDM in digital connections. FDM is used in cable or digital subscriber line (DSL) connections to allow the simultaneous use of multiple channels over the same wire.

NOTE   If you have cable television service at your home, the television channels are all carried (and multiplexed) over a single pair of wires. This includes both the audio signals and the video signals. All the channels are present on the cable wires all the time. When you select the channel you want to watch, your set-top cable tuner determines which channel is sent to your television.

Figure 1-11 *Frequency-Division Multiplexing*

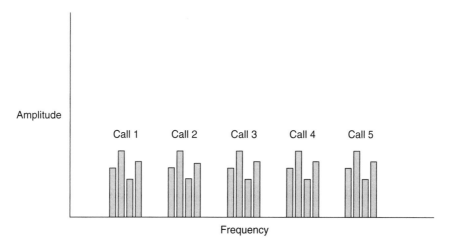

Fundamentals of Packet Telephony Networks

The increased efficiency of packet networks (for example, VoIP networks) and the ability to statistically multiplex voice traffic with data packets allows companies to maximize their return on investment (ROI) in data network infrastructures. Multiplexing voice traffic with data traffic reduces the number of costly circuits dedicated to servicing voice applications.

As demand for voice services expands, it is important to understand the different requirements of voice and data traffic. Previously, voice and data networks were separate and could not impact each other. Today, it is necessary to determine the protocols available to control voice calls and ensure that data flows are not negatively impacted.

This section delves into the benefits of packet telephony networks and provides an overview of basic packet telephony operations. Additionally, the fundamental components of packet networks are introduced. Finally, as a design consideration, this section considers the fragile nature of voice packets.

Benefits of Packet Telephony Networks

Traditionally, the potential savings on long-distance costs was the driving force behind the migration to converged voice and data networks. However, as the cost of long-distance calls has dropped in recent years, other factors have come to the forefront as benefits of converged networks.

The benefits of packet telephony versus circuit-switched telephony are as follows:

- **More efficient use of bandwidth and equipment**—Traditional telephony networks use a 64-kbps channel for every voice call. Packet telephony shares bandwidth among multiple logical connections and offloads traffic volume from existing voice switches.

- **Lower costs for telephony network transmission**—A substantial amount of equipment is needed to combine 64-kbps channels into high-speed links for transport across the network. Packet telephony statistically multiplexes voice traffic alongside data traffic. This consolidation represents substantial savings on capital equipment and operations costs.

- **Consolidated voice and data network expenses**—Data networks that function as separate networks to voice networks become major traffic carriers. The underlying voice networks are converted to utilize the packet-switched architecture to create a single integrated communications network with a common switching and transmission system.

- **Increased revenues from new services**—Packet telephony enables new integrated services, such as broadcast quality audio, unified messaging, and real-time voice and data collaboration. These services increase employee productivity and profit margins well above those of basic voice services. In addition, these services enable companies and service providers to differentiate themselves and improve their market position.

- **Greater innovation in services**—Unified communications use the IP infrastructure to consolidate communication methods that were previously independent; for example, fax, voice mail, e-mail, wireline telephones, cellular telephones, and the Web. The IP infrastructure provides users with a common method to access messages and initiate real-time communications, independent of time, location, or device.

- **Access to new communications devices**—Packet technology can reach devices that are largely inaccessible to the TDM infrastructures of today. Examples of such devices are computers, wireless devices, household appliances, personal digital assistants (PDAs), and cable set-top boxes. Intelligent access to such devices enables companies and service providers to increase the volume of communications they deliver, the breadth of services they offer, and the number of subscribers they serve. Packet technology, therefore, enables companies to market new devices, including videophones, multimedia terminals, and advanced IP phones.

- **Flexible new pricing structures**—Companies and service providers with packet-switched networks can transform their service and pricing models. Because network bandwidth can be dynamically allocated, network usage no longer needs to be measured in minutes or distance. Dynamic allocation gives service providers the flexibility to meet the needs of their customers in ways that bring them the greatest benefits.

Although packet technology has clear benefits, you should carefully consider the following points before migrating to this technology:

- ROI, when based on the new system features, can be difficult to prove.

- Generally, voice and data staffs use different terminology to describe the network.

- Current voice telephony components have not yet fully depreciated.

- Potential upgrade costs will override potential savings benefits.

Packet Telephony Components

The basic components of a packet voice network, as shown in Figure 1-12, include the following:

- **IP phones**—Provide IP voice to the desktop.

- **Gatekeeper**—Provides Call Admission Control (CAC), bandwidth control and management, address translation, and call routing.

- **Gateway**—Provides translation between VoIP and non-VoIP networks, such as the PSTN. It also provides physical access for local analog and digital voice devices, such as telephones, fax machines, key sets, and PBXs.

- **Multipoint control unit (MCU)**—Provides real-time connectivity for participants in multiple locations to attend the same videoconference or meeting.

- **Call agent**—Provides call control for IP phones, CAC, bandwidth control and management, and address translation. The call agent also serves as a repository for call routing information.

- **Application servers**—Provide services such as voice mail, unified messaging, or call center support.

- **Videoconference station**—Provides access for end-user participation in video-conferencing. The videoconference station contains a video capture device for video input and a microphone for audio input. The user can view video streams and hear the audio that originates at a remote user station. Cisco targets its VT Advantage product at desktop videoconferencing applications.

Figure 1-12 *Packet Telephony Network Components*

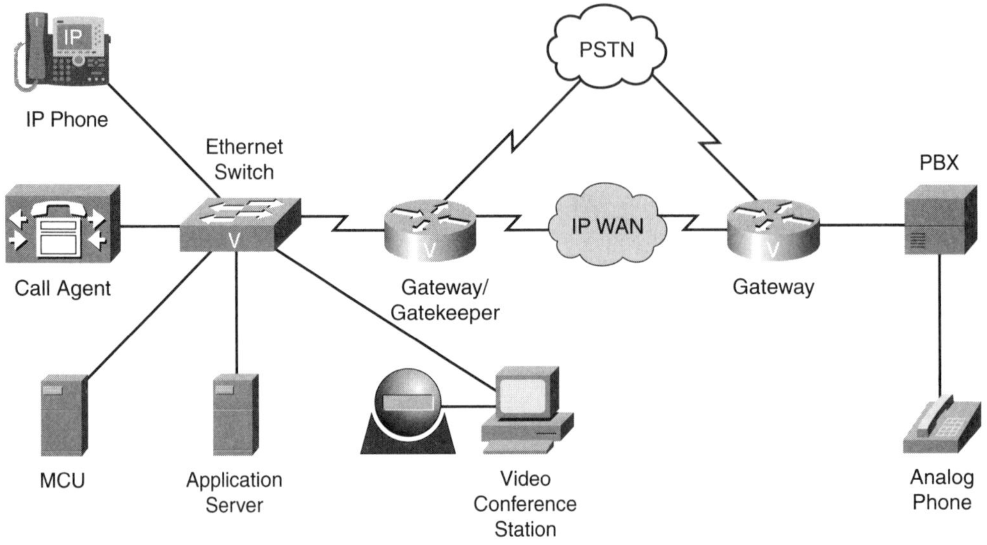

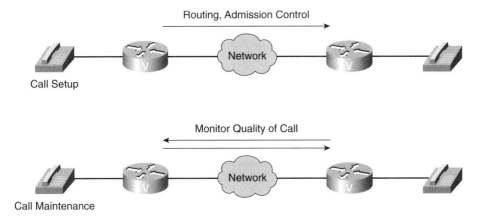

Other components, such as software voice applications, interactive voice response (IVR) systems, and softphones, provide additional services to meet the needs of enterprise sites.

Call Control

Call control allows users to establish, maintain, and disconnect a voice flow across a network, as shown in Figure 1-13.

Figure 1-13 *Call Control*

Although different protocols address call control in different ways, they all provide a common set of services. The following are the basic components of call control:

- **Call setup**—Checks call-routing configuration to determine the destination of a call. The configuration specifies the bandwidth requirements for the call. When the bandwidth requirements are known, CAC determines if sufficient bandwidth is available to support the call. If bandwidth is available, call setup generates a setup message and sends it to the destination. If bandwidth is not available, call setup notifies the initiator by presenting a busy signal. Different call control protocols, such as H.323, Media Gateway Control Protocol (MGCP), and Session Initiation Protocol (SIP), define different sets of messages to be exchanged during setup.

- **Call maintenance**—Tracks packet count, packet loss, and interarrival jitter, or delay, when the call is set up. Information passes to the voice-enabled devices to determine if connection quality is good or if it has deteriorated to the point where the call should be dropped.

- **Call teardown**—Notifies voice-enabled devices to free resources and make them available for the next call when either side terminates a call.

From a design perspective, you can set up call control in either a distributed or centralized architecture. The following sections describe both types.

Distributed Call Control

Distributed call control, an example of which is shown in Figure 1-13, offers an environment where call control is handled by multiple components in the network. This approach to call control is possible where the voice-capable device is configured to support call control directly. This is the case with a voice gateway when protocols, such as H.323 or SIP, are enabled on the device. In Figure 1-14, each location contains a Cisco Unified CallManager cluster. Each cluster is capable of handling call processing. Therefore, the topology shown demonstrates one example of distributed call control.

Distributed call control enables the gateway to perform the following procedure:

1. Recognize the request for service

2. Process dialed digits

3. Route the call

4. Supervise the call

5. Terminate the call

Figure 1-14 *Distributed Call Control*

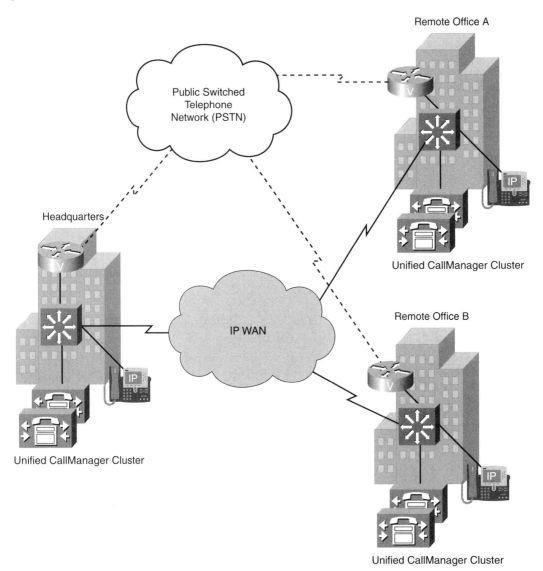

Centralized Call Control

Centralized call control, an example of which is illustrated in Figure 1-15, allows an external device (call agent) to handle the signaling and call processing, leaving the gateway to translate audio signals into voice packets after call setup. The call agent is responsible for all aspects of signaling, thus instructing the gateways to send specific signals at specific times. Also, the centralized call control model can leverage Cisco's Survivable Remote Site Telephony (SRST) feature to provide redundancy in the event of a WAN outage by having the voice-enabled router at the remote site perform basic call processing functions. In the figure, a Cisco Unified CallManager cluster located at the Headquarters location is in charge of call control. Therefore, the topology shown demonstrates an example of centralized call control.

Figure 1-15 *Centralized Call Control*

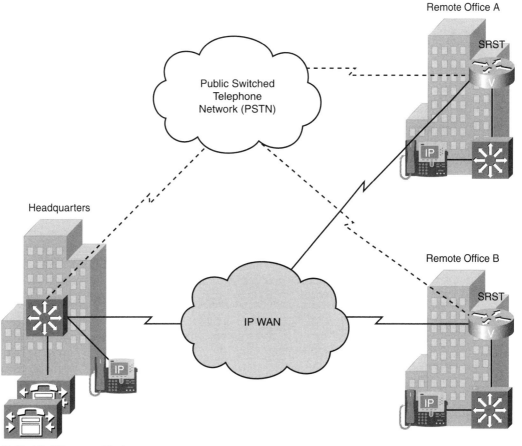

When the call is set up, the following occur:

- The voice path runs directly between the two gateways and does not involve the call agent.
- When either side terminates the call, the call agent signals the gateways to release resources and wait for another call.

The use of centralized call control devices is beneficial in several ways:

- It centralizes the configuration for call routing and CAC. In a large voice environment, centralization can be extremely beneficial.
- The call agent is the only device that needs the intelligence to understand and participate in call control functions. These call control functions enable the customer to purchase less expensive voice-gateway devices and point to a single device to handle call control.

MGCP is one example of a centralized call control model.

Real-Time versus Best-Effort Traffic

Voice and data can share the same medium. However, their traffic characteristics differ widely: Voice is real-time traffic and data is typically sent as best-effort traffic.

Traditional telephony networks were designed for real-time voice transmission, and therefore they cater to the need for a constant voice flow over the connection. Resources are reserved end to end on a per-call basis and are not released until the call is terminated. These resources guarantee that voice flows in an orderly manner. Good voice quality depends on the capacity of the network to deliver voice with guaranteed delay and timing.

Traditional data networks were designed for best-effort packet transmission. Packet telephony networks transmit with no guarantee of delivery, delay, or timing. Data handling is effective in this scenario because upper-layer protocols, such as TCP, provide for reliable, although untimely, packet transmission. TCP trades delay for reliability. Data can typically tolerate a certain amount of delay and is not affected by interpacket jitter.

A well-engineered, end-to-end network is required when converging delay-sensitive traffic, such as VoIP, with best-effort data traffic. Fine-tuning the network to adequately support VoIP involves a series of protocols and features to improve quality of service (QoS). Because the IP network is, by default, best effort, steps must be taken to ensure proper behavior of both the real-time and best-effort traffic. Packet telephony networks succeed, in large part, based on the QoS parameters that are implemented network-wide.

IP Telephony Applications

As customers migrate their voice networks, they face a myriad of choices regarding interface types, components, and topologies. A good network design incorporates solutions for current requirements and allows room for future growth. It is important to understand how voice interfaces with a network and how the components fit together to provide service in any environment.

Analog Interfaces

A Foreign Exchange Station (FXS) interface, as depicted in Figure 1-16, provides a direct connection to an analog telephone, a fax machine, or a similar device. From a telephone perspective, the FXS interface functions like a telephone switch (for example, a PBX); therefore, it must supply line power, ring voltage, and dial tone.

Figure 1-16 *Foreign Exchange Station (FXS) Interface*

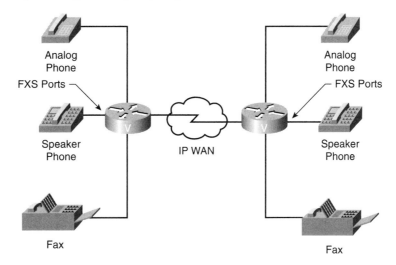

The FXS interface contains the coder-decoder (CODEC), which converts the spoken analog voice wave into a digital format for processing by the voice-enabled device.

The Foreign Exchange Office (FXO) interface, shown in Figure 1-17, allows an analog connection to be directed at the CO of a PSTN or to a station interface on a PBX. The switch recognizes the FXO interface as a telephone because the interface plugs directly into the line side of the switch. The FXO interface provides either pulse or DTMF digits for outbound dialing.

Figure 1-17 *Foreign Exchange Office (FXO) Interface*

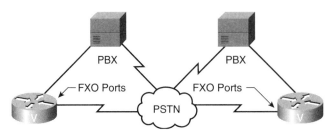

In PSTN terminology, an FXO-to-FXS connection is also referred to as a foreign exchange (FX) trunk. An FX trunk is a CO trunk that has access to a distant CO. Because this connection is FXS at one end and FXO at the other end, it acts as a long-distance extension of a local telephone line. In this instance, a local user can pick up the telephone and get a dial tone from a foreign city. Users in the foreign city can dial a local number and have the call connect to the user in the local city.

The E&M interface, shown in Figure 1-18, provides signaling for analog trunking. Analog trunk circuits connect automated systems (PBXs) and networks (COs). E&M signaling is also referred to as "ear and mouth," but its origin comes from the term "Earth and Magneto." Earth represents the electrical ground, and magneto represents the electromagnet used to generate tone.

Figure 1-18 *Earth and Magneto (E&M) Interface*

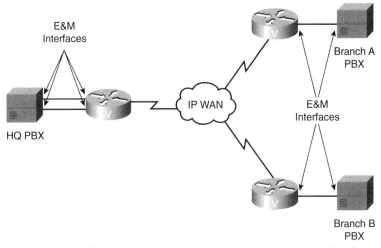

E&M signaling defines a trunk-circuit side and a signaling-unit side for each connection, similar to the DCE and DTE reference types. The PBX is usually the trunk-circuit side, and the telco, CO, channel bank, or Cisco voice-enabled platform is the signaling-unit side.

Digital Interfaces

In a corporate environment with a large volume of voice traffic, connections to the PSTN and to PBXs are primarily digital. Examples of digital interfaces include T1, E1, and BRI interfaces.

T1 Interface

A T1 interface, as illustrated in Figure 1-19, is a form of digital connection that can simultaneously carry up to 24 conversations using two-wire pairs. When a T1 link operates in full-duplex mode, one wire pair sends and the other wire pair receives. The 24 channels are grouped together to form a frame. The frames are then grouped together into Super Frames (groups of 12 frames) or into Extended Superframes (groups of 24 frames).

Figure 1-19 *T1 Interface*

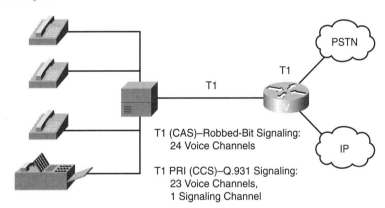

The T1 interface carries either CAS or CCS. When a T1 interface uses CAS, the signaling robs a sampling bit for each channel to convey in band. When a T1 interface uses CCS, Q.931 signaling is used on a single channel, typically the last channel.

To configure CAS, you must specify the type of signaling that the robbed bits carry (for example, E&M Wink Start). This signaling must match the PSTN requirements or the PBX configuration. This is considered in-band signaling because the signal shares the same channel as the voice.

To configure CCS, you must configure the interface for PRI signaling. This level of configuration makes it possible to use channels 1 to 23 (called B channels) for voice traffic. Channel 24 (called the D channel) carries the Q.931 call control signaling for call setup, maintenance, and teardown. This type of signaling is considered out-of-band signaling because the Q.931 messages are sent in the D channel only.

E1 Interface

An E1 interface, shown in Figure 1-20, has 32 channels and simultaneously carries up to 30 conversations. The other two channels are used for framing and signaling. The 32 channels are grouped to form a frame. The frames are then grouped together into multiframes (groups of 16 frames). In Europe and Mexico, the E1 interface is most often used, while in the United States the T1 interface is most commonly used.

Figure 1-20 *E1 Interface*

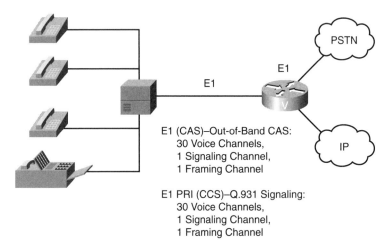

Although you can configure the E1 interface for either CAS or CCS, the most common usage is CCS.

When an E1 interface uses CAS, signaling travels out of band in the signaling channel but follows a strict association between the signal carried in the signaling channel and the channel to which the signaling is being applied. The signaling channel is channel 16.

In the first frame, channel 16 carries 4 bits of signaling for channel 1 and 4 bits of signaling for channel 17. In the second frame, channel 16 carries 4 bits of signaling for channel 2 and 4 bits for channel 18, and so on. This process makes it out-of-band CAS.

When an E1 interface uses CCS, Q.931 signaling is used on a single channel, typically channel 17. When configuring for CCS, configure the interface for PRI signaling. When E1 is configured for CCS, channel 16 carries Q.931 signaling messages only.

BRI Interface

Figure 1-21 depicts an Integrated Services Digital Network (ISDN) Basic Rate Interface (BRI). You can use a BRI to connect the PBX voice into the network. Used primarily in

Europe for PBX connectivity, BRI provides a 16-kbps D channel for signaling and two 64-kbps B channels for voice. BRI uses Q.931 signaling in the D channel for call signaling.

Figure 1-21 *Basic Rate Interface (BRI)*

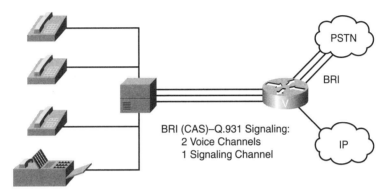

BRI (CAS)–Q.931 Signaling:
2 Voice Channels
1 Signaling Channel

IP Phones

Figure 1-22 depicts physical connection options for IP phones. The IP phone connects to the network through a Category 5 or better cable that has RJ-45 connectors. The power-enabled switch port or an external power supply provides power to an IP phone. The IP phone functions like other IP-capable devices sending IP packets to the IP network. Because these packets are carrying voice, you must consider both logical and physical configuration issues.

At the physical connection level, there are three options for connecting the IP phone:

- **Single cable**—A single cable connects the telephone and the PC to the switch. Most enterprises install IP phones on their networks using a single cable for both the telephone and a PC. Reasons for using a single cable include ease of installation and cost savings on cabling infrastructure and wiring-closet switch ports.

- **Multiple cables**—Separate cables connect the telephone and the PC to the switch. Users often connect the IP phone and PC using separate cables. This connection creates a physical separation between the voice and data networks.

- **Multiple switches**—Separate cables connect the telephone and the PC to separate switches. With this option, IP phones are connected to separate switches in the wiring closet. By using this approach, you can avoid the cost of upgrading the current data switches and keep the voice and data networks completely separate.

Figure 1-22 *Physical Connectivity Options for IP Phones*

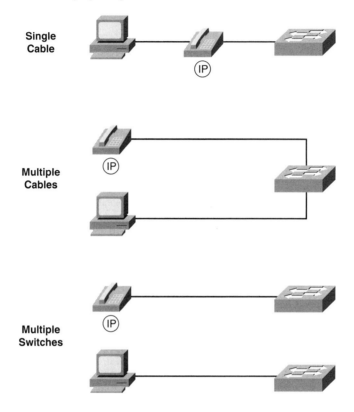

Multiple switches are used to do the following:

- Provide inline power to IP phones without having to upgrade the data infrastructure
- Reduce the amount of Cisco IOS Catalyst software upgrades needed in the network
- Limit the spanning-tree configuration in the wiring-closet switches

The physical configuration for connecting an IP phone must address the following issues:

- Speed and duplex settings
- Inline power settings

The logical configuration for connecting an IP phone must address the following issues:

- IP addressing
- VLAN assignment
- Spanning tree
- Classification and queuing

Many Cisco IP phones, such as the 7970G shown in Figure 1-23, contain a three-port 10/100 switch. One port is an internal port that connects the voice electronics in the telephone. A second port connects a daisy-chained PC, and the third port uplinks to the Ethernet switch in the wiring closet.

Figure 1-23   *Cisco 7970G IP Phone*

If a computer is connected to an IP phone, data packets traveling to and from the computer, and to and from the phone, share the same physical link to the access layer switch and the same port on the access layer switch. This shared physical link has the following implications for the VLAN network configuration:

- Current VLANs may be configured on an IP subnet basis. However, additional IP addresses may not be available for assigning the telephone to the same subnet as the other devices that are connected to the same port.

- Data traffic that is supporting phones on the VLAN may reduce the quality of VoIP traffic.

You can resolve these issues by isolating the voice traffic on a separate VLAN for each of the ports connected to a telephone. The switch port configured for connecting a telephone would have separate VLANs configured to carry the following types of traffic:

- Voice traffic to and from the IP phone (auxiliary VLAN)
- Data traffic to and from the PC connected to the switch through the IP phone access port (native VLAN)

NOTE   In some VoIP literature, you might see *auxiliary VLANs* referred to as *voice VLANs*.

Isolating the telephones on a separate auxiliary VLAN increases voice traffic quality and allows a large number of telephones to be added to an existing network that has a shortage of IP addresses. Additionally, the IP phone marks the voice and data frames with different priority levels, thus allowing the access switch to give priority treatment to the voice frames, as compared to the data frames.

NOTE   Cisco IP phones deployed in an office environment attach to Ethernet switches. The IP phone uses the existing cable infrastructure, or the infrastructure is updated to allow one connection for the phone and one for the desktop PC. The connections from the phone and the PC may lead to the same switch or to different switches. In either case, the IP phone has the capability to prioritize voice frames.

Types of Deployment

When deploying VoIP technologies, design decisions should take into account the environment in which VoIP is being installed. This section considers three typical environments: the campus LAN, enterprise, and service provider environments.

Campus LAN Environment

Campus LAN environments, an example of which is illustrated in Figure 1-24, have grown tremendously in the past several years due to the demand for networked resources, instant business communication, and VoIP applications.

Components for integrated voice and data campus networks, as discussed previously in the "Packet Telephony Components" section, include the following:

- IP Phone
- Gateway
- MCU
- Application server

Figure 1-24 *Campus LAN Environment*

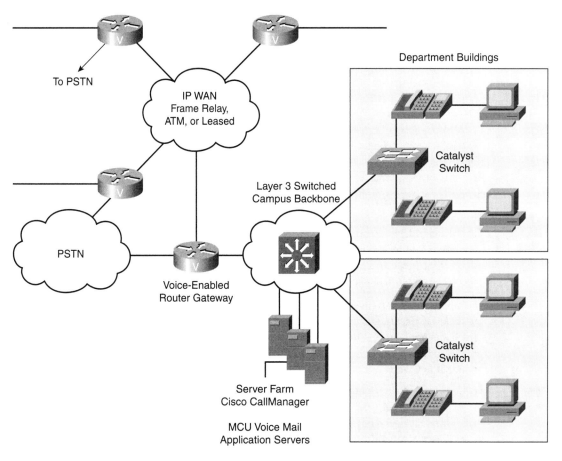

When you are designing the campus infrastructure for voice, you must consider the following key issues:

- Robust, fault-tolerant, highly available network design
- Ability to power IP phones
- Redundant power supply for network components
- Ease of IP addressing
- QoS enhancements

NOTE	Cisco Systems' internal telephone network in San Jose can be considered a campus LAN environment. All desktop phones connect to Ethernet switches and are controlled by Unified CallManager applications. Unified CallManager also controls the gateways and other application servers, such as the Unity server.

Enterprise Environment

Enterprise networks grow and evolve as company services and locations change and expand. Heavy reliance on information processing and universal access to corporate information has driven network designs to provide reliable access, redundancy, reachability, and manageability. These same principles apply to designing corporation-wide voice access in the enterprise environment.

Enterprise networks can be either centralized or distributed call processing environments. In the centralized call processing environment, all of the components of the voice system are controlled by a single centralized call agent, such as Unified CallManager, regardless of their physical location. In a distributed call processing environment, the components of the voice network at each location can act independently.

Figure 1-25 depicts an enterprise centralized call processing environment. Centralized voice networks provide enterprise-wide voice access for calls and voice services controlled from a central site. In this environment, the central site provisions all voice services, such as Cisco Unified CallManager, voice mail, and unified messaging. IP phones at remote sites connect to Cisco Unified CallManager through the IP WAN for call processing.

Components for centralized voice enterprise networks include the following:

- IP phone
- Cisco Unified CallManager cluster (central site only)
- Gateway (all sites)
- MCU (central site only)
- Application server (central site only)
- SRST based on Cisco IOS software (remote sites only)
- IP WAN

Figure 1-26 shows an enterprise distributed call processing environment. Distributed voice networks place voice components at each site and utilize the WAN for intersite calls only.

Figure 1-25 *Enterprise Centralized Call Processing Environment*

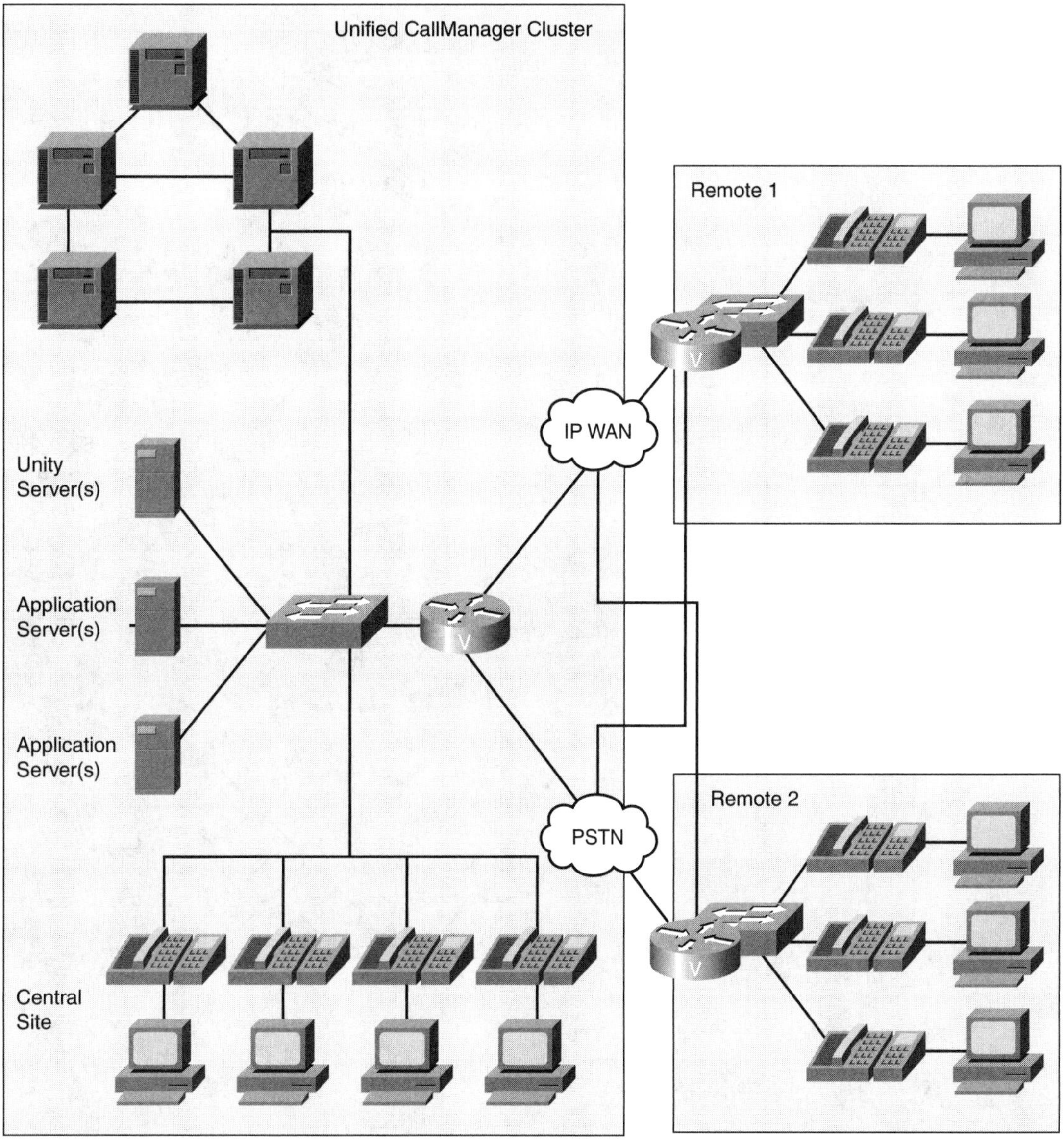

Figure 1-26   *Enterprise Distributed Call Processing Environment*

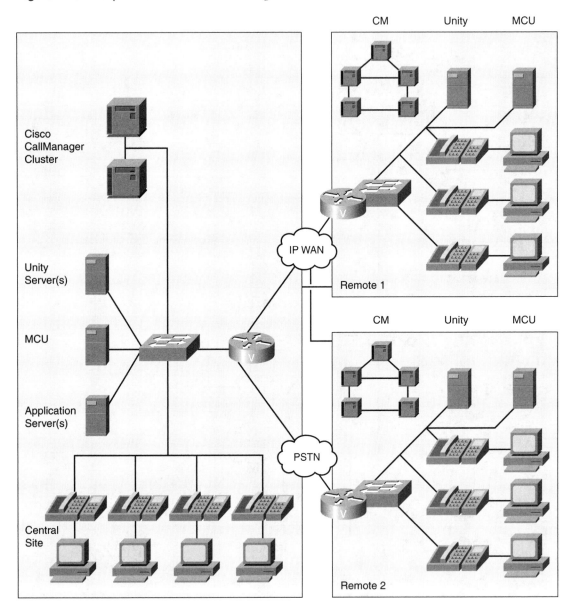

Components for distributed voice enterprise networks include the following:

- IP phone
- Cisco Unified CallManager cluster
- Gateway
- MCU
- Application server (all sites)
- IP WAN

Modern enterprise network applications include:

- E-business
- E-learning
- Customer care
- Unified messaging
- Videoconferencing
- Voice calls placed from web pages

Service Provider Environment

Service provider environments, an example of which is illustrated in Figure 1-27, add another level of complexity to the voice environment. To be competitive, service providers must provide their business customers with more efficient, less expensive alternatives to the PSTN for voice and data services.

Requirements in the service provider arena include:

- **Carrier class performance**—Voice gateways must provide service that minimizes latency and controls jitter. This level of performance allows customers to maintain voice quality as they migrate from circuit-switched voice to IP-based services.

- **Scalability**—Design must accommodate rapid growth to enable service providers to grow with their customer base. An important aspect of scalability is the automation, configuration, and administration of IP networks and gateways for seamless expansion.

- **Comprehensive call records supporting flexible service pricing**—This is the ability to extract IP session and transaction information from multiple network devices and from all layers of the network, in real time, to produce detailed billing records.

- **Signaling System 7 (SS7) interconnect capabilities**—Tariffs favor interconnection using SS7 signaling because Inter-Machine Trunks (IMTs) are less expensive than ISDN-based facilities. This financial benefit equates to lower monthly expenses, reduced cost of goods that are sold, and higher margins for service providers.

Figure 1-27 *Service Provider Environment*

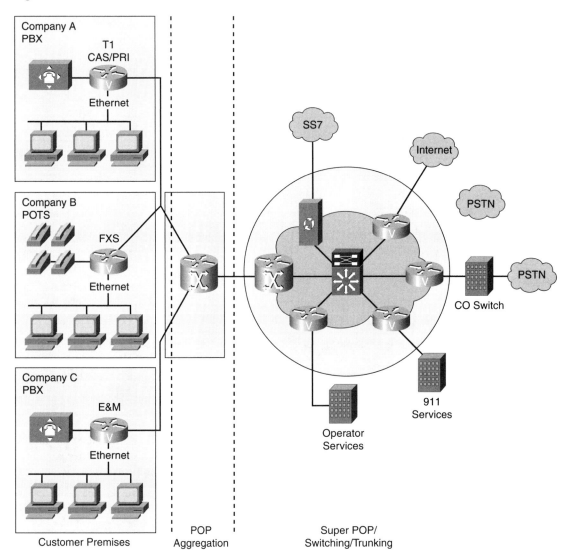

Summary

This chapter explored the fundamental concepts surrounding traditional telephony services, including privately owned and publicly owned telephone switches, call signaling, and multiplexing techniques. Also, the chapter identified foundational IP telephony concepts (for example, centralized and distributed call processing models) and components (for example, analog and digital interfaces).

Chapter Review Questions

The following questions test your knowledge of topics explained in this chapter. You can find the answers to the questions in Appendix A, "Answers to Chapter Review Questions."

1. Which type of trunk connects two local telephone company COs?

   a   tie trunk

   b   CO trunk

   c   interoffice trunk

   d   OPX trunk

2. What type of "tone" is used by a touch-tone phone to dial digits?

   a   CAS

   b   DTMF

   c   SF

   d   TDM

3. Which multiplexing process is used by TDM?

   a   Timeslots are assigned to different channels, regardless of whether there is data to transmit.

   b   Timeslots are assigned to different channels depending on which traffic has a higher priority at that time.

   c   All timeslots are used by the channel that is transmitting data at that time.

   d   Timeslots are assigned to the channel that starts transmitting first and are used by the other channels as timeslots become available.

4. DSL is an example of which style of multiplexing?

   a   frequency-division

   b   phase-division

   c   time-division

   d   statistical time-division

5. When discussing call control, what function does call setup use to ensure that there is enough bandwidth to place a call?

   a   call routing

   b   call maintenance

   c   call supervision

   d   Call Admission Control

6. Which two protocols are examples of distributed call control?

   a   MGCP

   b   H.323

   c   SIP

   d   Megaco

7. In the centralized call control model, signaling is performed by which component?

   a   gateway

   b   gatekeeper

   c   MCU

   d   call agent

8. To what does the FXS interface provide a direct connection?

   a CO

   b E&M trunk

   c telephone

   d gatekeeper

9. What is the function of the SRST component of a centralized voice enterprise network?

   a Connects IP phones on remote sites to Cisco Unified CallManager

   b Provides local call-processing capabilities in case of a WAN outage

   c Configures routing plans for the gateways

   d Serves as the primary voice path between sites

10. An E1 interface can carry up to how many simultaneous conversations?

   a 16

   b 24

   c 30

   d 32

After reading this chapter, you should be able to perform the following tasks:

- Select the appropriate analog voice connection for a Cisco device
- Choose a voice compression scheme that best suits your needs
- Describe the appropriate signaling method to deploy in a telephony system
- Implement an effective method of transporting fax and modem traffic over a VoIP network

CHAPTER 2

Analog and Digital Voice Connections

Cisco voice devices must support a wide variety of connection types. This chapter describes the various analog and digital connections, describes common compression schemes, and concludes with a description of fax-over-IP and modem-over-IP voice networks.

Upon completing this chapter, you will be able to explain the processes and standards for voice digitization, compression, digital signaling, and fax/modem transport as they relate to Voice over IP (VoIP) networks.

Analog Voice Fundamentals

Interfacing Cisco Systems equipment with traditional analog telephony devices requires an understanding of the various interfaces used in the industry. This section introduces analog interfaces that you can select from, including Foreign Exchange Station (FXS), Foreign Exchange Office (FXO), and ear and mouth (E&M).

Local-Loop Connections

A subscriber home telephone connects to the telephone company central office (CO) via an electrical communication path called a *local loop*, as illustrated in Figure 2-1. The loop consists of a pair of twisted wires. One is called *tip;* the other is called *ring*, as shown in Figure 2-2.

Figure 2-1   *Local Loops*

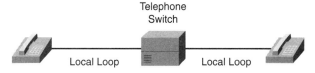

The names *tip* and *ring* come from the plug used by the operators of yesteryear to interconnect calls. As you can see in Figure 2-2, the plug used by these operators resembles the plug you might use to connect your headphones to your home stereo equipment. There are three conductors on this plug. The conductor (that is, wire) connected to the tip of the plug is called the *tip wire*, and the conductor connected to the ring in the middle of the plug is called the *ring wire*.

Figure 2-2 *Tip and Ring*

In most arrangements, the ring wire ties to the negative side of a power source, called the *battery*, while the tip wire connects to the ground. When you take your telephone off hook, current flows around the loop, allowing dial tone to reach your handset. Your local loop, along with all others in your neighborhood, connects to the CO in a cable bundle, either buried underground or strung on poles.

NOTE Your home telephone service is provided to you from your service provider by way of two wires. Your home telephone controls whether the service on these wires is activated via the switch hook inside the telephone.

Local-Loop Signaling

A subscriber and telephone company notify each other of the call status through audible tones and an exchange of electrical current. This exchange of information is called *local-loop signaling*. Local-loop signaling consists of supervisory signaling, address signaling, and informational signaling, each of which has its own characteristics and purpose. The three types of local-loop signaling appear on the local loop and serve to prompt the subscriber and the switch into a certain action.

Supervisory Signaling

Resting the handset on the telephone cradle opens the switch hook and prevents the circuit current from flowing through the telephone, as seen in Figure 2-3. Regardless of the signaling type, a circuit goes on hook when the handset is placed on the telephone cradle and the switch hook is toggled to an open state. When the telephone is in this position, only the ringer is active.

Figure 2-3   *On Hook*

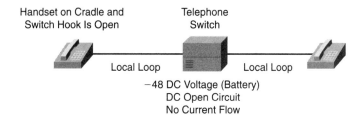

To place a call, a subscriber must lift the handset from the telephone cradle. Removing the handset from the cradle places the circuit off hook, as shown in Figure 2-4. The switch hook is then toggled to a closed state, causing circuit current to flow through the electrical loop. The current notifies the telephone company that someone is requesting to place a telephone call. When the telephone network senses the off-hook connection by the flow of current, it provides a signal in the form of the dial tone to indicate that it is ready.

Figure 2-4   *Off Hook*

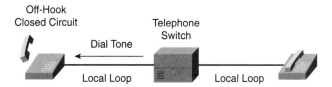

When a subscriber makes a call, the telephone switch sends voltage to the ringer to notify the other subscriber of an inbound call, as illustrated in Figure 2-5. The telephone company also sends a ringback tone to the caller, alerting the caller that it is sending ringing voltage to the recipient telephone.

Figure 2-5   *Ringing*

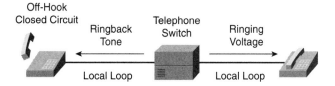

The pattern of the ring signal, or *ring cadence*, varies around the world. As depicted in Figure 2-6, the ring cadence (that is, ringing pattern) in the United States is 2 seconds of ringing followed by 4 seconds of silence. The United Kingdom uses a double ring of 0.4 seconds separated by 0.2 seconds of silence, followed by 2 seconds of silence.

Figure 2-6   *Ring Cadences*

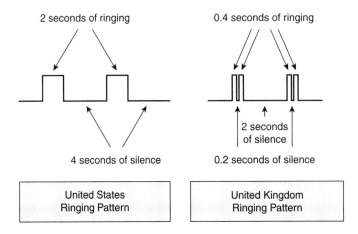

Address Signaling

Although somewhat outdated, rotary-dial telephones are still in use and easily recognized by their large numeric dial-wheel. When placing a call, the subscriber spins the large numeric dial-wheel to send digits. These digits must be produced at a specific rate and within a certain level of tolerance. Each pulse consists of a "break" and a "make," as detailed in Figure 2-7. The *break* segment is the time that the circuit is open. The *make* segment is the time during which the circuit is closed. In the United States, the break-and-make cycle must correspond to a ratio of 60 percent break to 40 percent make.

A governor inside the dial controls the rate at which the digits are pulsed. The dial pulse signaling process occurs as follows:

1. When a subscriber calls someone by dialing a digit on the rotary dial, a spring winds.

2. When the dial is released, the spring rotates the dial back to its original position.

3. While the spring rotates the dial back to its original position, a cam-driven switch opens and closes the connection to the telephone company. The number of consecutive opens and closes (that is, breaks and makes) represents the dialed digit.

A more modern approach to address signaling is touch-tone dialing. Users who have a touch-tone pad or a push-button telephone must push the keypad buttons to place a call, rather than rotating a dial as they did with pulse dialing. Each button on the keypad is associated with a set of high and low frequencies. Each row of keys on the keypad is identified by a low-frequency tone; each column of keys on the keypad is identified by a high-frequency tone. The combination of both tones notifies the telephone company of the number being called, hence the term *dual-tone multifrequency (DTMF)*. Figure 2-8 illustrates the combination of tones generated for each button on the keypad.

Figure 2-7   *Pulse Dialing*

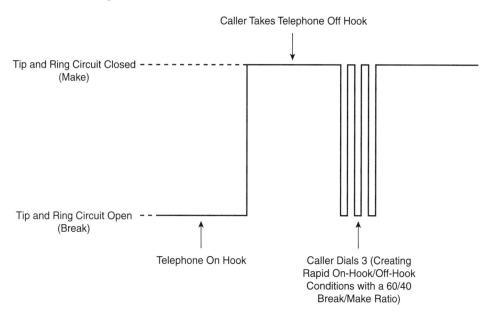

Figure 2-8   *Dual-Tone Multifrequency*

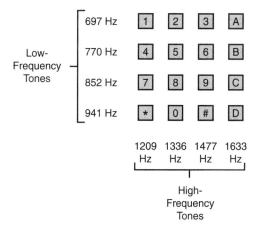

Informational Signaling

DTMF tones are used not just for address signaling but also for informational signaling. Specifically, call-progress indicators in the form of tone combinations are used to notify subscribers of call status. Each combination of tones represents a different event in the call process, as follows:

- **Dial tone**—Indicates that the telephone company is ready to receive digits from the user telephone. Cisco routers provide dial tone as a method of showing that the hardware is installed. In a PBX or key telephone system, the dial tone indicates the system is ready to receive digits.

- **Busy**—Indicates that a call cannot be completed because the telephone at the remote end is already in use.

- **Ringback (CO or PBX)**—Indicates that the telephone switch is attempting to complete a call on behalf of a subscriber.

- **Congestion**—Indicates that congestion in the long-distance telephone network is preventing a telephone call from being processed. The congestion tone is sometimes known as the *all-circuits-busy tone*.

- **Reorder**—Indicates that all of the local telephone circuits are busy, thus preventing a telephone call from being processed. The reorder tone is known to the user as *fast-busy* and is familiar to anyone who operates a telephone from a PBX.

- **Receiver off hook**—Indicates that the receiver has been off hook for an extended period without placing a call.

- **No such number**—Indicates that a subscriber placed a call to a nonexistent number.

Trunk Connections

Before a telephone call terminates at its final destination, the call is routed through multiple switches. When a switch receives a call, it determines whether the destination telephone number is within a local switch or if the call needs to go through another switch to a remote destination. Trunks interconnect the telephone company and PBX switches, as shown in Figure 2-9.

The primary function of the trunk is to provide the path between switches. The switch must route the call to the correct trunk or telephone line. Although many different subscribers share a trunk, only one subscriber uses it at any given time. As telephone calls end, they release trunks and make them available to the switch for subsequent calls. There can be several trunks between two switches.

Figure 2-9   *Trunks*

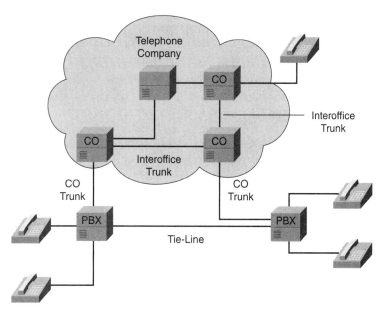

The following are examples of the more common trunk types:

- **Private trunk lines (tie-lines)**—Companies with multiple PBXs often connect them with tie trunk lines. Generally, tie trunk lines serve as dedicated circuits that connect PBXs. On a monthly basis, subscribers lease trunks from the telephone company to avoid the expense of using telephone lines on a per-extension basis. These types of connections, known as *tie-lines*, typically use special interfaces called recEive and transMit, or E&M interfaces.

- **CO trunks**—A CO trunk serves as a direct connection between a PBX and the local CO that routes calls; for example, the connection from a private office network to the public switched telephone network (PSTN). When users dial 9, they are connecting through their PBX to the CO trunk to access the PSTN. CO trunks typically use Foreign Exchange Office interfaces. Certain specialized CO trunks are frequently used on the telephony network. A *direct inward dial* trunk, for example, allows outside callers to reach specific internal destinations without having to be connected via an operator.

- **Interoffice trunks**—An interoffice trunk is a circuit that connects two local telephone company COs.

- **Foreign exchange (FX) trunks**—FX trunks are interfaces that are connected to switches supporting connections to either office equipment or station equipment. Office equipment includes other switches (to extend the connection) and Cisco devices. Station equipment includes telephones, fax machines, and modems. The two FX trunk interfaces are:

  — **Foreign Exchange Office (FXO) interfaces**—An FXO interface connects a PBX to another switch or Cisco device. The purpose of an FXO interface is to extend the telephony connection to a remote site; for example, if a user on a corporate PBX wanted a telephone installed at home instead of in the local office where the PBX is located, an FXO interface would be used. The FXO interface would connect to a Cisco voice router, which would serve to extend the connection to the user's home. This connection is an Off-Premises eXtension (OPX).

  — **Foreign Exchange Station (FXS) interfaces**—An FXS interface connects station equipment: telephones, fax machines, and modems. A telephone connected directly to a switch or Cisco device requires an FXS interface. Because a home telephone connects directly to the telephone company CO switch, an FXS interface is used.

NOTE   The service provided by local telephone companies for residential phones uses a foreign exchange interface, specifically FXS. This service is provided on two wires. The service is considered a station-side connection because the interface terminates with a telephone.

Trunk Signaling

Lines and trunks must adhere to signaling standards just as telephony networks and telephone companies do. Trunk signaling serves to initiate the connection between the switch and the network. There are five different types of trunk signaling, and each applies to different kinds of interfaces, such as FXS, FXO, and E&M:

- Loop-start signaling
- Ground-start signaling
- E&M wink-start signaling
- E&M immediate-start signaling
- E&M delay-start signaling

The following sections explain these signaling types.

Loop-Start Signaling

Loop-start signaling allows a user or the telephone company to seize a line or trunk when a subscriber is initiating a call. It is primarily used on local loops connecting to residences rather than on trunks interconnecting telephone switches.

A telephone connection exists in one of the following states, as illustrated in Figure 2-10:

- Idle (on hook)
- Telephone seizure (off hook)
- CO seizure (ringing)

Figure 2-10 *Loop-Start Signaling*

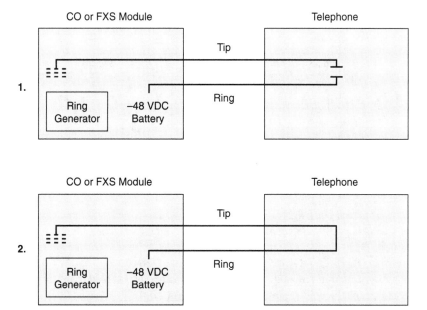

A summary of the loop-start signaling process is as follows:

1. When the line is in the idle state, or on hook, the telephone or PBX opens the two-wire loop. The CO or FXS has *battery* on ring and *ground* on tip.

2. If a user lifts the handset off the cradle to place a call, the switch hook goes off hook and closes the loop (line seizure). The current can now flow through the telephone circuit. The CO or FXS module detects the current and returns a dial tone.

3. When the CO or FXS module detects an incoming call, it applies AC ring voltage superimposed over the –48 VDC battery, causing the ring generator to notify the recipient of a telephone call. When the telephone or PBX answers the call, thus closing the loop, the CO or FXS module removes the ring voltage.

Loop-start signaling is a poor solution for high-volume trunks because it leads to *glare*, which is the simultaneous seizure of the trunk from both ends. Glare occurs, for example, when you pick up your home telephone and find that someone is already at the other end.

Glare is not a significant problem at home. It is, however, a major problem when it occurs between switches at high-volume switching centers, such as long-distance carriers or large PBX systems.

Ground-Start Signaling

Ground-start signaling, illustrated in Figure 2-11, is a modification of loop-start signaling that corrects for the probability of glare. It solves the problem by providing current detection at both ends.

Figure 2-11 *Ground-Start Signaling*

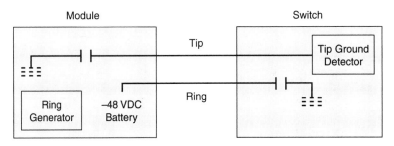

Although loop-start signaling works when you use your telephone at home, ground-start signaling is preferable when there are high-volume trunks involved at telephone switching centers. Because ground-start signaling uses a request or confirm switch at both ends of the interface, it is preferable over other signaling methods on high-usage trunks, such as FXOs. FXOs require implementation of answer supervision (reversal or absence of current) on the interface for the confirmation of on hook or off hook.

E&M Signaling

E&M signaling supports tie-line type facilities or signals between voice switches. Instead of superimposing both voice and signaling on the same wire, E&M uses separate paths, or leads, for each.

To call a remote office, your PBX must route a request for use of the trunk over its signal leads between the two sites. Your PBX makes the request by activating its M-lead. The other PBX detects the request when it detects current flowing on its E-lead. It then attaches a dial register to the trunk and your PBX, which sends the dialed digits. The remote PBX activates its M-lead to notify the local PBX that the call has been answered.

There are five types of E&M signaling: Type I, Type II, Type III, Type IV, and Type V. The E&M leads operate differently with each wiring scheme, as shown in Table 2-1 and Table 2-2. Keep in mind that any of the E&M supervisory signaling types (that is, wink-start, immediate-start, and delay-start) can operate over any of the following wiring schemes.

Table 2-1   *PBX to Intermediate Device*

Signaling Type	Lead	On Hook	Off Hook
I	M	Ground	Battery (-48 VDC)
II	M	Open	Battery (-48 VDC)
III	M	Ground	Battery (-48 VDC)
IV	M	Open	Ground
V	M	Open	Ground

Table 2-2   *Intermediate Device to PBX*

Signaling Type	Lead	On Hook	Off Hook
I	E	Open	Ground
II	E	Open	Ground
III	E	Open	Ground
IV	E	Open	Ground
V	E	Open	Ground

Four-wire E&M Type I signaling, shown in Figure 2-12, is actually a six-wire E&M signaling interface common in North America. One wire is the E-lead; the second wire is the M-lead, and the remaining two pairs of wires serve as the audio path. In this arrangement, the PBX supplies power, or *battery*, for both the M-leads and E-leads. This arrangement also requires that a common ground be connected between the PBX and the Cisco voice equipment.

With the Type I interface, the Cisco voice equipment (tie-line equipment) generates the E signal to the PBX by grounding the E-lead. The PBX detects the E signal by sensing the increase in current through a resistive load. Similarly, the PBX generates the M signal by sourcing a current to the Cisco voice equipment (tie-line equipment), which detects it via a resistive load. The signal battery (SB) lead provides battery, while the signal ground (SG) lead provides ground.

Figure 2-12 *E&M Type I*

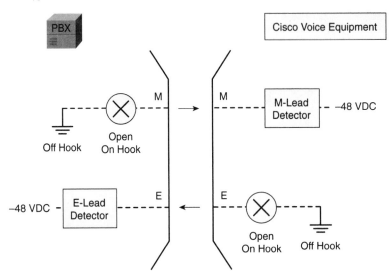

Type V, as illustrated in Figure 2-13, is another six-wire E&M signaling type and the most common E&M signaling form outside of North America. In Type V, one wire is the E-lead and the other wire is the M-lead.

Figure 2-13 *E&M Type V*

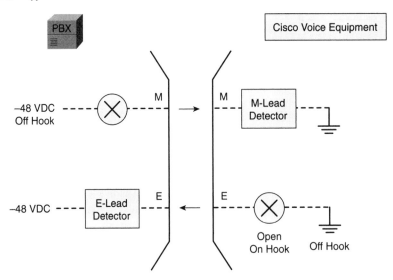

Type V is a modified version of the Type I interface. In the Type V interface, the Cisco voice equipment (tie-line equipment) supplies battery for the M-lead while the PBX supplies battery for the E-lead. As in Type I, Type V requires that a common ground be connected between the PBX and the Cisco voice equipment.

Types II, III, and IV are eight-wire interfaces, where the eight wires include the voice path. One wire is the E-lead; the other wire is the M-lead. Two other wires are SG and SB. In Type II, SG and SB are the return paths for the E-lead and M-lead, respectively.

The Type II interface, depicted in Figure 2-14, exists for applications where a common ground between the PBX and the Cisco voice equipment (tie-line equipment) is not possible or practical. For example, the PBX is in one building on a campus and the Cisco equipment is in another. Because there is no common ground, each of the signals has its own return. For the E signal, the tie-line equipment permits the current to flow from the PBX; the current returns to the PBX SG lead or reference. Similarly, the PBX closes a path for the current to generate the M signal to the Cisco voice equipment (tie-line equipment) on the SB lead.

Figure 2-14 *E&M Type II*

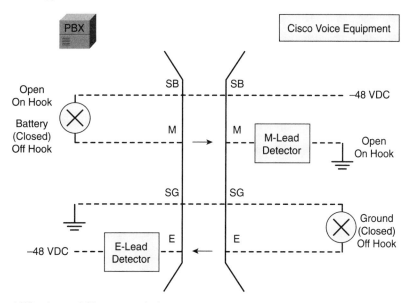

4-Wire, Looped, Nonsymmetrical

Type III, as demonstrated in Figure 2-15, is useful for environments where the M-lead is likely to experience electrical interference and falsely signal its attached equipment. When idle, Type III latches the M-lead via an electrical relay to the SG lead. When the PBX activates the M-lead, it first delatches the SG lead via the relay and signals normally, as in Type II. Type III is not a common implementation.

Figure 2-15 *E&M Type III*

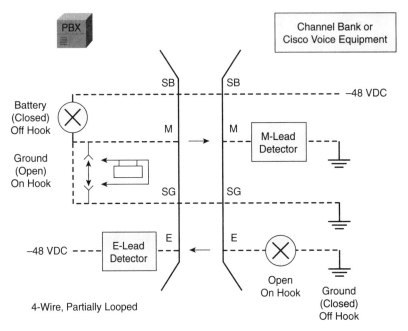

4-Wire, Partially Looped

Type IV, shown in Figure 2-16, is a variation of Type II. In this arrangement, the battery source and ground are reversed on the SB and M wires (as compared to Type II). This means that both the SB and SG wires are grounded. Type IV signaling is symmetric and requires no common ground. Each side closes a current loop to signal, which detects the flow of current through a resistive load to indicate the presence of the signal. Cisco voice equipment does not support Type IV.

E&M Wink-Start Signaling

Tie trunks have bidirectional supervisory signaling that allows either end to initiate a trunk seizure. In this way, one PBX seizes the trunk, which then waits for an acknowledgment reply from the remote end. The local end must differentiate between a return acknowledgment and a remote-end request for service. Wink-start signaling, shown in Figure 2-17, is the most common E&M trunk seizure signal type.

The following scenario summarizes the wink-start protocol event sequence:

- The calling office seizes the line by activating its M-lead.

- Instead of returning an off-hook acknowledgment immediately, the called switch allocates memory for use as a dial register, in the area of memory it uses to store incoming digits.

Figure 2-16 *E&M Type IV*

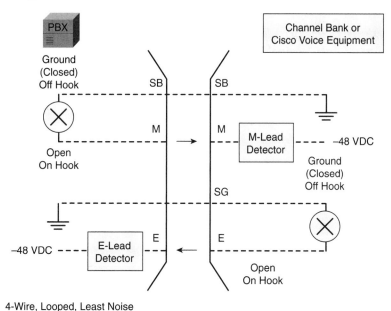

4-Wire, Looped, Least Noise

Figure 2-17 *Trunk Supervisory Signaling: Wink-Start*

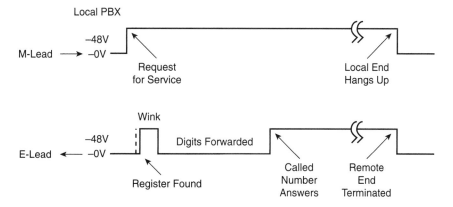

- The called switch toggles its M-lead on and off for a specific time (usually 170 to 340 ms). (This on-hook/off-hook/on-hook sequence constitutes the wink.)

- The calling switch receives the wink on its E-lead and forwards the digits to the remote end. DTMF tones are forwarded across the E&M link in the audio path, not on the M-lead.

- The called party answers the telephone, and the called PBX raises its M-lead for the duration of the call.

If the timing of the returned wink is too short or impossible to detect, the trunk uses immediate-start, which the following section describes.

E&M Immediate-Start Signaling

Immediate-start signaling occurs occasionally if a PBX vendor implements wink-start, shown in Figure 2-18, but does not conform to the standards.

Figure 2-18 *Trunk Supervisory Signaling: Immediate-Start*

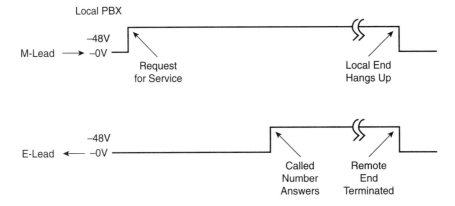

The following scenario summarizes the sequence of events for the immediate-start protocol:

- The calling PBX seizes the line by activating its M-lead.

- Instead of receiving an acknowledgment, the calling PBX waits a predetermined period (a minimum of 150 ms) and forwards the digits blindly. DTMF tones are forwarded across the E&M link in the audio path, not on the M-lead.

- The called PBX acknowledges the calling PBX only after the called party answers the call by raising its M-lead.

E&M Delay-Start Signaling

Delay-start signaling, as depicted in Figure 2-19, is the original start protocol for E&M.

Delay-start is used when all of the equipment is mechanical and requires time to process requests. The following scenario summarizes delay-start signaling:

- When you place a call, your calling switch goes off hook by activating its M-lead.

- The called switch acknowledges the request by activating its M-lead, and then rotates armatures and gears to reset its dial register to zero.

Figure 2-19 *Trunk Supervisory Signaling: Delay-Start*

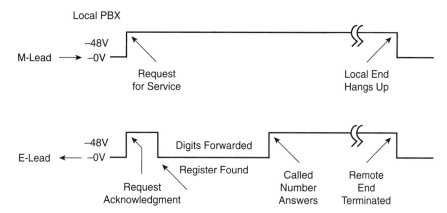

- When the dial register at the called switch is in the ready state, the called switch deactivates its M-lead.

- The calling switch then sends dialed digits. DTMF tones are forwarded across the E&M link in the audio path, not on the M-lead.

- When the called party answers, the called switch again activates its M-lead.

Echo

Although a local loop consists of two wires, when it reaches the switch, the connection changes to four wires with a two- to four-wire hybrid converter. Trunks then transport the signal across the network, as shown in Figure 2-20.

Figure 2-20 *Two-Wire to Four-Wire Conversion and Echo*

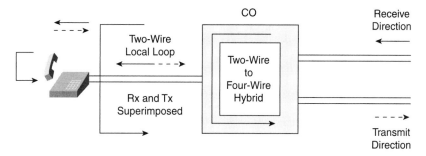

Telephone networks can experience two types of echo:

- **Acoustic echo**—Acoustic echo frequently occurs with speakerphones, when the received voice on the speaker excites the microphone and travels back to the speaker.

- **Electrical echo**—Electrical echo occurs when there is an electrical inconsistency in the telephony circuits. This electrical inconsistency is called an *impedance mismatch*.

If the lines have a good impedance match, the hybrid (that is, the two-wire to four-wire conversion circuit) is considered balanced, with little or no reflected energy. However, if the hybrid is inadequately balanced, and a portion of the transmit voice is reflected back toward the receive side, echo results.

Some form of echo is always present, as illustrated in Figure 2-21. However, echo can become a problem under the following conditions:

- The magnitude or loudness of the echo is high.
- The delay time between when you speak and when you hear your voice reflected is significant.
- The listener hears the speaker twice.

Figure 2-21 *Echo Is Always Present*

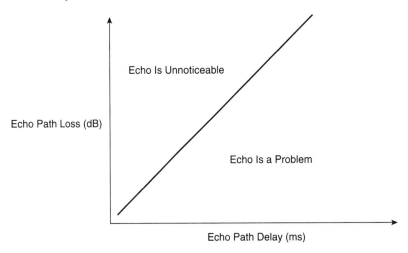

The two components of echo are loudness and delay. Reducing either component reduces overall echo. When a user experiences delay, the conversation can get choppy, and the words of the participants sometimes overlap.

NOTE   Echo tolerance varies. For most users, however, echo delay over 50 ms is problematic.

There are two ways to solve an echo problem in your telephone network:

- Echo suppression
- Echo cancellation

The echo suppressor, as depicted in Figure 2-22, works by transmitting speech in the forward direction and prohibiting audio in the return direction. The echo suppressor essentially breaks the return transmission path. This solution works sufficiently for voice transmission. However, for full-duplex modem connections, the action of the echo suppressor prevents communication. Therefore, when modems handshake, the answering modem returns a 2025 Hz tone to the calling modem, which serves to disable the echo suppressors along the transmission path.

Figure 2-22 *Echo Suppression*

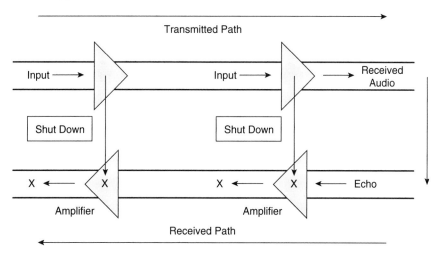

Echo suppression has shortcomings in addressing certain echo conflict situations. Echo cancellation, a schematic of which is shown in Figure 2-23, is a more sophisticated method of eliminating echo.

Rather than breaking or attenuating the return path (as in echo suppression), echo cancellation uses a special circuit to build a mathematical model of the transmitted speech pattern and subtracts it from the return path.

NOTE   Echo cancellation applies the same technology that is used in audio headphones to cancel ambient noise. The headsets used by airline pilots, for example, feature a suppression circuit that cancels ambient noise so that the pilot hears only the audio from the headset. Any ambient noise from the cockpit is cancelled. This is the same technology used in echo cancellers.

Echo cancellation is the most common method of removing echo in the telephone network today and is used when necessary to adjust for echo on a Cisco device.

Figure 2-23 *Echo Cancellation*

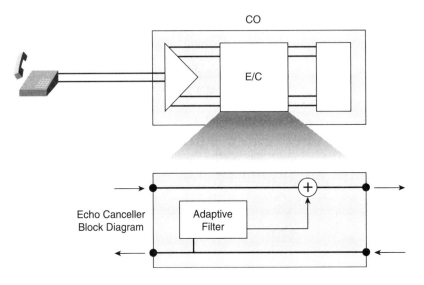

NOTE   The echo canceller removes the echo from one end of the circuit only. If echo is an issue at both ends of the circuit, you must apply another echo canceller at the other end.

Analog-to-Digital and Digital-to-Analog Voice Encoding

This section covers the fundamentals of digitally encoding voice, specifically, the basics of voice digitization and the various compression schemes that are used to transport voice while using less bandwidth.

Digitizing speech was a project first undertaken by the Bell System in the 1950s. The original purpose of digitizing speech was to deploy more voice circuits with a smaller number of wires. This evolved into the T1 and E1 transmission methods of today. Examples of analog and digital waveforms are presented in Figure 2-24.

Table 2-3 details the steps to convert an analog signal to a digital signal.

The three mandatory components in the analog-to-digital conversion process are further described as follows:

- **Sampling**—Sample the analog signal at periodic intervals. The output of sampling is a pulse amplitude modulation (PAM) signal.

- **Quantization**—Match the PAM signal to a segmented scale. This scale measures the amplitude (height) of the PAM signal and assigns an integer number to define that amplitude.

- **Encoding**—Convert the integer base-10 number to a binary number. The output of encoding is a binary expression in which each bit is either a 1 (pulse) or a 0 (no pulse).

Figure 2-24 *Analog and Digital Waveforms*

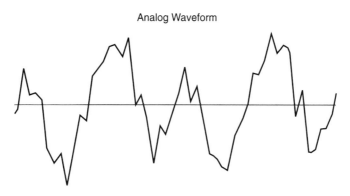

Analog Waveform

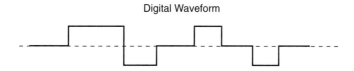

Digital Waveform

Table 2-3   *Analog-to-Digital Signal Conversion*

Step	Procedure	Description
1	Sample the analog signal regularly.	The sampling rate must be at least twice the highest frequency, to accurately represent the original signal.
2	Quantize the sample.	Quantization consists of a scale made up of 8 major divisions or chords. Each chord is subdivided into 16 equally spaced steps. The chords are not equally spaced but are actually finest near the origin. Steps are equal within the chords but different when they are compared between the chords. Finer graduations at the origin result in less distortion for low-level tones.
3	Encode the value into an 8-bit digital form.	PBX output is a continuous analog voice waveform. T1 digital voice is a snapshot of the wave encoded into binary digits (that is, ones and zeros).
4	(Optional) Compress the samples to reduce bandwidth.	Although not required to convert analog signals to digital, signal compression is widely used to reduce bandwidth requirements.

This three-step process is repeated 8000 times per second for telephone voice-channel service. Use the fourth optional step, compression, to save bandwidth. This optional step allows a single channel to carry more voice calls.

NOTE   The most commonly used method of converting analog to digital is pulse code modulation (PCM), as described later in the "Voice Compression Standards" section of this chapter.

After the receiving terminal at the far end receives the digital PCM signal, it must convert the PCM signal back into an analog signal. The process of converting digital signals back into analog signals includes the following two processes:

- **Decoding**—The received 8-bit word is decoded to recover the number that defines the amplitude of that sample. This information is used to rebuild a PAM signal of the original amplitude. This process is simply the reverse of the analog-to-digital conversion.

- **Filtering**—The PAM signal is passed through a filter to reconstruct the original analog wave form from its digitally coded counterpart.

With this basic understanding of analog to digital conversion, this chapter considers the sampling, quantization, and encoding processes more thoroughly, beginning with sampling.

Sampling and the Nyquist Theorem

One of the major issues with sampling is determining how often to take those samples (that is, "snapshots") of the analog wave. You do not want to take too few samples per second because when the equipment at the other end of the phone call attempts to reassemble and make sense of those samples, a different sound (that is, a lower frequency sound) signal might also match those samples, and the incorrect sound would be heard by the listener. This phenomenon is called *aliasing*, as shown in Figure 2-25.

With the obvious detrimental effect of undersampling, you might be tempted to take many more samples per second. While that approach, sometimes called *oversampling*, does indeed eliminate the issue of aliasing, it also suffers from a major drawback. If you take far more samples per second than actually needed to accurately recreate the original signal, you consume more bandwidth than is absolutely necessary. Because bandwidth is a scarce commodity (especially on a wide-area network), you do not want to perform the oversampling shown in Figure 2-26.

Figure 2-25 *Aliasing*

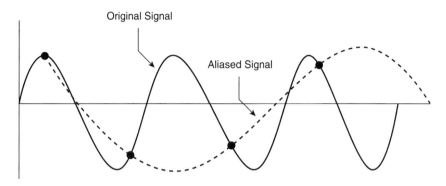

Figure 2-26 *Oversampling*

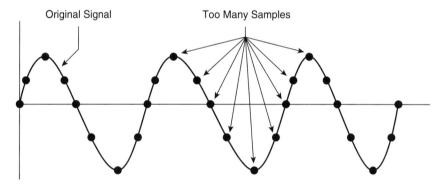

Digital signal technology is based on the premise stated in the Nyquist Theorem: When a signal is instantaneously sampled at the transmitter in regular intervals and has a rate of at least twice the highest channel frequency, then the samples will contain sufficient information to allow an accurate reconstruction of the signal at the receiver. Figure 2-27 illustrates sampling, as prescribed by the Nyquist Theorem.

While the human ear can sense sounds from 20 to 20,000 Hz, and speech encompasses sounds from about 200 to 9000 Hz, the telephone channel was designed to operate at about 300 to 3400 Hz. This economical range carries enough fidelity to allow callers to identify the party at the far end and sense their mood. Nyquist decided to extend the digitization to 4000 Hz, to capture higher-frequency sounds that the telephone channel may deliver. Therefore, the highest frequency for voice is 4000 Hz, or 8000 samples per second; that is, one sample every 125 microseconds.

Figure 2-27 *Nyquist Theorem*

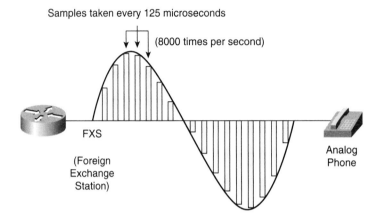

Quantization

Quantization involves dividing the range of amplitude values that are present in an analog signal sample into a set of discrete steps that are closest in value to the original analog signal, as illustrated in Figure 2-28. Each step is assigned a unique digital code word.

Figure 2-28 *Quantization*

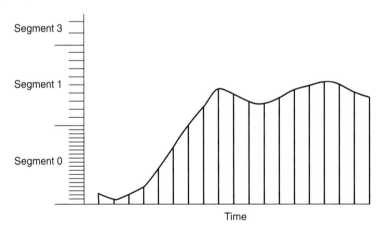

In Figure 2-28, the x-axis is time and the y-axis is the voltage value (PAM). The voltage range is divided into 16 segments (0 to 7 positive, and 0 to 7 negative). Starting with segment 0, each segment has fewer steps than the previous segment, which reduces the signal-to-noise ratio (SNR) and makes the segment uniform. This segmentation also corresponds closely to the logarithmic behavior of the human ear. If there is an SNR problem, it is resolved by using a logarithmic scale to convert PAM to PCM.

Linear sampling of analog signals causes small-amplitude signals to have a lower SNR, and therefore poorer quality, than larger amplitude signals. The Bell System developed the *μ-law* method of quantization, which is widely used in North America. The International Telecommunication Union (ITU) modified the original μ-law method and created *a-law*, which is used in countries outside of North America.

By allowing smaller step functions at lower amplitudes, rather than higher amplitudes, μ-law and a-law provide a method of reducing this problem. Both μ-law and a-law "compand" the signal; that is, they both compress the signal for transmission and then expand the signal back to its original form at the other end.

To calculate the bit rate of digital voice, you can use the formula:

2 * 4 kHz * 8 bits per sample = 64,000 bits per second (64 kbps).
64 kbps is a digital signal level 0 (DS-0) rate.

The result of using μ-law and a-law is a more accurate value for smaller amplitude and uniform signal-to-noise quantization ratio (SQR) across the input range.

NOTE   For communication between a μ-law country and an a-law country, the μ-law country must change its signaling to accommodate the a-law country.

Both μ-law and a-law are linear approximations of a logarithmic input/output relationship. They both generate 64-kbps bit streams using 8-bit code words to segment and quantize levels within segments.

The difference between the original analog signal and the quantization level assigned, as seen in Figure 2-29, is called quantization error, which is the source of distortion in digital transmission systems.

Due to the quantization error, the recreated signal at the receiving end will experience quantization noise. The quantization noise is mostly insignificant since a single sample represents only 1/8000th of a second. However, frequent quantization errors will cause perceptible quantization noise. For this reason, the recreated signal at the receiving end is sent through a low-pass filter, which filters out the noise.

Figure 2-29 *Quantization Error*

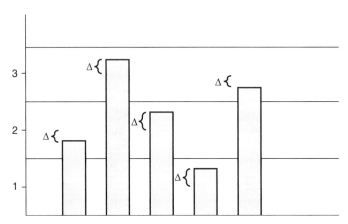

Voice Compression Standards

To conserve valuable WAN bandwidth, you can compress the quantized voice waveforms. Two categories of waveform encoding include:

- **Waveform algorithms (coders)**—Waveform algorithms have the following functions and characteristics:

    — Sample analog signals at 8000 times per second

    — Use predictive differential methods to reduce bandwidth

    — Highly impact voice quality because of reduced bandwidth

    — Do not take advantage of speech characteristics

    — Examples include: G.711 and G.726

- **Source algorithms (coders)**—Source algorithms have the following functions and characteristics:

    — Source algorithm coders are called *vocoders*, or voice coders. A vocoder is a device that converts analog speech into digital speech, using a specific compression scheme that is optimized for coding human speech.

    — Vocoders take advantage of speech characteristics.

    — Bandwidth reduction occurs by sending linear-filter settings.

    — Codebooks store specific predictive waveshapes of human speech. They match the speech, encode the phrases, decode the waveshapes at the receiver by looking up the coded phrase, and match it to the stored waveshape in the receiver codebook.

    — Examples include: G.728 and G.729

The following three common voice compression techniques are standardized by the ITU-T:

- **PCM**—Amplitude of voice signal is sampled and quantized at 8000 times per second. Each sample is then represented by one octet (8 bits) and transmitted. For sampling, you must use either a-law or μ-law to reduce the signal-to-noise ratio.

- **ADPCM**—The difference between the current sample and its predicted value (based on past samples). ADPCM is represented by 2, 3, 4, or 5 bits. This method reduces the bandwidth requirement at the expense of signal quality.

- **CELP**—Excitation value and a set of linear-predictive filters (settings) are transmitted. The filter setting transmissions are less frequent than excitation values and are sent on an as-needed basis.

Table 2-4 describes the CODECs and compression standards.

Table 2-4   *CODECs and Compression Standards*

CODEC	Compression Technique	Bit Rate (kbps)
G.711	PCM	64
G.726	ADPCM	16, 24, 32
G.728	LDCELP	16
G.729	CS-ACELP	8
G.729A	CS-ACELP	8

A common type of waveform encoding is pulse code modulation (PCM). Standard PCM is known as ITU standard G.711, which requires 64,000 bits per second of bandwidth to transport the voice payload (that is, not including any overhead), as shown in Figure 2-30.

Figure 2-30 shows that PCM requires 1 polarity bit, 3 segment bits, and 4 step bits, which equals 8 bits per sample. The Nyquist Theorem requires 8000 samples per second; therefore, you can figure the required bandwidth as follows:

8 bits * 8000 samples per second = 64,000 bits per second

Adaptive differential pulse code modulation (ADPCM) coders, like other waveform coders, encode analog voice signals into digital signals to adaptively predict future encodings by looking at the immediate past. The adaptive feature of ADPCM reduces the number of bits per second that the PCM method requires to encode voice signals. ADPCM does this by taking 8000 samples per second of the analog voice and turning them into linear PCM samples. ADPCM then calculates the predicted value of the next sample, based on the immediate past sample, and encodes the difference. The ADPCM process generates 4-bit words, thereby generating 16 specific bit patterns.

Figure 2-30 *Pulse Code Modulation*

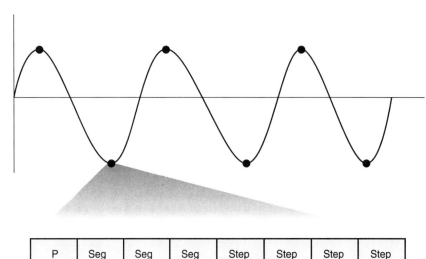

The ADPCM algorithm from the Consultative Committee for International Telegraph and Telephone (CCITT) transmits all 16 possible bit patterns. The ADPCM algorithm from the American National Standards Institute (ANSI) uses 15 of the 16 possible bit patterns. The ANSI ADPCM algorithm does not generate a 0000 pattern.

The ITU standards for compression are as follows:

- **G.711 rate:** 64 kbps = (2 * 4 kHz) * 8 bits/sample
- **G.726 rate:** 32 kbps = (2 * 4 kHz) * 4 bits/sample
- **G.726 rate:** 24 kbps = (2 * 4 kHz) * 3 bits/sample
- **G.726 rate:** 16 kbps = (2 * 4 kHz) * 2 bits/sample

NOTE   CCITT is now called International Telecommunication Union Telecommunication Standardization Sector (ITU-T).

Code excited linear prediction (CELP) compression transforms analog voice as follows:

1. The input to the coder is converted from an 8-bit to a 16-bit linear PCM sample.

2. A codebook uses feedback to continuously learn and predict the voice waveform.

3. The coder is excited (that is, begins its lookup process) by a white noise generator.

4. The mathematical result is sent to the far-end decoder for synthesis and generation of the voice waveform.

Two forms of CELP include Low-Delay CELP (LDCELP) and Conjugate Structure Algebraic CELP (CS-ACELP). LDCELP is similar to CS-ACELP, except for the following:

- LDCELP uses a smaller codebook and operates at 16 kbps to minimize delay, or look-ahead, from 2 to 5 ms, while CS-ACELP minimizes bandwidth requirements (8 kbps) at the expense of increasing delay (10 ms).

- The 10-bit code word is produced from every five speech samples from the 8 kHz input with no look-ahead.

- Four of these 10-bit code words are called a *subframe*. They take approximately 2.5 ms to encode. CS-ACELP uses eight 10-bit code words.

Two of these subframes are combined into a 5-ms block for transmission. CS-ACELP is a variation of CELP that performs these functions:

- Codes 80-byte frames, which take approximately 10 ms to buffer and process.

- Adds a look-ahead of 5 ms. A look-ahead is a coding mechanism that continuously analyzes, learns, and predicts the next waveshape.

- Adds noise reduction and pitch-synthesis filtering to processing requirements.

Cisco VoIP environments typically leverage the benefits of G.729 when transmitting voice traffic over the IP WAN. These benefits include the ability to minimize bandwidth demands, while maintaining an acceptable level of voice quality. Several variants of G.729 exist.

G.729 Variants

G.729, G.729 Annex A (G.729A), G.729 Annex B (G.729B), and G.729A Annex B (G.729AB) are variations of CS-ACELP. The G.729 Annex B (G.729B) variant adds voice activity detection (VAD) in strict compliance with G.729B standards. When this coder-decoder (CODEC) variant is used, VAD is not tunable for music threshold, meaning that a threshold volume level cannot be configured to pass voice while suppressing lower volume music on hold. However, when Cisco VAD is configured, music threshold is tunable.

There is little difference between the ITU recommendations for G.729 and G.729A. All of the platforms that support G.729 also support G.729A.

G.729 is the compression algorithm that Cisco uses for high-quality 8-kbps voice. When properly implemented, G.729 sounds as good as the 32-kbps ADPCM. G.729 is a high-complexity, processor-intensive compression algorithm that monopolizes processing resources.

Although G.729A is also an 8-kbps compression, it is not as processor intensive as G.729. It is a medium-complexity variant of G.729 with slightly lower voice quality. G.729A is not as high quality as G.729 and is more susceptible to network irregularities, such as delay, variation, and tandeming. Tandeming causes distortion that occurs when speech is coded, decoded, and then coded and decoded again, much like the distortion that occurs when a videotape is repeatedly copied.

CODEC Complexity

On Cisco IOS gateways, you must use the variant (G.729 or G.729A) that is related to the CODEC complexity configuration on the voice card. This variant does not show up explicitly in the Cisco IOS command-line interface (CLI) CODEC choice. For example, the CLI does not display g729r8 (alpha code) as a CODEC option. However, if the voice card is defined as medium-complexity, then the g729r8 option is the G.729A CODEC.

G.729B is a high-complexity algorithm, and G.729AB is a medium-complexity variant of G.729B with slightly lower voice quality. The difference between the G.729 and G.729B CODEC is that the G.729B CODEC provides built-in Internet Engineering Task Force (IETF) VAD and comfort noise generation (CNG).

The following G.729 CODEC combinations interoperate:

- G.729 and G.729A
- G.729 and G.729
- G.729A and G.729A
- G.729B and G.729AB
- G.729B and G.729B
- G.729AB and G.729AB

Signaling Systems

Configuring Cisco Systems voice equipment to interface with other equipment requires an understanding of the signaling that conveys supervision between the systems. Proper troubleshooting also requires an understanding of these signaling systems.

This section describes the various signaling systems used between telephony systems, such as common channel signaling and channel associated signaling. It also explores signaling between PBXs, signaling between PBXs and COs, and specialized signaling, such as ISDN.

Channel Associated Signaling

Channel associated signaling (CAS) is a signaling method commonly used between PBXs. Although this can manifest itself in many forms, some methods are more common than others. Signaling systems can also be implemented between a PBX and a Cisco voice device.

T1 Channel Associated Signaling

PBXs and Cisco devices use T1 and E1 interfaces to convey voice. Originally, this was the main purpose of T1, which carries signaling information using two methodologies: CAS and common channel signaling (CCS). Figure 2-31 illustrates the format of the T1 digital signal.

Figure 2-31 *T1 Digital Signal Format*

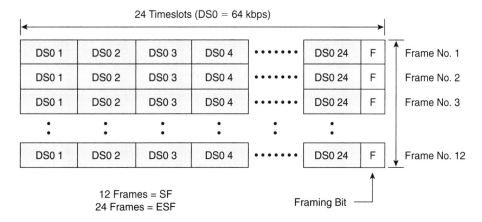

The characteristics of the T1 digital signal format are as follows:

- A T1 frame is 193 bits long, 8 bits from each of the 24 time slots (digital service zeros [DS0s]), plus 1 bit for framing. A T1 repeats every 125 microseconds, resulting in 8000 samples per second (8 bits * 24 time slots + 1 framing bit * 8000 samples per second = 1.544 Mbps).

- T1 has two major framing and format standards:

  — Super Frame (SF), or D4, specifies 12 frames in sequence. The D4 framing pattern used in the F position in Figure 2-31 is 100011011100 (a 1 goes with the first frame, a 0 goes with the second frame, a 0 goes with the third frame, and so on, all the way through 12 frames). This unique framing pattern allows the receiving T1 equipment to synchronize within four frames, since any four consecutive frame bits are unique within the 12-bit pattern. Because there are 8000 T1 frames transmitted per second, 8000 F bits are produced and used for framing.

  — Extended Superframe (ESF) format was developed as an upgrade to SF and is now dominant in public and private networks. Both types of formatting retain the basic frame structure of one framing bit followed by 192 data bits. However, ESF repurposes the use of the F bit. In ESF, of the total 8000 F bits used in T1, 2000 are used for framing, 2000 are used for cyclic redundancy check (CRC) (for error checking only), and 4000 are used as an intelligent supervisory channel to control functions end to end (such as loopback and error reporting).

Because each DS0 channel carries 64 kbps, and G.711 is 64 kbps, there is no room to carry signaling. Implemented for voice, the T1 uses every sixth frame to convey signaling information. In every sixth frame, the least significant bit (LSB) for each of the voice channels is used to convey the signaling, as shown in Figure 2-32. Although this implementation detracts from the overall voice quality (because only 7 bits represent a sample for that frame), the impact is not significant. This method is called *robbed-bit signaling (RBS)*. When SF employs this method, the signaling bits are conveyed in both the 6th (called the "A" bit) and 12th (called the "B" bit) frames. For control signaling, A and B bits provide both near- and far-end off-hook indication.

Figure 2-32 *Robbed-Bit Signaling*

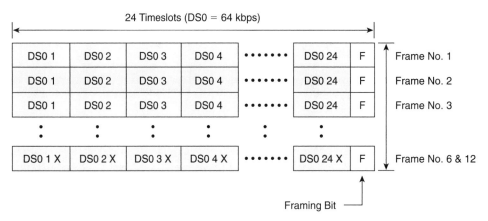

X = Least significant bit in each DS0 is "robbed" for signaling every sixth frame

The A and B bits can represent different signaling states or control features (on hook or off hook, idle, busy, ringing, and addressing). The robbed bit is the least significant bit from an 8-bit word.

ESF also uses RBS in frames 6, 12, 18, and 24 to yield four signaling bits, providing additional control and signaling information. These four bits are known as the A, B, C, and D bits.

Because the signaling occurs within each DS0, it is referred to as *in band*. Also, because the use of these bits is exclusively reserved for signaling each respective voice channel, it is referred to as CAS.

The robbed bits, depicted in Figure 2-33, are used to convey E&M status or FXS/FXO status and provide call supervision for both on hook and off hook.

Figure 2-33   *Channel Associated Signaling – T1*

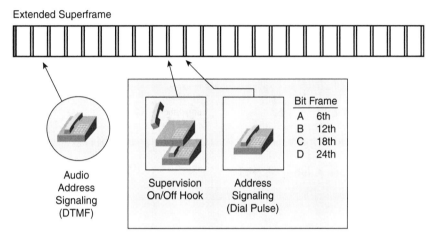

Extended Superframe

Audio
Address
Signaling
(DTMF)

Supervision
On/Off Hook

Address
Signaling
(Dial Pulse)

Bit Frame	
A	6th
B	12th
C	18th
D	24th

T1 CAS has the following characteristics:

* SF has a 12-frame structure and provides AB bits for signaling.

* ESF has a 24-frame structure and provides ABCD bits for signaling.

* DTMF, or tone, can be carried in band in the audio path. However, other supervisory signals must still be carried via CAS.

E1 Channel Associated Signaling

In E1 framing and signaling, 30 of the 32 available channels, or time slots, are used for voice and data. Framing information uses time slot 1, while time slot 17 (E0 16) is used for signaling by all the other time slots. This signaling format, illustrated in Figure 2-34, is also known as CAS because the use of the bits in the 17th time slot is exclusively reserved for the purpose of signaling each respective channel. However, this implementation of CAS is considered *out of band*, because the signaling bits are not carried within the context of each respective voice channel, as is the case with T1. E1 CAS is directly compatible with T1 CAS, because both methods use AB or ABCD bit signaling. Although the signaling for E1 CAS is carried in a single common time slot, it is still referred to as CAS because each individual signaling time slot represents a specific pair of voice channels.

Figure 2-34 *E1 Framing and Signaling*

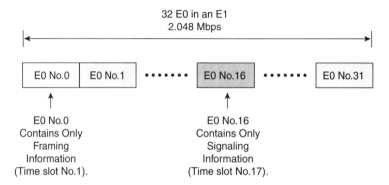

In the E1 frame format, 32 time slots make up a frame. A multiframe consists of 16 E1 frames, as depicted in Figure 2-35.

Figure 2-35 *Channel Associated Signaling - E1*

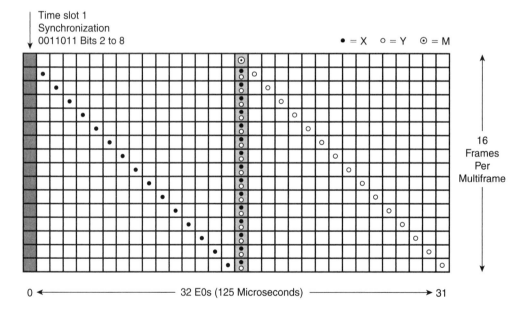

The time slots are numbered 1 though 32, although the channels are numbered 0 through 31, as shown in Figure 2-35. Multiframe time slots are configured as follows:

- Time slot 1 carries only framing information.

- Time slot 17, in the first frame of the 16-frame multiframe, declares the beginning of the multiframe, which is indicated by the M symbol in Figure 2-35.

- The remaining slot 17s carry signaling information for all the other time slots:
  - Slot 17 of the first frame declares the beginning of a 16-frame multiframe (M).
  - Slot 17 of the second frame carries ABCD for voice slot 2 (X) and ABCD for voice slot 18 (Y).
  - Slot 17 of the third frame carries ABCD for voice slot 3 (X) and ABCD for voice slot 19 (Y).

This process continues for all the remaining frames.

Common Channel Signaling Systems

Common channel signaling (CCS) differs from CAS in that all channels use a common channel and protocol for call setup. Using E1 as an example, a signaling protocol, such as ISDN Q.931, would be deployed in time slot 17 to exchange call-setup messages with its attached telephony equipment, as seen in Figure 2-36.

Figure 2-36 *Common Channel Signaling*

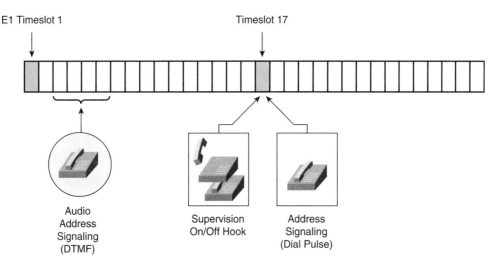

Examples of CCS signaling are as follows:

- **Proprietary implementations**—Some PBX vendors choose to use CCS for T1 and E1 and implement a proprietary CCS protocol between their PBXs. In this implementation, Cisco devices are configured for Transparent Common Channel Signaling (T-CCS) because the Cisco devices do not understand proprietary signaling information.

- **Integrated Services Digital Network (ISDN)**—ISDN uses Q.931 in a common channel to signal all other channels.

- **Q Signaling (QSIG)**—Like ISDN, QSIG uses a common channel to signal all other channels.

- **Digital Private Network Signaling System (DPNSS)**—DPNSS is an open standard developed by British Telecom for implementation by any vendor who chooses to use it. DPNSS also uses a common channel to signal all other channels.

- **Signaling System 7 (SS7)**—SS7 is an out-of-band network implemented and maintained by various telephone companies and used for signaling and other supplemental services.

The following discussions elaborate on various CCS implementations. Note that proprietary implementations are not discussed because they vary widely among vendors.

ISDN

ISDN (Integrated Services Digital Network) is an access specification to a network. You may have studied ISDN as an access method for dial-up data systems. Because it is a digital system, ISDN makes connections rapidly.

ISDN can be implemented in two different ways: BRI (Basic Rate Interface) and PRI (Primary Rate Interface). BRI features two bearer (B) channels, while PRI supports 23 (for T1) or 30 (for E1) B channels. Each implementation also supports a data (D) channel, used to carry signaling information (CCS).

The following are benefits of using ISDN to transmit voice:

- Each B channel is 64 kbps, making it perfect for G.711 PCM.

- ISDN has a built-in call control protocol known as ITU-T Q.931.

- ISDN can convey standards-based voice features, such as call forwarding.

- ISDN supports standards-based enhanced dial-up capabilities, such as Group 4 fax and audio channels.

NOTE   ISDN BRI voice is commonly used in Europe, while ISDN PRI voice is used worldwide.

Figure 2-37 shows the architecture of an ISDN network. The B channel carries information, such as voice, data, and video, at 64 kbps. The D channel carries call signaling between customer premises equipment (CPE) and the network, usually as the Q.931 protocol but sometimes as the QSIG protocol.

Figure 2-37 *ISDN Network Architecture*

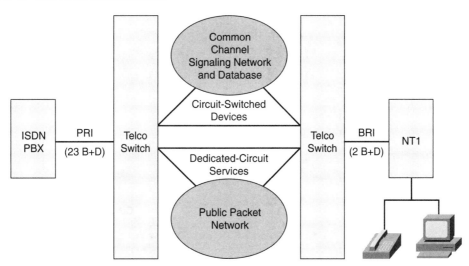

BRI operates using the average local copper pair. It uses two B channels and one signaling channel, which is written as *2 B + D*.

PRI implemented on T1 uses 23 B channels and one signaling channel, which is written as *23 B + D*. PRI implemented on E1 uses 30 B channels and one signaling channel, which is represented as *30 B + D*.

ISDN's Q.931 protocol, which operates at Layer 3 of the OSI (Open System Interconnection) model, uses a standard set of messages to communicate, as illustrated in Figure 2-38.

These standard messages cover the following areas:

- **Call establishment**—Initially sets up a call. Messages travel between the user and the network. Call establishment events include alerting, call proceeding, connect, connect acknowledgment, progress, setup, and setup acknowledgment.

- **Call information phase**—Data sent between the user and the network after the call is established. This allows the user to, for example, suspend and then resume a call. Events in the call information phase include hold, hold acknowledgment, hold reject, resume, resume acknowledgment, resume reject, retrieve, retrieve acknowledgment, retrieve reject, suspend, suspend acknowledgment, suspend reject, and user information.

- **Call clearing**—Terminates a call. The following events occur in the call-clearing phase: disconnect, release, release complete, restart, and restart acknowledgment.

Figure 2-38 *Layer 3 (Q.930/931) Messages*

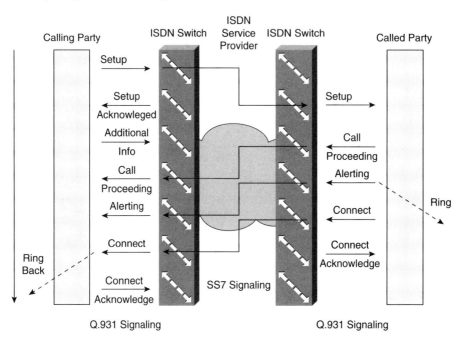

- **Miscellaneous messages**—Negotiates network features (supplementary services). Miscellaneous services include congestion control, facility, information, notify, register, status, and status inquiry.

NOTE ISDN Layer 3 messages, or Q.931, are carried within ISDN Layer 2 frames, called *Q.921*. Cisco ISDN equipment allows the administrator to monitor these messages as they occur using various **debug** commands.

QSIG

The QSIG (Q Signaling) protocol is based on the ISDN Q.931 standard and provides signaling for private integrated services network exchange (PINX) devices. Figure 2-39 shows how different QSIG operations map to the OSI model.

PINX includes everything from PBXs and multiplexers to Centrex. QSIG is implemented on PRI interfaces only. By using QSIG PRI signaling, a Cisco device can route incoming voice calls from a PINX across a WAN to a peer Cisco device, which can then transport the

Figure 2-39 *QSIG Protocol*

Layers 4–7	Remote Operations Service Element (ROSE) Association control service element (ACSE)		End-to-end protocol network transparent
Network	In progress		QSIG procedures for supplementary services
	ISO 11582, ETS300, 239 ECMA 165		QSIG generic functional procedures
	ISO 11574, ETS200 171/172, EDMA 142/143		QSIG basic call
Link Layer	ECMA 141, ETS300 402		
Physical	Basic Rate 1,430	Primary Rate 1,431	Interface-dependent protocols
Media	Copper	Copper	Optical

signaling and voice packets to a second PINX. ISDN PRI QSIG voice signaling provides the following benefits:

- Connects the Cisco device with digital PBXs that use the QSIG form of CCS

- Provides transparent support for supplementary PBX services so that proprietary PBX features are not lost when connecting PBXs to Cisco networks

- Provides QSIG support based on widely used ISDN Q.931 standards and the European Telecommunications Standards Institute (ETSI) implementation standards, which include the following specifications:

    — **European Computer Manufacturers Association (ECMA)-143**— Private Integrated Services Network (PISN) – Circuit Mode Bearer Services – Inter-Exchange Signalling Procedures and Protocol (QSIG-BC). The ECMA-143 standard addresses the signaling procedures and protocol used for circuit-switched call control at the Q-reference point between private integrated services network exchanges (PINXs) that are interconnected in a PISN.

    — **ECMA-142**—Private Integrated Services Network (PISN) – Circuit Mode 64-kbps Bearer Services – Service Description, Functional Capabilities and Information Flows (BCSD). The ECMA-142 standard addresses the service description and control aspects of standardized circuit-mode bearer services.

— **ECMA-165**—Private Integrated Services Network (PISN) – Generic Functional Protocol for the Support of Supplementary Services – Inter-Exchange Signalling Procedures and Protocol (QSIG-GF). The ECMA-165 standard addresses the signaling protocol used for supplementary service control and Additional Network Features (ANFs) at the Q reference point.

DPNSS

British Telecom and selected PBX manufacturers originally developed the Digital Private Network Signaling System (DPNSS) in the early 1980s. It was developed and put into use before the ISDN standards were completed because customers wanted to make use of digital facilities as soon as possible.

DPNSS operates over standard ISDN physical interfaces and is described in four documents:

● BTNR 188: Digital Private Networking Signalling System No 1, Issue 6, January 1995.

● BTNR 188-T: Digital Private Networking Signalling System No 1: Testing Schedule.

● BTNR 189: Interworking between DPNSS1 and other Signalling Systems, Issue 3, March 1988.

● BTNR 189-I: Interworking between DPNSS1 and ISDN Signalling Systems, Issue 1, December 1992.

NOTE   Cisco Systems supports DPNSS on various gateway platforms, such as the Cisco 2600, 3600, and 5300 series. DPNSS is not a common signaling system but is still in use in various parts of the world.

SIGTRAN

SIGTRAN, as illustrated in Figure 2-40, is a signaling protocol defined in RFC 2719 and RFC 2960. It describes the way the IP protocol carries SS7 messages in a VoIP network. SIGTRAN relies on the Stream Control Transport Protocol at Layer 4 of the TCP/IP protocol stack.

Using SIGTRAN, a service provider may interconnect a private VoIP network to the public switched telephone network (PSTN) and ensure that SS7 signals are conveyed end to end.

NOTE   SIGTRAN is implemented on Cisco IP Transfer Point (ITP) equipment as well as the Cisco SC 2200 Signaling Controller.

Figure 2-40 *SIGTRAN*

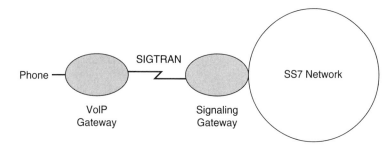

SS7

The ITU-T (formerly the CCITT) developed SS7 in 1981. The primary functions and benefits of SS7 are as follows:

* Fast call setup is handled by high-speed circuit-switched connections.

* PBX transaction capabilities (that is, call forwarding, call waiting, call screening, and call transfer) are extended to the entire network.

* A dedicated control channel exists for all signaling functions.

* Each associated trunk group needs only one set of signaling facilities.

* Information, such as address digits, can be transferred directly between control elements.

* There is no chance of mutual interference between voice and control channel because SS7 is out-of-band signaling.

* Because the control channel is not accessible by the user, possible fraudulent use of the network is avoided.

* Connections involving multiple switching offices can be set up more quickly.

Figure 2-41 depicts an implementation of SS7. As a function of customer networks, SS7 can be implemented as CCS across a telephony network enterprise. Using Cisco equipment, service providers can implement SS7 on their networks. Cisco has developed several solutions that support off-loading IP traffic from public networks and that support the direct connection of network access servers to the PSTN using SS7 links. These solutions utilize the Cisco SC2200, BTS 10200, and AS5x00, giving service providers a proven and cost-efficient SS7 solution for connecting dial-access servers and voice gateways to the PSTN.

The Cisco AS5x00 family provides carrier-class, high-density connectivity for VoIP and dial subscribers. The product set supports a wide range of IP services (including voice) and enables carriers and Internet service providers (ISPs) to cost-effectively support increased subscriber services and an increasing subscriber base.

Figure 2-41 *SS7 Application Example*

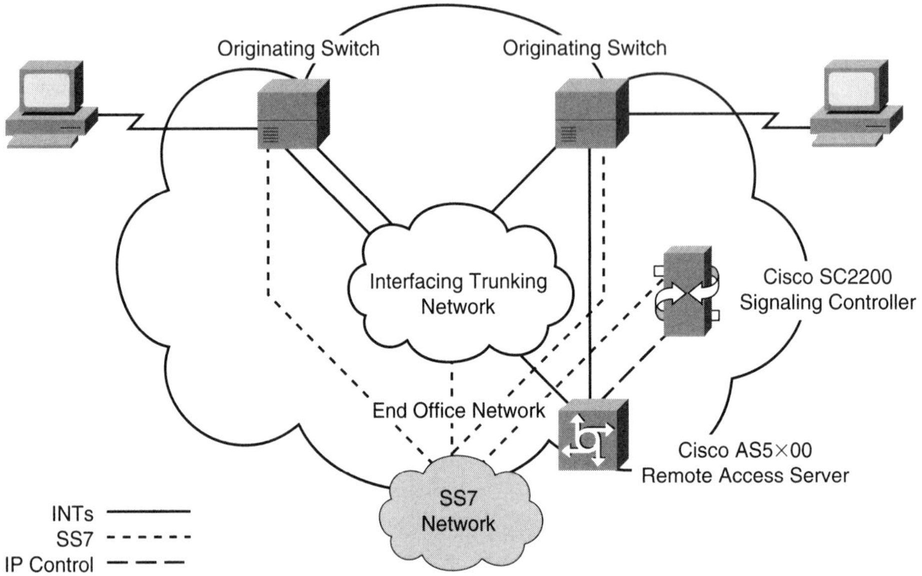

Originating Switch Originating Switch

Interfacing Trunking
Network

Cisco SC2200
Signaling Controller

End Office Network

SS7
Network

Cisco AS5×00
Remote Access Server

INTs ———
SS7 - - - - -
IP Control — — —

Signaling System Interoperability

In some implementations, it is necessary to convert from one signaling format to another.
Conversion is necessary to allow different systems to signal each other. Figure 2-42
illustrates an example of signal conversion.

Figure 2-42 *Signal Conversion Example*

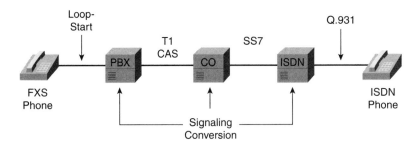

Loop-
Start

T1
CAS

SS7

Q.931

PBX CO ISDN

FXS
Phone

ISDN
Phone

Signaling
Conversion

The FXS phone is using FXS loop-start signaling to connect to the PBX. The user dials 9
for an outside line, which carries the call on the T1 by using CAS. After the call reaches the
CO, it travels via an SS7-signaled circuit to an ISDN switch. The call is then conveyed via
Q.931 to the ISDN telephone at the called party location. Other conversion applications
exist in voice telephony, and the telephony equipment must have the capability to perform
these conversions transparently to the end users.

Enabling VoIP Fax and Modem Transmission

This section describes the implementation of fax and modem traffic over a VoIP network. It explores both Cisco Systems and standard implementations of faxing, as well as various methods used to transport modem traffic over VoIP.

Cisco Fax Relay

Figure 2-43 depicts a VoIP network set up for fax relay. Initially, fax calls are digitized representations of the contents on paper. The digitized bit stream is then converted to analog for transmission over voice circuits. If Cisco equipment treated fax calls like voice calls, the analog waveform would then be converted to G.711 PCM at 64 kbps and subsequently compressed before transmission across the VoIP network. Treating fax calls like voice calls is impractical because there are too many conversions and because the coding and compression schemes are designed to convey human speech, not fax modem tones.

Figure 2-43 *Fax Relay*

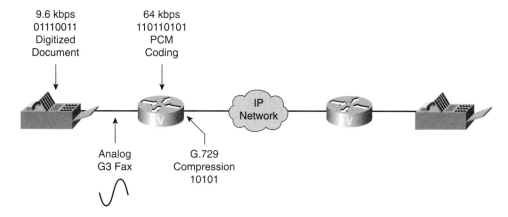

Using Cisco fax relay, as shown in Figure 2-44, the DSP (digital signal processor) chip first sets up the call as an end-to-end voice call. The DSP then recognizes the tones as those coming from a fax machine. The local DSP assumes the role of a fax modem, converting the analog data back to the original digitized bit stream. Acting as the fax modem, the DSP is downshifted in speed to 9.6 kbps to save bandwidth over the IP path. The bit stream is then packaged in VoIP packets and identified as a fax. The remote DSP assumes a similar role and converts the bit stream to analog for reception by the remote fax machine. Cisco fax relay is a proprietary protocol supported only on Cisco voice equipment. Cisco Systems pioneered this protocol in the early 1990s before standards were developed and ratified.

Figure 2-44 *Cisco Fax Relay*

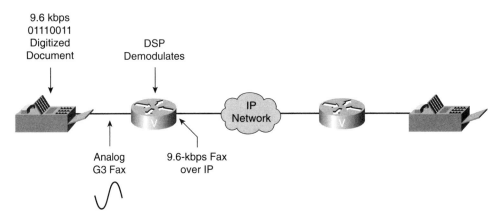

T.38 Fax Relay

The T.38 approach to fax relay is similar to the Cisco approach, but represents the industry standard. Because T.38 is an open standard from the ITU, it is compatible between different vendors. A Cisco voice-enabled router can be configured as a T.38 gateway, and the transmission methodology is similar to the Cisco fax relay method. However, with T.38 it is possible to deliver documents to virtual fax machines, such as PCs and servers that are configured with software that is compatible with T.38 fax.

As illustrated in Figure 2-45, a T.38 gateway is required at both ends. The T.38 method uses DSP chips to intercept the fax signal at each end and convert the signal to its original digital format, for example, 9600 bps Group 3 fax. The resulting bit stream is then packetized into the T.38 packet format and sent across the IP network.

Figure 2-45 *T.38 Fax Relay*

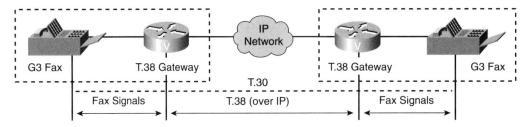

T.37 Fax Store and Forward

The T.37 standard for fax store and forward, as depicted in Figure 2-46, is a way of delivering faxed documents as e-mail attachments. T.37 works by scanning a document, converting that document to tagged image file format (TIFF), and sending it to an e-mail address as an attachment using Simple Mail Transfer Protocol (SMTP). Cisco implements T.37 fax store and forward by using special gateways that are configured as on-ramps (transmitters of faxes) or off-ramps (receivers of faxes).

Figure 2-46 *T.37 Fax Store and Forward*

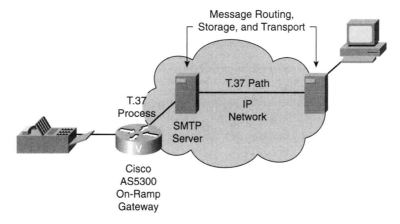

When configured on an on-ramp gateway, fax store and forward provides a way to transform standard fax messages into e-mail messages and TIFF attachments that travel to PCs on the network. When configured on an off-ramp gateway, e-mail with TIFF attachments transform into standard fax messages. These messages travel out of the packet network to standard Group 3 fax devices on the PSTN. When configured on both the on-ramp and off-ramp gateways of a network, fax store and forward allows temporary storage in the packet network for standard fax messages that cannot be delivered immediately.

Internet users are offered free store-and-forward faxes from various ISPs. Once subscribed, it is possible to send and receive fax messages using the service. If someone wants to send you a fax, they dial your assigned fax number from any standard fax machine. The store-and-forward on-ramp gateway at the service provider converts the fax back to its digital bit stream and then converts it into a graphics file (usually JPG). The completed graphics file is then e-mailed to you as an attachment.

Fax store and forward uses two different interactive voice response (IVR) applications for on-ramp and off-ramp functionality. The applications are implemented in two Tool Command Language (TCL) scripts that you can download from Cisco.com.

SMTP facilitates the basic functionality of fax store and forward, with additional functionality that provides confirmation of delivery using existing SMTP mechanisms such as Extended Simple Mail Transfer Protocol (ESMTP). Fax store and forward requires that you configure gateway dial peers and the following types of parameters:

- **IVR application parameters and IVR security and accounting parameters**—Load the applications on the router and enable accounting and authorization for the application.

- **Fax parameters**—Specify the cover sheet and header information for faxes that are generated in the packet network.

- **Message Transfer Agent (MTA) parameters**—Define delivery parameters for the e-mail messages that accompany fax TIFF images.

- **Message disposition notification (MDN) parameters**—Specify the generation of messages to notify e-mail originators when their fax e-mail messages are delivered.

- **Delivery status notification (DSN) parameters**—Instruct the SMTP server to send messages to e-mail originators to inform them of the status of their e-mail messages.

- **Gateway security and accounting parameters**—Define authentication, authorization, and accounting (AAA) for faxes that enter or exit the packet network.

Fax Pass-Through

Fax pass-through occurs when incoming T.30 fax data is not demodulated or compressed for its transit through the packet network, as shown in Figure 2-47. The two fax machines communicate directly with each other over a transparent IP connection.

Figure 2-47   *Fax Pass-Through*

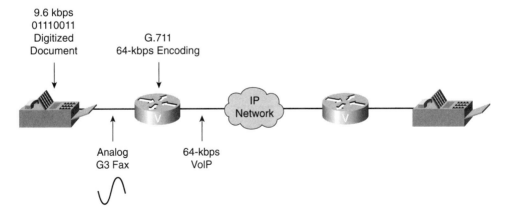

When a gateway detects a fax tone, it switches the call to a high-bandwidth CODEC. The fax traffic, still in PCM form, travels in band over VoIP using G.711 with no VAD. This method of transporting fax traffic takes a constant 64-kbps (payload) stream end to end for the duration of the call. It is very sensitive to packet loss, jitter, and latency in the IP network, although packet redundancy can be used to mitigate the effects of packet loss.

Fax pass-through is applicable when connecting to a third-party voice gateway that does not support T.38 fax relay. Fax pass-through treats the fax call as a simple G.711 voice call with no special handling for fax. When connecting a Cisco fax-enabled router to a third-party voice-enabled router that does not support fax, you should use fax pass-through. The originating Cisco router will treat the call as a G.711 voice call and will not compress, thus preserving the analog properties of the waveshape for the receiving fax machine.

Fax pass-through is supported under the following call control protocols:

- H.323
- Session initiation protocol (SIP)
- Media Gateway Control Protocol (MGCP)

NOTE   Echo cancellation is enabled and preferred for pass-through using Cisco IOS Release 12.0(3) T and later. Earlier versions of Cisco IOS software required that you disable echo cancellation.

Modem Pass-Through

Modem pass-through, as illustrated in Figure 2-48, is similar to fax pass-through, except that there is a computer modem at each end of the connection. The two modems communicate directly with each other over a transparent IP connection.

Figure 2-48 *Modem Pass-Through*

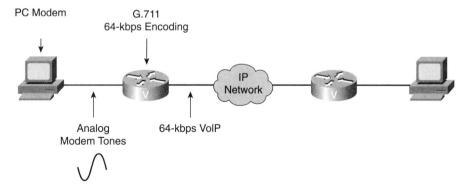

When a gateway detects a modem tone, it switches the call to a high-bandwidth CODEC. The modem traffic, still in PCM form, travels in band over VoIP using G.711 with no VAD. This method of transporting modem traffic takes a constant 64-kbps (payload) stream end to end for the duration of the call. It is highly sensitive to packet loss, jitter, and latency in the IP network, although packet redundancy can be used to mitigate the effects of packet loss. Packet redundancy is defined in RFC 2198 and describes a way in which RTP carries the modem audio essentially twice. The redundant packets are sent in case there is packet loss. This scheme produces significant overhead, therefore, and may not be acceptable in all applications. You can enable or disable packet redundancy when configuring modem pass-through.

The following call control protocols support modem pass-through:

- H.323
- SIP
- MGCP

Modem pass-through is utilized when the gateways serve as a dial-up application for terminals or alarm systems. If your company utilizes alarm systems in multiple buildings throughout a WAN application and the alarm system requires modems to dial in to a central server, you can use modem pass-through on your VoIP network. This application will eliminate the cost of separate long-distance dial telephone lines for the modems.

Modem Relay

When using modem relay, which is illustrated in Figure 2-49, computer modem signals are demodulated at one gateway, converted to digital form, and carried in Simple Packet Relay Transport (SPRT) protocol packets to the other gateway. When it reaches the other gateway, the modem signal is recreated and remodulated and then passed to the receiving computer modem. SPRT is a protocol running over User Datagram Protocol (UDP). At the end of the modem session, the voice ports revert to the previous configuration and the DSPs switch back to the original voice CODEC. This method uses less bandwidth (Real-Time Transport Protocol [RTP] is not required) and is much less sensitive to jitter and clocking mismatches than modem pass-through.

Figure 2-49 *Modem Relay*

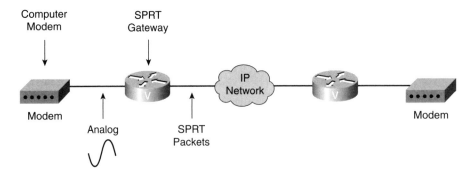

The following call control protocols support modem relay:

- H.323
- SIP
- MGCP

Summary

This chapter explored analog signaling technologies, such as loop-start, ground-start, and various E&M signaling approaches. Additionally, this chapter described digital signaling approaches, including CAS (channel associated signaling) and CCS (common channel signaling).

Conversion between analog and digital waveforms involves the process of sampling the original voice wave and converting that sample into a binary value. The Nyquist Theorem specifies the number of samples per second to take from an analog waveform. Specifically, the Nyquist Theorem states that samples should be taken at a rate that equals twice the highest frequency being sampled. For example, if the highest frequency being sampled is 4000 Hz (as it is in the VoIP world), 8000 samples (that is, 2 * 4000) should be taken per second.

Finally, this chapter considered the challenges associated with sending fax and modem transmissions over a network using compression technology (for example, the G.729 CODEC). Approaches for sending fax tones over the IP WAN included Cisco fax relay, T.38 fax relay, T.37 fax store and forward, and fax pass-through. Solutions for modem transmission included modem pass-through and modem relay.

Chapter Review Questions

The following questions test your knowledge of topics explained in this chapter. You can find the answers to the questions in Appendix A, "Answers to Chapter Review Questions."

1. What are the three different types of local-loop signaling?

   a address signaling

   b coding signaling

   c control signaling

   d informational signaling

   e remote signaling

   f supervisory signaling

2. What is the normal ring cadence in the United States?

   a   one 2-second ring followed by 2 seconds of silence

   b   one 2-second ring followed by 4 seconds of silence

   c   two 0.4-second rings separated by 0.2 seconds of silence, followed by 2 seconds of silence

   d   two 2-second rings separated by 4 seconds of silence

3. Which method is used to reduce echo on Cisco devices?

   a   echo suppression

   b   echo cancellation

   c   echo correction

   d   echo return loss

4. In telephone voice-channel service, how often is the analog-to-digital signal conversion sampling process repeated?

   a   8000 times per call

   b   8000 times per voice sample

   c   8000 times per second

   d   8000 times per minute

5. Which voice coding technique is used with G.711 CODECs?

   a   ADPCM

   b   CS-ACELP

   c   LDCELP

   d   PCM

6. Which two G.729 CODECs provide built-in IETF VAD and CNG?

   a   G.729

   b   G.729A

   c   G.729B

   d   G.729AB

7. How many time slots are there in an E1 frame using CAS?

   a 16

   b 24

   c 30

   d 32

8. How many B channels and D channels are implemented on a PRI T1?

   a 1 B channel and 1 D channel

   b 2 B channels and 1 D channel

   c 23 B channels and 1 D channel

   d 30 B channels and 1 D channel

9. At what speed does the fax modem operate in a Cisco fax relay environment?

   a 64 kbps

   b 52 kbps

   c 16 kbps

   d 9.6 kbps

10. Which protocol is used to carry modem signals across a VoIP network when using modem relay?

   a SMTP

   b SPRT

   c MGCP

   d RTP

Lab Exercise: Navigating Your Hands-On Lab

In this lab, you will construct and become familiar with the VoIP lab topology to be used in subsequent labs. The lab topology contains a total of three Cisco routers. However, some of the labs can be adapted to only two routers.

Following is a list of required lab equipment:

- Three Cisco routers running Cisco IOS Software Release 12.3(1) or later. (The IOS should support the H.323 Gateway and AutoQoS features.)
    - Router R1 should contain one serial interface and one FXS port.
    - Router R2 should contain two serial interfaces.
    - Router R3 should contain one serial interface and one FXS port.

NOTE   To identify an appropriate IOS image for your routers, visit Cisco's Feature Navigator, at www.cisco.com/go/fn, where you can specify the features you require for your specific router platform.

- Two DTE-to-DCE serial cables (with the appropriate serial connectors for your routers).
- Two analog telephones.

Figure 2-50 illustrates the lab's physical topology and IP addressing.

Figure 2-50 *Lab Topology*

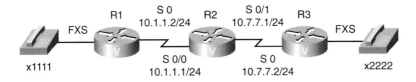

Task 1: Physical Connectivity

In this task, you will interconnect the lab routers.

Complete these steps:

1. Adapting the topology shown in Figure 2-50 to your own router interfaces, interconnect routers R1 and R2 using a DTE-to-DCE serial cable. The DTE end of the cable should be connected to router R1, and the DCE end of the cable should be connected to router R2.

2. Interconnect routers R2 and R3 using a DTE-to-DCE serial cable. The DTE end of the cable should be connected to router R2, and the DCE end of the cable should be connected to router R3.

3. Connect an analog telephone to the FXS port in router R1.

4. Connect an analog telephone to the FXS port in router R3.

Task 2: Initial Configuration

In this task, you will configure the routers in the lab topology for Layer 3 connectivity.

Complete these steps:

1. Adapting the topology shown in Figure 2-50 to your own router interface, assign an IP address to the serial interface on router R1 and configure the interface for PPP encapsulation. Set the bandwidth of the interface connecting to R2 to 128 kbps, using the **bandwidth 128** command. Administratively bring up the interface.

2. Assign IP addresses to the two serial interfaces on router R2 and configure the interfaces for PPP encapsulation. Set the bandwidth of the interface connecting to router R1 to 128 kbps, using the **bandwidth 128** command. Set the clock rate on the interface connecting to router R1 to 128 kbps with the **clock rate 128000** command. Set the bandwidth of the interface connecting to router R3 to 2 Mbps, using the **bandwidth 2000** command. Administratively bring up the interfaces.

3. Assign an IP address to the serial interface router R3, and configure the interface for PPP encapsulation. Set the clock rate on the serial interface to 2 Mbps with the **clock rate 2000000** command and indicate the interface bandwidth as 2 Mbps with the **bandwidth 2000** command. Administratively bring up the interface.

4. Configure a routing protocol of your choice on the routers such that all routers can see the networks associated with each of the serial interfaces in the topology.

Task 3: Exercise Verification

In this task, you will verify Layer 3 connectivity across your pod of routers.

Complete these steps:

1. Issue the **show ip route** command on R1, R2, and R3 to verify that the following networks are visible to each router:

    - 10.1.1.0/24

    - 10.7.7.0/24

2. From a console connection to the R1 router, **ping** the 10.7.7.2 interface (that is, R3's serial interface) to verify Layer 3 connectivity across the pod.

Suggested Solution

Although your physical hardware and selection of a routing protocol might differ, the following examples offer one solution. Example 2-1 shows a possible configuration for router R1.

Example 2-1   *Router R1's Configuration*

```
interface Serial0
 bandwidth 128
ip address 10.1.1.2 255.255.255.0
 encapsulation ppp
 !
router eigrp 100
 network 10.0.0.0
```

Example 2-2 shows a possible configuration for router R2.

Example 2-2   *Router R2's Configuration*

```
interface Serial0/0
bandwidth 128
 ip address 10.1.1.1 255.255.255.0
 encapsulation ppp
 clockrate 128000
 !
interface Serial0/1
 bandwidth 2000
 ip address 10.7.7.1 255.255.255.0
 encapsulation ppp
 !
router eigrp 100
network 10.0.0.0
```

Example 2-3 shows a possible configuration for R3.

Example 2-3   *Router R3's Configuration*

```
interface Serial0
 bandwidth 2000
ip address 10.7.7.2 255.255.255.0
 encapsulation ppp
 clock rate 2000000
 !
router eigrp 100
 network 10.0.0.0
```

The results of the **show ip route** command, issued on all routers, should be similar to the output shown in the following examples.

Example 2-4 shows the **show ip route** command output for router R1.

Example 2-4 *Router R1's* **show ip route** *Output*

```
R1#show ip route
Codes: C - connected, S - static, R - RIP, M - mobile, B - BGP
       D - EIGRP, EX - EIGRP external, O - OSPF, IA - OSPF inter area
       N1 - OSPF NSSA external type 1, N2 - OSPF NSSA external type 2
       E1 - OSPF external type 1, E2 - OSPF external type 2
       i - IS-IS, su - IS-IS summary, L1 - IS-IS level-1, L2 - IS-IS level-2
       ia - IS-IS inter area, * - candidate default, U - per-user static route
       o - ODR, P - periodic downloaded static route

Gateway of last resort is not set

     10.0.0.0/8 is variably subnetted, 4 subnets, 2 masks
D       10.7.7.2/32 [90/21024000] via 10.1.1.1, 00:14:05, Serial0
D       10.7.7.0/24 [90/21024000] via 10.1.1.1, 00:14:05, Serial0
C       10.1.1.0/24 is directly connected, Serial0
C       10.1.1.1/32 is directly connected, Serial0
C     192.168.0.0/24 is directly connected, Ethernet0
```

Example 2-5 shows the **show ip route** command output for router R2.

Example 2-5 *Router R2's* **show ip route** *Output*

```
R2#show ip route
Codes: C - connected, S - static, R - RIP, M - mobile, B - BGP
       D - EIGRP, EX - EIGRP external, O - OSPF, IA - OSPF inter area
       N1 - OSPF NSSA external type 1, N2 - OSPF NSSA external type 2
       E1 - OSPF external type 1, E2 - OSPF external type 2
       i - IS-IS, su - IS-IS summary, L1 - IS-IS level-1, L2 - IS-IS level-2
       ia - IS-IS inter area, * - candidate default, U - per-user static route
       o - ODR, P - periodic downloaded static route

Gateway of last resort is not set

     10.0.0.0/8 is variably subnetted, 4 subnets, 2 masks
C       10.7.7.2/32 is directly connected, Serial0/1
C       10.1.1.2/32 is directly connected, Serial0/0
C       10.7.7.0/24 is directly connected, Serial0/1
C       10.1.1.0/24 is directly connected, Serial0/0
```

Example 2-6 shows the **show ip route** command output for router R3.

Example 2-6   *Router R3's* **show ip route** *Output*

```
R3#show ip route
Codes: C - connected, S - static, R - RIP, M - mobile, B - BGP
       D - EIGRP, EX - EIGRP external, O - OSPF, IA - OSPF inter area
       N1 - OSPF NSSA external type 1, N2 - OSPF NSSA external type 2
       E1 - OSPF external type 1, E2 - OSPF external type 2
       i - IS-IS, su - IS-IS summary, L1 - IS-IS level-1, L2 - IS-IS level-2
       ia - IS-IS inter area, * - candidate default, U - per-user static route
       o - ODR, P - periodic downloaded static route

Gateway of last resort is not set

     10.0.0.0/8 is variably subnetted, 4 subnets, 2 masks
D       10.1.1.2/32 [90/21024000] via 10.7.7.1, 00:15:22, Serial0
C       10.7.7.0/24 is directly connected, Serial0
D       10.1.1.0/24 [90/21024000] via 10.7.7.1, 00:15:22, Serial0
C       10.7.7.1/32 is directly connected, Serial0
```

The result of the **ping 10.7.7.2** command, issued on router R1, should be similar to the output shown in Example 2-7.

Example 2-7   *Router R1's* **ping 10.7.7.2** *Output*

```
R1#ping 10.7.7.2

Type escape sequence to abort.
Sending 5, 100-byte ICMP Echos to 10.7.7.2, timeout is 2 seconds:
!!!!!
Success rate is 100 percent (5/5), round-trip min/avg/max = 16/19/24 ms
```

After reading this chapter, you should be able to perform the following tasks:

- Configure analog and digital voice interfaces as new devices are introduced into the voice path

- Configure analog and digital voice ports for optimal voice quality

CHAPTER 3

Voice Interface Configuration

Voice gateways bridge the gap between the VoIP world and the traditional telephony world (for example, a PBX, the PSTN, or an analog phone). Cisco voice gateways connect to traditional telephony devices via voice ports. This chapter introduces basic configuration of analog and digital voice ports, and demonstrates how to fine-tune voice ports with port-specific configurations.

Upon completing this chapter, you will be able to configure voice interfaces on Cisco voice-enabled equipment for connection to traditional, nonpacketized telephony equipment.

Configuring Voice Ports

Connecting voice devices to a network infrastructure requires an in-depth understanding of signaling and electrical characteristics that are specific to each type of interface. Improperly matched electrical components can cause echo and make a connection unusable. As another consideration, configuring devices for international implementation requires knowledge of country-specific settings. This section provides voice port configuration parameters for signaling and country-specific settings.

Before delving into the specific syntax of configuring these voice ports, this section begins by considering several examples of voice applications. The applications discussed help illustrate the function of the voice ports, whose configuration is addressed at the end of this section.

Voice Applications

Different types of applications require specific types of ports. In many instances, the type of port is dependent on the voice device connected to the network. Different types of voice applications include the following:

- Local calls
- On-net calls
- Off-net calls
- Private line, automatic ringdown (PLAR) calls

- PBX-to-PBX calls
- CallManager-to-CallManager calls
- On-net to off-net calls

The following sections describe each type and provide an illustration of each.

Local Calls

Local calls, as illustrated in Figure 3-1, occur between two telephones connected to one Cisco voice-enabled router. This type of call is handled entirely by the router and does not travel over an external network. Both telephones are directly connected to Foreign Exchange Station (FXS) ports on the router.

Figure 3-1 *Local Calls*

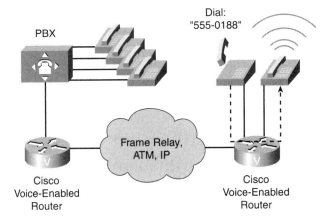

On-Net Calls

On-net calls occur between two telephones on the same data network, as shown in Figure 3-2. The calls can be routed through one or more Cisco voice-enabled routers, but the calls remain on the same data network. The edge telephones attach to the network through direct connections and FXS ports, or through a PBX, which typically connects to the network via a T1 connection. IP phones that connect to the network via switches place on-net calls through Cisco Unified CallManager. The connection across the data network can be a LAN connection, as in a campus environment, or a WAN connection, as in an enterprise environment.

Figure 3-2   *On-Net Calls*

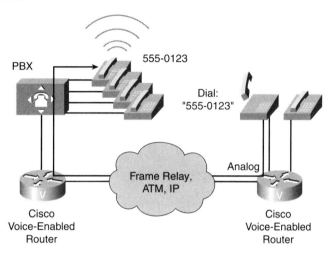

Off-Net Calls

Figure 3-3 shows an example of an off-net call. To gain access to the public switched telephone network (PSTN), the user dials an access code, such as 9, from a telephone that is directly connected to a Cisco voice-enabled router or PBX. The connection to the PSTN is typically a single analog connection via a Foreign Exchange Office (FXO) port or a digital T1 or E1 connection.

Figure 3-3   *Off-Net Calls*

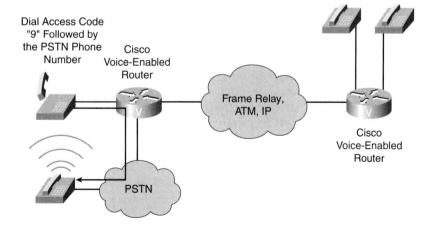

PLAR Calls

PLAR calls automatically connect a telephone to a second telephone when the first telephone goes off hook, as depicted in Figure 3-4. When this connection occurs, the user does not get a dial tone because the voice-enabled port that the telephone is connected to is preconfigured with a specific number to dial. A PLAR connection can work between any types of signaling, including receive and transmit (ear and mouth [E&M]), FXO, FXS, or any combination of analog and digital interfaces. As an example, you might have encountered a PLAR connection at an airline ticket counter, where you pick up a handset and are immediately connected with an airline representative.

Figure 3-4 *PLAR Calls*

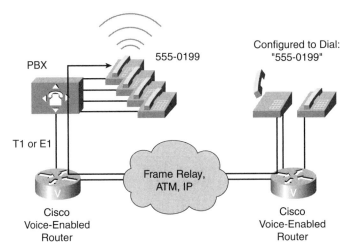

PBX-to-PBX Calls

PBX-to-PBX calls, as shown in Figure 3-5, originate at a PBX at one site and terminate at a PBX at another site while using the network as the transport between the two locations. Many business environments connect sites with private tie trunks. When migrating to a converged voice and data network, this same tie-trunk connection can be emulated across the IP network. Modern PBX connections to the network are typically digital T1 or E1 with channel associated signaling (CAS) or PRI signaling, although PBX connections can also be analog.

CallManager-to-CallManager Calls

As part of an overall migration strategy, a business might replace PBXs with a Cisco Unified CallManager infrastructure. This infrastructure includes IP telephones that

Figure 3-5 *PBX-to-PBX Calls*

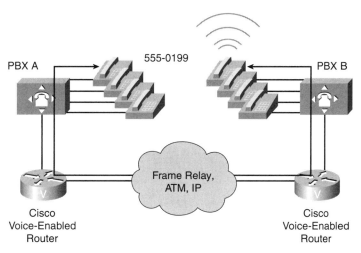

plug directly into the IP network. Cisco Unified CallManager performs the same call-routing functions formerly provided by the PBX. When an IP phone uses Cisco Unified CallManager to place a call, Cisco CallManager, based on its configuration, assesses whether the call is destined for another IP phone under its control or whether the call must be routed through a remote Cisco CallManager for call completion. Although the call stays on the IP network, it might be sent between zones. Every Cisco CallManager is part of a zone. A *zone* is a collection of devices that are under a common administration, usually a Cisco Unified CallManager or gatekeeper. Figure 3-6 provides an example of a CallManager-to-CallManager call.

On-Net to Off-Net Calls

When planning a resilient call-routing strategy, it might be necessary to reroute calls through a secondary path should the primary path fail. An on-net to off-net call, as illustrated in Figure 3-7, originates on an internal network and is routed to an external network, usually to the PSTN. On-net to off-net call-switching functionality might be necessary when a network link is down or if a network becomes overloaded and unable to handle all calls presented.

Figure 3-6 *CallManager-to-CallManager Calls*

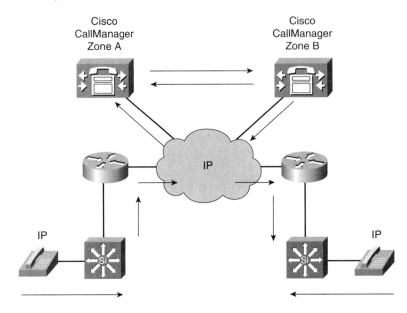

Figure 3-7 *On-Net to Off-Net Calls*

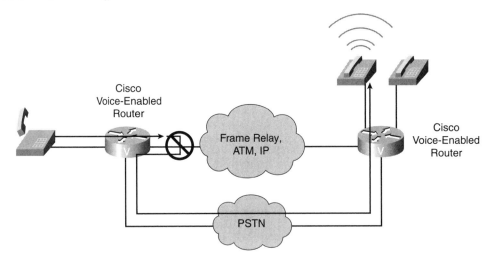

Summarizing Examples of Voice Port Applications

Table 3-1 lists application examples for each type of call.

Table 3-1   *Voice Port Call Types*

Type of Call	Example
Local call	One staff member calls another staff member at the same office. The call is switched between two ports on the same voice-enabled router.
On-net call	One staff member calls another staff member at a remote office. The call is sent from the local voice-enabled router, across the IP network, and terminated on the remote office voice-enabled router.
Off-net call	A staff member calls a client who is located in the same city. The call is sent from the local voice-enabled router, which acts as a gateway, to the PSTN. The call is then sent to the PSTN for call termination.
PLAR call	A client picks up a customer service telephone located in the lobby of an office and is automatically connected to a customer service representative without dialing any digits. The call is automatically dialed, based on the PLAR configuration of the voice port. In this case, as soon as the handset goes off hook, the voice-enabled router generates the prespecified digits to place the call.
PBX-to-PBX call	One staff member calls another staff member at a remote office. The call is sent from the local PBX, through a voice-enabled router, across the IP network, through the remote voice-enabled router, and terminated on the remote office PBX.
CallManager-to-CallManager call	One staff member calls another staff member at a remote office using IP phones. The call setup is handled by the Cisco Unified CallManagers at both locations. After the call is set up, the IP phones generate IP packets carrying voice between sites.
On-net to off-net call	One staff member calls another staff member at a remote office while the IP network is congested. When the originating voice-enabled router determines that it cannot terminate the call across the IP network, it sends the call to the PSTN with the appropriate dialed digits to terminate the call at the remote office via the PSTN network.

FXS Ports

FXS ports connect analog edge devices, such as analog phones, fax machines, and modems. In North America, the FXS port connection functions with default settings most of the time. The same cannot be said for other countries and continents. Remember, FXS ports look like switches to the edge devices that are connected to them. Therefore, the configuration of the FXS port should emulate the switch configuration of the local PSTN. For example, if the local PSTN uses loop-start signaling, the FXS port should use loop-start signaling.

Consider the scenario of an international company with offices in the United States and England. The PSTN of each country provides signaling that is standard for that country. In the United States, the PSTN provides a dial tone that is different from the dial tone in England. Also, when the telephone rings to signal an incoming call, the ring is different in the United States. Another instance when the default configuration might be changed is when the connection is a trunk to a PBX or key system. In that case, the FXS port must be configured to match the settings of that device.

FXS Configuration Parameters

FXS port configuration allows you to set parameters based on the requirements of the connection. You can alter the default settings and fine-tune the parameters for specific needs. For example, you might need to connect an older phone with a mechanical ringer to a router, and the FXS port's default ringing frequency does not work for the older phone's ringer. You could adjust the ringing frequency parameter to fix that problem. You can set the following configuration parameters for an FXS port:

- **signal**—Sets the signaling type for the FXS port. In most cases, the default signaling of loop-start works well. If the connected device is a PBX or a key system, the preferred signaling is ground start. Modern PBXs and key systems do not normally use FXS ports as connections to the network, but older systems might still have these interfaces. When connecting the FXS port to a PBX or key system, you must check the configuration of the voice system and set the FXS port to match the system setting.

- **cptone**—Configures the appropriate call-progress tone for the local region. The call-progress tone setting determines the dial tone, busy tone, and ringback tone to the originating party.

- **description**—Configures a description for the voice port. You can use the description setting to describe the voice port in **show** command output. It is almost always useful to provide some information about the usage of a port. The description could specify the type of equipment that is connected to the FXS port.

- **ring frequency**—Configures a specific ring frequency (in Hz) for an FXS voice port. You must select the ring frequency that matches the connected equipment. If set incorrectly, the attached telephone might not ring or might buzz. In addition, the ring frequency is usually country dependent, and you should take into account the appropriate ring frequency for your area before you configure this command.

NOTE   Typically, the ring frequency parameter is an issue only for electromechanical bell ringers. Back in the days of party lines (that is, where multiple residences shared a local loop connection going back to the CO), these mechanical ringers were tuned to ring at different frequencies. However, most modern piezoelectric ringers are unaffected by the ring frequency setting.

- **ring cadence**—Configures the ring cadence for an FXS port. The ring cadence defines how ringing voltage is sent to signal a call. The normal ring cadence in North America is 2 seconds of ringing followed by 4 seconds of silence. The United Kingdom uses a double ring of 0.4 seconds separated by 0.2 seconds of silence, followed by 2 seconds of silence. When configured, the **cptone** setting automatically sets the ring cadence to match that country. You can manually set the ring cadence if you want to override the default country value. You might have to shut down and reactivate the voice port before the configured value takes effect.

- **disconnect-ack**—Configures an FXS voice port to remove line power if the equipment on an FXS loop-start trunk disconnects first. This removal of line power is not something the user hears, but instead is a method for electrical devices to signal that one side has ended the call.

- **busyout**—Configures the ability to busy out an analog port, perhaps for maintenance purposes.

- **station id name**—Provides the station name associated with the voice port. This parameter is passed as a calling name to the remote end if the call is originated from this voice port. Maximum string length is limited to 15.

- **station id number**—Provides the station number that is to be used as the calling number associated with the voice port. This parameter is optional and, if provided, will be used as the calling number if the call is originated from this voice port. If not specified, the calling number will be used from a reverse dial-peer search. Maximum string length is 15.

Configuring FXS Ports

Figure 3-8 shows an FXS port of a router connecting into a PBX.

Figure 3-8   *FXS Voice Port Configuration*

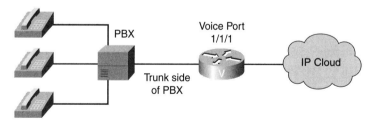

The syntax given in Example 3-1 shows how the British office, in Figure 3-8, is configured to enable ground-start signaling on a router on FXS voice port 1/1/1. Notice the call-progress tones are set for Great Britain, and the ring cadence is set for pattern 1.

Example 3-1 *FXS Voice Port Configuration on a Voice-Enabled Router*

```
Router#configure terminal
Router(config)#voice-port 1/1/1
!Enters voice-port configuration mode
Router(config-voiceport)#signal ground-start
!Enables ground-start signaling
Router(config-voiceport)#cptone GB
!Sets call-progress tones for Great Britain
Router(config-voiceport)#ring cadence pattern01
!Specifies ring cadence pattern 1
```

FXO Ports

FXO ports act like telephones and connect to central office (CO) switches or to a station port on a PBX. This section describes FXO port configuration parameters and provides a sample FXO port configuration.

FXO Configuration Parameters

In most instances, the FXO port connection functions with default settings. FXO port configuration allows you to set parameters based on the requirements of the connection. As with FXS ports, you can alter default settings and fine-tune parameters. You can set the following configuration parameters for an FXO port:

- **signal**—Sets the signaling type for the FXO port. If the FXO port is connected to the PSTN, the default setting of *loop start* is usually appropriate. If the FXO port is connected to a PBX, the signal setting must match the PBX.

- **ring number**—Configures the number of rings before an FXO port answers a call. This is useful when you have other equipment available on the line to answer incoming calls. The FXO port answers if the equipment that is online does not answer the incoming call within the configured number of rings.

- **dial-type**—Configures the appropriate dial type for outbound dialing. Older PBXs or key sets might not support dual-tone multifrequency (DTMF) dialing. If you are connecting an FXO port to this type of device, you might need to set the dial type for pulse dialing.

- **description**—Configures a description for the voice port. Use the description setting to describe the voice port in **show** command output.

- **supervisory disconnect**—Configures supervisory disconnect signaling on the FXO port. Supervisory disconnect signaling is a power denial from the switch that lasts at least 350 ms. When this condition is detected, the system interprets this as a disconnect indication from the switch and clears the call. You should disable supervisory disconnect on the voice port if there is no supervisory disconnect available from the switch. Typically, supervisory disconnect is available when connecting to the PSTN and is enabled by default. When the connection extends out to a PBX, you should verify the documentation to ensure that supervisory disconnect is supported.

Configuring FXO Ports

Figure 3-9 shows a router's FXO port connecting into a PBX.

Figure 3-9   *FXO Voice Port Configuration*

The configuration in Example 3-2 enables loop-start signaling on the router, on FXO voice port 1/0/0. The ring-number setting of 3 specifies that the FXO port does not answer the call until after the third ring, and the dial type is set to DTMF.

Example 3-2   *FXO Voice Port Configuration on a Voice-Enabled Router*

```
Router#configure terminal
Router(config)#voice-port 1/0/0
!Enters voice-port configuration mode
Router(config-voiceport)#signal loop-start
!Enables loop-start signaling
Router(config-voiceport)#ring number 3
!Sets FXO port to answer after three rings
Router(config-voiceport)#dial-type dtmf
!Specifies dial type of DTMF
```

E&M Ports

E&M ports provide signaling that is used generally for switch-to-switch or switch-to-network trunk connections. This section describes E&M configuration parameters and provides an example of an E&M port configuration.

E&M Configuration Parameters

Although E&M ports have default parameters, you must usually configure these parameters to match the device that is connected to the E&M port.

You can set the following configuration parameters:

- **signal**—Configures the signal type for E&M ports which defines the signaling used when notifying a port to send dialed digits. This setting must match that of the PBX to which the port is connected. You must shut down and reactivate the voice port before the configured value takes effect.

  With wink-start signaling, the router listens on the M-lead to determine when the PBX wants to place a call. When the router detects current on the M-lead, it waits for availability of digit registers and then provides a short wink on the E-lead to signal the PBX to start sending digits.

  With delay-start, the router provides current on the E-lead immediately upon seeing current on the M-lead. When current is stopped for the digit-sending duration, the E-lead stays high until digit registers are available. With immediate-start, the PBX simply waits a short time after raising the M-lead and then sends the digits without a signal from the router.

- **operation**—Configures the cabling scheme for E&M ports. The **operation** command affects the voice path only. The signaling path is independent of two-wire versus four-wire operation settings. If the wrong cable scheme is specified, the user might get voice traffic in one direction only. You must check with the PBX configuration to ensure that the settings match. You must then shut down and reactivate the voice port for the new value to take effect.

- **type**—Configures the E&M interface type for a specific voice port. The type defines the electrical characteristics for the E- and M-leads. The E- and M-leads are monitored for on-hook and off-hook conditions. From a PBX perspective, when the PBX attempts to place a call, it goes high (off hook) on the M-lead. The switch monitors the M-lead and recognizes the request for service. If the switch attempts to pass a call to the PBX, the switch goes high on the E-lead. The PBX monitors the E-lead and recognizes the request for service by the switch. To ensure that the settings match, you must check them against the PBX configuration.

- **auto-cut-through**—Configures the ability to enable call completion when a PBX does not provide an M-lead response. For example, when the router is placing a call to the PBX, even though they might have the same correct signaling configured, not all PBXs provide the wink with the same duration or voltage. Therefore, the router might not understand the PBX wink. The **auto-cut-through** command allows the router to send digits to the PBX, even when the expected wink is not detected.

- **description**—Configures a description for the voice port. Use the description setting to describe the voice port in **show** command output.

Configuring E&M Ports

Figure 3-10 shows a router's E&M port connecting to a PBX's E&M interface.

Figure 3-10 *E&M Voice Port Configuration*

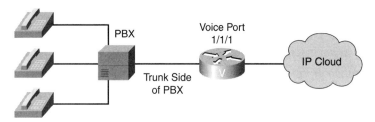

The configuration in Example 3-3 enables wink-start signaling on the router, on E&M voice port 1/1/1. The operation is set for the two-wire voice-cabling scheme, meaning the voice path consists of two wires, and the type is set to 1.

Example 3-3 *E&M Voice Port Configuration on a Voice-Enabled Router*

```
Router#configure terminal
Router(config)#voice port 1/1/1
!Enters voice port configuration mode
Router(config-voiceport)#signal wink-start
!Enables Wink-Start signaling
Router(config-voiceport)#operation 2-wire
!Sets operation for two-wire cabling scheme
Router(config-voiceport)#type 1
!Configures type 1 E&M port
```

Timers and Timing

A variety of default timer settings are configured for various voice ports. Under normal use, these timers do not need adjusting. In instances where ports are connected to a device that does not properly respond to dialed digits or hookflash (that is, quickly transitioning from the off-hook state to the on-hook state and back to the off-hook state) or where the connected device provides automated dialing, these timers can be configured to allow more or less time for a specific function.

Timers and Timing Configuration Parameters

You can set a number of timers and timing parameters for fine-tuning the voice port. Following are voice port configuration parameters that you can set:

- **timeouts initial**—Configures the initial digit timeout value in seconds. This value controls how long the dial tone is presented before the first digit is expected. This timer typically does not need to be changed from its default of 10 seconds.

- **timeouts interdigit**—Configures the number of seconds for which the system will wait for the caller to input a subsequent digit of the dialed digits after the caller has input the initial digit. If the digits are coming from an automated device and the dial plan is a variable-length dial plan, you can shorten this timer so that the call proceeds without having to wait the full default of 10 seconds for the interdigit timer to expire.

- **timeouts ringing**—Configures the length of time that a caller can continue ringing a telephone when there is no answer. You can configure this setting to be less than the default of 180 seconds so that you do not tie up the voice port when it is evident that the call is not going to be answered.

- **timing digit**—Configures the DTMF digit-signal duration for a specified voice port. You can use this setting to fine-tune a connection to a device that might have trouble recognizing dialed digits. If a user or device dials too quickly, the digit might not be recognized. By changing the timing on the digit timer, you can provide for a shorter or longer DTMF duration.

- **timing interdigit**—Configures the DTMF interdigit duration for a specified voice port. You can change this setting to accommodate faster or slower dialing characteristics.

- **timing hookflash-in and hookflash-out**—Configures the maximum duration (in milliseconds) of a hookflash indication. *Hookflash* is an indication by a caller that the caller wishes to do something specific with the call, such as transfer the call or place the call on hold.

    For **hookflash-in**, if the hookflash lasts longer than the specified limit, the FXS interface processes the indication as on hook. If you set the value too low, the hookflash might be interpreted as a hang up; if you set the value too high, the handset has to be left hung up for a longer period to clear the call.

    For **hookflash-out**, the setting specifies the duration (in milliseconds) of the hookflash indication that the gateway generates outbound. You can configure this to match the requirements of the connected device.

Configuring Timers

The installation in Figure 3-11 serves as a solution in a home for the elderly, where users might need more time to dial digits than in other residences. Also, there is a requirement to allow the telephone to ring, unanswered, for only one minute. Figure 3-11 shows an analog phone connecting into FXS port 1/0/0 on a voice-enabled router.

Figure 3-11 *Timers and Timing Configuration*

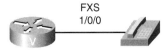

FXS
1/0/0

The FXS port's configuration, as shown in Example 3-4, enables several timing parameters for this voice port. The initial timeout is lengthened to 15 seconds, the interdigit timeout is lengthened to 15 seconds, the ringing timeout is set to 60 seconds, and the hookflash-in timer is set to 500 ms.

Example 3-4 *Timer Voice Port Configuration on a Voice-Enabled Router*

```
Router#configure terminal
Router(config)#voice-port 1/0/0
!Enters voice-port configuration mode
Router(config-voiceport)#timeouts initial 15
!Sets initial timeout to 15 seconds
Router(config-voiceport)#timeouts interdigit 15
!Sets interdigit timeouts to 15 seconds
Router(config-voiceport)#timeouts ringing 60
!Sets ringing timeout to 60 seconds
Router(config-voiceport)#timing hookflash-in 500
!Sets hookflash-in to 500 ms duration
```

Digital Voice Ports

While analog voice ports typically carry a single voice call on a single port, digital voice ports often carry multiple voice conversations over a single voice port. Therefore, digital voice ports might be more appropriate for environments with a high call volume. As a rule of thumb, if a design requires more than seven voice connections, the designer should consider a digital voice port, as opposed to multiple analog voice ports, due to the economies of scale offered by the higher-density digital voice ports.

Digital Voice Configuration Parameters

When you purchase a T1 or E1 connection, make sure that your service provider gives you the appropriate settings. Before you configure a T1 or E1 controller to support digital voice ports, you must enter the following basic configuration parameters to bring up the interface:

- **framing**—Selects the frame type for a T1 or E1 data line. The framing configuration differs between T1 and E1, as follows:

  — **Options for T1**—Super Frame (SF) or Extended Superframe (ESF). SF is the default.

  — **Options for E1**—4-bit cyclic redundancy check (CRC4), no-CRC4, or Australia. CRC4 is the default.

- **linecode**—Configures the line-encoding format for the DS1 link. The linecode configuration differs for T1 and E1, as follows:

  — **Options for T1**—Alternate mark inversion (AMI) or binary 8-zero substitution (B8ZS). AMI is the default.

  — **Options for E1**—AMI or high-density binary 3 (HDB3). HDB3 is the default.

- **clock source**—Configures clocking for individual T1 or E1 links. Line and internal are the options for both T1 and E1. Line is the default.

You must create a digital voice port in the T1 or E1 controller to make the digital voice port available for specific voice port configuration parameters. You must also assign timeslots and signaling to the logical voice port. The first step is to create the T1 or E1 digital voice port with the **ds0-group** *ds0-group-no* **timeslots** *timeslot-list* **type** *signal-type* command. The following list describes the command syntax:

- The **ds0-group** command automatically creates a logical voice port that is numbered as *slot/port*:*ds0-group-no*.

- The *ds0-group-no* parameter identifies the DS0 group (number from 0 to 23 for T1 and from 0 to 30 for E1). This group number is used as part of the logical voice port numbering scheme.

- The **timeslots** command allows the user to specify which timeslots are part of the DS0 group.

- The *timeslot-list* parameter is a single timeslot number, a single range of numbers, or multiple ranges of numbers separated by commas.

- The **type** command defines the emulated analog signaling method that the router uses to connect to the PBX or PSTN. The type depends on whether the interface is T1 or E1.

- The *signal-type* parameter is the signaling type being used by all channels in the DS0 group. For example, the signaling type could be configured as *e&m-wink-start*, which would cause each channel in the DS0 group to use E&M wink-start signaling.

After you specify a **ds0-group** command, the system creates a logical voice port. You must then enter the voice-port configuration mode to configure port-specific parameters. To enter voice port configuration mode, use the **voice-port** *slot/port*:*ds0-group-no* command.

To delete a DS0 group, you must first shut down the logical voice port. When the port is in shutdown state, you can remove the DS0 group from the T1 or E1 controller with the **no ds0-group** *ds0-group-no* command.

Configuring a T1 Controller

Figure 3-12 illustrates how specific channels within a T1 can be defined as a DS0 group.

Figure 3-12 *Digital Voice Configuration*

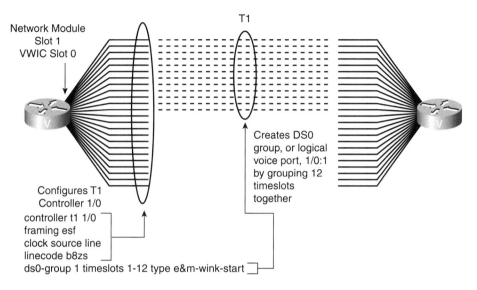

The syntax for the topology shown is presented in Example 3-5. The example configures the T1 controller for ESF framing, B8ZS line coding, and timeslots 1 through 12 with E&M wink-start signaling. The resulting logical voice port is **1/0:1**, where **1/0** is the module and slot number and **:1** is the *ds0-group-no* value that was assigned during configuration. You can configure the remaining timeslots for other signaling types or leave them unused.

Example 3-5 *DS0 Group Configuration on a Voice-Enabled Router*

```
Router#configure terminal
Router(config)#controller t1 1/0
!Enters controller configuration mode
Router(config-controller)#framing esf
!Sets the framing to Extended Superframe
Router(config-controller)#clock source line
!Specifies that the controller receives clocking from the network
Router(config-controller)#linecode b8zs
!Sets the linecoding to Bipolar 8 Zero Substitution
Router(config-controller)#ds0-group 1 timeslots 1-12 type e&m-wink-start
!Defines a DS0 group, which contains the first 12 channels of the T1, and configures
the signaling for those channels as E&M Wink Start signaling
```

ISDN

Cisco voice-capable devices provide support for both PRI and BRI voice connections. Many PBX vendors support either T1/E1 PRI or BRI connections. In Europe, where ISDN is more popular, many PBX vendors support BRI connections. When designing how the PBX passes voice to the network, you must ensure that the router supports the correct connection.

ISDN Configuration Parameters

The first step in configuring ISDN capabilities for T1 or E1 PRI is to configure the T1 or E1 controller basics. After the clock source, framing, and line code are configured, ISDN voice functionality requires the following configuration commands:

- **isdn switch-type**—Configures the ISDN switch type. You can enter this parameter in global configuration mode or in interface configuration mode. If you configure both, the interface switch type takes precedence over the global switch type. This parameter must match the provider ISDN switch. This setting is required for both BRI and PRI connections.

- **pri-group**—Configures timeslots for the ISDN PRI group. T1 allows for timeslots 1 to 23, with timeslot 24 allocated to the D channel. E1 allows for timeslots 1 to 31, with timeslot 16 allocated to the D channel. You can configure the PRI group to include all available timeslots, or you can configure a select group of timeslots for the PRI group.

- **isdn incoming-voice voice**—Configures the interface to send all incoming calls to the digital signal processor (DSP) card for processing.

- **QSIG signaling**—Configures the use of Q Signaling (QSIG) signaling on the D channel. You typically use this setting when connecting via ISDN to a PBX. The command to enable QSIG signaling is **isdn switch-type primary-qsig** for PRI and **isdn switch-type basic-qsig** for BRI connections.

Configuring ISDN

Figure 3-13 shows an ISDN port on a voice-enabled router connecting into an ISDN port on a PBX.

Figure 3-13 *ISDN Configuration*

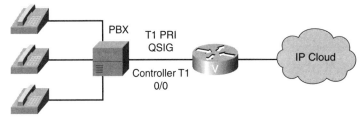

Example 3-6 shows the configuration for this connection. The connection is configured for QSIG signaling across all 23 timeslots.

Example 3-6 *ISDN Voice Port Configuration on a Voice-Enabled Router*

```
Router (config)#isdn switch-type primary-qsig
!QSIG signaling support
Router (config)#controller T1 0/0
Router (config-controller)#pri-group timeslots 1-23
!PRI timeslot allocation
Router (config)#interface serial 0/0:23
Router (config-if)#isdn incoming-voice voice
!Sends incoming calls to DSPs
```

Common Channel Signaling Options

Proprietary signaling can be passed between two PBXs through the use of Transparent Common Channel Signaling (T-CCS), an example of which is provided in Figure 3-14.

Figure 3-14 *CCS Options*

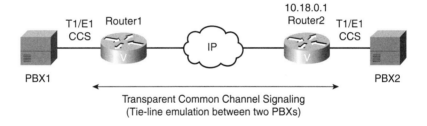

The syntax for the configuration shown is provided in Example 3-7. The **dial-peer** and **voice-port** commands are covered in Chapter 4, "Voice Dial Peer Configuration." For now, consider the **ds0-group 1 timeslots 24 type ext-sig** command, entered in controller configuration mode. This command specifies that the 24th channel of the T1 is going to be carrying external signaling, which the router should not attempt to interpret. Also, notice the **codec clear-channel** command. This command tells the router to pass the signaling information through the DSP transparently, without any compression or processing.

Example 3-7 *Transparent Common Channel Signaling Configuration*

```
Router(config)#controller T1 1/0
Router(config-controller)#ds0-group 1 timeslots 24 type ext-sig
!Configures the signaling channel for external signaling
Router(config-controller)#exit
Router config)#dial-peer voice 1 voip
!Creates a VoIP dial peer
Router(config-dialpeer)#codec clear-channel
!Specifies clear-channel CODEC to pass signaling through the DSP without
!compression or processing
Router(config-dialpeer)#destination-pattern 1000
```

continues

Example 3-7 *Transparent Common Channel Signaling Configuration (Continued)*

```
!Specifies a destination pattern
Router(config-dialpeer)#session target ipv4:10.18.0.1
!Specifies IP address of remote site router
Router(config-dialpeer)#exit
Router(config)#voice-port 1/0:1
Router(config-voiceport)#connection trunk 1000 answer-mode
!Creates a trunk on voice-port 1/0:1 and ties it to the VoIP dial peer with
!a destination pattern of 1000
```

In many cases, PBXs support proprietary signaling that is used to signal supplementary services only, such as making a light on the telephone blink when voice mail is waiting. Because the router does not understand this proprietary signaling, the signaling must be carried transparently across the network without interpretation. T-CCS allows the connection of two PBXs with digital interfaces that use a proprietary or unsupported common channel signaling (CCS) protocol. T1 and E1 traffic is transported transparently through the data network, and the T-CCS feature preserves proprietary signaling. From the PBX standpoint, this type of communication is accomplished through a point-to-point connection.

The configuration for T-CCS in a Voice over IP (VoIP) environment calls for the following three-step process:

1. To define the DS0 group, configure the command **ds0-group** *ds0-group-no* **timeslots** *timeslot-list* **type ext-sig** in the T1 or E1 controller configuration mode. The **timeslots** command specifies the D channel that carries call signaling. The **type ext-sig** command specifies that the signaling is coming from an external source.

2. Create the dial peer, as follows:

   a Configure a VoIP dial peer that points to the IP address of the remote voice-enabled router that connects to the remote PBX.

   b Configure the dial peer for clear-channel codec that signals the DSP to pass the signaling without interpretation.

   c Specify the destination pattern for the dial peer, which is used to create the trunk in Step 3. The number entered here must match the number entered in the **trunk** command.

   d Configure the session target to point to the IP address of the remote voice-enabled router.

   e Configure the dial peer to point to the IP address of the remote site voice-enabled router using the **session target** command.

3. Create the voice port trunk.

NOTE	Chapter 4 covers dial peers in depth.

Configure the **connection trunk** *digits* **answer-mode** command at the logical voice port to create a trunk from that port through the VoIP dial peer and across the IP network to the remote router. The *digits* parameter must match the destination pattern in the VoIP dial peer created in Step 2. The **answer-mode** parameter specifies that the router should not attempt to initiate a trunk connection but should wait for an incoming call before establishing the trunk.

The process for passing the signal transparently through the IP network is as follows:

1. PBX1 sends proprietary signaling across the signaling channel to router 1.

2. The logical voice port that corresponds to the signaling channel is configured for trunking, so the router looks for the dial peer that matches the **trunk** *digits* parameter.

3. The VoIP dial peer is configured for clear-channel codec and points to the IP address of the remote router (router 2) connecting the remote PBX (PBX2).

4. The remote router has a plain old telephone service (POTS) dial peer configured that points to the logical voice port associated with the signaling channel of PBX2. The signal arrives at PBX2 in its native form.

This process shows the T-CCS signaling part of the configuration only. Additional DS0 group and dial-peer configuration is necessary for transport of the voice channels.

Monitoring and Troubleshooting

After physically connecting analog or digital devices to a Cisco voice-enabled router, you might need to issue **show**, **test**, or **debug** commands to verify or troubleshoot your configuration. For example, the following list enumerates six steps to monitor and troubleshoot voice ports:

1. Pick up the handset of an attached telephony device and check for a dial tone. If there is no dial tone, check the following:
   - Is the plug firmly seated?
   - Is the voice port enabled?
   - Is the voice port recognized by the Cisco IOS?
   - Is the router running the correct version of Cisco IOS in order to recognize the module?

2. If you have a dial tone, check for DTMF voice band tones, such as touch-tone detection. If the dial tone stops when you dial a digit, the voice port is probably configured properly.

3. Use the **show voice port** command to verify that the data configured is correct. If you have trouble connecting a call and you suspect that the problem is associated with voice port configuration, you can try to resolve the problem by performing Steps 4 through 6.

4. Use the **show voice port** command to make sure that the port is enabled. If the port is administratively down, use the **no shutdown** command. If the port was working previously and is not working now, it is possible that the port is in a hung state. Use the **shutdown/no shutdown** command sequence to reinitialize the port.

5. If you have configured E&M interfaces, make sure that the values associated with your specific PBX setup are correct. Specifically, check for two-wire or four-wire wink-start, immediate-start, or delay-start signaling types, and the E&M interface type. These parameters need to match those set on the PBX for the interface to communicate properly.

6. You must confirm that the voice network module (VNM) (that is, the module in the router that contains the voice ports) is correctly installed. With the device powered down, remove the VNM and reinsert it to verify the installation. If the device has other slots available, try inserting the VNM into another slot to isolate the problem. Similarly, you must move the voice interface card (VIC) to another VIC slot to determine if the problem is with the VIC card or with the module slot.

For your reference, Table 3-2 lists six **show** commands for verifying the voice port configuration.

Table 3-2 *Commands to Verify Voice Ports*

Command	Description
show voice port	Shows all voice port configurations in detail
show voice port *slot/ subunit/port*	Shows one voice port configuration in detail
show voice port summary	Shows all voice port configurations in brief
show voice busyout	Shows all ports configured as busyout
show voice dsp	Shows status of all DSPs
**show controller T1	E1**	Shows the operational status of a controller

For your further reference, Table 3-3 provides a series of commands used to test Cisco voice ports. The **test** commands provide the ability to analyze and troubleshoot voice ports on voice-enabled routers. As Table 3-3 shows, there are five **test** commands to force voice ports into specific states to test the voice port configuration. The **csim start** *dial-string* command simulates a call to any end station for testing purposes.

Table 3-3   test *Commands*

Command	Description
test voice port *port_or_DS0-group_identifier* **detector** {**m-lead** | **battery-reversal** | **ring** | **tip-ground** | **ring-ground** | **ring-trip**} {**on** | **off** | **disable**}	Forces a detector into specific states for testing.
test voice port *port_or_DS0-group_identifier* **inject-tone** {**local** | **network**} {**1000hz** | **2000hz** | **200hz** | **3000hz** | **300hz** | **3200hz** | **3400hz** | **500hz** | **quiet** | **disable**}	Injects a test tone into a voice port. A call must be established on the voice port under test. When you are finished testing, be sure to enter the **disable** command to end the test tone.
test voice port *port_or_DS0-group_identifier* **loopback** {**local** | **network** | **disable**}	Performs loopback testing on a voice port. A call must be established on the voice port under test. When you finish the loopback testing, be sure to enter the **disable** command to end the forced loopback.
test voice port *port_or_DS0-group_identifier* **relay** {**e-lead** | **loop** | **ring-ground** | **battery-reversal** | **power-denial** | **ring** | **tip-ground**} {**on** | **off** | **disable**}	Tests relay-related functions on a voice port.
test voice port *port_or_DS0-group_identifier* **switch** {**fax** | **disable**}	Forces a voice port into fax or voice mode for testing. If the voice port does not detect fax data, the voice port remains in fax mode for 30 seconds and then reverts automatically to voice mode. After you enter the **test voice port switch fax** command, you can use the **show voice call** command to check whether the voice port is able to operate in fax mode.
csim start *dial-string*	Simulates a call to the specified dial string. It is most useful when testing dial plans.

Table 3-4 lists ISDN **show** and **debug** commands specific to the monitoring and troubleshooting of ISDN connections.

Table 3-4 *ISDN Commands*

Command	Description
show isdn active	Shows ISDN calls in progress
show isdn history	Shows ISDN call history
show isdn status	Shows ISDN line status
show isdn timers	Shows ISDN timer values
debug isdn events	Displays ISDN events in real time
debug isdn q921	Displays ISDN Q.921 packets in real time
debug isdn q931	Displays ISDN Q.931 packets in real time

Tuning Voice Quality

User acceptance of the converged voice and data network depends on the quality of current calls compared to the quality through their original providers. As new devices are introduced in the voice path, it is important to understand how the electrical characteristics of interfaces impact voice quality. This section discusses these electrical characteristics and how to fine-tune them for improved voice quality.

Electrical Characteristics

Voice signal power in a long-distance connection must be tightly controlled. The delivered signal power must be high enough to be clearly understood, but not so strong that it leads to instabilities such as echo. In the traditional telephony network, telephone companies control the signal power levels at each analog device. Now that the IP network is carrying voice, it might be necessary to adjust signal power on a voice interface to fine-tune the voice quality.

Echo

Most initial voice signals enter the network through a two-wire local loop. Most switches connect to other switches through a four-wire connection. As voice travels through the network for delivery to the remote telephone, the voice signal must be passed from the two-wire local loop to the four-wire connection at the first switch, and from the four-wire connection at the switch to a two-wire local loop at the remote end. If the impedance at these two-wire to four-wire connections is not matched exactly, some of the voice signal reflects back in the direction of the source. As a result, originating callers hear their own voice reflected back. Sometimes, the reflected signal is reflected again, causing the destination to hear the same conversation twice.

In a traditional voice network, voice can reflect back. It usually goes unnoticed, however, because the delay is so low. In a VoIP network, echo is more noticeable because both packetization and compression contribute to delay. Specifically, for echo to be a problem, all of the following conditions must exist:

- An analog leakage path between analog Tx and Rx paths
- Sufficient delay in echo return for echo to be perceived as annoying
- Sufficient echo amplitude to be perceived as annoying

Two types of echo might exist in a telephony network: *talker echo* and *listener echo*. Talker echo, which is the most common type of echo, occurs when the speech energy of a talker, transmitted down the primary signal path, is coupled into the receiving path from the far end (or *tail circuit*), as illustrated in Figure 3-15. Talkers then hear their own voice, delayed by the total echo path delay time. If the "echoed"'signal has sufficient amplitude and delay, the result can be annoying to the user and can interfere with the normal speech process. Talker echo is usually a direct result of the two-wire to four-wire conversion that takes place through "hybrid" transformers.

Figure 3-15 *Talker Echo*

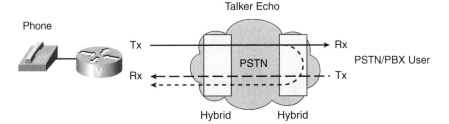

Listener echo is less common than talker echo. As shown in Figure 3-16, listener echo occurs at the far end by circulating voice energy and is generally caused by the two-wire and four-wire hybrid transformers (caused by the "echo being echoed"). The voice of the talker is echoed by the far-end hybrid, and when the echo comes back to the listener, the hybrid on the side of the listener echoes the echo back toward the listener. The effect is that the person listening hears both the talker and an echo of the talker.

Figure 3-16 *Listener Echo*

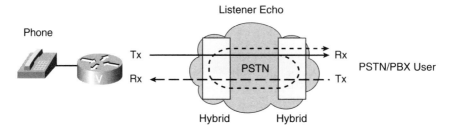

Signal Strength

Another problem is inconsistent volume at different points in the network. Both echo and volume inconsistency might be caused by a voice port generating a signal level that is too high or too low. You can adjust signal strength, either in the inbound direction from an edge telephone or switch into the voice port, or in the outbound direction from the voice port to the edge telephone or switch. Echo results from incorrect input or output levels, or from an impedance mismatch. Although these adjustments are available on the Cisco voice equipment, they are also adjustable on PBX equipment.

Too much input gain can cause clipped or fuzzy voice quality. If the output level is too high at the remote router voice port, the local caller hears echo. If the local router voice port input decibel level is too high, the remote side hears clipping. If the local router voice port input decibel level is too low, or the remote router output level is too low, the remote-side voice can become distorted at a very low volume and DTMF tones might be missed.

Calculating Decibel Levels

Change in signal strength is measured in decibels (dBs). You can either boost the signal or attenuate it by configuring the voice port for input gain or output attenuation. You must be aware of what a voice port connects to and know at what dB level that device works best.

Calculating network dB levels is often an exercise in simple number line arithmetic. Table 3-5 provides common dB levels.

Table 3-5 *Calculating Decibel Levels*

Source 1 Out/In	Router 1 Adjustment	Net at Router 1	WAN	Net at Router 2	Router 2 Adjustment	Destination 1 In/Out
0 dB →	-3 dB →	-3 dB	--	-3 dB	+/-6 dB →	→ -9 dB
-9 dB ←	← +/- 6 dB	-3 dB	--	-3 dB	-3 dB	← 0 dB

Baselining Input and Output Power Levels

Considerations for baselining input and output power levels are as follows:

- Analog voice routers operate best when the receive level from an analog source is set at approximately –3 dB.

- In the United States and most of Europe, the receive level normally expected for an analog telephone is approximately –9 dB. In Asian and South American countries, receive levels are closer to –14 dB. To accommodate these differences, the output levels to the router are set over a wide range.

- Overdriving the circuit can cause analog clipping. Clipping occurs when the power level is above available pulse code modulation (PCM) codes, and a continuous repetition of the last PCM value is passed to the DSP.

- Echo occurs when impedance mismatches reflect power back to the source.

Adjustment of decibel levels might be necessary throughout a voice network. A station connected to a PBX might experience one level of loudness when calling a local extension, a different level when dialing an outside line, and different levels when calling remote sites via VoIP. Adjustments might be necessary in this case.

Voice Port Tuning

In an untuned network, a port configuration that delivers perceived good quality for a call between two dial peers might deliver perceived poor quality for a call between two other dial peers.

Voice quality adjustment is a defined, step-by-step procedure that is implemented after the network is up and running. It is ineffective for you to begin changing the default voice port configurations until full cross-network calls are established; a correctly implemented procedure results in a quality compromise between various sources that the customer accepts as good overall quality.

A variety of different factors, including input gain and output attenuation, can affect voice quality, as illustrated in Figure 3-17. Notice that *input gain* occurs as the signal goes into the echo canceller, and *output attenuation* occurs as the signal comes out of the echo canceller.

A loss plan looks at the required dB levels at specific interfaces, such as an analog FXS port connecting to a telephone or an FXO port connecting to the PSTN. An analog voice router works best with a receive level of –3 dB. An analog telephone in North America and Europe works best with a receive level of –9 dB. Therefore, if the device connecting to that router provides a different level than the expected –3 dB, then input gain can be set to equalize it to –3 dB. If the output at the other end is a telephone that expects –9 dB, then the output voice port has to provide –6 dB output attenuation in addition to the –3 dB to send signaling to the telephone at the expected –9 dB levels. A system-wide loss plan looks at the dB levels

Figure 3-17 *Configuring Voice Port Voice-Quality Tuning*

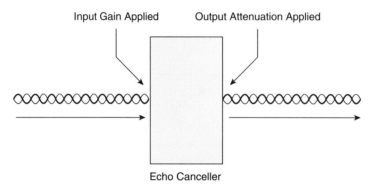

of the initial input and the remote output ports and plans for the appropriate adjustments for end-to-end signal levels. You must consider other equipment (including PBXs) in the system when creating a loss plan.

Voice Port Tuning Configuring Parameters

Parameters for configuring voice port voice quality tuning are as follows:

- **input-gain**—Configures a specific input gain, in decibels, to insert into the receiver side of the interface. The default value for this command assumes that a standard transmission loss plan is in effect, meaning that there must be an attenuation of –6 dB between telephones. The standard transmission plan defines country-specific dB levels and assumes that interfaces already provide the expected dB levels. For example, there must be attenuation of –6 dB between two telephones so that the input gain and output attenuation is 0, if the interfaces provide the required –6 dB attenuation.

- **output-attenuation**—Configures the output attenuation value in decibels for the transmit side. The value represents the amount of loss to be inserted at the transmit side of the interface.

- **impedance**—Configures the terminating impedance of a voice port interface. The impedance value selected must match the setting from the specific telephony system or device to which it is connected. Impedance standards vary between countries. CO switches in the United States are predominantly 600 ohms real (600r). PBXs in the United States are normally 600r or 900 ohms complex (900c).

    Incorrect impedance settings or an impedance mismatch generates a significant amount of echo. You can mask the echo by entering the **echo-cancel** command. In addition, gains often do not work correctly if there is an impedance mismatch.

NOTE   The **input-gain** and **output-attenuation** commands accommodate network equipment and are not end-user volume controls for user comfort.

Configuring Voice Port Tuning

Figure 3-18 shows a voice-enabled router connecting to a PBX via an E&M port, specifically, port 1/0/0. Additionally, the router connects into the PSTN via FXO port 1/1/0.

Figure 3-18 *Voice Port Tuning Example*

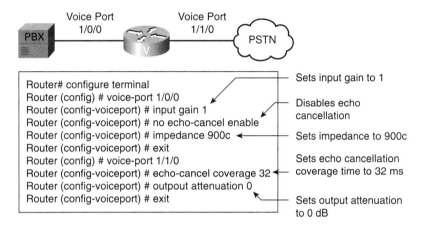

Example 3-8 illustrates voice port tuning parameters on the E&M and FXO ports in the router shown in Figure 3-18. In the example, the PBX output is –4 dB, whereas the voice router functions best at –3 dB. Therefore, the adjustment is made in the inbound path to the router using the **input-gain** command. The impedance setting on the router needs to be changed from the default of 600r to match the 900c impedance setting of the PBX. Because this is an E&M port, echo cancellation is disabled. The FXO port connecting to the PSTN has an adjustment for echo coverage that allows for longer-distance echo cancellation.

Example 3-8 *Configuring Voice Port Tuning*

```
Router#configure terminal
Router(config)#voice-port 1/0/0
Router (config-voiceport)#input gain 1
!Sets input gain to 1
Router (config-voiceport)#no echo-cancel enable
!Disables echo cancellation
Router (config-voiceport)#impedance 900c
!Sets impedance to 900c
Router (config-voiceport)#exit
Router(config)#voice-port 1/1/0
Router (config-voiceport)#output attenuation 0
!Sets output attenuation to 0 decibels
Router (config-voiceport)#exit
```

E&M voice port parameters used in Example 3-8 include:

- **input-gain**—Increases the inbound voice level by 1 dB before the voice is transmitted across the network

- **no echo-cancel enable**—Disables echo cancellation

- **impedance**—Sets the impedance to match the connecting hardware

FXO voice port parameters used in Example 3-8 include:

- **echo-cancel coverage**—Adjusts the cancellation coverage time to 32 ms. This allows for cancellation of echo that has greater delay.

- **output-attenuation**—Specifies that there is no attenuation as the signal is passed out of the interface to the PSTN.

Configuring Echo Cancellation

Echo cancellation is configured at the voice port level. It is enabled by default, and its characteristics are configurable. Echo cancellation commands are as follows:

- **echo-cancel enable**—Enables cancellation of voice that is sent out through the interface and received back on the same interface. Sound that is received back in this manner is perceived by the listener as echo. Echo cancellation keeps a certain-sized sample of the outbound voice and calculates what that same signal looks like when it returns as an echo. Echo cancellation then attenuates the inbound signal by that amount to cancel the echo signal. If you disable echo cancellation, it will cause the remote side of a connection to hear echo. Because echo cancellation is an invasive process that can minimally degrade voice quality, you should disable this command if it is not needed. There is no echo path for a four-wire E&M interface. The echo canceller should be disabled for this interface type.

- **echo-cancel coverage**—Adjusts the coverage size of the echo canceller. This command enables cancellation of voice that is sent out through the interface and received back on the same interface within the configured amount of time. If the *local loop* (the distance from the interface to the connected equipment that is producing the echo) is longer, the configured value of this command should be extended.

  If you configure a longer value for this command, it takes the echo canceller longer to converge. In this case, the user might hear a slight echo when the connection is initially set up. If the configured value for this command is too short, the user might hear some echo for the duration of the call because the echo canceller is not canceling the longer-delay echoes. There is no echo or echo cancellation on the network side (for example, the non-POTS side of the connection).

- **non-linear**—The function enabled by the **non-linear** command is also known as residual echo suppression. This command effectively creates a half-duplex voice path. If voice is present on the inbound path, then there is no signal on the outbound path. This command is associated with the echo canceller operation. The **echo-cancel enable** command must be enabled for the **non-linear** command to take effect. Use the **non-linear** command to shut off any signal if near-end speech is not detected.

  Enabling the **non-linear** command normally improves performance. However, some users encounter truncation of consonants at the ends of sentences when this command is enabled. This occurs when one person is speaking and the other person starts to speak before the first person finishes. Because the nonlinear cancellation allows speech in one direction only, it must switch directions on the fly. This might clip the end of the sentence spoken by the first person or the beginning of the sentence spoken by the second person.

ITU standard G.164 defines the performance of echo suppressors, which are the predecessors of echo cancellation technology. G.164 also defines the disabling of echo suppressors in the presence of 2100-Hz tones that precede low-bit-rate modems.

ITU standard G.165 defines echo cancellation and provides a number of objective tests that ensure a minimum level of performance. These tests check convergence speed of the echo canceller, stability of the echo canceller filter, performance of the nonlinear processor, and a limited amount of double-talk testing. The signal used to perform these tests is white noise. Additionally, G.165 defines the disabling of echo cancellers in the presence of 2100-Hz signals with periodic phase reversals in order to support echo-canceling modem technology (for example, V.34), which does not work if line echo cancellation is performed in the connection.

ITU standard G.168 allows more rigorous testing and satisfies more testing requirements. White noise is replaced with a pseudo-speech signal for the convergence tests. Most echo cancellation algorithms use a least mean square algorithm to adapt the echo cancellation filter. This algorithm works best with random signals and slows down with more correlated signals such as speech. Use of the pseudo-speech signal in testing provides a more realistic portrayal of the echo canceller's performance in real use.

If you speak into your telephone and hear your own voice a short time later, you are experiencing talker echo. As you learned earlier in the "Echo" section, talker echo is caused by the remote telephony circuitry's two-wire to four-wire hybrid circuit. Enabling echo-cancellation on your voice port will eliminate the problem. Depending on the return time of the echoed voice, you can further adjust using the **echo-cancel coverage** command. Table 3-6 compares echo cancellation standards.

Table 3-6 *Comparing Echo Cancellation Standards*

	G.165 EC	G.168 EC
Tail Coverage	Up to 32 ms	Up to 64 ms
Minimum Echo Return Loss (ERL)	Greater than or equal to -6 dB	Configurable to greater than or equal to -0 dB, -3 dB, or -6 dB
Echo Suppression	Up to 10 seconds	Not required due to faster convergence
Minimum Cisco IOS Software Release	12.2(11)T, 12.2(8)T5, 12.2(12), and higher	12.2(13)T, 12.2(8)YN, 12.2(15)T, 12.3(4)T, 12.3(4)XD, and higher

Summary

This chapter discussed the configuration of various analog and digital voice ports. For example, analog voice ports, such as FXS and FXO ports, need an appropriate signaling type (that is, loop-start or ground-start) to communicate with attached equipment. E&M port configurations also need to match the configurations of the equipment connecting to the E&M ports (for example, a PBX E&M interface). This chapter also reviewed various analog port timing parameters.

Digital port configuration included parameters such as line coding and framing. Additionally, this chapter introduced how DS-0 groups logically combine multiple channels in a digital circuit (for example, a T1), thus reducing the number of required configuration steps. Several **show**, **debug**, and **test** commands assist in the monitoring and troubleshooting of voice ports.

Echo often causes significant quality issues in VoIP networks. Typically, echo results from an impedance mismatch in a two-wire to four-wire hybrid circuit. Fortunately, Cisco voice-enabled routers combat echo via echo suppression and echo cancellation technologies. This chapter explored the commands used to influence the effect of echo on voice calls.

Chapter Review Questions

The following questions test your knowledge of topics explained in this chapter. You can find the answers to the questions in Appendix A, "Answers to Chapter Review Questions."

1. If a client picked up a customer service handset and was automatically connected to customer service without dialing any digits, what kind of call would it be?

   a Cisco CallManager-to-Cisco CallManager call

   b PBX-to-PBX call

   c on-net call

d local call

e PLAR call

2. Which configuration parameter would you change to set the dial tone, busy tone, and ringback tone on an FXS port?

a cptone

b ring frequency

c ring cadence

d description

e signal

3. What are the two options for the **linecode** command on an E1 connection?

a SF

b ESF

c CRC4

d AMI

e B8ZS

f HDB3

4. What are the two options for the **framing** command on a T1 connection?

a SF

b ESF

c CRC4

d AMI

e B8ZS

f HDB3

5. What is the purpose of T-CCS?

a To route calls between PBXs

b   To provide point-to-point connections between PBXs

c   To pass proprietary signaling between PBXs

d   To specify a channel for standards-based call signaling

6.   What is the best time to change default voice port configurations to tune voice quality?

a   Before you set up the network

b   After the network is up and running

c   After two dial peers experience poor quality

d   When there is a network failure

7.   Which command is used to enable residual echo suppression?

a   **echo-cancel enable**

b   **echo-cancel coverage**

c   **non-linear**

d   **no echo-cancel enable**

8.   Which two of the following are echo cancellation standards?

a   G.114

b   G.165

c   G.168

d   G.400

9.   Which of the following statements best describes when echo occurs?

a   When there is a mismatch in signaling types

b   When impedance mismatches reflect power back to the source

c   When the far-end impedance absorbs the signal

d   When the router processor utilization is too high to run the companding algorithm in a timely manner

10.   Why does echo usually go unnoticed in a traditional telephony network?

a   The volume of the echo is high.

    b   The delay between the original voice signal and the echo is low.

    c   Traditional telephony networks do not suffer from impedance mismatches.

    d   Traditional telephony networks negate inductance through the use of load coils.

Lab Exercise: Voice Port Configuration

In this lab, you will configure and test router R1's FXS port using the topology you constructed in the lab exercise for Chapter 2, "Analog and Digital Voice Connections." Recall that an FXS port allows you to connect end stations, such as analog phones, fax machines, and modems, into a voice-enabled router.

Figure 3-19 illustrates the lab's physical topology and IP addressing.

Figure 3-19 *Lab Topology*

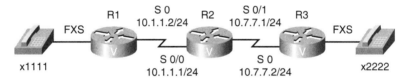

Task 1: Configure FXS Port Parameters

In this task, you will issue commands to configure various parameters on an FXS port.

Complete these steps:

    1. Enter voice port configuration mode for the FXS port on router R1.

    2. To ensure the appropriate signaling type on this voice port, configure the signaling to the default value of **loopstart**.

    3. Assume the analog phone connected to this voice port is located in one of several adjoining cubicles and you wish to create a distinctive ring for this phone so that the phone's user can distinguish their phone's ringing pattern from other phones' ringing patterns. Create a distinctive ringing pattern that causes the analog phone to ring for 5 seconds, be silent for 1 second, and then repeat this pattern. To make sure this change takes effect, shut down and then bring up the voice port, using the **shutdown** command, followed by the **no shutdown** command.

    4. Assume that several thousand feet of cable separate the analog phone from the FXS port, and as a result, some electrical capacitance has built up in the line. This capacitance can lead to an impedance mismatch, thus causing echo. To help counteract this capacitance, change the impedance value of the voice port from the default value of 600r (that is, 600 purely resistive ohms) to 600c (that is, 600 ohms of impedance that contains both a resistive and a capacitive component).

NOTE	At this point, you have not configured your voice-enabled routers with call routing intelligence. Therefore, you cannot place a call between the two analog phones. However, the parameters you configured in this lab will be in effect at the completion of the lab exercise for Chapter 4.

Task 2: Exercise Verification

In this task, you will verify the parameters you configured are in effect and that the FXS port is functioning properly.

Complete these steps:

1. To verify that the appropriate signaling, ring cadence, and impedance settings are applied to R1's FXS port, use the **show voice port** *port_id* command to view the port settings.

2. To verify that the voice port is functioning, lift the handset of the attached analog phone. You should hear dial tone. If you do not hear dial tone, you might need to administratively bring up the port with the **no shutdown** command.

3. To verify that the voice port can send a ringing signal at an appropriate voltage and frequency as to alert the attached analog phone, enter the **test voice port** *port_id* **relay ring on** command, followed by the **test voice port** *port_id* **relay ring disable** command.

Suggested Solution

Although your physical hardware might differ, Example 3-9 offers one solution to the preceding exercise.

Example 3-9 *Router R1's Configuration*

```
R1#configure terminal
Enter configuration commands, one per line.  End with CNTL/Z.
R1(config)#voice-port 1/1
R1(config-voiceport)#signal loopstart
R1(config-voiceport)#ring cadence define 50 10
R1(config-voiceport)#shutdown
R1(config-voiceport)#no shutdown
R1(config-voiceport)#impedance 600c
R1(config-voiceport)#end
```

The results of the **show voice port** *port_id* command, issued on router R1, should be similar to the output shown in Example 3-10. Note that the shaded lines in the output reflect the parameters configured in this exercise

Example 3-10 *Router R1's* **show voice port 1/1** *Output*

```
R1#show voice port 1/1
FXS 1/1 Slot is 1, Port is 1
 Type of VoicePort is FXS
 Operation State is DORMANT
 Administrative State is UP
 No Interface Down Failure
 Description is not set
 Noise Regeneration is enabled
 Non Linear Processing is enabled
 Non Linear Mute is disabled
 Non Linear Threshold is -21 dB
 Music On Hold Threshold is Set to -38 dBm
 In Gain is Set to 0 dB
 Out Attenuation is Set to 0 dB
 Echo Cancellation is enabled
 Echo Cancellation NLP mute is disabled
 Echo Cancellation NLP threshold is -21 dB
 Echo Cancel Coverage is set to 64 ms
 Echo Cancel worst case ERL is set to 6 dB
 Playout-delay Mode is set to adaptive
 Playout-delay Nominal is set to 60 ms
 Playout-delay Maximum is set to 200 ms
 Playout-delay Minimum mode is set to default, value 40 ms
 Playout-delay Fax is set to 300 ms
 Connection Mode is normal
 Connection Number is not set
 Initial Time Out is set to 10 s
 Interdigit Time Out is set to 10 s
 Call Disconnect Time Out is set to 60 s
 Supervisory Disconnect Time Out is set to 750 ms
 Ringing Time Out is set to 180 s
 Wait Release Time Out is set to 30 s
 Companding Type is u-law
```

continues

Example 3-10 *Router R1's* **show voice port 1/1** *Output (Continued)*

```
Coder Type is g729ar8
Voice Activity Detection is enabled
Nominal Playout Delay is 60 milliseconds
Maximum Playout Delay is 200 milliseconds
Region Tone is set for US

Analog Info Follows:
Currently processing none
Maintenance Mode Set to None (not in mtc mode)
Number of signaling protocol errors are 0
Impedance is set to 600c Ohm
Analog interface A-D gain offset = -3.0 dB
Analog interface D-A gain offset = -3.0 dB
FXS idle voltage set to low
Station name None, Station number None
Translation profile (Incoming):
Translation profile (Outgoing):

Voice card specific Info Follows:
Signal Type is loopStart
Ring Frequency is 20 Hz
Hook Status is On Hook
Ring Active Status is inactive
Ring Ground Status is inactive
Tip Ground Status is active
Digit Duration Timing is set to 100 ms
InterDigit Duration Timing is set to 100 ms
Hookflash-in Timing is set to 1000 ms
Hookflash-out Timing is set to 400 ms
No disconnect acknowledge
Ring Cadence is User defined
Ring Cadence are [50 10] * 100 msec
Ringer Equivalence Number is set to 1
InterDigit Pulse Duration Timing is set to 500 ms
```

After reading this chapter, you should be able to perform the following tasks:

- Describe call establishment principles
- Configure POTS and VoIP dial peers
- Explain special purpose connections

CHAPTER 4

Voice Dial Peer Configuration

Configuring dial peers is the key to setting up dial plans and implementing voice in a VoIP network. In some situations, a router might also need to manipulate digits in a dial string before passing the dial string to a telephony device. For example, a 9 might need to be added to a dial string before the dial string passes out the router to a PBX, or perhaps a dialed area code and office code needs to be removed from a dial string. This chapter introduces plain old telephone service (POTS) and Voice over IP (VoIP) dial peers, which make an end-to-end VoIP call possible. Additionally, this chapter discusses various approaches to manipulating dialed digits.

Consider a call center environment. Calls coming into a call center need to be distributed among available customer service agents. A *hunt group* takes calls coming into a single number and logically distributes those calls across hunt group members. This chapter also describes how to configure hunt groups and similarly how to reroute a call across the PSTN during times when an IP WAN connection is unavailable.

Finally, this chapter addresses the configuration of special purpose connections such as private line, automatic ringdown (PLAR) and connections that interconnect existing PBX systems.

Configuring Dial Peers

As a call is set up across the network, the existence of various parameters is checked and negotiated. A mismatch in parameters can cause call failure. Therefore, it is important to understand how routers interpret call legs and how call legs relate to inbound and outbound dial peers. Successful implementation of a VoIP network relies heavily on the proper application of dial peers, the digits they match, and the services they specify. A network designer needs in-depth knowledge of dial peer configuration options and their uses. This section discusses the proper use of digit manipulation and the configuration of dial peers.

Understanding Call Legs

Call legs are logical connections between any two telephony devices, such as gateways, routers, Cisco Unified CallManagers, or telephony endpoint devices. Additionally, call legs are router-centric. When an inbound call arrives, it is processed separately until the destination is determined. Then a second outbound call leg is established, and the inbound call leg is switched to the outbound voice port. The topology shown in Figure 4-1 illustrates the four call legs involved in an end-to-end call between two voice-enabled routers.

Figure 4-1 *Call Legs*

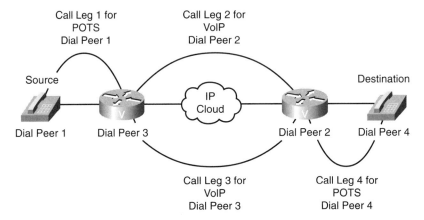

An end-to-end call consists of four call legs: two from the source router's perspective and two from the destination router's perspective. To complete an end-to-end call from either side and send voice packets back and forth, you must configure all four dial peers. Dial peers are only used to set up calls. After the call is established, dial peers are no longer employed.

An inbound call leg occurs when an incoming call comes *into* the router or gateway. An outbound call leg occurs when a call is placed *from* the router or gateway, as depicted in Figure 4-2.

Figure 4-2 *End-to-End Calls*

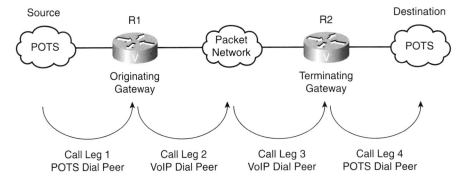

A call is segmented into call legs, and a dial peer is associated with each call leg. The process for call setup, as diagramed in Figure 4-2, is:

1. The POTS call arrives at R1, and an inbound POTS dial peer is matched.

2. After associating the incoming call to an inbound POTS dial peer, R1 creates an inbound POTS call leg and assigns it a call ID (call leg 1).

3. R1 uses the dialed string to match an outbound VoIP dial peer.

4. After associating the dialed string to an outbound voice network dial peer, R1 creates an outbound voice network call leg and assigns it a call ID (call leg 2).

5. The voice network call request arrives at R2, and an inbound VoIP dial peer is matched.

6. After R2 associates the incoming call to an inbound VoIP dial peer, R2 creates the inbound voice network call leg and assigns it a call ID (call leg 3). At this point, both R1 and R2 negotiate voice network capabilities and applications, if required. The originating router or gateway might request nondefault capabilities or applications. When this is the case, the terminating router or gateway must match an inbound VoIP dial peer that is configured for such capabilities or applications.

7. R2 uses the dialed string to match an outbound POTS dial peer.

8. After associating the incoming call setup with an outbound POTS dial peer, R2 creates an outbound POTS call leg, assigns it a call ID, and completes the call (call leg 4).

Understanding Dial Peers

When a call is placed, an edge device generates dialed digits as a way of signaling where the call should terminate. When these digits enter a router voice port, the router must decide whether the call can be routed and where the call can be sent. The router does this by searching a list of dial peers.

A *dial peer* is an addressable call endpoint. The address is called a *destination pattern* and is configured in every dial peer. Destination patterns use both explicit digits and wildcard variables to define one telephone number or range of numbers.

Dial peers define the parameters for the calls that they match. For example, if a call is originating and terminating at the same site and is not crossing through slow-speed WAN links, then the call can cross the local network uncompressed and without special priority. A call that originates locally and crosses the WAN link to a remote site may require compression with a specific coder-decoder (CODEC). In addition, this call may require that voice activity detection (VAD) be turned on and will need to receive preferential treatment by specifying a higher priority level.

Cisco voice-enabled routers support four types of dial peers, including POTS, VoIP, VoFR, and VoATM. However, this book focuses on POTS and VoIP dial peers:

- **POTS dial peers**—Connect to a traditional telephony network, such as the public switched telephone network (PSTN) or a PBX, or to a telephony edge device such as a telephone or fax machine. POTS dial peers perform these functions:

  — Provide an address (telephone number or range of numbers) for the edge network or device

  — Point to the specific voice port that connects the edge network or device

- **VoIP dial peers**—Connect over an IP network. VoIP dial peers perform these functions:

  — Provide a destination address (telephone number or range of numbers) for the edge device that is located across the network

  — Associate the destination address with the next-hop router or destination router, depending on the technology used

In Figure 4-3, the telephony device connects to the Cisco voice-enabled router. The POTS dial peer configuration includes the telephone number of the telephony device and the voice port to which it is attached. The router determines where to forward incoming calls for that telephone number.

Figure 4-3   *Dial Peers*

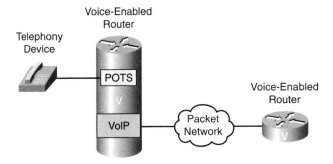

The Cisco voice-enabled router VoIP dial peer is connected to the packet network. The VoIP dial peer configuration includes the destination telephone number (or range of numbers) and the next-hop or destination voice-enabled router network address.

Follow these steps to enable a router to complete a VoIP call:

1. Configure a compatible dial peer on the source router that specifies the recipient destination address.

2. Configure a POTS dial peer on the recipient router that specifies which voice port the router uses to forward the voice call.

Configuring POTS Dial Peers

Before the configuration of Cisco IOS dial peers can begin, you must have a good understanding of where the edge devices reside, what type of connections need to be made between these devices, and what telephone numbering scheme is applied to the devices.

Follow these steps to configure POTS dial peers:

1. Configure a POTS dial peer at each router or gateway, where edge telephony devices connect to the network.

2. Use the **destination-pattern** command in dial peer configuration mode to configure the telephone number.

3. Use the **port** command in dial peer configuration mode to specify the physical voice port that the POTS telephone is connected to.

The dial peer type will be specified as POTS because the edge device is directly connected to a voice port, and the signaling must be sent from this port to reach the device. There are two basic parameters that need to be specified for the device: the telephone number and the voice port. When a PBX is connecting to the voice port, a range of telephone numbers can be specified.

Figure 4-4 shows POTS dial peers. Example 4-1 illustrates proper POTS dial peer configuration on the Cisco voice-enabled router shown in Figure 4-4. The **dial-peer voice 1 pots** command notifies the router that dial peer 1 is a POTS dial peer with a tag of 1. The tag is a number that is locally significant to the router. Although the tag does not need to match the phone number specified by the **destination-pattern** command, many administrators recommend configuring a tag that does match a dial-peer's phone number, to help make the configuration more intuitive. The **destination-pattern 7777** command notifies the router that the attached telephony device terminates calls destined for telephone number 7777. The **port 1/0/0** command notifies the router that the telephony device is plugged into module 1, voice interface card (VIC) slot 0, and voice port 0.

Figure 4-4 *POTS Dial Peers*

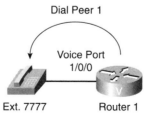

Dial Peer 1

Voice Port
1/0/0

Ext. 7777   Router 1

Example 4-1 *Configuration for Dial Peer 1 on Router 1*

```
Router1#configure terminal
Router1(config)#dial-peer voice 1 pots
Router1(config-dialpeer)#destination-pattern 7777
Router1(config-dialpeer)#port 1/0/0
Router1(config-dialpeer)#end
```

Practice Scenario 1: POTS Dial Peer Configuration

Throughout this chapter, you will practice what you have learned. In this scenario, assume that there is a data center at the R1 site and executive offices at the R2 site. Using the diagram shown in Figure 4-5, create POTS dial peers for the four telephones shown. Notice that three configuration commands are required for R1, and nine configuration commands are required for R2. You might want to use a separate sheet of paper to write your configuration commands.

Figure 4-5   *POTS Dial Peer Configuration*

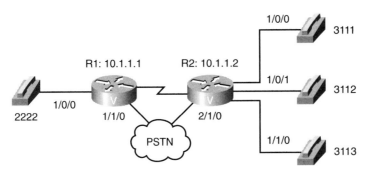

R1:

_____

_____

_____

R2:

_____

_____

_____

R2:

Practice Scenario 1: Suggested Solution

Although your choice of dial peer tags might vary, the following offers a suggested solution to Practice Scenario 1:

R1:

```
dial-peer voice 2222 pots
        destination-pattern 2222
        port 1/0/0
```

R2:

```
dial-peer voice 3111 pots
        destination-pattern 3111
        port 1/0/0
dial-peer voice 3112 pots
        destination-pattern 3112
        port 1/0/1
dial-peer voice 3113 pots
        destination-pattern 3113
        port 1/1/0
```

Configuring VoIP Dial Peers

The administrator must know how to identify the far-end voice-enabled device that will terminate the call. In a small network environment, the device might be the IP address of the remote device. In a large environment, identifying the device might mean pointing to a Cisco Unified CallManager or gatekeeper for address resolution and call admission control (CAC) to complete the call.

Follow these steps to configure VoIP dial peers:

1. Configure the path across the network for voice data.

2. Specify the dial peer as a VoIP dial peer.

3. Use the **destination-pattern** command to configure a range of numbers reachable by the remote router or gateway.

4. Use the **session target** command to specify an IP address of the terminating router or gateway.

5. As a best practice, use the remote device loopback address as the IP address.

The dial peer specified as a VoIP dial peer alerts the router that it must process a call according to the various dial peer parameters. The dial peer must then send the call setup information in IP packets for transport across the network. Specified parameters might include the CODEC used for compression (for example, VAD) or marking the packet for priority service.

The **destination-pattern** parameter configured for this dial peer is typically a range of numbers that are reachable via the remote router or gateway.

Because this dial peer points to a device across the network, the router needs a destination IP address to put in the IP packet. The **session target** parameter allows the administrator to specify either an IP address of the terminating router or gateway or another device. For example, a gatekeeper or Cisco Unified CallManager might return an IP address of that remote terminating device.

To determine which IP address a dial peer should point to, Cisco recommends you use a loopback address. The loopback address is always up on a router as long as the router is powered on and the interface is not administratively shut down. The reason an interface IP address is not recommended is that if the interface goes down the call will fail, even if there is an alternate path to the router.

Figure 4-6 shows VoIP dial peers. Example 4-2 lists the proper VoIP dial peer configuration on Router 1, which is a Cisco voice-enabled router shown in Figure 4-6. The **dial-peer voice 2 voip** command notifies the router that dial peer 2 is a VoIP dial peer with a tag of 2. The **destination-pattern 8888** command notifies the router that this dial peer defines an IP voice path across the network for telephone number 8888. The **session target ipv4:10.18.0.1** command defines the IP address of the router that is connected to the remote telephony device.

Figure 4-6   *VoIP Dial Peers*

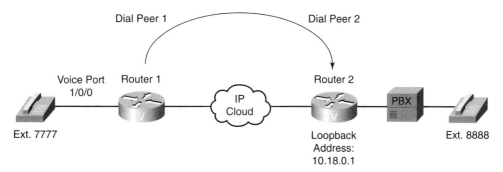

Example 4-2   *Configuration for Dial Peer 2 on Router 1*

```
Router1#configure terminal
Router1(config)#dial-peer voice 2 voip
Router1(config-dialpeer)#destination-pattern 8888
Router1(config-dialpeer)#session target ipv4:10.18.0.1
Router1(config-dialpeer)#end
```

Practice Scenario 2: VoIP Dial Peer Configuration

Create VoIP dial peers for each of the R1 and R2 sites based on the diagram presented in Figure 4-7.

Figure 4-7   *VoIP Dial Peer Configuration*

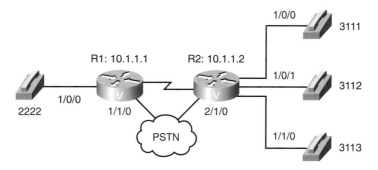

R1:

R2:

Practice Scenario 2: Suggested Solution

Although your choice of dial peer tags might vary, the following offers a suggested solution to Practice Scenario 2:

R1:

```
dial-peer voice 3111 voip
      destination-pattern 3111
      session target ipv4:10.1.1.2
dial-peer voice 3112 voip
      destination-pattern 3112
      session target ipv4:10.1.1.2
dial-peer voice 3113 voip
      destination-pattern 3113
      session target ipv4:10.1.1.2
```

R2:

```
dial-peer voice 2222 voip
      destination-pattern 2222
      session target ipv4:10.1.1.1
```

The next section of this chapter introduces you to the use of wildcards to minimize the number of dial peers you must configure.

Configuring destination-pattern Options

As previously discussed, the destination pattern associates a telephone number with a given dial peer. It also determines the dialed digits that the router collects and forwards to the remote telephony interface, such as a PBX, Cisco Unified CallManager, or PSTN. You must configure a destination pattern for each POTS and VoIP dial peer that you define on the router.

The destination pattern can indicate a complete telephone number or a partial telephone number with wildcard digits, or it can point to a range of numbers defined in a variety of ways.

Destination-pattern options include the following:

- **Plus sign (+)**—An optional character that indicates an E.164 standard number. E.164 is the ITU-T recommendation for the international public telecommunication numbering plan. The plus sign in front of a destination-pattern string specifies that the string must conform to E.164.

- *string*—A series of digits specifying the E.164 or private dial-plan telephone number. The following examples show the use of special characters that are often found in destination pattern strings:

  — **Asterisk (*) and pound sign (#)**—An asterisk (*) and pound sign (#) appear on standard touch-tone dial pads. These characters may need to be used when passing a call to an automated application that requires these characters to signal the use of a special feature. For example, when calling an interactive voice response (IVR) system that requires a code for access, the number dialed might be 5551212888#, which would initially dial the telephone number 5551212 and input a code of 888 followed by the pound key to terminate the IVR input query.

— **Comma (,)**—A comma (,) inserts a one-second pause between digits. The comma can be used, for example, where a 9 is dialed to signal a PBX that the call should be processed by the PSTN. The 9 is followed by a comma to give the PBX time to open a call path to the PSTN, after which the remaining digits are played out. An example of this string is 9,5551212.

— **Period (.)**—A period (.) matches any single entered digit from 0 to 9 and is used as a wildcard. The wildcard can be used to specify a group of numbers that might be accessible via a single destination router, gateway, PBX, or Cisco Unified CallManager. A pattern of 200. allows for ten uniquely addressed devices, while a pattern of 20.. can point to 100 devices. If one site has the numbers 2000 through 2049 and another site has the numbers 2050 through 2099, then a bracket notation would be more efficient, as described next.

— **Brackets ([ ])**—Brackets ([ ]) indicate a range. A range is a sequence of characters that are enclosed in the brackets. Only single numeric characters from 0 through 9 are allowed in the range. In the previous example, the bracket notation could be used to specify exactly which range of numbers is accessible through each dial peer. For example, the first site pattern would be 20[0 – 4]., and the second site pattern would be 20[5-9]. Note that in both cases, a dot is used in the last digit position to represent any single digit from 0 through 9. The bracket notation offers much more flexibility in how numbers can be assigned.

• **T**—An optional control character indicating that the destination-pattern value is a variable-length dial string. In cases where callers might be dialing local, national, or international numbers, the destination pattern must provide for a variable-length dial plan. If a particular voice gateway has access to the PSTN for local calls and access to a transatlantic connection for international calls, then calls being routed to that gateway have a varying number of dialed digits. A single dial peer with a destination pattern of ".T" could support the different call types. The **interdigit timeout** determines when a string of dialed digits is complete. The router continues to collect digits until there is an interdigit pause longer than the configured value, which by default is 10 seconds.

When the calling party finishes entering dialed digits, there is a pause equal to the interdigit timeout value before the router processes the call. The calling party can immediately terminate the interdigit timeout by entering the pound character (#), which is the default termination character. Because the default interdigit timer is set to 10 seconds, users might experience a long call setup delay.

NOTE	Cisco IOS software does not check the validity of the E.164 telephone number. It accepts any series of digits as a valid number.

Table 4-1 demonstrates the use of various destination pattern wildcards, including the period, brackets, and the ".T."

Table 4-1   *Destination Pattern Options*

Destination Pattern	Matching Telephone Numbers
5550124	Matches one telephone number exactly, 5550124.
	This is typically used when there is a single device, such as a telephone or fax, connected to a voice port.
55501[1-3].	Matches a seven-digit telephone number where the first five digits are 55501; the sixth digit can be a 1, 2, or 3; and the last digit can be any valid digit.
	This type of destination pattern is used when telephone number ranges are assigned to specific sites. In this example, the destination pattern is used in a small site that does not need more than 30 numbers assigned.
.T	Matches any telephone number that has at least one digit and can vary in length from 1 through 32 digits total.
	This destination pattern is used for a dial peer that services a variable-length dial plan, such as local, national, and international calls. It can also be used as a default destination pattern so that any calls that do not match a more specific pattern will match this pattern and can be directed to an operator.

Characteristics of the Default Dial Peer

When a matching inbound dial peer is not found, the router resorts to a virtual dial peer called the *default dial peer*. The default dial peer is often referred to as *dial peer 0*.

NOTE	Default dial peers are used for inbound matches only. They are not used to match outbound calls that do not have a dial peer configured.

Dial peer 0 for inbound VoIP peers has the following characteristics:

- Any CODEC
- IP precedence 0
- VAD enabled
- No RSVP support
- **fax-rate** service

For inbound POTS peers, dial peer 0 has no IVR application.

You cannot change the default configuration for dial peer 0. Default dial peer 0 fails to negotiate nondefault capabilities or services. When the default dial peer is matched on a VoIP call, the call leg that is set up in the inbound direction uses any supported CODEC for voice compression that is based on the requested CODEC capability coming from the source router. When a default dial peer is matched, the voice path in one direction may have different parameters than the voice path in the return direction. This might cause one side of the connection to report good quality voice while the other side reports poor quality voice. For example, the outbound dial peer has VAD disabled, but the inbound call leg is matched against the default dial peer, which has VAD enabled. VAD would be on in one direction and off in the return direction.

When the default dial peer is matched on an inbound POTS call leg, there is no default IVR application with the port. As a result, the user gets a dial tone and proceeds with dialed digits. Interestingly, the default dial peer cannot be viewed using **show** commands.

In Figure 4-8, only one-way dialing is configured. Example 4-3 and Example 4-4 illustrate the configuration for this topology. The caller at extension 7777 can call extension 8888 because there is a VoIP dial peer configured on Router 1 to route the call across the network. However, there is no VoIP dial peer configured on Router 2 to point calls across the network toward Router 1. Therefore, there is no dial peer on Router 2 that will match the calling number of extension 7777 on the inbound call leg. If no incoming dial peer matches the calling number, the inbound call leg automatically matches to a default dial peer (POTS or VoIP).

Figure 4-8 *Default Dial Peer 0*

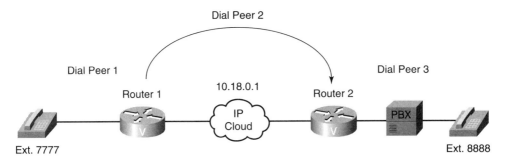

Example 4-3 *Router 1 Configuration*

```
Router1(config)# dial-peer voice 1 pots
Router1(config-dial-peer)# destination-pattern 7777
Router1(config-dial-peer)# port 1/0/0
Router1(config-dial-peer)# exit
Router1(config)# dial-peer voice 2 pots
Router1(config-dial-peer)# destination-pattern 8888
Router1(config-dial-peer)# session target ipv4: 10.18.0.1
```

Example 4-4 *Router 2 Configuration*

```
Router2(config)# dial-peer voice 3 pots
Router2(config-dial-peer)# destination-pattern 8888
Router2(config-dial-peer)# port 1/1/0
```

Matching Inbound Dial Peers

When determining how inbound dial peers are matched on a router, it is important to note whether the inbound call leg is matched to a POTS or VoIP dial peer. Matching occurs in the following manner:

- Inbound POTS dial peers are associated with the incoming POTS call legs of the originating router or gateway.

- Inbound VoIP dial peers are associated with the incoming VoIP call legs of the terminating router or gateway.

Three information elements sent in the call setup message are matched against four configurable **dial-peer** command attributes. Table 4-2 describes the three call setup information elements.

Table 4-2 *Call Setup Information Elements*

Call Setup Element	Description
Called number dialed number identification service	This is the call-destination dial string, and it is derived from the ISDN setup message or channel associated signaling dialed number identification service (DNIS).
Calling number automatic number identification	This is a number string that represents the origin, and it is derived from the ISDN setup message or channel associated signaling (CAS) automatic number identification (ANI). The ANI is also referred to as the calling line ID (CLID).
Voice port	This represents the POTS physical voice port.

The four configurable dial peer command attributes are detailed in Table 4-3.

Table 4-3 *Command Attributes for the **dial-peer** Command*

dial-peer **Command Attribute**	Description
incoming called-number	Defines the called number or DNIS string
answer-address	Defines the originating calling number or ANI string
destination-pattern	Uses the calling number (originating or ANI string) to match the incoming call leg to an inbound dial peer
Port	Attempts to match the configured dial peer port to the voice port associated with the incoming call (POTS dial peers only)

When the Cisco IOS router or gateway receives a call setup request, it looks for a dial peer match for the incoming call. This is not digit-by-digit matching. Instead, the router uses the full digit string received in the setup request for matching against the configured dial peers.

The router or gateway matches call setup element parameters in the following order:

1. The router or gateway attempts to match the called number of the call setup request with the configured **incoming called-number** of each dial peer.

2. If a match is not found, the router or gateway attempts to match the calling number of the call setup request with the **answer-address** of each dial peer.

3. If a match is not found, the router or gateway attempts to match the calling number of the call setup request to the **destination-pattern** of each dial peer.

4. The voice port uses the voice port number associated with the incoming call setup request to match the inbound call leg to the configured dial peer **port** parameter.

5. If multiple dial peers have the same port configured, then the router or gateway matches the first dial peer added to the configuration.

6. If a match is not found in the previous steps, then dial peer 0 is matched.

Because call setups always include DNIS information, it is recommended that you use the **incoming called-number** command for inbound dial peer matching. Configuring **incoming called-number** is useful for a company that has a central call center providing support for a number of different products. Purchasers of each product get a unique toll-free number to call for support. All support calls are routed to the same trunk group destined for the call center. When a call comes in, the computer telephony system uses the DNIS to flash the appropriate message on the computer screen of the agent to whom the call is routed. The agent will then know how to customize the greeting when answering the call.

The calling number ANI with **answer-address** is useful when you want to match calls based on the originating calling number. For example, when a company has international customers who require foreign-language-speaking agents to answer the call, the call can be routed to the appropriate agent based on the country of call origin.

You must use the calling number ANI with **destination-pattern** when the dial peers are set up for two-way calling. In a corporate environment, the head office and remote sites must be connected. As long as each site has a VoIP dial peer configured to point to each site, inbound calls from each remote site will match against that dial peer.

Practice Scenario 3: Matching Inbound Dial Peers

In this practice scenario, assume that you are setting up a technical support center for desktop PCs, printers, and laptops. Customers who dial specific numbers need to reach the appropriate technical support staff. Using the diagram in Figure 4-9, create dial peers on R1 to route incoming calls (that is, from the PSTN) by the incoming called number to the appropriate site. Because the focus of this practice scenario is dial peer configuration, as opposed to digit manipulation, assume the DNIS has already been truncated to four digits.

Figure 4-9   *Matching Inbound Dial Peers*

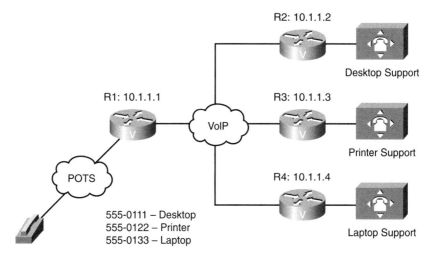

R1:

_____

_____

_____

_____

_____

_____

_____

_____

Practice Scenario 3: Suggested Solution

Although your choice of dial peer tags might vary, the following offers a suggested solution to Practice Scenario 3:

R1:

```
dial-peer voice 111 voip
        incoming called-number 5550111
        session target ipv4:10.1.1.2
dial-peer voice 122 voip
        incoming called-number 5550122
        session target ipv4:10.1.1.3
dial-peer voice 133 voip
        incoming called-number 5550133
        session target ipv4:10.1.1.4
```

Matching Outbound Dial Peers

Outbound dial peer matching is completed on a digit-by-digit basis. Therefore, the router or gateway checks for dial peer matches after receiving each digit and then routes the call when a full match is made.

The router or gateway matches outbound dial peers in the following order:

1. The router or gateway uses the dial peer **destination-pattern** command to determine how to route the call.

2. The **destination-pattern** command routes the call in the following manner:

   — On POTS dial peers, the **port** command forwards the call.

   — On VoIP dial peers, the **session target** command forwards the call.

3. Use the **show dialplan number** *string* command to determine which dial peer is matched to a specific dialed string. This command displays all matching dial peers in the order that they are used.

In Example 4-5, dial peer 1 matches any digit string that does not match the other dial peers more specifically. Dial peer 2 matches any seven-digit number in the 30 and 40 range of numbers starting with 55501. Dial peer 3 matches any seven-digit number in the 20 range of numbers starting with 55501. Dial peer 4 matches the specific number 5550124 only. When the number 5550124 is dialed, dial peers 1, 3, and 4 all match that number, but dial peer 4 places that call because it contains the most specific destination pattern.

Example 4-5 *Matching Outbound Dial Peers*

```
Router(config)# dial-peer voice 1 voip
Router(config-dial-peer)# destination-pattern .T
Router(config-dial-peer)# session target ipv4:10.1.1.1

Router(config)# dial-peer voice 2 voip
Router(config-dial-peer)# destination-pattern 55501[3-4].
Router(config-dial-peer)# session target ipv4:10.2.2.2

Router(config)# dial-peer voice 3 voip
Router(config-dial-peer)# destination-pattern 555012.
Router(config-dial-peer)# session target ipv4:10.3.3.3

Router(config)# dial-peer voice 4 voip
Router(config-dial-peer)# destination-pattern 5550124
Router(config-dial-peer)# session target ipv4:10.4.4.4
```

Configuring Hunt Groups

Cisco voice-enabled routers support the concept of *hunt groups*, sometimes called *rotary groups*, in which multiple dial peers are configured with the same destination pattern. The destination of each POTS dial peer is a single voice port to a telephony interface so hunt groups help ensure that calls get through even when a specific voice port is busy. If the router is configured to hunt, it can forward a call to another voice port that is not busy.

The following is a listing of hunt group commands:

- **preference** *value*—Sets priority for dial peers. The destination with the lowest setting has the highest priority. Values range from 0 through 10, and 0 is the default.
- **huntstop**—Disables dial peer hunting on the dial peer.
- **dial-peer hunt** *hunt-group-order*—Changes the default selection order for hunting through dial peers. Table 4-4 lists the possible values for the *hunt-group-order* parameter.

Table 4-4 *Supported* **hunt-group-order** *Values*

hunt-group-order Number	Description
0	Longest match in phone number, explicit preference, random selection. This is the default hunt order number.
1	Longest match in phone number, explicit preference, least recent use.
2	Explicit preference, longest match in phone number, random selection.
3	Explicit preference, longest match in phone number, least recent use.
4	Least recent use, longest match in phone number, explicit preference.
5	Least recent use, explicit preference, longest match in phone number.
6	Random selection.
7	Least recent use.

In some business environments, such as call centers or sales departments, there may be a group of agents available to answer calls coming in to a single number. Scenario 1 may randomly distribute the calls between all agents. Scenario 2 may send calls to the senior agents first and to the junior agents only when all senior agents are busy. Both of these scenarios can be serviced by configuring a hunt group with specific commands to control the hunt actions.

Follow these steps to configure hunt groups:

1. Configure the same destination pattern across multiple dial peers.

2. Use the **preference** command if the destination pattern of the dial peer is the same for several dial peers. If the **preference** does not act as the tiebreaker, then the router picks the matching dial peer randomly.

You must use the **dial-peer hunt** global configuration command to change the default selection order of the procedure or to choose different methods for hunting through dial peers. To view the current setting for **dial-peer hunt**, use the **show dial-peer voice summary** command.

If you do not want to hunt through a range of dial peers, the **huntstop** command disables dial peer hunting. After you enter this command, no further hunting is allowed if a call fails on the selected dial peer. This is useful in situations where it is undesirable to hunt to a less-specific dial peer if the more specific dial peer fails. For example, if a call is destined for a particular staff member and the person is on the phone, the router searches for any other dial peer that might match the dialed number. If there is a more generic destination pattern in another dial peer that also matches, the call is routed to the more generic destination pattern. Configuring the **huntstop** command in the more specific dial peer will send the caller a busy signal and stop hunting.

You can mix POTS and VoIP dial peers when creating hunt groups. This is useful if you want incoming calls sent over the IP network but network connectivity fails. You can then reroute the calls back through the PBX, or through the router, to the PSTN. By default, the router selects dial peers in a hunt group according to the following criteria, in the order listed:

1. The router matches the most specific telephone number.
2. The router matches according to the preference setting.
3. The router matches randomly.

The destination pattern that matches the greatest number of dialed digits is the first dial peer selected by the router. For example, if one dial peer is configured with a dial string of 345.... and a second dial peer is configured with 3456789, the router selects 3456789 first because it has the longest explicit match of the two dial peers. Without a PBX, if the line is currently in use, the desired action is to send a call to a voice-mail system or a receptionist, instead of giving the caller a busy signal.

If the destination pattern is the same for several dial peers, you can configure the priority by using the **preference** dial peer command. This would be the configuration for scenario 2, where the dial peers connecting to the senior agents would have **preference 0** and the dial peers connecting to the junior agents would have **preference 1**. The lower the preference is set, the more likely that dial peer will handle the call.

By default, if all destination patterns are equal, the preference is set to 0 on all dial peers. If the preference does not act as the tiebreaker, then a dial peer matching the called number will be picked randomly.

Example 4-6 shows an example of configuring a hunt group to send calls to the PSTN if the IP network fails, as shown in Figure 4-10. For all calls going to 555-0188, VoIP dial peer 2 is matched first because the preference is set to 0. If the path through the IP network fails, POTS dial peer 3 is matched and the call is forwarded through the PSTN. The **forward-**

digits command forwards all digits to the PSTN to automatically complete the call without a secondary dial tone.

Example 4-6 *Hunt-Group Configuration*

```
Router(config)# dial-peer voice 1 pots
Router(config-dial-peer)# destination-pattern 5550111
Router(config-dial-peer)# port 1/0/0
Router(config-dial-peer)# exit
Router(config)# dial-peer voice 2 voip
Router(config-dial-peer)# destination-pattern 5550188
Router(config-dial-peer)# session target ipv4:10.18.0.1
Router(config-dial-peer)# preference 0
!VoIP dial peer 2 will be matched first because preference is 0
Router(config-dial-peer)# exit
Router(config)# dial-peer voice 3 pots
Router(config-dial-peer)# destination-pattern 5550188
Router(config-dial-peer)# port 1/1/0
Router(config-dial-peer)# preference 1
Router(config-dial-peer)# forward-digits all
!POTS dial peer 3 will be matched next if dial peer 2 is busy or not available
```

Figure 4-10 *PSTN Fallback Using a Hunt Group*

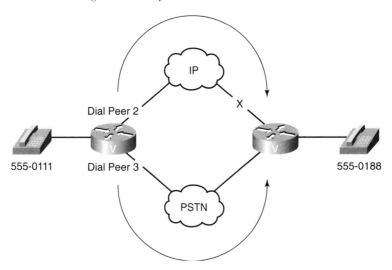

Practice Scenario 4: Configuring Hunt Groups

Consider the diagram presented in Figure 4-11. Create a hunt group using the **preference** command on R2. Configure it so that if extension 3111 is busy, the call rings extension 3112. Assume that you have POTS dial peers for all three extensions already configured.

Figure 4-11 *Configuring Hunt Groups*

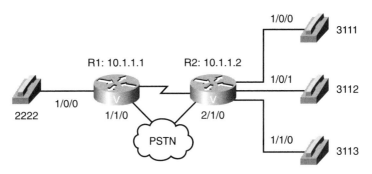

R2: Already configured

```
dial-peer voice 1 pots
destination-pattern 3111
port 1/0/0
!
dial-peer voice 2 pots
destination-pattern 3112
port 1/0/1
!
dial-peer voice 3 pots
destination-pattern 3113
port 1/1/0
```

R2: Hunt group dial peer

Practice Scenario 4: Suggested Solution

Although your choice of a dial peer tag and priority value might vary, the following offers a suggested solution to Practice Scenario 4:

R2:

```
dial-peer voice 4 pots
      destination-pattern 3111
      port 1/0/1
      preference 1
```

Collecting and Analyzing Digits

Effective destination-pattern design requires an understanding of how a voice-enabled router collects and analyzes digits. By default, when the terminating router matches a dial string to an outbound POTS dial peer, the router strips off the left-justified digits that explicitly match the destination pattern. The remaining wildcard digits are forwarded to the telephony interface, which connects devices such as a PBX or the PSTN.

Use the **no digit-strip** command to disable the automatic digit-stripping function. This allows the router to match digits and pass them to the telephony interface.

However, digit stripping is the desired action in some situations. There is no need to forward digits out of a POTS dial peer if it is pointing to a Foreign Exchange Station (FXS) port that connects a telephone or fax machine. When digit stripping is turned off on this type of port, the user will hear tones after answering the call because any unconsumed and unmatched digits are passed through the voice path after the call is answered.

When a PBX or the PSTN is connected through the POTS dial peer, digit stripping is not desired because these devices need additional digits to further direct the call. In these situations, the administrator must assess the number of digits that need to be forwarded for the remote device to correctly process the call. With a VoIP dial peer, all digits are passed across the network to the terminating voice-enabled router.

When a voice call enters the network, the router collects digits as follows:

1. The originating router collects dialed digits until it matches an outbound dial peer.

2. The router immediately places the call and forwards the associated dial string.

3. The router collects no additional dialed digits.

Example 4-7 and Example 4-8 demonstrate the impact that overlapping destination patterns have on the call routing decision. In Example 4-7, the destination pattern in dial peer 1 is a subset of the destination pattern in dial peer 2. The router matches one digit at a time against available dial peers. This means that an exact match will always occur on dial peer 1, and dial peer 2 will never be matched. Only the collected digits of 555 will be forwarded.

Example 4-7 *Dial Peer Digit Consumption with Variable-Length Destination Patterns*

```
Router(config)# dial-peer voice 1 voip
Router(config-dial-peer)# destination-pattern 555
Router(config-dial-peer)# session target ipv4:10.18.0.1
Router(config-dial-peer)# exit
Router(config)# dial-peer voice 2 voip
Router(config-dial-peer)# destination-pattern 5550124
Router(config-dial-peer)# session target ipv4:10.18.0.2
```

In Example 4-8, the length of the destination patterns in both dial peers is the same. Dial peer 2 has a more specific value than dial peer 1, so it will be matched first. If the path to IP address 10.18.0.2 is unavailable, dial peer 1 will be used when 5550124 is dialed. Collected digits of 5550124 will be forwarded.

Example 4-8 *Dial Peer Digit Consumption with Fixed-Length Digit Consumption*

```
Router(config)# dial-peer voice 1 voip
Router(config-dial-peer)# destination-pattern 555....
Router(config-dial-peer)# session target ipv4:10.18.0.1
Router(config-dial-peer)# exit
Router(config)# dial-peer voice 2 voip
Router(config-dial-peer)# destination-pattern 5550124
Router(config-dial-peer)# session target ipv4:10.18.0.2
```

Destination patterns are matched based on the longest explicit number match. Digits collected are dependant on the configured destination pattern. Table 4-5 describes how different number combinations are matched and collected.

Table 4-5 *Matching Destination Patterns*

Dialed Digits	Destination Pattern	Dialed Digits Collected
5550124	5......	5550124
5550124	555....	5550124
5550124	555	555
5550124	555T	5550124

In the first row of Table 4-5, the destination pattern specifies a seven-digit string. The first digit must be a five, and the remaining six digits can be any valid digits. All seven digits must be entered before the destination pattern is matched.

In the second row, the destination pattern specifies a seven-digit string. The first three digits must be 555, and the remaining four digits can be any valid digits. All seven digits must be entered before the destination pattern is matched.

In the third row, the destination pattern specifies a three-digit string. The dialed digits must be exactly 555. When the user begins to dial the seven-digit number, the destination pattern matches after the first three digits are entered. The router then stops collecting digits and places the call. If the call is set up quickly, the answering party at the other end may hear the remaining four digits as the user finishes dialing the string, because after a call is set up, any dual-tone multifrequency (DTMF) tones are sent through the voice path and played out at the other end.

In the last row, the destination pattern specifies a variable-length digit string that is at least three digits long. The first three digits must be exactly 555, and the remaining digits can be any valid digits. The "T" tells the router to continue collecting digits until the interdigit timer expires. The router stops collecting digits when the timer expires or when the user presses the pound (#) key.

Manipulating Digits

Digit manipulation is the task of adding or subtracting digits from the original dialed number to accommodate user dialing habits or gateway needs. The digits can be manipulated before matching an inbound or outbound dial peer. The following list describes digit manipulation commands issued in dial peer configuration mode:

- **prefix**—Adds digits to the front of the dial string before it is forwarded to the telephony interface. This occurs after the outbound dial peer is matched but before digits get sent out of the telephony interface. Use the **prefix** command when the dialed digits leaving the router must be changed from the dialed digits that had originally matched the dial peer. For example, a call is dialed using a four-digit extension such as 0123, but the call needs to be routed to the PSTN, which requires ten-digit dialing. If the four-digit extension matches the last four digits of the actual PSTN number, then you can use the **prefix 902555** command to prepend the six additional digits needed for the PSTN to route the call to 902-555-0123. After the POTS dial peer is matched with the destination pattern of 0123, the **prefix** command prepends the additional digits and the string "9025550123" is sent out of the voice port to the PSTN.

- **forward-digits**—Specifies the number of digits that must be forwarded to the telephony interface, regardless of whether they match explicitly or with wildcards. This command occurs after the outbound dial peer is matched but before the digits are sent out of the telephony interface. When a specific number of digits are configured for forwarding, the count is right-justified. For example, the POTS dial peer has a destination pattern configured to match all extensions in the 1000 range (**destination-pattern 1...**). By default, only the last three digits are forwarded to the PBX that is connected to the specified voice port. If the PBX needs all four digits to route the call, you can use the command **forward-digits 4** or **forward-digits all** so that the appropriate number of digits are forwarded. To restore the **forward-digits** command to its default setting, use the **default forward-digits** command. Using the **no forward-digits** command specifies that no digits are to be forwarded.

- **num-exp**—The **num-exp** global command expands an extension into a full telephone number or replaces one number with another. The number expansion table manipulates the called number. This command occurs before the outbound dial peer is matched. Therefore, you can configure a dial peer with the expanded number in the destination pattern for the call to go through. The number expansion table becomes useful when the PSTN changes the dialing requirements from seven-digit dialing to ten-digit dialing. In this scenario, you can do one of the following:

    — Make all the users dial all ten digits to match the new POTS dial peer that is pointing to the PSTN.

    — Allow the users to continue dialing the seven-digit number as they have before but expand the number to include the area code before the ten-digit outbound dial peer is matched.

NOTE You can use the **show num-exp** command to view the configured number-expansion table. You can use the **show dialplan number** *number* command to confirm the presence of a valid dial peer to match the newly expanded number.

- **translation-rule**—Digit translation is a two-step configuration process. First, the translation rule is defined at the global level. Then, the rule is applied at the dial peer level either as inbound or outbound translation on either the called or calling number. Specifically, translation rules manipulate the ANI or DNIS digits for a voice call. They also convert a telephone number into a different number before the call is matched to an inbound dial peer or before the outbound dial peer forwards the call. For example, an employee may dial a five-digit extension to reach another employee of the same company at another site. If the call is routed through the PSTN to reach the other site, the originating gateway might use translation rules to convert the five-digit extension into the ten-digit format that is recognized by the central office (CO) switch.

You can also use translation rules to change the numbering type for a call. For example, some gateways may tag a number with more than 11 digits as an international number, even when the user must dial 9 to reach an outside line. In this case, the number that is tagged as an international number needs to be translated into a national number, without the 9, before it is sent to the PSTN.

As illustrated in this section, there are numerous ways to manipulate digits at various stages of call completion. The administrator needs to determine which command will be most suitable and the requirements that are necessary for manipulation.

NOTE To test configured translation rules, you can use the **test translation** command.

Example 4-9 shows a sample configuration using the **prefix** command.

Example 4-9   *The **prefix** Command*

```
Router(config)# dial-peer voice 1 pots
Router(config-dial-peer)# destination-pattern 555....
Router(config-dial-peer)# prefix 555
Router(config-dial-peer)# port 1/0/0
```

In the sample configuration using the **prefix** command, the device attached to port 1/0/0 needs all seven digits to process the call. On a POTS dial peer, only wildcard-matched digits are forwarded by default. Use the **prefix** command to send the prefix numbers 555 before forwarding the four wildcard-matched digits.

Example 4-10 illustrates a sample configuration using the **forward-digits** command.

Example 4-10   *The **forward-digits** Command*

```
Router(config)# dial-peer voice 1 pots
Router(config-dial-peer)# destination-pattern 555....
Router(config-dial-peer)# forward-digits 7
Router(config-dial-peer)# port 1/0/0
```

In the sample configuration using the **forward-digits** command, the device attached to port 1/0/0 needs all seven digits to process the call. On a POTS dial peer, only wildcard-matched digits are forwarded by default. The **forward-digits** command allows the user to specify the total number of digits to forward.

Example 4-11 provides a sample configuration using the number expansion table (**num-exp**) command.

Example 4-11   *The **num-exp** Command*

```
Router(config)# num-exp 2... 5552...
Router(config)# dial-peer voice 1 pots
Router(config-dial-peer)# destination-pattern 5552...
Router(config-dial-peer)# port 1/1/0
```

In the sample configuration using the **num-exp** command, the extension number 2... is expanded to 5552... before an outbound dial peer is matched. For example, the user dials 2401, but the outbound dial peer 1 is configured to match 5552401.

Example 4-12 presents a sample configuration using the **translation-rule** command.

Example 4-12   *The **translation-rule** Command*

```
Router(config)# translation-rule 5
Router(config-translate)# rule 1 2401 5552401
Router(config-translate)# exit
Router(config)# dial-peer voice 1 pots
Router(config-dial-peer)# translate-outgoing called-number 5
```

In the sample configuration using the **translation-rule** command, the rule is defined to translate 2401 into 5552401. The dial peer **translate-outgoing called-number 5** command notifies the router to use the globally defined translation rule 5 to translate the number before sending the string out the port. The translation rule is applied as an outbound translation from the POTS dial peer.

Example 4-13 demonstrates a translation rule that converts any called number that starts with 91 and is tagged as an international number into a national number without the 9 before sending it to the PSTN.

Example 4-13 *Sample* **translation-rule** *Configuration*

```
Router(config)# translation-rule 20
Router(config-translate)# rule 1 91 1 international national
Router(config-translate)#exit
Router(config)# dial-peer voice 10 pots
Router(config-dial-peer)# destination-pattern 91..........
Router(config-dial-peer)# translate-outgoing called 20
Router(config-dial-peer)# port 1/1:5
Router(config-dial-peer)# forward-digits all
```

The IOS can also leverage regular expression characters, as shown in Table 4-6, to create powerful translation rules.

Table 4-6   *Translation Rule Regular Expressions*

Regular Expression Characters	Match Condition
^	Match the expression at the beginning of the line.
$	Match the expression at the end of the line.
/	Delimiter that marks the beginning and ending of both the matching and replacement strings.
\	Escape the special meaning of the next character.
-	Indicates a range, used with the brackets.
[list]	Match a single character in a list.
[^list]	Do not match a single character specified in the list.
.	Match any single character.
*	Repeat the previous regular expression 0 or more times.
+	Repeat the previous regular expression 1 or more times.
?	Repeat the previous regular expression 0 or 1 time. (Use CTRL-V to enter in the IOS CLI.)
()	Groups regular expressions.

Example 4-14 offers an example of a translation rule using regular expressions.

Example 4-14 *Sample* **translation-rule** *Using Regular Expressions*

```
Router(config)# voice translation-rule 1
Router(config-translate)# rule 1 /^555\(....\)/ /444\1/
Router(config-translate)# rule 2 /^\(555\)\(....\)/ /444\2/
```

To interpret rule 1, consider the following:

- Matching pattern /^555\(....\)/

  Notice that the parentheses are escaped out with the \ character. If the \ was not used, the parentheses would be matched as part of the string instead of being used to group the expression. The parentheses are used to group portions of the expression into sets so you can manipulate it. Since the 555 is not in a set, it is ignored, and the first set consists of the four digits following 555.

- Replacement pattern /444\1/

  This replacement pattern makes the new string start with 444 and then appends \1. The \1 means that you take the first set from the matching pattern and put it here. For this replacement, the number looks like 444.... If the dialed string was 5551212, then the replacement string would be 4441212.

Rule 2 is functionally equivalent to rule 1. The matching pattern in rule 2 is divided into two sets. The first set is 555 and the second set is the four digits following the 555. The replacement pattern starts with 444 and then appends the \2, which adds the second set from the matching pattern.

For illustrative purposes, Table 4-7 shows several examples of translation rule regular expressions.

Table 4-7 *Regular Expression Examples*

Match String	Replace String	Dialed String	Replaced String	Comments
/^$/	//	NULL	NULL	Simple null-to-null translation.
/^.$/	//	9195551212	NULL	Any-to-null translation.
/^\(555\)\(....\)/	/444\2/	5551212	4441212	Match beginning of the line. Second parentheses structure is pulled to the new string.

Table 4-7   *Regular Expression Examples   (Continued)*

Match String	Replace String	Dialed String	Replaced String	Comments
/^555\(....\)/	/444\1/	5551212	4441212	Match beginning of the line. Notice the \1 replaces the first grouping of the regular expression within parenthesis.
/\(^...\)555\(....\)/	/\1444\2/	9195551212	9194441212	Match middle of a string.
/ \(^...\)\(555\)\(....\)/	/\1444\3/	9195551212	9194441212	Match middle of a string.
/\(.*\)1212$/	/\13434/	9195551212 555121212	9195553434 555123434	Match end of string.
/444/	/555/	4441212 44441212 44414441212	5551212 55541212 55514441212	Match substring.

Practice Scenario 5: Digit Manipulation

Assume that all POTS and VoIP dial peers are configured for the topology illustrated in Figure 4-12. Create a dial peer to divert calls from R1 to R2 across the PSTN in the event of failure of the VoIP network. Assume that digits must be forwarded to the PSTN, and a prefix of 555 is necessary.

Figure 4-12 *Digit Manipulation*

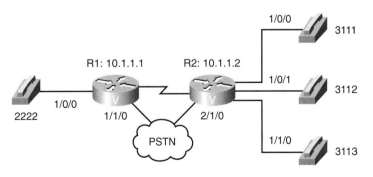

R1:

_____

_____

_____

_____

_____

Practice Scenario 5: Suggested Solution

Although your choice of a dial peer tag might vary, the following offers a suggested solution to Practice Scenario 5:

R1:

```
dial-peer voice 5 pots
      destination-pattern 311[1-3]
      port 1/1/0
      prefix 555311
      preference 1
```

Special-Purpose Connections

Integrating VoIP technologies with legacy PBXs and the public switched telephone network (PSTN) often requires voice port configuration for certain connection types. The original design of a PBX might have called for tie-lines between PBXs. When replacing tie-lines with a VoIP solution, special configuration at the voice port level can emulate the original tie-line design. In many cases, telecommuters require access to PBX services that resemble other extensions of the PBX, regardless of where the telecommuters actually reside. In other instances, telephones, such as lobby customer-service telephones, need to be connected directly to customer-service staff.

You can configure voice ports to support special connection requirements. These requirements usually reflect the needs of a specific business environment that must connect to the network in a special way. The following list describes the available connection types and their application:

- **Private line, automatic ringdown (PLAR)**—PLAR is an autodialing mechanism that permanently associates a voice port with a far-end voice port, allowing call completion to a specific telephone number or PBX.

- **PLAR-OPX**—Most frequently, a PLAR-OPX (Off Premises eXtension) is a PBX extension not located on the business site, even though it operates as though it is directly connected to the PBX.
- **Trunk**—The trunk connection type specifies a connection that emulates a permanent trunk connection between two PBXs, a PBX and a local extension, or some combination of telephony interfaces with signaling passed transparently through the packet data network.
- **Tie-line**—The tie-line connection type specifies a connection that emulates a temporary tie-line trunk to a PBX.

Table 4-8 illustrates the use of the **connection** command to establish these special purpose connections.

Table 4-8 *Options for the **connection** Command*

Command Option	Description
connection plar *digits*	*digits* represent the destination number to be automatically dialed.
connection plar-opx *digits*	*digits* represent the off-premise extension number to be automatically dialed.
connection trunk *digits* [**answer-mode**]	*digits* represent the trunk number to be used to create the virtual trunk across the network.
answer-mode (optional) specifies that the router should wait for an incoming call before establishing the trunk.	**connection tie-line** *digits*
digits represent the tie-line number to be used to create the temporary tie-line.	

The next sections describe each connection type in more detail.

PLAR

With a PLAR connection, when the calling telephone goes off hook, a predefined network dial peer is automatically matched, which sets up a call to the destination telephone or PBX. Callers do not hear a dial tone nor do they have to dial a number. PLAR connections are widely used in the business world. One common use is to connect stockbrokers with trading floors. Timing is critical when dealing with stock transactions; the amount of time it takes to dial a number and get a connection can be costly in some cases.

Another common use is in the travel sector, directly connecting travelers with services. Often, at places like airports, the traveler will see display boards advertising taxi companies, car rental companies, and local hotels. These displays often have telephones that connect the traveler directly with the service of choice. The device is preconfigured with the telephone number of the desired service. One obvious difference between these telephones and a normal telephone is that they lack a dial mechanism. Figure 4-13 shows a PLAR topology whose syntax is provided in Example 4-15 and Example 4-16.

Figure 4-13 *PLAR Connection*

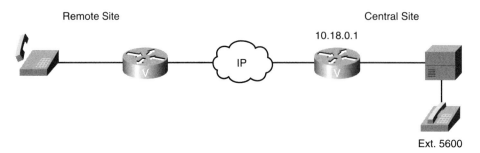

Example 4-15 *Remote Site Router Configuration*

```
Router(config)# voice-port 1/0/0
Router(config-voiceport)# connection plar 5600
Router(config-voiceport)# exit
Router(config)# dial-peer voice 5 voip
Router(config-dial-peer)# destination-pattern 5...
Router(config-dial-peer)#session target ipv4:10.18.0.1
```

Example 4-16 *Central Site Router Configuration*

```
Router(config)# dial-peer voice 1 pots
Router(config-dial-peer)# destination-pattern 5...
Router(config-dial-peer)# port 1/0:1
Router(config-dial-peer)# forward-digits 4
```

The following actions occur during the establishment of the PLAR connection illustrated in Figure 4-13:

1. A user at the remote site lifts the handset.

2. A voice port at the remote site router automatically generates the digits 5600 for a dial peer lookup.

3. The router at the remote site matches digits 5600 to VoIP dial peer 5 and sends the setup message with the digits 5600 to IP address 10.18.0.1 as designated in the **session target** command.

4. The router at the central site matches received digits 5600 to POTS dial peer 1 and forwards digits 5600 out voice port 1/0:1. At the same time, the central site router sends a call-complete setup message to the router at the remote site, because both the inbound and outbound call legs on the central site router were processed correctly.

5. The PBX receives digits 5600 and rings the appropriate telephone.

PLAR-OPX

With a PLAR-OPX connection, company staff can dial an extension and reach the remote telephone as though it were on site. The remote telephone has access to PBX services such as voice mail and extension dialing. This functionality is most often used when on-site staff become telecommuters. Many companies are cutting back on office space in expensive locations and are setting up their staff with home offices. A PLAR-OPX connection is configured between the office and the remote site so that a telecommuter can continue to access all the corporate telephony services in the same manner as before. This approach allows a telecommuter to dial the same extensions to reach other staff and to have access to long-distance dialing and other voice services via the same calling codes. From the office perspective, on-site staff can reach the telecommuter by dialing the same extension as before.

One OPX connection feature is that when a call is being attempted the voice-enabled router or gateway that takes the call from the PBX or Cisco Unified CallManager will not report a call completion until the far end has answered the call. Without the OPX configuration, the PBX or Cisco Unified CallManager passes the call to the local gateway or router. Then the gateway or router routes the call to the PSTN. After the PSTN sends ringing current to the telephone, the router reports call completion back to the PBX or Cisco Unified CallManager. At this point, the call is completed. The problem is that if the call is not answered, there is no way to reroute the call to the corporate voice mail server. From the PBX or Cisco Unified CallManager perspective, the call is completed. When you configure the OPX, however, the gateway or router will not report call completion until the telephone is actually answered. Figure 4-14 illustrates a PLAR-OPX topology whose syntax is provided in Example 4-17 and Example 4-18.

Figure 4-14 *PLAR-OPX Connection*

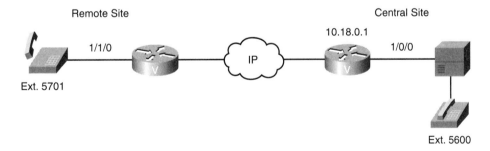

Example 4-17 *Remote Site Router Configuration*

```
Router(config)# dial-peer voice 1 pots
Router(config-dial-peer)# destination-pattern 5701
Router(config-dial-peer)# port 1/1/0
```

Example 4-18 *Central Site Router Configuration*

```
Router(config)# voice-port 1/0/0
Router(config-voiceport)# connection plar-opx 5701
Router(config-voiceport)# exit
Router(config)# dial-peer voice 10 voip
Router(config-dial-peer)# destination-pattern 5701
Router(config-dial-peer)# session target ipv4:10.0.0.1
```

1. The series of steps occurring during the PLAR-OPX connection, illustrated in Figure 4-14, are as follows:

2. A user at the central site calls a user at a remote site using the extension 5701.

3. The central site PBX routes the call to the central site router port 1/0/0, which is configured for PLAR-OPX and points to extension 5701.

4. The central site router matches VoIP dial peer 10 and sends a setup message to the corresponding IP address. In the meantime, port 1/0/0 does not respond immediately to the PBX with a seizure or off-hook indication, but waits for the remote site call setup complete message.

5. After the remote router sends the call setup complete message, the central site router sends a trunk seizure indication to the PBX and opens a voice path.

Trunk Connection

A trunk connection remains permanent in the absence of active calls and is established immediately after configuration. The ports on either end of the connection are dedicated until you disable trunking for that connection. If, for some reason, the link between the two voice ports goes down, the virtual trunk reestablishes itself after the link comes back up. This trunk configuration is useful when a permanent connection is desired between two devices. For example, a caller at one end of the trunk connection can pick up the telephone and speak into it without dialing any digits or waiting for call setup. This is analogous to the red telephone to the Kremlin that is depicted in vintage movies. With a trunk connection, there is no digit manipulation performed by the gateway or router. Because this is a permanent connection, digit manipulation is not necessary. Figure 4-15 shows the establishment of a trunk connection. The syntax for the topology is provided in Examples 4-19 and 4-20.

Example 4-19 *Router R1's Configuration*

```
R1(config)# voice-port 1/0:1
R1(config-voiceport)# connection trunk 55
R1(config-voiceport)# exit
R1(config)# dial-peer voice 55 voip
R1(config-dial-peer)# destination-pattern 55
R1(config-dial-peer)# session target ipv4:10.18.0.1
R1(config-dial-peer)# exit
R1(config)# dial-peer voice 44 pots
R1(config-dial-peer)# destination-pattern 44
R1(config-dial-peer)# port 1/0:1
```

Figure 4-15 *Trunk Connection*

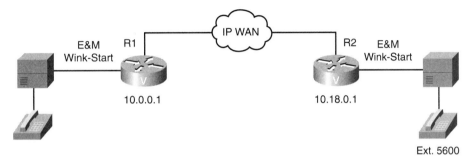

The syntax for the topology shown in Figure 4-15 is provided in Example 4-19 and Example 4-20.

Example 4-20 *Router R2's Configuration*

```
R2(config)# voice-port 1/0:5
R2(config-voiceport)# connection trunk 44
R2(config-voiceport)# exit
R2(config)# dial-peer voice 44 voip
R2(config-dial-peer)# destination-pattern 44
R2(config-dial-peer)# session target ipv4:10.0.0.1
R2(config-dial-peer)# exit
R2(config)# dial-peer voice 55 pots
R2(config-dial-peer)# destination-pattern 55
R2(config-dial-peer)# port 1/0:5
```

In Example 4-19, router R1 is configured to set up a trunk connection from voice port 1/0:1 to a remote voice-enabled router with the IP address of 10.18.0.1 (router R2). This is done by specifying the same number in the **connection trunk** voice port command as in the appropriate dial peer **destination-pattern** command. In this example, router R1 uses **connection trunk 55**, which matches VoIP dial peer 55. The call is routed to router R2, which matches the 55 in a POTS dial peer. Router R2 is also configured to set up a trunk connection from its voice port, 1/0:5, to a remote voice-enabled router with the IP address of 10.0.0.1 (router R1). Router R2 uses 44 as its connection trunk number. These trunk connections are set up when the routers power on and remain up until a router is powered down or the ports are shut down.

The following conditions must be met for a VoIP network to support virtual trunk connections:

- You must use the following voice port combinations:

    — E&M to E&M (same type)

    — Foreign Exchange Station (FXS) to Foreign Exchange Office (FXO)

    — FXS to FXS (with no signaling)

- You must not perform number expansion on the destination-pattern telephone numbers configured for a trunk connection.

- You must configure both end routers for trunk connections.

Tie-Line Connection

In traditional telephony networks, companies often had dedicated circuits called *tie-lines* connecting two PBXs. This, in effect, allowed callers at one site to reach callers at a remote site through that tie-line connection. Now that the IP network is replacing the traditional telephony connection, the two sites are logically tied together through the use of the **connection tie-line** command at both sites. Callers at one site can still reach callers at the remote site, but the call goes over the IP network. The **connection tie-line** command emulates tie-lines between PBXs.

Although a tie-line connection is similar to a trunk connection, it is automatically set up for each call and torn down when the call ends. Another difference is that digits are added to the dial string *before* matching an outbound dial peer. For example, if a user were to dial extension 8000, which terminates at a remote office, the voice port is configured with an identifying number for that remote office. If that office ID is the number 7, then the digits that are sent to be matched against the outbound dial peer would be 78000. This new five-digit number would be carried across the network to the remote site. At the remote site, the number 7 can be stripped off or, if necessary, passed to the destination device.

As demonstrated in Figure 4-16, with the syntax provided in Example 4-21 and Example 4-22, the following procedure is used to establish a tie-line connection:

1. Use the **connection tie-line** command when the dial plan requires the addition of digits in front of any digits dialed by the PBX.

2. Use the combined set of digits to route the call onto the network.

3. The tie-line port waits to collect digits from the PBX.

4. The terminating router automatically strips the tie-line digits.

Figure 4-16 *Tie-Line Connection*

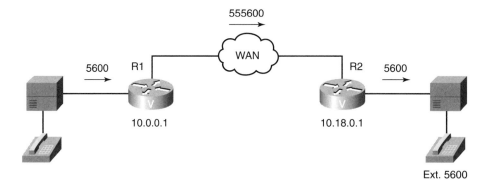

Example 4-21 *Router R1's Configuration*

```
R1(config)# voice-port 1/0:1R1
(config-voiceport)# connection tie-line 55
R1(config-voiceport)# exit
R1(config)# dial-peer voice 55 voip
R1(config-dial-peer)# destination-pattern 55....
R1(config-dial-peer)# session target ipv4:10.18.0.1
R1(config-dial-peer)# exit
R1(config)# dial-peer voice 44 voip
R1(config-dial-peer)# destination-pattern 44....
R1(config-dial-peer)# port 1/0:1
```

Example 4-22 *Router R2's Configuration*

```
R2(config)# voice-port 1/0:5
R2(config-voiceport)# connection tie-line 44....
R2(config-voiceport)# exit
R2(config)# dial-peer voice 44 voip
R2(config-dial-peer)# destination-pattern 44....
R2(config-dial-peer)# session target ipv4:10.0.0.1
R2(config-dial-peer)# exit
R2(config)# dial-peer voice 55 voip
R2(config-dial-peer)# destination-pattern 55....
R2(config-dial-peer)# port 1/0:5
```

In Figure 4-16, the caller off of router R1 picks up the telephone and dials the four-digit extension, 5600. Because the voice port on router R2 is configured for **connection tie-line**, the router collects the four digits and prepends the tie-line digits 55 to make a six-digit number, 555600. That number is then matched to a VoIP dial peer and sent to the appropriate IP address. After the call reaches router R2, it is matched against a POTS dial peer with a destination pattern of 55.... Because POTS dial peers, by default, forward only wildcard digits, only the four-digit extension 5600 is passed to the PBX.

Summary

This chapter introduced the concept of *dial peers*. Dial peers provide voice-enabled routers with call-forwarding intelligence. Specifically, a POTS dial peer points to a locally attached device, while a VoIP dial peer points across the network to the IP address of a remote device, such as another voice-enabled router Cisco Unified CallManager.

Some circumstances require the manipulation of dialed digits. For example, if a call originally intended to travel across the IP WAN is rerouted across the PSTN, additional digits, such as an area code and an office code, might need to be added to the originally dialed numbers. This chapter explored various methods of manipulating the originally dialed digits.

Finally, this chapter considered special purpose connections. These connections included PLAR, PLAR-OPX, trunk, and tie-line connections.

Chapter Review Questions

The following questions test your knowledge of topics explained in this chapter. You can find the answers to the questions in Appendix A, "Answers to Chapter Review Questions."

1. When an end-to-end call is established, how many inbound call legs are associated with the call?

   a   one

   b   two

   c   three

   d   four

2. A POTS dial peer performs which of the following two functions?

   a   Provides a phone number for the edge network or device

   b   Provides a destination address for the edge device that is located across the network

   c   Routes the call across the network

   d   Identifies the specific voice port that connects the edge network or device

   e   Associates the destination address with the next-hop router or destination router, depending on the technology used

3. Which command is used to specify the address of the terminating router or gateway?

   a   **destination-port**

   b   **destination-pattern**

   c   **session target**

   d   **destination address**

   e   **dial-peer terminal**

4. What happens if there is no matching dial peer for an outbound call?

  a The default dial peer is used.

  b Dial peer 0 is used.

  c The POTS dial peer is used.

  d The call is dropped.

5. A dial peer is configured with the **prefix** command. When are digits added to the front of the dial string?

  a Before the outbound dial peer is matched

  b After the outbound dial peer is matched

  c After the digits are sent out of the telephony interface

  d When the digits are received on the dial peer

6. Which Cisco IOS command would you use if you wanted a site ID number to be prepended to the dialed digits before they are trunked across the network?

  a **connection plar**

  b **connection plar-opx**

  c **connection tie-line**

  d **connection trunk**

7. What happens when a dial peer is configured with the **connection plar** command?

  a The caller hears a dial tone, and the number is automatically dialed.

  b The caller does not hear a dial tone, and the call is automatically set up.

  c The caller dials an extension and reaches a telephone at a remote site.

  d The caller does not hear a dial tone, and the call is set up after dialing.

8. The voice port at the remote site is configured with this command:

voice-port 1/0/0
connection plar 5678

What is the next step in making a call after the user at the remote site lifts the handset?

a   The user must dial extension 5678 to make the call.

b   The telephone will automatically dial 5678, and the user need only dial the extension.

c   The voice port will automatically generate digits 5678 for a dial peer lookup.

d   The voice port has been permanently associated with dial peer 5678, and the call is already established.

9. How do tie-line connections over IP networks differ from tie-line connections over traditional telephony networks?

a   The calls go over the IP network.

b   Callers can dial a shorter number.

c   Callers at one site can reach callers at any other site.

d   Callers at one site can reach callers at the remote site only.

10. On which POTS voice ports must the **connection trunk** parameter be configured?

a   The voice ports connecting the two FXS trunks

b   The voice ports connecting the FXS trunk to the FXO trunk

c   The voice ports connecting the two PBX trunks

d   The voice ports connecting the E&M trunk to the FXS trunk

Lab Exercise: POTS and VoIP Dial Peers

In this lab, you will configure four dial peers. Routers R1 and R3, which are illustrated in Figure 4-17, each need a POTS and a VoIP dial peer. The POTS dial peers should point to the locally attached analog phones, and the VoIP dial peers should point to the remote voice gateways.

Figure 4-17 *Lab Topology*

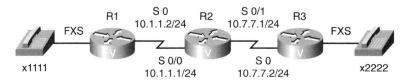

Task 1: Configure POTS Dial Peers

In this task, you will configure two POTS dial peers, one on router R1 and one on router R3.

Complete these steps:

1. Create a POTS dial peer on R1 that specifies a destination-pattern of 1111. The **port** parameter should be configured to match the physical hardware on your router.

2. Create a VoIP dial peer on R1 that specifies a destination-pattern of 2222 and a session target of ipv4:10.7.7.2.

3. Create a POTS dial peer on R3 that specifies a destination-pattern of 2222. The **port** parameter should be configured to match the physical hardware on your router.

4. Create a VoIP dial peer on R3 that specifies a destination-pattern of 1111 and a session target of ipv4:10.1.1.2.

Task 2: Exercise Verification

In this task, you will verify the configuration of your POTS and VoIP dial peers.

Complete these steps:

1. To verify the status of your POTS and VoIP dial peers, issue the **show dial-peer voice summary** command on routers R1 and R3. The ADMIN (that is, administrative) status and the OPER (that is, operational) status should both be "up."

2. At this point, you should be able to place a call between the analog phones. Take extension 1111 (that is, the analog phone attached to router R1) off hook and dial 2222. The analog phone attached to router R3 should ring. Take the other analog phone (that is, the analog phone attached to router R3) off hook. You should now have a bidirectional conversation.

3. Repeat Step 2, but initiate the phone call from extension 2222 and call extension 1111.

Suggested Solution

Although your physical hardware might differ, and your selection of dial peer tags might vary, Example 4-23 and Example 4-24 offer one solution to the preceding exercise.

Example 4-23 *Router R1's Configuration*

```
R1#configure terminal
R1(config)#dial-peer voice 1111 pots
R1(config-dial-peer)#destination-pattern 1111
R1(config-dial-peer)#port 1/1
R1(config-dial-peer)#exit
R1(config)#dial-peer voice 2222 voip
R1(config-dial-peer)#destination-pattern 2222
R1(config-dial-peer)#session target ipv4:10.7.7.2
```

Example 4-24 *Router R3's Configuration*

```
R1#configure terminal
R1(config)#dial-peer voice 2222 pots
R1(config-dial-peer)#destination-pattern 2222
R1(config-dial-peer)#port 1/1
R1(config-dial-peer)#exit
R1(config)#dial-peer voice 1111 voip
R1(config-dial-peer)#destination-pattern 1111
R1(config-dial-peer)#session target ipv4:10.1.1.2
```

The **show dial-peer voice summary** results for routers R1 and R3, using the preceding suggested solution, are shown in Example 4-25 and Example 4-26.

Example 4-25 *Router R1's* **show dial-peer voice summary** *Result*

```
R1#show dial-peer voice summary
dial-peer hunt 0
                 AD                                    PRE PASS              OUT
TAG    TYPE  MIN  OPER PREFIX    DEST-PATTERN      FER THRU SESS-TARGET     STAT
PORT
1111   pots  up   up             1111              0                         up
1/1
2222   voip  up   up             2222              0   syst ipv4:10.7.7.2
```

Example 4-26 *Router R3's* **show dial-peer voice summary** *Result*

```
R3#show dial-peer voice summary
dial-peer hunt 0
                 AD                                    PRE PASS              OUT
TAG    TYPE  MIN  OPER PREFIX    DEST-PATTERN      FER THRU SESS-TARGET     STAT
PORT
2222   pots  up   up             2222              0                         up
1/1
1111   voip  up   up             1111              0   syst ipv4:10.1.1.2
```

Lab Exercise: PLAR Connection

In this lab, you will configure the FXS voice port on router R1 for PLAR. The PLAR configuration will cause router R1 to dial extension 2222 when extension 1111 goes off hook, as shown earlier in the topology depicted in Figure 4-17.

Task 1: Configure PLAR

In this task, you will configure PLAR on router R1's FXS port.

Complete these steps:

1. Enter voice port configuration mode for the FXS port on router R1.

2. Configure the voice port to automatically dial extension 2222 whenever the phone attached to the voice port goes off hook, by issuing the **connection plar 2222** command.

Task 2: Exercise Verification

In this task, you will verify router R1's PLAR configuration.

Complete these steps:

1. Issue the **show voice port** command for the FXS port on your R1 router. Note the Connection Mode in the output, which should be PLAR.

2. To verify the proper operation of PLAR, take router R1's analog phone off hook. The analog phone attached to router R3 should then ring.

Suggested Solution

Although your physical hardware might differ, Example 4-27 offers one solution to the preceding exercise.

Example 4-27 *Router R1's PLAR Configuration*

```
R1#configure terminal
R1(config)#voice-port 1/1
R1(config-voiceport)#connection plar 2222
```

The **show voice port 1/1** command on router R1 yields the output shown in Example 4-28. Note that the connection mode is PLAR.

Example 4-28 *Router R1's* **show voice port 1/1** *Output (Continued)*

```
R1#show voice port 1/1

FXS 1/1 Slot is 1, Port is 1
 Type of VoicePort is FXS
 Operation State is DORMANT
 Administrative State is UP
 No Interface Down Failure
 Description is not set
 Noise Regeneration is enabled
 Non Linear Processing is enabled
 Non Linear Mute is disabled
 Non Linear Threshold is -21 dB
 Music On Hold Threshold is Set to -38 dBm
 In Gain is Set to 0 dB
 Out Attenuation is Set to 0 dB
 Echo Cancellation is enabled
 Echo Cancellation NLP mute is disabled
 Echo Cancellation NLP threshold is -21 dB
 Echo Cancel Coverage is set to 64 ms
```

continues

Example 4-28 *Router R1's* **show voice port 1/1** *Output (Continued)*

```
Echo Cancel worst case ERL is set to 6 dB
Playout-delay Mode is set to adaptive
Playout-delay Nominal is set to 60 ms
Playout-delay Maximum is set to 200 ms
Playout-delay Minimum mode is set to default, value 40 ms
Playout-delay Fax is set to 300 ms
Connection Mode is plar
Connection Number is 2222
Initial Time Out is set to 10 s
Interdigit Time Out is set to 10 s
Call Disconnect Time Out is set to 60 s
Supervisory Disconnect Time Out is set to 750 ms
Ringing Time Out is set to 180 s
Wait Release Time Out is set to 30 s
Companding Type is u-law
Coder Type is g729ar8
Voice Activity Detection is enabled
Nominal Playout Delay is 60 milliseconds
Maximum Playout Delay is 200 milliseconds
Region Tone is set for US

Analog Info Follows:
Currently processing none
Maintenance Mode Set to None (not in mtc mode)
Number of signaling protocol errors are 0
Impedance is set to 600r Ohm
Analog interface A-D gain offset = -3.0 dB
Analog interface D-A gain offset = -3.0 dB
FXS idle voltage set to low
Station name None, Station number None
Translation profile (Incoming):
Translation profile (Outgoing):

Voice card specific Info Follows:
Signal Type is loopStart
Ring Frequency is 20 Hz
Hook Status is On Hook
Ring Active Status is inactive
Ring Ground Status is inactive
Tip Ground Status is active
Digit Duration Timing is set to 100 ms
InterDigit Duration Timing is set to 100 ms
Hookflash-in Timing is set to 1000 ms
Hookflash-out Timing is set to 400 ms
No disconnect acknowledge
Ring Cadence is defined by CPTone Selection
Ring Cadence are [20 40] * 100 msec
Ringer Equivalence Number is set to 1
InterDigit Pulse Duration Timing is set to 500 msdial-peer hunt 0
```

After reading this chapter, you should be able to perform the following tasks:

- Describe how key VoIP technologies overcome data network challenges to provide cost-efficient and feature-rich voice-enabled networks.

- Describe the key components of a VoIP network in centralized and distributed architectures.

- Develop scalable dial plans to meet both domestic and foreign requirements.

- Given the CODEC and sample size for a specific VoIP application, calculate the total bandwidth requirement, including overhead and potential bandwidth savings using voice activity detection (VAD).

- Given voice and data network statistics and network objectives, provision an appropriate amount of bandwidth for voice and data traffic.

- Describe the implications of implementing security measures in IP networks that will transport voice packets.

CHAPTER 5

VoIP Fundamentals

Voice over IP (VoIP) enables a voice-enabled router to carry voice traffic, such as telephone calls and faxes, over an IP network. This chapter introduces the fundamentals of VoIP, architecture types, and available voice-signaling protocols. Numbering plans, dial plans, and VoIP access to 911 emergency services are explained. The role of gateways and their use in integrating VoIP with traditional voice technologies is described. Traffic engineering and bandwidth calculations are discussed. Finally, the impact of security threats and the components required for a secure voice network are also explained.

Understanding VoIP Requirements

The increased efficiency of IP networks and the ability to statistically multiplex voice traffic with data packets allows companies to maximize their return on investment (ROI) in data network infrastructures. Decreased cost and an increase in the availability of differentiated services are two major reasons companies are evaluating the implementation of VoIP.

As demand for voice services in the IP network expands, it is important to understand the components and functionality that must be present for a successful implementation. Several protocols and tools are available for carrying voice in a data network. In defining the VoIP protocol stack, you must understand at which layer these tools and protocols reside and how they interact with other layers. When voice is packaged into IP packets, additional headers are created to carry voice-specific information. These headers can create significant additional overhead in the IP network.

Understanding which protocols to use and knowing how to limit overhead is crucial in carrying voice efficiently across an IP network.

Business Case for VoIP

Business advantages that are driving implementations of VoIP networks have changed over time. Starting with simple media convergence, these advantages have evolved to include the convergence of call-switching intelligence and the total user experience.

Originally, ROI calculations centered on toll-bypass and converged-network savings. Although these savings are still relevant today, advances in voice technologies allow organizations and service providers to differentiate their product offerings by providing advanced features.

VoIP business drivers include the following:

- **Cost savings**—Traditional time-division multiplexing (TDM), which is used in the public switched telephone network (PSTN) environment, dedicates 64 kbps bandwidth per voice channel. This approach results in bandwidth being wasted when there is no voice to transmit. VoIP shares bandwidth among multiple logical connections, which makes more efficient use of the bandwidth, thereby reducing bandwidth requirements. A substantial amount of equipment is needed to combine 64 kbps channels into high-speed links for transport across the network. Packet telephony statistically multiplexes voice traffic alongside data traffic. This consolidation results in substantial savings on capital equipment and operations costs.

- **Flexibility**—The sophisticated functionality of IP networks allows organizations to be flexible in the types of applications and services they provide to their customers and users. Service providers can easily segment customers, which helps the service providers provide different applications, custom services, and rates that depend on the traffic volume needs of the customer and other factors.

- **Advanced features**—Current VoIP applications provide advanced features such as the following:

  - **Advanced call routing**—When multiple paths exist to connect a call to its destination, some of these paths might be preferred over others based on cost, distance, quality, partner handoffs, traffic load, or various other considerations. Least-cost routing and time-of-day routing are two examples of advanced call routing that can be implemented to determine the best possible route for each call.

  - **Unified messaging**—Unified messaging improves communications and boosts productivity. It delivers this advantage by providing a single-user interface to messages that have been delivered over a variety of mediums. For example, users can read their e-mail, hear their voice mail, and view fax messages by accessing a single inbox.

  - **Integrated information systems**—Organizations are using VoIP to affect business process transformation. Centralized call control, geographically dispersed virtual-contact centers, and access to resources and self-help tools are examples of VoIP technology that have enabled organizations to draw from a broad range of resources to service customers.

  - **Long-distance toll bypass**—Long-distance toll bypass is an attractive solution for organizations that are charged long-distance fees for a significant number of calls between sites. In this case, it might be more cost effective to use VoIP to place those calls across the IP network. If the IP WAN becomes congested, the calls can overflow into the PSTN, ensuring that there is no degradation in voice quality.

— **Encryption**—Security mechanisms in the IP network allow the administrator to ensure that IP conversations are secure. Encryption of sensitive signaling header fields and the message body protects the packet in case of unauthorized packet interception.

— **Customer relationship**—The ability to provide customer support through multiple mediums, such as telephone, chat, and e-mail, builds solid customer satisfaction and loyalty. A pervasive IP network allows organizations to provide contact-center agents with consolidated and up-to-date customer records along with the related customer communication. Access to this information allows quick problem solving, which, in turn, builds strong customer relationships.

VoIP Functional Components

In the traditional PSTN telephony network, all the elements that are required to complete the call are transparent to the end user. Migration to VoIP necessitates an awareness of these required elements and a thorough understanding of the protocols and components that provide the same functionality in an IP network.

Required VoIP functionality includes the following features:

* Signaling
* Database services
* Bearer control
* CODECs

The following sections describe each required functional component.

Signaling

Signaling is the ability to generate and exchange control information to establish, monitor, and release connections between two endpoints. Voice signaling requires the ability to provide supervisory, address, and alerting functionality between nodes. PSTN uses Signaling System 7 (SS7) to transport control messages in an out-of-band signaling network. VoIP presents several options for signaling, including H.323, Session Initiation Protocol (SIP), Megaco/H.248, and Media Gateway Control Protocol (MGCP). Some VoIP gateways are also capable of initiating SS7 signaling directly to the PSTN network.

Signaling protocols are classified either as peer-to-peer or client/server architectures. SIP and H.323 are examples of peer-to-peer signaling protocols where the end devices or gateways contain the intelligence to initiate and terminate calls and interpret call control messages. Megaco/H.248 and MGCP are examples of client/server protocols where the endpoints or gateways do not contain call control intelligence but send or receive event notifications to the server commonly referred to as the *call agent*. For example, when an MGCP gateway detects that a telephone has gone off hook, the gateway does not know to automatically provide a dial tone. The gateway sends an event notification to the call agent, telling the agent that an off-hook condition has been detected. The call agent then notifies the gateway to provide a dial tone.

Database Services

Access to services such as 1-800 numbers or caller ID requires the ability to query a database to determine whether the call can be placed or the information can be made available. Database services include access to billing information, calling name (CNAM) delivery, toll-free database services (1-8xx), and calling card services. VoIP service providers can differentiate their services by providing access to numerous and unique database services. For example, to simplify fax access to mobile users, a provider might build a service that converts fax to e-mail. Another example might be to provide a call notification service that places outbound calls with prerecorded messages at specific times to notify users of such events as school closures, wake-up calls, or appointment reminders.

Bearer Channel Control

Bearer channels are the channels that carry voice calls. Proper supervision of these channels requires that the appropriate call connect and call disconnect signaling be passed between end devices. Correct signaling ensures that the channel is allocated to the current voice call and that the channel is properly de-allocated when either side terminates the call. These connect and disconnect messages are carried in SS7 within the PSTN network, and in SIP, H.323, Megaco/H.248, or MGCP within an IP network.

CODECs

Coder-decoders (CODECs) provide the coding and decoding translation between analog and digital facilities. Each CODEC type defines the method of voice coding and the compression mechanism that is used to convert the voice stream. The PSTN uses TDM to carry each voice call. Each voice channel reserves 64 kbps of bandwidth and uses the G.711 CODEC to convert the analog voice wave to a TDM voice stream. G.711 creates a 64 kbps digitized voice stream. In VoIP design, CODECs often compress voice beyond the 64 kbps voice stream to allow more efficient use of network resources. The most widely used CODEC in the WAN environment is G.729, which compresses the voice stream (that is, the voice payload only) to 8 kbps.

VoIP Protocols

VoIP employs a variety of protocols to set up a call, tear down a call, and send information (for example, the actual spoken voice) during a call. The following are the major VoIP protocols:

- **H.323**—An ITU standard protocol for interactive conferencing. H.323 was originally designed for multimedia in a connectionless environment, such as a LAN. H.323 serves as an umbrella of standards that define all aspects of synchronized voice, video, and data transmission. H.323 defines end-to-end call signaling.

- **Media Gateway Control Protocol (MGCP)**—A method for PSTN gateway control or thin device control. Specified in RFC 2705, MGCP defines a protocol to control VoIP gateways that are connected to external call-control devices, referred to as *call agents.* MGCP provides the signaling capability for less-expensive edge devices, such as gateways, that might not have implemented a full voice-signaling protocol such as H.323. For example, any time an event such as an off-hook condition occurs at the voice port of a gateway, the voice port reports that event to the call agent. The call agent then signals that device to provide a service, such as dial-tone signaling.

- **Megaco/H.248**—A joint Internet Engineering Task Force (IETF) and ITU standard that is based on the original MGCP standard. Megaco defines a single gateway control approach that works with multiple gateway applications including PSTN gateways, ATM interfaces, analog-like and telephone interfaces, interactive voice response (IVR) servers, and others. Megaco provides full call control intelligence and implements call level features such as transfer, conference, call forward, and hold. The basic operation of Megaco is very similar in nature to MGCP. However, Megaco provides more flexibility by interfacing with a wider variety of applications and gateways.

- **Session Initiation Protocol (SIP)**—A detailed protocol that specifies the commands and responses to set up and tear down calls. SIP also details features such as security, proxy, and transport (TCP or User Datagram Protocol [UDP]) services. SIP and its partner protocols, Session Announcement Protocol (SAP) and Session Description Protocol (SDP), can provide announcements and information about multicast sessions to users on a network. SIP defines end-to-end call signaling between devices. SIP is a text-based protocol that borrows many elements of HTTP, using the same transaction request and response model, and similar header and response codes. It also adopts a modified form of the URL-addressing scheme used within e-mail that is based on Simple Mail Transfer Protocol (SMTP).

- **Real-Time Transport Protocol (RTP)**—An IETF standard media-streaming protocol. RTP carries the voice payload across the network. RTP provides sequence numbers and time stamps for the orderly processing of voice packets. In addition to voice packets, RTP can also carry streaming video packets.

- **RTP Control Protocol (RTCP)**—Provides out-of-band control information for an RTP flow. Every RTP flow has a corresponding RTCP flow that reports statistics on the call. RTCP is used for quality of service (QoS) reporting.

Successfully integrating connection-oriented voice traffic in a connectionless IP network requires enhancements to the signaling stack. In some ways, the user voice protocol must make the connectionless network appear more connection oriented through the use of sequence numbers. Table 5-1 provides examples of how various VoIP components and protocols map to the seven-layer OSI model.

Table 5-1 *Mapping VoIP Components and Protocols to the OSI Model*

OSI Layer	VoIP Component and Protocol
Application	IP Communicator, CallManager, and human speech
Presentation	CODECs
Session	H.323, SIP, MGCP, and Megaco
Transport	RTP and UDP (media); TCP and UDP (signal)
Network	IP
Data link	Any data link technology that supports the transport of IP packets. Examples include Frame Relay, ATM, Ethernet, Point-to-Point Protocol (PPP), Multilink PPP (MLP), and High-Level Data Link Control (HDLC).
Physical	Any physical technology that supports the transport of the data link frames or cells listed in the preceding row. Examples include Category 5 unshielded twisted-pair (UTP), T1, E1, ISDN BRI, and ISDN PRI.

Applications such as Cisco IP Communicator and CallManager provide the interface for users to originate voice at their PCs or laptops and convert and compress the voice before passing it to the network. If a gateway is used, a standard telephone becomes the interface to users, and human speech becomes the application.

CODECs define how voice is compressed. Users can configure which CODEC to use or negotiate a CODEC according to what is available.

The VoIP components that reside at the session layer are the signaling methods. H.323 and SIP define end-to-end call-signaling methods. MGCP and Megaco/H.248 define a method to separate the signaling function from the voice call function. This last approach is referred to as client/server architecture for voice signaling. The client/server architecture uses a call agent to control signaling on behalf of the endpoint devices, such as gateways. The central control device participates in the call setup only. Voice traffic still flows directly from endpoint to endpoint.

A constant in VoIP implementation is that voice uses RTP inside UDP to carry the voice payload across the network. IP voice packets can reach the destination out of order and unsynchronized. The packets must be reordered and resynchronized before playing them out to the user. Because UDP does not provide services such as sequence numbers or time stamps, RTP provides the sequencing functionality.

Once voice packets have been encapsulated at the transport layer, they are ready for transmission across an IP network. This network layer IP traffic can be transmitted across nearly any data-link and physical layer technology, which are capable of transmitting data.

VoIP Service Considerations

In traditional telephony networks, dedicated bandwidth for each voice stream provides voice with a guaranteed delay across the network. Because bandwidth is guaranteed in the TDM environment, there is no variable delay (jitter). Configuring voice in a data network requires network services with low delay, minimal jitter, and minimal packet loss. Bandwidth requirements must be properly calculated based on the CODEC that is used and the number of concurrent connections. QoS must be configured to minimize jitter and loss of voice packets. The PSTN offers uptime of 99.999 percent, also known as the *five nines of availability*. A system that is up 99.999 percent of the time experiences only five minutes of down time in an entire year. To match the availability of the PSTN, the IP network must be designed with redundancy and failover mechanisms. Additionally, security policies must be established to address both network stability and voice-stream security.

Table 5-2 lists the issues associated with implementing VoIP in a converged network and solutions that address these issues.

Table 5-2   *Issues and Solutions for VoIP in a Converged Network*

Issue	Solution
Latency	Increase bandwidth.
	Choose a different CODEC type.
	Fragment data packets.
	Prioritize voice packets.
Jitter	Use dejitter buffers.
Bandwidth	Calculate bandwidth requirements, including voice, payload, overhead, and data.
Packet loss	Design the network to minimize congestion.
	Prioritize voice packets.
	Drop lower priority traffic more aggressively than voice traffic.

continues

Table 5-2 *Issues and Solutions for VoIP in a Converged Network (Continued)*

Issue	Solution
Reliability	Provide redundancy for the following: • Hardware • Links • Power (uninterruptible power supply [UPS]) • Perform proactive network management.
Security	Secure the following components: • Netw ork infrastructure • Call-processing systems • Endpoints • Applications

RTP and RTCP

Real-Time Transport Protocol (RTP) provides end-to-end network transport functions intended for applications transmitting real-time payloads, such as audio and video. Those functions include payload-type identification, sequence numbering, time stamping, and delivery monitoring.

RTP typically runs on top of UDP to use the multiplexing and checksum services of UDP. Although RTP is often used for unicast sessions, it was primarily designed for multicast sessions. In addition to the roles of sender and receiver, RTP also defines the roles of translator and mixer to support multicast requirements.

RTP is a critical component of VoIP because it enables the destination device to reorder and retime the voice packets before they are played out to the user. An RTP header contains a time stamp and sequence number, which allows the receiving device to buffer and remove jitter and latency by synchronizing the packets to play back a continuous stream of sound. RTP uses sequence numbers to properly order the packets. However, RTP does not request retransmission if a packet is lost. Rather, a voice-enabled router can use a loss-concealment algorithm to interpolate approximately what the lost packet would have sounded like. This synthetically generated packet can then be sent in place of the dropped packet. While this loss-concealment approach minimizes the impact of a single dropped voice packet, multiple voice packets, dropped in succession, result in poor voice quality, as perceived by the listener.

While RTP streams the actual audio, RTP Control Protocol (RTCP) monitors the quality of the data distribution and provides control information.

RTCP provides the following feedback on current network conditions:

- RTCP provides a mechanism for hosts involved in an RTP session to exchange information about monitoring and controlling the session. RTCP monitors the quality of elements such as packet count, packet loss, delay, and interarrival jitter. RTCP transmits packets as a percentage of session bandwidth, but at a specific rate of at least every five seconds.

- The RTP standard states that the Network Time Protocol (NTP) time stamp is based on synchronized clocks. The corresponding RTP time stamp is randomly generated and based on data-packet sampling. Both NTP and RTP information are included in RTCP packets by the sender of the data.

- When a voice stream is assigned UDP port numbers, RTP is typically assigned an even-numbered port, and RTCP is assigned the next odd-numbered port. Each voice call has four ports assigned: RTP plus RTCP in the transmit direction and RTP plus RTCP in the receive direction.

RTP and RTCP Application

As voice packets are placed on the network to reach a destination, they might take one or more paths to reach their destination. Each path might have a different length and transmission speed, which results in the packets being out of order when they arrive at their destination. As the packets were placed on the wire at the source of the call, RTP tagged the packets with a time stamp and sequence number. At the destination, RTP can reorder the packets and send them to the digital signal processor (DSP) at the same pace as they were placed on the wire at the source.

NOTE   For more information on RTP, refer to RFC 1889, "RTP: A Transport Protocol for Real-Time Applications," which you can find at ftp://ftp.rfc-editor.org/in-notes/rfc1889.txt.

Throughout the duration of each RTP call, the RTCP report packets are generated at least every five seconds. In the event of poor network conditions, a call might be disconnected due to high packet loss. When viewing packets using a packet analyzer, a network administrator could check information in the RTCP header, which includes packet count, octet count, number of packets lost, and jitter. The RTCP header information might shed light on why a call was disconnected.

RTP Header Compression

RTP, a Layer 4 protocol, is encapsulated inside of UDP, another Layer 4 protocol. This UDP segment is then encapsulated inside of an IP packet. The combined IP, UDP, and RTP header overhead is 40 bytes. However, in a default G.729 implementation, the voice payload is only 20 bytes, half the size of the header. Fortunately, Cisco offers a feature called *RTP header compression*, which reduces the 40-byte header down to only two or four bytes, as illustrated in Figure 5-1.

Figure 5-1   *RTP Header Compression*

NOTE   RTP header compression is often abbreviated as cRTP.

RTP header compression technology does not actually compress the header. Rather, cRTP makes the observation that most information contained in the IP, UDP, and RTP headers does not change during a conversation. For example, the source and destination IP addresses, the source and destination UDP port numbers, and the RTP payload type fields do not change during a conversation. Therefore, instead of transmitting this redundant information in each and every packet, cRTP allows routers at each end of a link to cache this information and only send such header information as UDP checksums and a session context ID (CID), which identifies the RTP session to which a particular packet belongs.

An administrator can configure cRTP for an interface, using the **ip rtp header-compression** [**passive**] command. This command should be entered, in interface configuration mode, for the interfaces on both ends of a link. Also, note the optional **passive** keyword. The **passive** keyword tells an interface not to send compressed headers unless it first receives a compressed header. Therefore, the **passive** keyword should only be entered on one of the two interfaces connected to a link. If the **passive** keyword were entered on both interfaces connected to a link, cRTP would not function because neither interface would initiate the sending of compressed headers.

VoIP Network Architectures

One benefit of VoIP technology is that it allows networks to be built using either a centralized or a distributed architecture. Corporate business requirements dictate the architecture and functionality that is required. This section discusses centralized and distributed architectures and the gateway requirements to support these architectures in enterprise and service provider environments.

Support for protocols, signaling capabilities, voice features, and voice applications is changing and growing quickly. You must have a good understanding of voice network architectures to know which business requirements each architecture addresses. Also, gateways play an important role in providing access to the right mix of functionality. You must understand the main features and functions required in enterprise and service provider environments to choose the appropriate gateway.

Centralized Network Architectures

One benefit of VoIP technology is that it works with centralized and distributed architectures. This flexibility allows companies to build networks characterized by both simplified management and endpoint innovation. It is important to understand the protocols that are used to achieve this type of VoIP network agility.

The multisite WAN model with centralized call processing, as illustrated in Figure 5-2, consists of the following components:

- **Central gateway controller (call agent)**—The call agent handles switching logic and call control for all sites under the central controller. A central gateway controller includes both centralized configuration and maintenance of call-control functionality. When new functionality needs to be added, only the controller needs to be updated.

- **Media gateways**—Media gateways provide physical interconnection between the telephone network, individual endpoints, and the IP network. Media gateways communicate with the call agent to notify it of an event. An example is a telephone going off hook. The gateway also expects direction from the call agent on what action to take as a result of the event. For example, the call agent tells the gateway to provide a dial tone to the port that sees the off-hook condition. After the call-control exchange is completed, the gateways route and transmit the audio or media portion of the calls. This is the actual voice information.

- **IP WAN**—The IP WAN carries both call control signaling and voice payload between the central site and the remote sites. QoS configuration is highly recommended when voice packets are transported across a WAN to ensure that the voice packets get priority over data packets in the same network. To minimize bandwidth use for voice streams that are crossing the WAN, the G.729 coder-decoder (CODEC) is used to compress the voice payload. G.729 compresses voice to 8 kbps per call as opposed to the 64 kbps traditionally used in LAN and PSTN environments.

Centralized call-processing deployments typically offer the following characteristics:

- MGCP or Megaco/H.248 protocol for call control
- Cisco CallManager at central site for managing call control

- Centralized applications pointed to by remote sites
- Up to 30,000 IP phones per cluster
- Call Admission Control (CAC) to limit number of calls per site
- Survivable Remote Site Telephony (SRST) for remote branches

Figure 5-2 *Centralized Network Architectures*

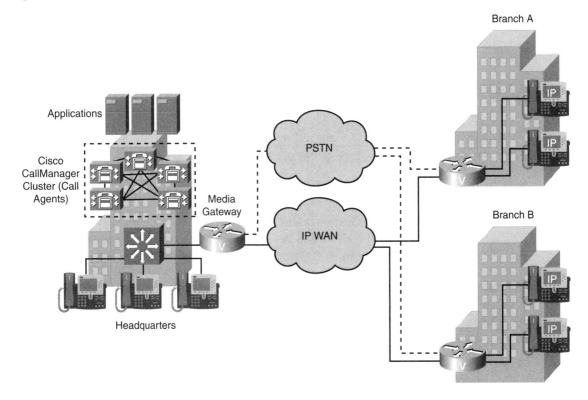

A typical use for centralized architecture is a main site with many smaller remote sites. The remote sites are connected via a QoS-enabled WAN but do not require full features and functionality during a WAN outage. MGCP and Megaco/H.248 are the prevalent signaling protocols used in centralized architectures to control gateways and endpoints.

Applications such as voice mail and IVR systems are typically centralized to reduce the overall cost of administration and maintenance.

Cisco CallManager clusters can support up to 30,000 IP phones per cluster, providing for a scalable solution in enterprise environments. For even more scalability, clusters can be interconnected via intercluster trunks.

CAC is administered by the Cisco CallManager cluster. CAC is critical in enterprise implementations that include WAN connections because these connections typically have limited bandwidth that is shared between voice and data users. Control must be established over the number of calls that can flow concurrently across the WAN at any given time so that as the call volume grows, overall call quality does not diminish.

One disadvantage of implementing a centralized architecture is that if the WAN connection fails between the remote site and the central site that houses Cisco CallManager, no further voice calls can be processed by the remote site. Additional steps need to be taken to ensure that data and voice services at the remote sites remain available. One option is to implement redundant WAN links between the remote sites and the central site. In many cases, this solution is not financially feasible. Alternatively, Survivable Remote Site Telephony (SRST) provides high availability for voice services. SRST provides a subset of the call-processing capabilities within the remote-office gateway. It also enhances the IP phones with the ability to "re-home" to the call-processing functions in the local gateway if a WAN failure is detected. This feature allows the remote site to continue to provide voice connectivity in the absence of the WAN link.

Most centralized VoIP architectures use MGCP or Megaco/H.248 protocols. You can also build session initiation protocol (SIP) or H.323 networks in a centralized fashion. This is done using back-to-back user agents (B2BUAs) or gatekeeper-routed call signaling (GKRCS), respectively.

Figure 5-2 shows a typical centralized call-processing deployment, with a Cisco CallManager cluster acting as the call agent at the central site and an IP WAN with QoS enabled to connect all the sites. The remote sites rely on the centralized Cisco CallManager cluster to handle their call processing but have local voice-enabled routers to perform the voice-gateway translations for media streams. Each remote site connects locally to the PSTN. Long-distance (LD) service might be provided from the head office or through each local PSTN connection.

H.323 Distributed Network Architectures

The multisite WAN architecture with distributed call processing consists of multiple independent sites. Each site has its own call-processing agent, which is connected to an IP WAN that carries voice traffic between the distributed sites.

Each site in the distributed call-processing architecture using H.323 can be comprised of one of the following:

- A single site with its own call-processing agent
- A centralized call-processing site and all its associated remote sites
- A legacy PBX with a VoIP gateway

Figure 5-3 provides an example of a distributed call-processing architecture. Notice, in the figure, that each site contains its own call-processing agents (in the form of CallManager clusters). This type of call-processing approach has the following characteristics:

- No call control signaling for intrasite and off-net calls through the IP WAN
- Transparent use of the PSTN if the IP WAN is unavailable
- Logical hub-and-spoke topology for the directory gatekeeper
- Only one type of CODEC configured for the IP WAN

Figure 5-3   *Distributed Network Architectures*

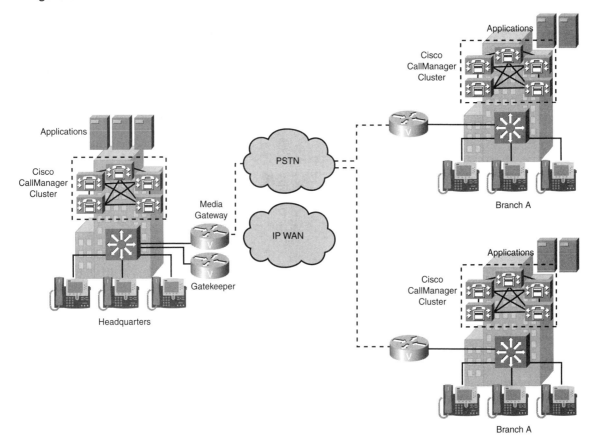

Multisite distributed call processing allows each site to be completely self-contained. The IP WAN in this model does not carry call-control signaling for intranet and off-net calls because each site has its own Cisco CallManager cluster. Typically, the PSTN serves as a backup connection between the sites in case the IP WAN connection fails or does not have any more bandwidth available.

Distributed architectures are associated with H.323 and SIP protocols. These protocols allow network intelligence to be distributed between endpoints and call control devices. Intelligence in this instance refers to any aspect of call handling including the following:

- Call state
- Calling features
- Call routing
- Provisioning
- Billing

The endpoints can be VoIP gateways, IP phones, media servers, or any device that can initiate and terminate an H.323 VoIP call. The call control devices are called *gatekeepers (GKs)* in an H.323 network. In an enterprise environment where many gatekeepers are required, a second level of hierarchy is achieved through the use of directory gatekeepers *(DGKs)*. Directory gatekeepers provide summarization capabilities for multiple configured gatekeepers.

The multisite WAN architecture with distributed call processing consists of the following components:

- **Media gateways**—Media gateways provide physical interconnection between the telephone network, individual endpoints, and the IP network. The media gateway translates call signaling between the PSTN or local endpoints and the IP network. The media gateway must contain the call-processing intelligence to perform all call-handling functions related to H.323. Media gateways communicate with gatekeepers for call address resolution and CAC.

- **Gatekeeper**—A gatekeeper is an H.323 device that provides CAC and E.164 number resolution. Gatekeepers are among the key elements in the multisite WAN model that have distributed call processing. Gatekeepers provide dial plan resolution, which improves scalability in an H.323 network. Without gatekeepers, each gateway would need to be configured to know where all other reachable telephone numbers were located. The gatekeeper provides a central repository of telephone numbers and the gateways associated with those numbers. When the network is configured for gatekeepers, the learning process is dynamic, because all participating gateways register with the gatekeeper and notify it of available telephone numbers. The gatekeeper also provides CAC to ensure that voice quality is not diminished when a large number of calls enter the network.

- **IP WAN**—The IP WAN carries call control signaling and voice payload for intersite voice communication only. Call signaling and voice transmission for all intrasite calls and off-net calls that are going to the local PSTN remain local to the site. QoS configuration is highly recommended when voice packets are transported across a WAN, to ensure the voice packets get priority over data packets in the same network. As in the centralized system, to minimize bandwidth use for voice streams that are crossing the WAN, the G.729 CODEC is typically used to compress the voice payload. G.729 compresses voice to 8 kbps per call as opposed to the 64 kbps that is traditionally used in LAN and PSTN environments.

Few implementations of call control are totally distributed. Although H.323 and SIP operate in a purely distributed mode, for scalability reasons both are most often deployed with common control components that give endpoints many of the advantages of a centralized call control environment. As a result, these implementations also inherit many of the disadvantages of centralized call control.

SIP Distributed Network Architectures

The rapid evolution of voice and data technology is significantly changing the business environment. The introduction of services such as instant messaging, integrated voice and e-mail, and follow-me services has contributed to a work environment where employees can communicate much more efficiently, thus increasing productivity. To meet the demands of the changing business environment, businesses are beginning to deploy converged voice-and-data networks based on SIP.

SIP was originally defined in 1999 by the Internet Engineering Task Force (IETF) in RFC 2543. SIP is the IETF standard for multimedia conferencing over IP, and SIP is an ASCII-based, application-layer control protocol that can be used to establish, maintain, and terminate calls between two or more endpoints. Service development in the SIP environment is made easier because of its use of, and similarity to, Internet technologies such as HTTP, Domain Name System (DNS), and addressing in the form of e-mail addresses. SIP enables the integration of traditional voice services with web-based data services, including self-based provisioning, instant messaging, presence, and mobility services.

A SIP-based network is made up of several components, as depicted in Figure 5-4, including:

- **SIP user agent**—Any network endpoint that can originate or terminate a SIP session. This device could be a SIP-enabled telephone, a SIP PC client (known as a softphone), or a SIP-enabled gateway.
- **SIP proxy server**—A call control device that provides many services, such as routing of SIP messages between SIP user agents.

- **SIP redirect server**—A call control device that provides routing information to user agents when requested, giving the user agent an alternate uniform resource identifier (URI) or destination user agent server (UAS).

- **SIP registrar server**—A device that stores the logical location of user agents within that domain or subdomain. A SIP registrar server stores the location of user agents and dynamically updates its data via REGISTER messages.

Figure 5-4   *SIP Network Components*

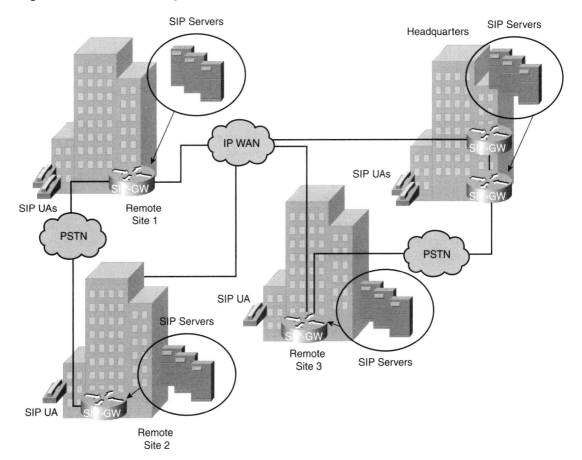

Additionally, SIP provides the following capabilities:

- **Determines the location of the target endpoint**—SIP supports address resolution, name mapping, and call redirection.

- **Determines the media capabilities of the target endpoint**—Via the Session Description Protocol (SDP), SIP determines the "lowest level" of common services between the endpoints. Conferences are established using only those media capabilities that can be supported by all endpoints.

- **Determines the availability of the target endpoint**—If a call cannot be completed because the target endpoint is unavailable, SIP determines whether the called party is already on the phone or did not answer in the allotted number of rings. SIP then returns a message that indicates why the target endpoint was unavailable.

- **Establishes a session between the originating and target endpoint**—If the call can be completed, SIP establishes a session between the endpoints. SIP also supports midcall changes, such as the addition of another endpoint to the conference or the changing of a media characteristic or CODEC.

- **Handles the transfer and termination of calls**—SIP supports the transfer of calls from one endpoint to another. During a call transfer, SIP simply establishes a session between the transferee and a new endpoint specified by the transferring party. SIP then terminates the session between the transferee and the transferring party. At the end of a call, SIP terminates the sessions between all parties.

As a protocol used in a distributed architecture, SIP allows companies to build large networks that are scalable, resilient, and redundant. The SIP protocol provides mechanisms for interconnecting with other VoIP networks and for adding intelligence and new features on either the endpoints or the SIP proxy or redirect servers.

Comparing Network Architectures

Both the centralized and distributed models have advantages and disadvantages. Features that are considered advantages of one type of call control model might be disadvantages of the other type. The main differences between the two models are in the following areas:

- **Configuration**—The centralized call control model provides superior control of the configuration and maintenance of the dial plan and endpoint database. It simplifies the introduction of new features and supplementary services. The centralized call control model also provides a convenient location for the collection and dissemination of call detail records (CDRs).

  The distributed model requires distributed administration of the configuration and management of endpoints. This approach complicates the administration of a dial plan. Distributed call control simplifies the deployment of additional endpoints while making new features and supplementary services difficult to implement.

- **Security**—Centralized call control requires that endpoints be known to a central authority. This approach avoids or reduces security concerns.

  The autonomy of endpoints in the distributed model elevates security concerns.

- **Reliability**—The centralized model has two points of vulnerability: single point of failure and contention. It places high demands on the availability of the underlying data network, possibly requiring a fault-tolerant WAN design.

The distributed call control model minimizes the dependence on shared common control components and network resources. This approach reduces exposure to single points of failure and contention for network resources.

- **Efficiency**—Centralized call control fails to take full advantage of call routing intelligence that resides in the endpoints. It also consumes bandwidth through the interaction of the call agent and its endpoints.

  Distributed call control takes advantage of the inherent call routing intelligence in endpoints.

Because the centralized model is more sensitive to IP WAN outages, a centralized model design mandates the implementation of survivability and load management strategies. Few implementations of call control are totally distributed. For example, H.323 and SIP operate in a purely distributed mode, but for scalability reasons, both are most often deployed with common control components that give endpoints many of the advantages of a centralized call control environment. Unfortunately, these implementations also inherit many of the disadvantages of centralized call control.

Simple Multisite IP Telephony Network

To help solidify the concepts of the various call-processing models, consider a case study company, Span Engineering LLC. Span Engineering LLC is migrating to a Cisco IP telephony solution. It has three sites in the United States and a fourth site in Brazil. Figure 5-5 shows the distributed architecture implemented by Span Engineering. Notice in the figure that Post, Telephone, and Telegraph (PTT) is the international term for PSTN. Also, the term LD refers to a long-distance network.

Span Engineering is a company based in the United States, with headquarters in Chicago and branches in Dallas and on the west coast of the United States. It has recently expanded internationally to Sao Paulo, Brazil. The plan for migrating to Cisco IP telephony includes eliminating all PBXs and migrating to full VoIP in the near future. The overall deployment model used by Span Engineering is multisite distributed and contains both centralized and single-site locations:

- **Centralized call control (Chicago)**—Span Engineering has three separate locations in Illinois, with the Chicago location serving as the headquarters. A centralized network architecture is used for the Illinois sites. The Cisco CallManager cluster in Chicago manages call address resolution and CAC for the three Illinois locations.

- **Centralized call control (West Coast)**—Span Engineering has recently acquired three West Coast companies. The companies consist of a 12-story location in San Francisco, a 2-story location in Oakland, and a single-story location in San Jose. The San Francisco location houses the Cisco CallManager cluster that serves all three West Coast locations.

Figure 5-5 *Distributed Architecture: Span Engineering Case Study*

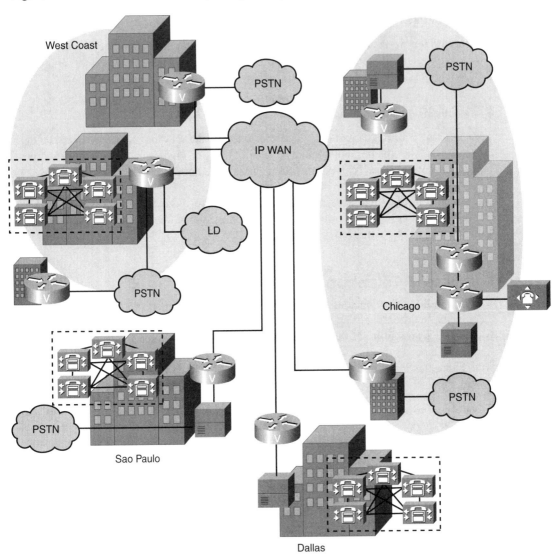

- **Single-site call control (Sao Paulo and Dallas)**—Span Engineering currently has no plans to expand in these locations but wants to ensure high availability of voice communication capabilities. The company has chosen to put Cisco CallManager clusters in each of these locations as single-site locations. Both the Dallas and Sao Paulo sites have local connections to telephone service providers for local dial tone. In non–North American countries, the telephone service provider is referred to as the PTT provider.

Interconnecting VoIP Protocols

Just as companies choose various protocols for their data networks based on business and technical requirements, they also need to choose one or more protocols for their VoIP requirements. In an environment where more than one VoIP protocol is present, companies must support the interconnection between the differing VoIP protocols.

Choices for interconnecting the segments that use differing VoIP protocols typically fall into one of the following three categories:

- **Translation through TDM**—In this method, a company uses either TDM equipment or VoIP gateways to translate from one protocol domain to another. The benefit of this method is the widespread availability of devices that provide this translation. The downside is that it introduces latency into the VoIP network and introduces an additional translation (TDM) into the voice path between two protocol domains. This method is usually considered a short-term solution until VoIP translators become available.

- **Single-protocol architecture**—In this method, a company moves all its VoIP devices and services to a single protocol, simplifying the network as a whole. The downside to this approach is that it might not be possible to migrate existing equipment to support the new protocol. This situation can limit the ability of the company to take advantage of some existing services. In addition, this method limits the potential connectivity to other networks that are using other VoIP signaling protocols.

- **Protocol translation**—In this method, a company uses IP-based protocol translators to interconnect two or more VoIP protocol domains. IP translators allow a company to retain the flexibility of using multiple VoIP protocols. They do not introduce the delay problems that additional TDM interconnections do. IP translators also do not require the wholesale replacement of existing equipment.

    The negative aspect of this approach is that there is no standard for protocol translation. Not all VoIP protocol translators are exactly the same. Although the IETF attempted to define a model for translating H.323 to SIP, this model involves more than just building a protocol-translation box. Vendors of protocol translators need in-depth knowledge of all the protocols that are being used in the VoIP network. They must be aware of how various VoIP components use different aspects of the protocol. For example, H.323 and SIP can send dual-tone multifrequency (DTMF) digits in either the signaling path or the media path via RTP. H.323 mandates only that the H.245 signaling path be used. SIP does not specify how DTMF should be carried. This design means that SIP devices could be sending DTMF in the media path (RFC 2833) and H.323 devices could be sending DTMF in the signaling path (H.245). If the VoIP protocol translator cannot properly recognize both the signaling path and the media path, the protocol translator might not function properly.

Understanding Gateways

A gateway is a device that translates one type of signal to a different type of signal. There are different types of gateways, including the voice gateway, as illustrated in Figure 5-6.

Figure 5-6 *Gateway Interfaces*

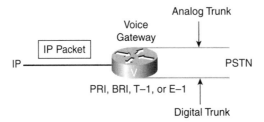

A voice gateway is a router or switch that converts IP voice packets to analog or digital signals that are understood by TDM trunks or stations. Gateways are used in several situations (for example, to connect the PSTN, a PBX, or a key system to a VoIP network).

In Figure 5-6, the voice-enabled router (that is, the voice gateway) examines the incoming IP packet to determine whether it is a voice packet and determine the packet's destination. Based on information inside the voice packet, the router translates the digitized signal or voice into the appropriate analog or digital signal to be sent to the PSTN. For a call coming from the PSTN, the gateway interprets the dialed digits and determines the IP destination for the call.

Guidelines for Selecting an Appropriate Gateway

Understanding gateways and being able to select the correct gateway out of numerous gateway options is challenging. Factors to consider include the protocols that are supported, the density and types of interfaces on the gateway, and the features that are required. Knowing the requirements will guide you to the correct solution.

One criterion involves defining the type of site that the gateway supports. Is it a small office/home office (SOHO), branch office, enterprise campus environment, or service provider? Each type of site has its own set of requirements.

A key objective is to identify the number and type of voice interfaces that are necessary and to verify the protocol support. Are supplementary services supported? Which CODECs must be supported? Is fax relay necessary? Many of these functions are features of specific Cisco IOS software releases. Identification of the proper IOS software release necessary to support the features is critical.

Another key consideration is whether the gateway is acting as a gateway only or needs to combine the functions of gateway and router within one device. This will point to a specific set of hardware and software.

When planning gateways for placement in other countries, verify that the device meets the government standards for PSTN connection in that country. If the device supports encryption capabilities, verify the legality of export to the destination country.

For example, consider a network where the requirements are to support Foreign Exchange Station (FXS) and E&M connections. The trunk is to be a T1 PRI from the PBX. In this case, a suitable choice would be a Cisco 3745 Multiservice Access Router with a two-slot voice network module (VNM), 1 FXS voice interface card (VIC), 1 E&M VIC, and a High Density Voice (HDV) module.

Enterprise Central and Remote Site Gateway Interconnection Requirements

As IP telephony services become a standard in the corporate setting, a broad mix of requirements surface in the enterprise environment. The IP telephony deployment is typically initiated by connecting to the PSTN to manage off-net calls while using a Cisco CallManager infrastructure to manage on-net calls.

Table 5-3 shows example questions that you might ask to determine the requirements for gateway interconnections.

Table 5-3   *Determining Gateway Interconnection Requirements*

Question	Reasoning
How do you control the gateways?	You must ensure support for proper call processing, such as MGCP, SIP, or H.323.
Is cost an issue?	Distributed call processing is easier to implement, but costs are higher when deploying intelligent devices at each site.
Is remote site survivability an issue?	Remote site survivability is not an issue with a distributed model unless there is a need for redundancy. This is an issue for a centralized model that can be addressed by providing SRST. This means ensuring that the version of Cisco IOS software supports the feature.
Are gatekeepers in the design, and if so, how are the zones structured?	Gatekeepers are normally used in enterprise sites for scalability and manageability. The design must include proper planning for zone configurations.
Are the gateways switches or routers?	This question determines how other features, such as QoS, are implemented. Numerous switches and routers are available that have voice gateway functionality along with other core services. These services include Layer 2 and Layer 3 QoS implementations, inline power, and security features.
How will fax and modem transmission be supported?	In a Cisco environment, fax support options include Cisco Fax Relay, T.37, T.38, and Fax Pass-Through. Modem support options include Cisco Modem Relay and Modem Pass-Through.

At the central site, several specific issues need addressing. These issues include:

- **Dial plan integration**—Consistent reachability demands that the new dial plan for the IP voice network must integrate with the existing dial plan. It is essential that you have a thorough understanding of how the dial plans interact.

- **Voice-mail integration**—After a voice-mail application is selected, the designer must ensure that all users can seamlessly reach the voice mail server. It is also vital that all incoming calls be properly forwarded when the recipient does not answer the telephone. This might mean dedicating gateway connections for an existing voice mail server or dedicating an entire gateway for the express purpose of voice mail server integration.

- **Gateway for PBX interconnect**—When the IP voice network interconnects PBXs, the designer must determine which type of connection is supported by the PBX and which gateway will support that connection.

- **Inline power requirements for IP phones**—When the design includes IP phones, you need to consider the power requirements. In many cases, it is desirable to provide inline power to the telephones. A number of devices provide inline power, such as routers, switches, and midspan devices. A midspan device sits between an IP phone and a switch and injects in-line power over the non-Ethernet leads, in the cable connecting back to the IP phone. The decision about in-line power requirements is based on capacity and the current power options.

Service Provider Gateway Interconnection Requirements

Service providers must provide a level of service that meets or exceeds PSTN standards. The gateways that service providers implement must offer reliable, high-volume voice traffic with acceptable levels of latency and jitter. The following functions address those requirements:

- **Signaling interconnection type**—SS7 interconnect supports a high volume of call setup and benefits from redundant interconnect capabilities directly into the PSTN network.

- **Carrier-class performance**—Carrier-class performance can be provided through the proper redundant design for high availability, in addition to the proper implementation of QoS features, to ensure acceptable delay and jitter.

- **Scalability**—Scalability is a critical factor in the service provider arena. Customers requesting network access should be serviced promptly. Choosing a gateway with capacity for rapid growth is an important design decision. Gateways can scale upward to T3 capabilities for large-scale environments.

Consider a scenario where an IP telephony service provider needs to upgrade its existing gateway platforms because of business growth. The service provider sells a managed IP telephony service to small- and medium-sized businesses and provides connections to many different low-cost, long-distance carriers. Their issues are call quality over the IP network. Delay and jitter need to be controlled. Service providers must also consider scalability and the ability to provide differentiated levels of service through QoS. They also need connectivity to the SS7 networks of long-distance carriers to reduce costs. Finally, the service provider needs to consider the overall cost of implementation. SS7 capabilities and a redundant design enable the service provider to deliver a reliable level of service.

Practice Scenarios: Network Architecture

Throughout this chapter, practice scenarios will help reinforce what you have learned. In this scenario, Span Engineering is assessing VoIP network architectures and reviewing components and functionality associated with each type of architecture. Your task is to view each scenario and determine the network architecture type and the protocols that are commonly used in support of the network architecture.

Practice Scenario 1: Network Architecture and Protocol Selection

The network shown in Figure 5-7 has the following characteristics:

- Cisco CallManager acts as the call agent.
- The voice gateway provides physical connectivity for end devices.
- The voice gateway does not contain full call-signaling protocol implementation.
- The call agent manages voice gateways.
- Call control signaling for all calls crosses the IP WAN.
- CAC limits the number of calls per site.
- SRST is used for remote branches.

Based on the figure and on the preceding characteristics, identify the network architecture type and protocols that are commonly used to support that architecture.

Network architecture: _____

Protocols: _____

Figure 5-7 *Practice Scenario 1*

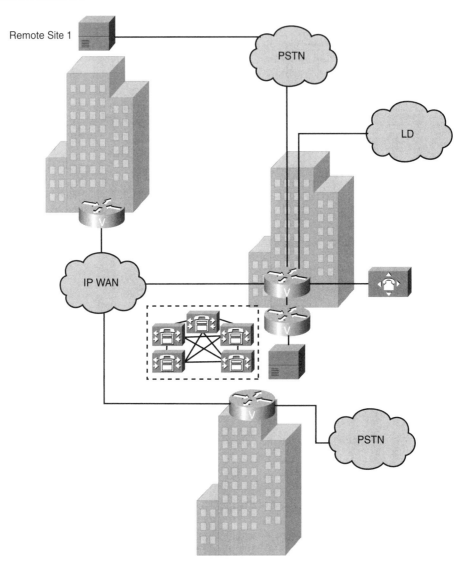

Practice Scenario 2: Network Architecture and Protocol Selection

The network shown in Figure 5-8 has the following characteristics:

- The voice gateway provides physical connectivity for end devices.
- The voice gateway performs call setup and teardown.
- Gatekeepers provide call control and dial-plan resolution.
- No call control signaling exists for intrasite and off-net calls through the IP WAN.

Based on the figure and on the preceding characteristics, identify the network architecture type and protocols that are commonly used to support that architecture.

Network architecture: _____

Protocols: _____

Figure 5-8   *Practice Scenario 2*

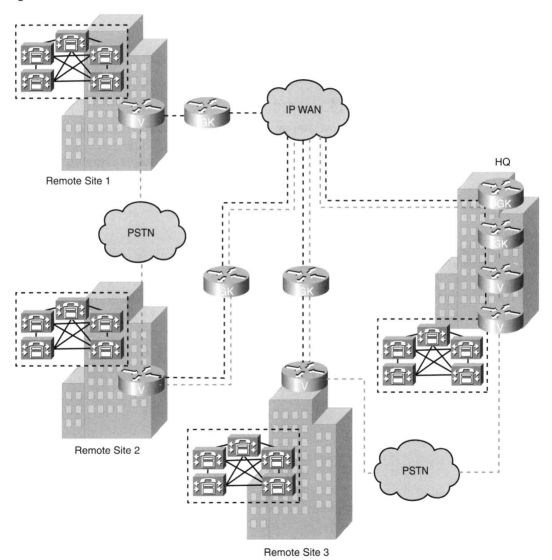

Practice Scenarios 1 and 2: Solutions

Scenario 1:

- Network architecture: Centralized
- Protocols: MGCP and Megaco/H.248

Scenario 2:

- Network architecture: Distributed
- Protocols: H.323

Building Scalable Dial Plans

To integrate VoIP networks into existing voice networks, network administrators must have the skills and knowledge to implement a scalable numbering plan and a comprehensive, scalable, and logical dial plan. This section describes the attributes of numbering plans and scalable dial plans for voice networks, addresses the challenges of designing these plans, and identifies the methods of implementing dial plans.

Numbering Plans and Dial Plans

Implementing a VoIP network involves designing a numbering plan for all endpoints or reviewing an existing numbering plan for scalability and completeness. A dial plan can be designed only after the numbering plan has been completed and call patterns and connectivity to the PSTN are understood. All implementations of VoIP require both a numbering plan and a dial plan:

- **Numbering plan**—A numbering plan identifies each VoIP endpoint and application in the network with a unique telephone number. Numbering plan design should evaluate both current requirements and potential growth requirements to avoid the need to renumber as more users connect to the voice network. Types of numbering plans include the following:

   — **The Public International Telecommunications Numbering Plan (E.164)**—The E.164 standard defines the use of a one-, two-, or three-digit country code, followed by the national destination code, followed by the subscriber number.

   — **National numbering plans**—A national numbering plan defines the numbering structure for a specific country or group of countries. An example is the North American Numbering Plan (NANP). It defines a ten-digit numbering plan. First is a three-digit Numbering Plan Area (NPA) commonly referred to as the area code. Next is a three-digit central office code. Finally, there is a four-digit subscriber line number. The United States, Canada, and parts of the Caribbean all use the NANP for number assignment. Other countries have differing national numbering plans. Familiarity with these plans is required when planning an international voice network.

— **Private numbering plans**—Private numbering plans are used to address endpoints and applications within private networks. Private numbering plans are not required to adhere to any specific format and can be created to accommodate the needs of the network. Because most private telephone networks connect to the PSTN at some point in the design, it is good practice to plan the private numbering plan to coincide with publicly assigned number ranges. Number translation might be required when connecting private voice networks to the PSTN.

- **Dial plan**—The dial plan is a key element of an IP telephony system and an integral part of all call-processing agents. Generally, the dial plan is responsible for instructing the call-processing agent on how to route calls. Primary functions of a dial plan include:

  — **Endpoint addressing**—Reachability of internal destinations is provided by assigning directory numbers (DNs) to all endpoints (such as IP phones, fax machines, and analog phones) and applications (such as voice mail systems, auto attendants, and conferencing systems). DN assignment is based on the implemented numbering plan.

  — **Path selection**—Depending on the calling device, different paths can be selected to reach the same destination. Moreover, a secondary path can be used when the primary path is not available. For example, a call can be transparently rerouted over the PSTN during an IP WAN outage.

  — **Calling privileges**—Different groups of devices can be assigned to different classes of service by granting or denying access to certain destinations. For example, lobby phones might be allowed to reach only internal and local PSTN destinations, while executive phones could have unrestricted PSTN access.

  — **Digit manipulation**—In some cases, it is necessary to manipulate the dialed string before routing the call. One example would be when rerouting a call over the PSTN that was originally dialed using the on-net access code. Another would be expanding an abbreviated code, such as expanding a 0 for the operator, to an extension.

— **Call coverage**—Special groups of devices can be created to handle incoming calls for a certain service according to different algorithms. These call coverage algorithms might include top-down, circular hunt, longest idle, or broadcast.

— **Overlapping number processing**—In some cases, administrators are tasked with connecting two or more voice networks with overlapping number ranges. For example, when two companies merge, company X might have a user number range of 1*xxx*, and company Y might also use the number range of 1*xxx*. When dealing with overlapping number ranges, one solution is to assign a unique site-access code to each individual location. Users would then dial the access code, followed by the extension number. The number of digits used for the access code would depend on the total number of locations affected.

Figure 5-9 shows the topology for Span Engineering LLC, the previously introduced fictitious company being used for illustrative purposes. Span Engineering's numbering plan is presented in Table 5-4.

Table 5-4   *Span Engineering Numbering Plan Example*

Location	Numbering Plan
Cicero	708-555-1*xxx*
	708-555-2*xxx*
	708-555-3*xxx*
Woodridge	331-555-4*xxx*
ORD	630-555-5*xxx*
Dallas	972-555-1*xxx*
	972-555-2*xxx*

Span Engineering has multiple locations and is currently evaluating the numbering plan associated with its Chicago campuses and the Dallas location. The numbering plan design process includes enumerating the number of current users at each location and evaluating future growth requirements. The internal numbering plan will use the PSTN-assigned direct inward dial (DID) numbers that have been allocated at each site.

Figure 5-9   *Span Engineering's Numbering Plan*

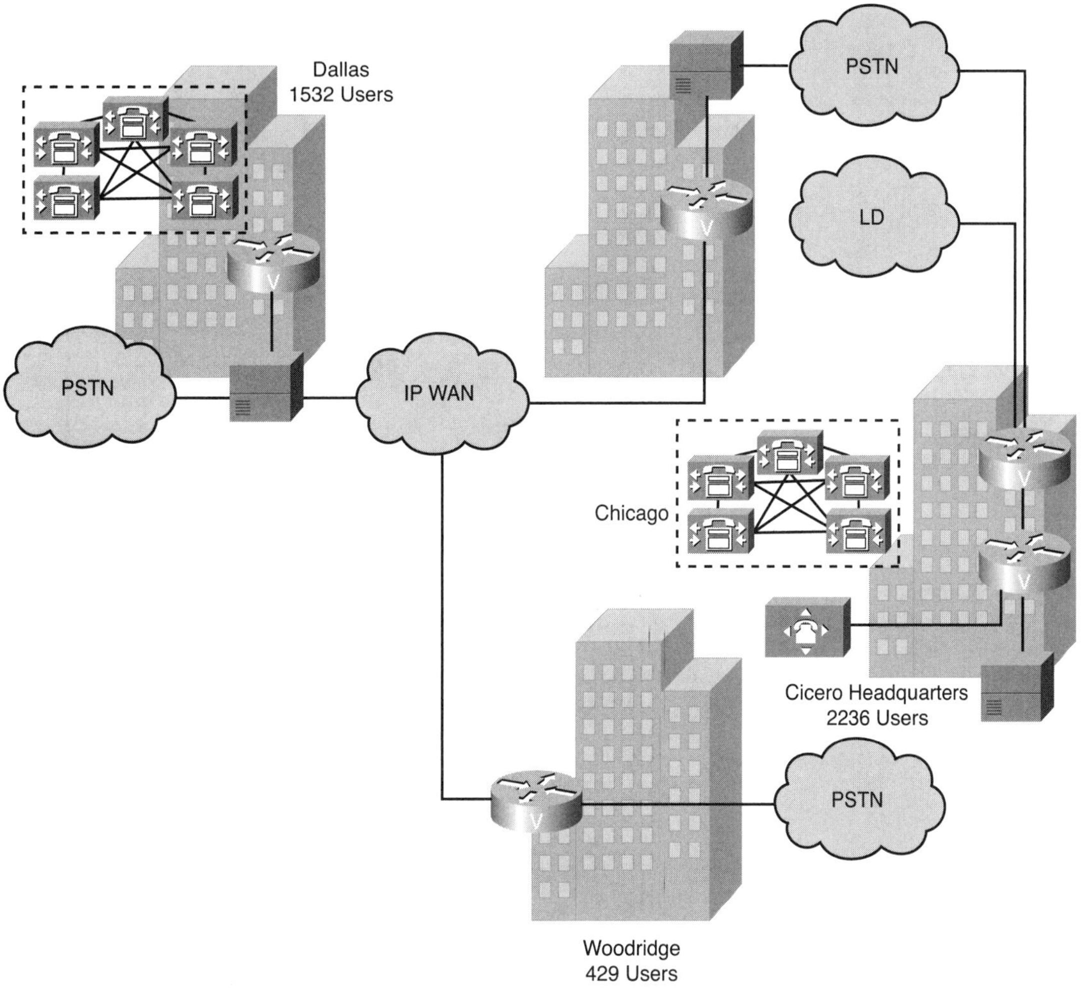

Dallas
1532 Users

PSTN

IP WAN

PSTN

LD

Chicago

Cicero Headquarters
2236 Users

PSTN

Woodridge
429 Users

Figure 5-10 depicts Span Engineering's dial plan requirements.

Figure 5-10 *Span Engineering's Dial Plan Requirements*

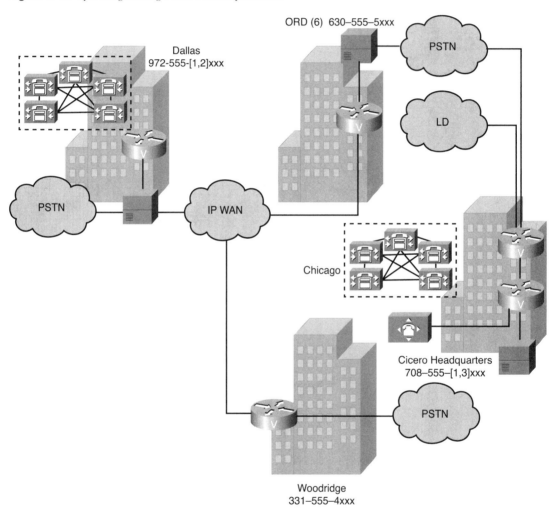

Span Engineering's dial plan requirements include the following:

- Single-digit [1–8] access code identifying each campus
- Single-digit [9] access code that directs calls to the local PSTN
- Intrasite dialing that is based on the four-digit extension
- Intersite dialing that is based on the access code plus the four-digit extension
- Local PSTN access that requires the access code 9 followed by the ten-digit number and also requires that the 9 be stripped and the ten digits passed to the PSTN switch

- Long-distance PSTN access that requires the access code 9 followed by the digit 1, followed by the ten-digit number and also requires the 9 be stripped and the 11 digits passed to the PSTN switch

With this basic understanding of numbering plans and dial plans, the following sections discuss design considerations surrounding hierarchical numbering plans, internal numbering, and public numbering plan integration.

Hierarchical Numbering Plans

The previous section discussed the Public International Telecommunications Numbering Plan (E.164), national numbering plans, and private numbering plans. Each of the numbering plans can benefit, in terms of scalability, from a hierarchical design. A hierarchical design has the following advantages:

- **Simplified provisioning**—Refers to the ability to easily add new groups and modify existing groups

- **Simplified routing**—Keeps local calls local and uses a specialized number, such as an area code, for long-distance calls

- **Summarization**—Establishes groups of numbers in a specific geographical area or functional group

- **Scalability**—Provides additional high-level number groups

- **Management**—Controls number groups from a single point in the overall network

The North American Numbering Plan (NANP) serves as a good role model for a scalable numbering plan. Consider how the NANP might be adapted to your environment. To illustrate the operation of the NANP, examine Figure 5-11.

Figure 5-11 *Hierarchical Numbering Plan*

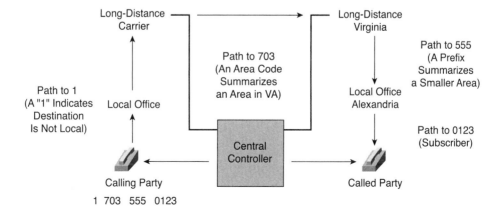

In Figure 5-11, the calling party dials 1-703-555-0123. The calling party's local central office (CO) forwards the call to a long-distance carrier because the first digit (that is, the 1) indicated the call was a long-distance call. The long-distance carrier then forwards the call, based on the dialed area code, to a Virginia long-distance office. The Virginia long-distance office forwards the call, based on the CO code (that is, the *NXX* code), to an Alexandria CO. Finally, the Alexandria CO, based on the last four digits, forwards the call out to the called party.

While the NANP acts as a good starting point in designing a numbering plan, it is not always easy to design a hierarchical numbering plan. Existing numbering plans in the network might include proprietary PBXs, key systems, and telephony services such as a Centrex service. The necessity to conform to the PSTN at the gateways also contributes to the complexity of the design. Translation between these systems is a difficult task. If possible, avoid retraining system users. The goal is to design a numbering plan that has the following attributes:

- Minimal impact on existing systems
- Minimal impact on users of the system
- Minimal translation configuration
- Consideration of anticipated growth

Span Engineering LLC will use the full ten-digit DID numbers that are assigned by the PSTN for the company's internal numbering plan. Using the ten-digit numbers provides Span Engineering with the following benefits:

- Allows easy integration to the PSTN at each local campus with minimal digit manipulation
- Allows dial plans to summarize call routing for sites that use multiple number ranges
- Provides flexibility for the dial plan to use shorter dialing patterns as extensions within the voice network

Internal Numbering and Public Numbering Plan Integration

Numbering plans vary greatly throughout the world. Different countries use different number lengths and hierarchical plans within their borders. Telephony equipment manufacturers and service providers use nonstandard numbering. In an attempt to standardize numbering plans, the ITU developed the E.164 worldwide prefix scheme.

Numbering plan integration from an internal system such as a VoIP and PBX system to the PSTN requires careful planning. The hierarchical structure of the numbering plan and the problems associated with varying number lengths in different systems make numbering plan integration complex.

The challenges faced with numbering plan integration include the following:

- **Varying number lengths**—Within the IP network, consideration is given to varying number lengths that exist outside the IP network. Local, long-distance, key-system, and Centrex dialing from within the IP network might require digit manipulation.

- **Specialized services**—Services such as Centrex and their equivalents typically have four- or five-digit numbers. Dialing from the PSTN into a private VoIP network and then out to a Centrex extension can also require extensive digit manipulation.

- **Voice mail**—When a called party cannot be reached, the network might have to redirect the call to voice mail. Since the voice mail system can require a completely different numbering plan than the endpoint telephones, translation is necessary.

- **Necessity of prefixes or area codes**—It can be necessary to strip or add area codes, or prepend or replace prefixes. Rerouting calls from the IP network to the PSTN for failure recovery can require extra digits.

- **International dialing consideration**—Country codes and numbering plans vary in length within countries. Dialing through an IP network to another country requires careful consideration.

In Figure 5-12, Span Engineering LLC uses the PSTN as a backup route for calls between Cicero and Dallas.

Figure 5-12 *Span Engineering Integration of Internal and Public Numbering Plans*

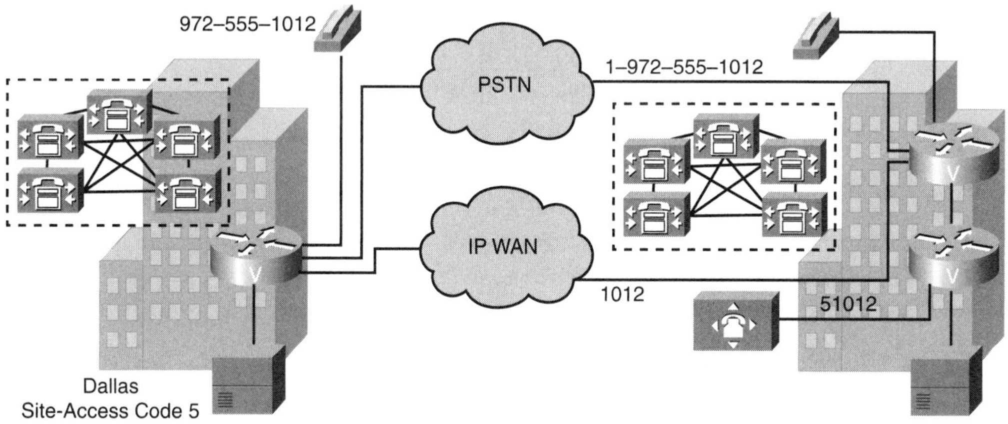

The following list enumerates the call setup steps shown in Figure 5-12:

1. The Cicero caller dials the site-access code for Dallas (5) followed by the four-digit extension number of the destination phone (1012).

2. The voice gateway determines whether the call can be completed using the IP WAN or whether it must be routed via the PSTN.

3. Digit manipulation occurs based on the path chosen.

4. The gateway strips the site-access code and sends four digits if completing the call across the IP WAN.

5. The gateway strips the site-access code and prepends 1-972-555 if completing the call across the PSTN.

Scalable Dial Plans

The North American telephone network is designed around a ten-digit numbering plan that consists of three-digit area codes and seven-digit telephone numbers, as shown in Figure 5-13. For telephone numbers that are located within an area code, the PSTN often uses a seven-digit dial plan. Features within a CO-based PBX, such as Centrex, allow the use of a custom five-digit dial plan for customers who subscribe to that service. PBXs are more flexible and allow for variable-length dial plans containing 3 to 11 digits.

Figure 5-13 *Dial Plan Example*

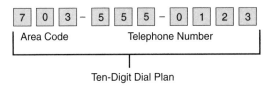

Dial plans contain specific dialing patterns for a user who wants to reach a particular telephone number. Dial plans also contain access codes, area codes, specialized codes, and combinations of the numbers of digits dialed.

Dial plans require knowledge of the customer network topology, current telephone number dialing patterns, proposed router and gateway locations, and traffic-routing requirements. If the dial plans are for a private internal voice network that is not accessed by the outside voice network, the telephone numbers can be any number of digits.

Typically, companies that implement VoIP networks carry voice traffic within the least expensive systems and paths. Implementing this type of system involves routing calls through IP networks, private trunks, PBXs, key systems, and the PSTN. The numbering plan to support the system is scalable, easily understood by the user, and transportable between all of the system components. The use of alternate path components reduces instances of call failure. Finally, the numbering plan conforms to all applicable standards and formats for all of the systems involved.

Scalable Dial Plan Attributes

When designing a large-scale dial plan, Cisco recommends you adhere to the following attributes:

- **Logic distribution**—Good dial plan architecture relies on the effective distribution of the dial plan logic among the various components. Devices that are isolated to a specific portion of the dial plan reduce the complexity of the configuration. Each component focuses on a specific task accomplishment. Generally, the local switch or gateway handles details that are specific to the local point of presence (POP). Higher-level routing decisions are passed along to the gatekeepers and PBXs. A well-designed network places the majority of the dial plan logic at the gatekeeper devices.

- **Hierarchical design (scalability)**—You should attempt to keep the majority of the dial plan logic (routing decisions and failover) at the highest-component level. Maintaining a hierarchical design makes the addition and deletion of number groups more manageable. Scaling the overall network is much easier when configuration changes are made to a single component.

- **Simplicity in provisioning**—Keep the dial plan simple and symmetrical when designing a network. Try to keep consistent dial plans on the network by using translation rules to manipulate the local digit dialing patterns. These number patterns are normalized into a standard format or pattern before the digits enter the VoIP core. Putting digits into a standard format simplifies provisioning and dial-peer management.

- **Reduction in postdial delay**—Consider the effects of postdial delay in the network when you design a large-scale dial plan. Postdial delay is the time between the last digit dialed and the moment the phone rings at the receiving location. In the PSTN, people expect a short postdial delay and to hear ringback within seconds. The more translations and lookups that take place, the longer the postdial delay becomes. Overall network design, translation rules, and alternate pathing affect postdial delay. Therefore, you should efficiently use these tools to reduce postdial delay.

- **Availability and fault tolerance**—Consider overall network availability and call success rates when you design a dial plan. Fault tolerance and redundancy within VoIP networks are most important at the gatekeeper level. By using an alternate path you help provide redundancy and fault tolerance in the network.

- **Conformance to public standards**—Different geographical locations might impose restrictions to your dial plan. Therefore, familiarize yourself with any such limitations prior to designing your dial plan.

Practice Scenario 3: Span Engineering Dial Plan Worksheet

Following is a list of specifications for the Span Engineering dial plan:

- The Cicero Campus number ranges are 708-555-1*xxx*, 708-555-2*xxx*, and 708-555-3*xxx*.
- The Cicero Campus site-access code is 7.
- The Dallas campus number ranges are 972-555-1*xxx* and 972-555-2*xxx*.
- The Dallas campus site-access code is 5.
- The ORD (Span Engineering Chicago airport location) number range is 630-555-5*xxx*.
- The ORD site-access code is 6.
- The PSTN requires ten-digit dialing for local calls.
- The PSTN requires 1 + ten digits for long-distance calls.
- Cicero to ORD is local through PSTN.
- Cicero to Dallas is long distance through PSTN.
- Intrasite calls require a four-digit extension.
- Intersite calls require an access code and a four-digit extension.

Based on the dial plan worksheet, fill in the appropriate information in each space in Table 5-5. The first row has been filled in for you as an example.

Table 5-5 *Practice Scenario 3: Span Engineering Dial Plan*

Call Information	Number Dialed	Number Sent to Remote Gateway Through WAN	Number Sent to PSTN
Cicero caller calls Dallas extension 2312	52312	2312	1-972-555-2312
Cicero caller calls ORD extension 5087			
Dallas caller calls Cicero extension 3312			
Dallas caller calls Dallas extension 2887			

Practice Scenario 3: Solution

Table 5-6 shows the solution for Practice Scenario 3.

Table 5-6   *Solution: Span Engineering Dial Plan*

Call Information	Number Dialed	Number Sent to Remote Gateway Through WAN	Number Sent to PSTN
Cicero caller calls Dallas extension 2312	52312	2312	1-972-555-2312
Cicero caller calls ORD extension 5087	65087	5087	630-555-5087
Dallas caller calls Cicero extension 3312	73312	3312	1-708-555-3312
Dallas caller calls Dallas extension 2887	2887	N/A	972-555-2887

Enhancing and Extending an Existing Plan to Accommodate VoIP

There are many ways that you can enhance and extend an existing numbering plan to accommodate the VoIP network. All of these ways require careful planning and consideration. This section discusses two of these ways: number normalization and technology prefixes. First, consider number normalization.

Number Normalization

Number normalization is a technique where dial strings can be modified to match the expected dial string length of the next hop device. For example, when a router passes a dial string to a PBX, the router should pass the number of digits that are meaningful to the PBX. Similarly, if a router passes a dial string to the PSTN, the router might need to add digits (for example, a 1, an area code, and an office code) to the dial string. Consider the topology in Figure 5-14, whose configuration is provided in Table 5-7. When site E (703555....) dials 7275550199, the full ten-digit dialed string is passed through the Centrex to the router at site D. Router D matches the destination pattern 7275550199 and forwards the ten-digit dial string to router A. Router A matches the destination pattern 727555...., strips off the matching 727555, and forwards the remaining four-digit dial string to the PBX. The PBX matches the correct station and completes the call to the proper extension.

Figure 5-14 *Number Normalization*

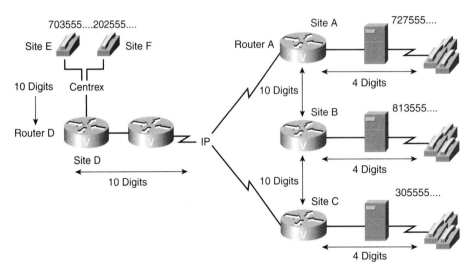

Table 5-7 *Router Digit Stripping Comparison*

Router A	Router D
dial-peer voice 1 pots	dial-peer voice 4 pots
destination-pattern 727555....	destination-pattern 703555....
port 1/0:1	no digit-strip
!	port 1/0:1
dial-peer voice 4 voip	!
destination-pattern 703555....	dial-peer voice 5 pots
session target ipv4:10.10.10.2	destination-pattern 202555....
!	no digit-strip
dial-peer voice 5 voip	port 1/0:1
destination-pattern 202555....	!
session target ipv4:10.10.10.3	dial-peer voice 1 voip
!	destination-pattern 727555....
	session target ipv4:10.10.10.1
	!

Calls in the reverse direction are handled similarly. However, because the Centrex service requires the full ten-digit dial string to complete calls, the plain old telephone service (POTS) dial peer at router D is configured with digit stripping disabled. An alternate solution involves enabling digit stripping and configuring the dial peer with a six-digit prefix (for example, 703555), which results in forwarding the full dial string to the Centrex service.

Technology Prefixes Applied

Another method, called *technology prefixes*, allows you to include special characters in the called number. These special characters (most commonly designated as 1#, 2#, 3#, and so on) are prepended to the called number on the outgoing VoIP dial peer. The gatekeeper then checks its gateway technology prefix table for gateways that are registered with that particular technology prefix. Technology prefixes also identify a type, class, or pool of gateways.

Voice gateways typically register with technology prefix 1#, H.320 gateways with technology prefix 2#, and voice mail gateways with technology prefix 3#. Multiple gateways can register with the same type prefix. When this happens, the gatekeeper makes a random selection among gateways of the same type.

If the callers know the type of device that they are trying to reach, they can include the technology prefix in the destination address to indicate the type of gateway to use to get to the destination. For example, if a caller knows that address 7275550111 belongs to a regular telephone, the caller can use the destination address of 1#7275550111, where 1# indicates that the address should be resolved by a voice gateway. When the voice gateway receives the call for 1#7275550111, it strips off the technology prefix and routes the next leg of the call to the telephone at 7275550111.

You can enter technology prefix commands on gateways and gatekeepers in two places, depending on how you want to design the technology prefix decision intelligence:

- The gateway VoIP interface
- The gateway dial peer

You can implement this type of digit manipulation and management of dialed numbers in various ways, depending on the infrastructure of the network. All of the components, including the gatekeepers, gateways, Cisco CallManagers, PBXs, key systems, and other systems, might need to be included in the process.

Accounting for Caller Mobility for 911 Services

To understand how VoIP networks can provide the location and telephone number for 911 services, you need to understand the basic component functions. The basic components of 911 services are as follows:

- **Automatic number identification (ANI)**—ANI is the calling-party number that is included with each call to identify where the call originated. Often, in a business environment, the original ANI might be changed by the service provider at the first switch to reflect the billing number of the company instead of reflecting the calling number of the original party. Discussions with the service provider need to ensure that the original ANI is transmitted with all calls. Internal extensions or private numbering plans require mapping or translation for outbound ANI.

- **Automatic location identification (ALI)**—The ALI database contains the records that map telephone numbers to geographic locations. The ALI database resides in the service provider network. Updates to the ALI database are submitted any time there is a move, add, or change event in a telephony network. Updates can require up to 48 hours to take effect, thereby making dynamic ALI updates unsuitable in a mobile environment.

- **Public safety answering point (PSAP)**—The PSAP is the answer point where an emergency call is terminated. Calls are directed to specific PSAPs based on the geographic location of the call origination point.

- **Emergency response location (ERL)**—ERL is the location from which an emergency call is placed. In a network where VoIP mobility is common, the ANI of the calling telephone does not always identify the location of the emergency because the callers retain the same extension regardless of where they are actually located. The ERL is used in mobile environments by associating ports and devices to an ERL group. The recommendation is to define an ERL group for each floor in a building, each unit in a hotel or motel, or each tenant in a multitenant building.

- **Emergency location identification number (ELIN)**—An ELIN is a NANP telephone number used for routing an emergency call to the appropriate PSAP. In a mobile environment where the ANI is the mobile extension of the user, the ELIN is substituted for the ANI when the call is sent to the PSAP. This substitution enables the PSAP to record the calling number and be able to call the number back if the need arises. Each ERL has a unique ELIN associated with it. When a mobile caller logs into the VoIP phone, the ELIN for the call is determined based on the ERL with which the port is associated.

- **Master street address guide (MSAG)**—MSAG is a database maintained by a government agency. This database maps geographic locations to the PSAPs responsible for handling emergency calls for those locations.

- **Selective router**—A selective router is a dedicated 911 switch in the service provider network that routes 911 calls to the appropriate PSAP based on the calling number. This approach is different from normal call routing, which routes calls based on the called number. When a call is routed to the selective router, the router looks at the ANI and determines which PSAP to send the cacell to.

- **Centralized automated message accounting (CAMA)**—A CAMA is an analog truck that connects a customer switch directly to the selective router in the service provider network. A CAMA trunk carries 911 calls only. It does not carry other user calls.

- **Cisco Emergency Responder (CER)**—CER is an application that automatically tracks and updates moves and changes of equipment, thereby removing this burden from the administrative staff and providing cost savings. Through a real-time, location-tracking database, the Cisco Emergency Responder also allows emergency personnel to identify locations of 911 callers. The Cisco Emergency Responder works in conjunction with Cisco CallManager.

It is critical that the network designer understand and adhere to local, municipal, state, and federal laws regarding compliance to 911 requirements.

The following sections describe 911 call processing in nonmobile and mobile environments.

911 Call Processing in a Nonmobile Environment

Figure 5-15 shows an environment where telephony end devices remain in their permanent location.

The call illustrated in Figure 5-15 is processed as follows:

1. The emergency call originates from the device with the ANI of 555-1234.

2. The call is routed via Cisco CallManager to the main PSTN gateway at the company's headquarters.

3. The PSTN gateway either routes the call directly to the selective router via the CAMA trunk (if present) or routes the call via the normal PRI connection to the CO switch.

4. The CO switch retains the original ANI and does not replace it with the billing number.

5. The CO switch routes the call to the selective router.

6. The selective router queries the database to determine which PSAP is responsible for the location of the ANI.

7. The selective router routes the call to the PSAP.

8. The PSAP queries the ALI database to determine the exact location of the caller.

Figure 5-15 *911 Call Processing in a Nonmobile Environment*

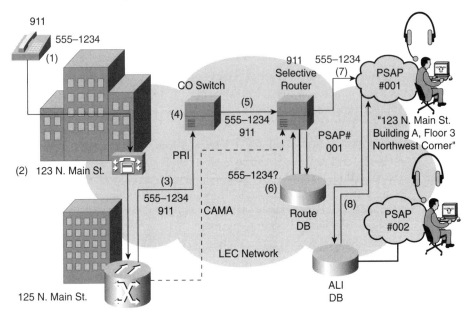

911 Call Processing in a Mobile Environment

Cisco Emergency Responder (CER) is used to dynamically update location information for mobile users. In Figure 5-16, the user with extension 1000 is normally located at 123 N. Main St. but is working on a project with a team at headquarters, which is located at 125 N. Main St. The emergency call is placed by the user of extension 1000 at the 125 N. Main St. location.

The call shown in Figure 5-16 is processed as follows:

1. The user with extension 1000 logs into a VoIP phone plugged into a switch that is configured for ERL 2.

2. The ERL 2 has ELIN 555-5679 associated with it.

3. The CER queries Cisco CallManager to determine when new users log into a VoIP telephone. Cisco Emergency Responder queries Cisco Catalyst switches to determine the port that the user is plugged into.

4. The CER determines the ELIN based on the ERL configuration for the port.

5. The CER replaces the original ANI of 1000 with the ELIN of ERL 2 (which is 555-5679) and forwards the call to the gateway connected to the PSTN.

6. The CO switch routes the call to the selective router.

Figure 5-16 *911 Call Processing in a Mobile Environment*

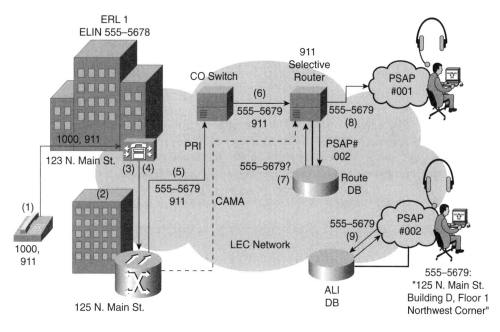

7. The selective router queries the database to determine which PSAP is responsible for the location of the ANI.

8. The selective router routes the call to the PSAP.

9. The PSAP queries the ALI database to determine the exact location of the caller.

Practice Scenario 4: Numbering Plan for Span Engineering

To confirm your understanding of numbering plan issues, this practice scenario revisits the Span Engineering network. Specifically, you will answer questions regarding Span Engineering's Chicago airport and London locations.

Chicago Airport Location

The Span Engineering Chicago airport location (referred to as ORD) uses the number range of 630-555-5000 through 630-555-5999. Before the start of the VoIP migration, all employees at ORD are connected to each other and to the PSTN through the local PBX. The first phase of migration consists of moving a small group of ten users off the PBX and onto the VoIP infrastructure. The ten users who are to be migrated use the extension range of 5100 through 5110. Define the new numbering ranges that will be used for connectivity to all staff at ORD:

ORD numbering range(s) for PBX: _____

ORD numbering range(s) for VoIP phones: _____

London Location

Span Engineering collaborates with several companies in London, England. The telephone number range to reach the London facilities is 7946-0300 through 7946-0350. The area code for London is 020, and the country code is 44. All calls that originate in the United States and are destined for international carriers must begin with the international access code of 011. This access code must be followed by the country code, the area code, and the local telephone number.

The internal code within Span Engineering for dialing London locations is 2 plus a four-digit extension, which is the last four digits of the telephone number. Define the requested dialing patterns for users located at ORD who are dialing the London offices, based on a call from ORD to London extension 0344:

Number dialed by ORD staff: _____

Number that needs to be sent to the PSTN to complete the overseas call:

_____

Practice Scenario 4: Solution

The correct answers for the Chicago airport location scenario follow:

- ORD numbering range(s) for PBX: 630-555-0000 through 630-555-5099 and 630-555-5111 through 630-555-5999
- ORD numbering range for VoIP phones: 630-555-5100 through 630-555-5110

The correct answers for the London location scenario follow:

- Number dialed by ORD staff: 20344
- Number that needs to be sent to the PSTN to complete the overseas call: 0114402079460344

Calculating Bandwidth Requirements

Because WAN bandwidth is probably the most expensive component of an enterprise network, network administrators must know how to calculate the total bandwidth required for voice traffic and how to reduce overall bandwidth consumption.

This section describes, in detail, VoIP bandwidth requirements. You learn about several variables affecting total bandwidth and the method of calculating and reducing the total required bandwidth.

CODEC Payload Bandwidth Requirements

One of the most important factors for the network administrator to consider while building voice networks is proper capacity planning. Network administrators must understand how much bandwidth is used for each VoIP call. With a thorough understanding of VoIP bandwidth, the network administrator can apply capacity-planning tools.

Following is a list of CODECs and their associated bandwidth:

- **G.711**—The G.711 pulse code modulation (PCM) coding scheme uses the most bandwidth. G.711 takes samples 8000 times per second, each of which is 8 bits in length, for a total bandwidth of 64,000 bps.

- **G.726**—The G.726 adaptive differential pulse code modulation (ADPCM) coding schemes use somewhat less bandwidth. While each coding scheme takes samples 8000 times per second like PCM, G.726 ADPCM uses 4, 3, or 2 bits for each sample, thereby resulting in total required bandwidths of 32,000, 24,000, or 16,000 bps.

- **G.728**—The G.728 low-delay code excited linear prediction (LDCELP) coding scheme compresses PCM samples using codebook technology. It uses a total bandwidth of 16,000 bps.

- **G.729**—The G.729 and G.729A conjugate structure algebraic code excited linear prediction (CS-ACELP) coding scheme also compresses PCM using advanced codebook technology. It uses 8000 bps of total bandwidth.

- **G.723**—The G.723 and G.723A multipulse maximum likelihood quantization (MPMLQ) coding schemes use a look-ahead algorithm. These compression schemes result in a required bandwidth of 6300 or 5300 bps.

The network administrator should balance the need for voice quality against the cost of bandwidth in the network when choosing CODECs. The higher the CODEC bandwidth is, the higher the cost of each call across the network will be.

Impact of Voice Samples and Packet Size on Bandwidth

Voice sample size is a variable that can affect total bandwidth used. A voice sample is defined as the digital output from a CODEC digital signal processor (DSP) encapsulated into a protocol data unit (PDU). Cisco uses DSPs that output samples based on digitization of 10 ms worth of audio. Cisco voice equipment encapsulates 20 ms of audio in each PDU by default, regardless of the CODEC used. You can apply an optional configuration command to the dial peer to vary the number of samples encapsulated. When you encapsulate more samples per PDU, the total bandwidth is reduced. However, encapsulating more samples per PDU comes at the risk of larger PDUs, which can cause variable delay and severe gaps if PDUs are dropped. Table 5-8 demonstrates how the number of packets required to transmit one second of audio varies with voice sample sizes.

Table 5-8 *Impact of Voice Samples*

CODEC	Bandwidth (bps)	Sample Size (Bytes)	Packets
G.711	64,000	240	33
G.711	64,000	160	50
G.726r32	32,000	120	33
G.726r32	32,000	80	50
G.726r24	24,000	80	25
G.726r24	24,000	60	33
G.726r16	16,000	80	25
G.726r16	16,000	40	50
G.728	16,000	80	13
G.728	16,000	40	25
G.729	8000	40	25
G.729	8000	20	50
G.723r63	6300	48	16
G.723r63	6300	24	33
G.723r53	5300	40	17
G.723r53	5300	20	33

Using a simple formula, it is possible for you to determine the number of bytes encapsulated in a PDU based on the CODEC bandwidth and the sample size (20 ms is the default):

Bytes_per_Sample = (Sample_Size * CODEC_Bandwidth) / 8

If you apply G.711 numbers, the formula reveals the following:

Bytes_per_Sample = (.020 * 64000) / 8
Bytes_per_Sample = 160

Notice from Table 5-8 that the larger the sample size, the larger the packet, and the fewer the encapsulated samples that have to be sent (which reduces bandwidth).

Data Link Overhead

Another contributing factor to bandwidth is the Layer 2 protocol used to transport VoIP. VoIP alone carries a 40-byte IP/User Datagram Protocol/Real-Time Transport Protocol (IP/UDP/RTP) header, assuming uncompressed RTP. Depending on the Layer 2 protocol used, the overhead could grow substantially. More bandwidth is required to transport VoIP frames with larger Layer 2 overhead. The following illustrates the Layer 2 overhead for various protocols:

- **Ethernet II**—Carries 18 bytes of overhead: 6 bytes for source MAC, 6 bytes for destination MAC, 2 bytes for type, and 4 bytes for cyclic redundancy check (CRC)

- **Multilink Point-to-Point Protocol (MLP)**—Carries 6 bytes of overhead: 1 byte for flag, 1 byte for address, 2 bytes for control (or type), and 2 bytes for CRC

- **Frame Relay Forum Standard 12 (FRF.12)**—Carries 6 bytes of overhead: 2 bytes for data-link connection identifier (DLCI) header, 2 bytes for FRF.12 header, and 2 bytes for CRC

Security and Tunneling Overhead

Certain security and tunneling encapsulations also add overhead to voice packets and should be considered when calculating bandwidth requirements. When using a virtual private network (VPN), IP Security (IPSec) will add 50 to 57 bytes of overhead, a significant amount when considering the relatively small voice packet size. Layer 2 Tunneling Protocol/generic routing encapsulation (L2TP/GRE) adds 24 bytes. When using MLP, 6 bytes will be added to each packet. Multiprotocol Label Switching (MPLS) adds a 4-byte label to every packet. All these specialized tunneling and security protocols must be considered when planning for bandwidth demands.

For example, many companies have their employees telecommute from home. These employees often initiate a VPN connection into their enterprise for secure Internet transmission. When deploying a remote telephone at the employee's home using a router and a PBX Off-Premises eXtension (OPX), the voice packets experience additional overhead associated with the VPN.

Calculating the Total Bandwidth for a VoIP Call

CODEC choice, data-link overhead, sample size, and RTP header compression have positive and negative impacts on total bandwidth, as demonstrated in Table 5-9.

Table 5-9 *Total Bandwidth Required*

CODEC	CODEC Speed (bps)	Sample Size (Bytes)	Frame Relay (bps)	Frame Relay with cRTP (bps)	Ethernet (bps)
G.711	64,000	240	76,267	66,133	79,467
G.711	64,000	160	82,400	67,200	87,200
G.726r32	32,000	120	44,267	34,133	47,467
G.726r32	32,000	80	50,400	35,200	55,200
G.726r24	24,000	80	37,800	26,400	41,400
G.726r24	24,000	60	42,400	27,200	47,200
G.726r16	16,000	80	25,200	17,600	27,600
G.726r16	16,000	40	34,400	19,200	39,200
G.728	16,000	80	25,200	17,600	27,600
G.728	16,000	40	34,400	19,200	39,200
G.729	8000	40	17,200	9600	19,600
G.729	8000	20	26,400	11,200	31,200
G.723r63	6300	48	12,338	7350	13,913
G.723r63	6300	24	18,375	8400	21,525
G.723r53	5300	40	11,395	6360	12,985
G.723r53	5300	20	17,490	7420	20,670

To perform the calculations, you must consider these contributing factors as part of the equation:

- More bandwidth required for the CODEC requires more total bandwidth
- More overhead associated with the data link requires more total bandwidth
- Larger sample size requires less total bandwidth
- RTP header compression requires significantly less total bandwidth

Consider a total bandwidth calculation for Span Engineering. The company is implementing VoIP to carry voice calls between all sites. WAN connections between sites will carry both data and voice. To use bandwidth efficiently and keep costs to a minimum, voice traffic traversing the WAN will be compressed using the G.729 CODEC with 20-byte voice samples. WAN connectivity will be through a Frame Relay provider.

The following calculation is used to calculate total bandwidth required per call:

Total_Bandwidth = ([Layer_2_Overhead + IP_UDP_RTP Overhead + Sample_Size] / Sample_Size) * CODEC_Speed

Calculation for the G.729 CODEC, 20-byte sample size, using Frame Relay *without* Compressed RTP (cRTP) is as follows:

Total_Bandwidth = ([6 + 40 + 20] / 20) * 8000
Total_Bandwidth = 26,400 bps

Calculation for G.729 CODEC, 20-byte sample size, using Frame Relay *with* cRTP is as follows:

Total_Bandwidth = ([6 + 2 + 20] / 20) * 8000
Total_Bandwidth = 11,200 bps

Effects of Voice Activity Detection on Bandwidth

On average, an aggregate of 24 calls or more might contain 35 percent silence. With traditional telephony voice networks, all G.711 voice calls use 64 kbps fixed-bandwidth links regardless of how much of the conversation is speech and how much is silence. In Cisco VoIP networks, all conversations and silences are packetized. Voice activity detection (VAD) can suppress packets containing silence. Instead of sending VoIP packets of silence, VoIP gateways interleave data traffic with VoIP conversations to more effectively use network bandwidth. Table 5-10 illustrates the type of bandwidth savings VAD offers.

Table 5-10   *The Impact of VAD on Required Bandwidth*

CODEC	CODEC Speed (bps)	Sample Size (Bytes)	Frame Relay (bps)	Frame Relay with VAD (bps)
G.711	64,000	240	76,267	49,573
G.711	64,000	160	82,400	53,560
G.726r32	32,000	120	44,267	28,773
G.726r32	32,000	80	50,400	32,760
G.726r24	24,000	80	37,800	24,570
G.726r24	24,000	60	42,400	27,560
G.726r16	16,000	80	25,200	16,380
G.726r16	16,000	40	34,400	22,360
G.728	16,000	80	25,200	16,380
G.728	16,000	40	34,400	22,360

continues

Table 5-10 *The Impact of VAD on Required Bandwidth (Continued)*

CODEC	CODEC Speed (bps)	Sample Size (Bytes)	Frame Relay (bps)	Frame Relay with VAD (bps)
G.729	8000	40	17,200	11,180
G.729	8000	20	26,400	17,160
G.723r63	6300	48	12,338	8019
G.723r63	6300	24	18,375	11,944
G.723r53	5300	40	11,395	7407
G.723r53	5300	20	17,490	11,369

NOTE Bandwidth savings of 35 percent is an average figure and does not take into account loud background sounds, differences in languages, and other factors.

NOTE For the purposes of network design and bandwidth engineering, VAD should not be taken into account, especially on links that carry fewer than 24 voice calls simultaneously.

Various features, such as music on hold (MOH) and fax, render VAD ineffective. When the network is engineered for the full voice call bandwidth, all savings provided by VAD are available to data applications.

VAD is enabled by default for all VoIP calls. Not only does VAD reduce the silence in VoIP conversations, but it also provides comfort noise generation (CNG). In some cases silence might be mistaken for a disconnected call. CNG provides locally generated *white noise* to make the call appear normally connected to both parties.

Span Engineering LLC is assessing the effect of VAD in a Frame Relay VoIP environment. The company plans to use G.729 for all voice calls crossing the WAN. Previously, it was determined that each voice call compressed with G.729 uses 26,400 bps. VAD can reduce the bandwidth utilization to approximately 17,160 bps, which constitutes a bandwidth savings of 35 percent.

Practice Scenario 5: Span Engineering Voice Bandwidth Requirement

Span Engineering is planning to carry intrasite VoIP calls across the LAN at each site. The company plans to use the G.711 CODEC with a 30 ms voice sample for voice coding. Your task is to calculate how much bandwidth per call will be required to implement the design specifications.

1. Calculate the voice sample size in bytes, given that the CODEC will be G.711 with a 30 ms sample size.

   _____

2. Calculate the bandwidth per call for the G.711 call, including Ethernet overhead.

   _____

3. Calculate the bandwidth per call, reflecting a 35 percent VAD savings.

   _____

Practice Scenario 5: Solution

1. Calculate the voice sample size in bytes, given that the CODEC will be G.711 with a 30 ms sample size.

   Bytes_per_Sample = (*Sample_Size * CODEC_Bandwidth*) / 8

   Bytes per sample = (.030 * 64,000) / 8

   Bytes per sample = 240

2. Calculate the bandwidth per call for the G.711 call, including Ethernet overhead.

   Total_Bandwidth = ([Layer_2_Overhead + IP_UDP_RTP Overhead + Sample_Size] / Sample_Size) * CODEC_Speed

   Total bandwidth = ([18 + 40 + 240] / 240) * 64,000

   Total bandwidth = 79,467 bps

3. Calculate the bandwidth per call, reflecting 35 percent VAD savings.

   Total bandwidth = *Bandwidth* – (*Bandwidth* * 35%)

   Total bandwidth = 79,467 – (79,467 * .35)

   Total bandwidth = 51,653 bps

Cisco Voice CODEC Bandwidth Calculator

Although the charts presented in this section aid in determining the required bandwidth for a call, you might prefer to use Cisco's web-based Voice CODEC Bandwidth Calculator located at the following URL:

http://tools.cisco.com/Support/VBC/do/CodecCalc1.do

NOTE   A Cisco.com account is required in order to use this tool. You can register for a Cisco.com account by pointing your web browser to the Cisco home page at http://www.cisco.com and clicking the Register link. You need a maintenance contract or a partner agreement with Cisco in order to access this tool. A guest account does not have permission to access the Voice CODEC Bandwidth Calculator.

Follow these steps to use Cisco's Voice Bandwidth Calculator:

1. Point a web browser to:

   http://tools.cisco.com/Support/VBC/do/CodecCalc1.do

   From the initial screen, as shown in Figure 5-17, select the CODEC being used (typically G.711 on a high-speed local area network or G.729 on a lower-speed wide area network), the voice protocol (VoIP for this discussion), and the number of simultaneous calls you need to support. Then click the Next button.

Figure 5-17 *Voice Bandwidth Calculator – Screen 1*

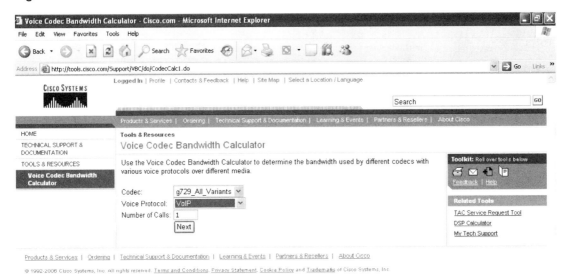

2. Complete the next screen, as shown in Figure 5-18, by entering the voice payload size (the number of bytes used to encode a single voice sample, which is typically 20 bytes for the G.729 CODEC), clicking a check box if you are using RTP header compression, selecting the media access (for example, Frame Relay, Ethernet, or PPP), and indicating any additional overhead that increases the size of the packet (for example, tunneling or security overhead). Then click the Submit button.

Figure 5-18 *Voice Bandwidth Calculator – Screen 2*

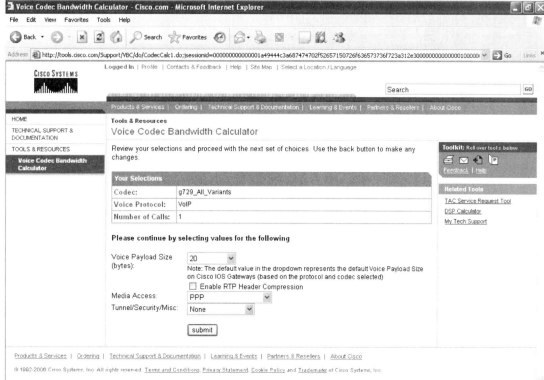

3. From the final screen, as shown in Figure 5-19, note the Total Bandwidth (Including Overhead) value. This value gives you the amount of bandwidth required to support the number of simultaneous calls you indicated, with the network characteristics you specified.

Figure 5-19 *Voice Bandwidth Calculator – Screen 3*

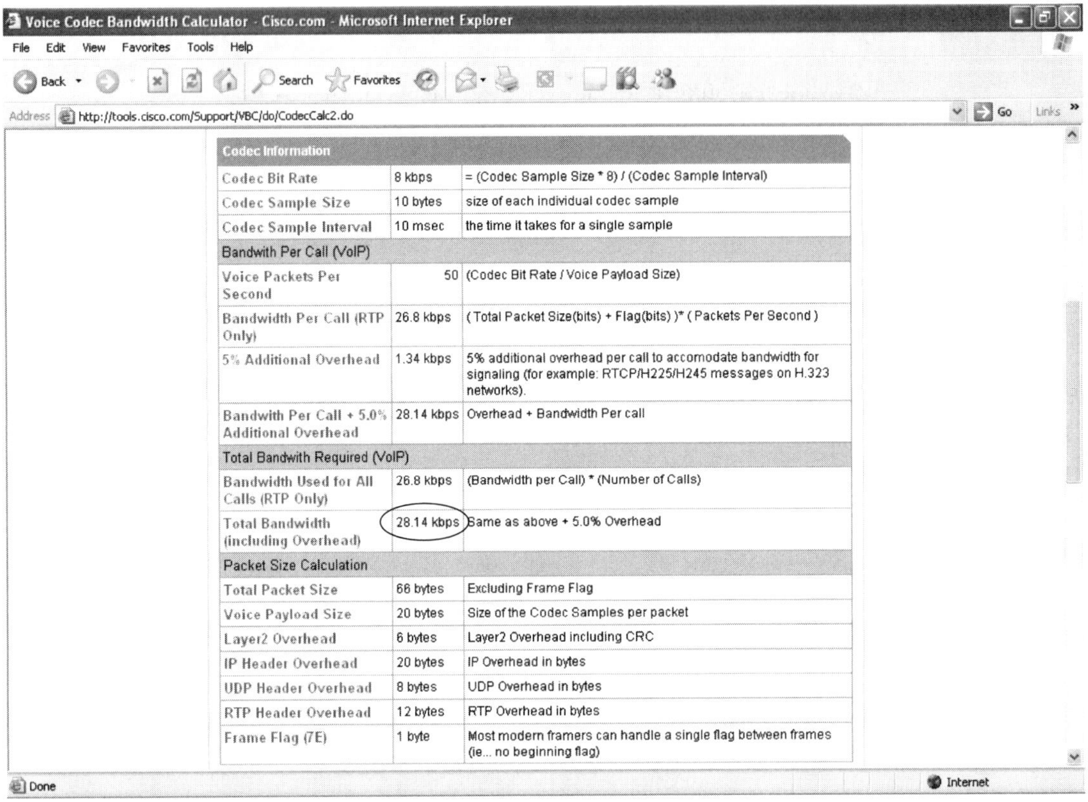

Codec Information		
Codec Bit Rate	8 kbps	= (Codec Sample Size * 8) / (Codec Sample Interval)
Codec Sample Size	10 bytes	size of each individual codec sample
Codec Sample Interval	10 msec	the time it takes for a single sample
Bandwith Per Call (VoIP)		
Voice Packets Per Second	50	(Codec Bit Rate / Voice Payload Size)
Bandwidth Per Call (RTP Only)	26.8 kbps	(Total Packet Size(bits) + Flag(bits))* (Packets Per Second)
5% Additional Overhead	1.34 kbps	5% additional overhead per call to accomodate bandwidth for signaling (for example: RTCP/H225/H245 messages on H.323 networks).
Bandwith Per Call + 5.0% Additional Overhead	28.14 kbps	Overhead + Bandwidth Per call
Total Bandwith Required (VoIP)		
Bandwidth Used for All Calls (RTP Only)	26.8 kbps	(Bandwidth per Call) * (Number of Calls)
Total Bandwidth (including Overhead)	28.14 kbps	Same as above + 5.0% Overhead
Packet Size Calculation		
Total Packet Size	66 bytes	Excluding Frame Flag
Voice Payload Size	20 bytes	Size of the Codec Samples per packet
Layer2 Overhead	6 bytes	Layer2 Overhead including CRC
IP Header Overhead	20 bytes	IP Overhead in bytes
UDP Header Overhead	8 bytes	UDP Overhead in bytes
RTP Header Overhead	12 bytes	RTP Overhead in bytes
Frame Flag (7E)	1 byte	Most modern framers can handle a single flag between frames (ie... no beginning flag)

Allocating Bandwidth for Voice and Data Traffic

Network administrators must be able to calculate existing bandwidth and forecast additional voice bandwidth that is required to implement VoIP. This section describes the importance of proper bandwidth engineering, sometimes called *traffic engineering*. Simply adding voice to an existing IP network is not acceptable. You must take proper precautions to ensure enough bandwidth for existing data applications and the additional voice traffic.

Traffic Statistics

Traffic engineering, as it applies to traditional voice networks, involves determining the number of trunks necessary to carry a required number of voice calls during a specific time period. For designers of a VoIP network, the goal is to properly calculate the number of trunks and provision the appropriate amount of bandwidth necessary to carry the data equivalent of the number of trunks determined. To determine the number of required voice trunks, you must first have statistics showing the current voice traffic. These statistics can be collected from various sources, as detailed in the following section.

Gathering Voice Statistics

You can gather voice traffic statistics from several sources, including:

- PSTN carriers
- PBX call detail records (CDRs)
- Telephone bills

From the PSTN carrier, you can often gather the following information:

- **Peg counts**—For calls offered, calls abandoned, and all trunks busy. A peg count is a telephony term that dates back to the days of mechanical switches. A mechanical counter was attached to a peg to measure the number of events on that peg. The peg might be energized (that is, sent a signal) for any one of several reasons, including call overflow and trunk seizure. Today, electronic switches record peg counts by way of software programs in their common control components.
- **Total traffic**—Carried voice traffic per trunk group.

In the absence of this detailed information, you could use a telephone bill to approximate the total traffic, but telephone bills do not show you the lost calls or the grade of service (that is, the percentage of calls rejected during the busiest hour of the day).

The internal telecommunications department provides CDRs for PBXs. This information typically records calls that are offered, but might not provide information on calls that were blocked because all trunks were busy.

Ideally, all call statistics are provided on a time-of-day basis. The number of trunks required to carry voice traffic is based on the *peak* daily traffic, not the *average* daily traffic.

Gathering Data Statistics

The total data traffic after migrating voice to the data network is the sum of the data traffic and the newly introduced voice traffic. The only exception is when the data network is accommodating voice and data on separate facilities. Therefore, you need to know how much bandwidth is required for data applications. You can gather data traffic statistics from the following:

- Network management systems (NMSs)
- Sniffers
- **show interfaces** commands
- Router-based accounting

Establishing Network Objectives for Voice and Data

To provide an acceptable level of access to telephone and data services in a combined voice and data network, you should establish guidelines for the acceptable performance of each.

In a data network, users can reasonably expect to achieve a level of throughput in bits per second (bps) or a network transit delay in milliseconds (ms). Unfortunately, few networks have stated objectives for throughput and delay. In planning a combined voice and data network, voice is sharing the same paths as data. Voice is given first access to the network resources because of its real-time requirements. However, service to the data users will be affected. You will be unable to judge the suitability of the combined voice and data network without a target for throughput and delay.

Traffic engineering for voice is based on a target grade of service (GoS). GoS is a unit that measures the chance that a call will be blocked. The GoS is usually defined for the peak or busiest period in the business day when demand for service is at its highest. This approach means that GoS is naturally better during off-peak hours. This GoS value is an important parameter when calculating the number of trunks required to carry a particular quantity of voice traffic.

As an example, a GoS of P(.01) means that one call is blocked in 100 call attempts, and a GoS of P(.001) means that one call is blocked in 1000 attempts.

Meeting the Current Network Objective

The first step to provision an appropriate number of trunks is to measure the level of voice and data traffic in the networks and set the objectives for throughput, delay (data traffic), and GoS (voice traffic). The next step is to determine whether you are meeting these objectives in the current network.

You might discover through your analysis of the voice and data networks that you are providing a poor GoS to your voice users, or that the throughput and delay are below the standards for your data users. Without recognizing these shortcomings, you might be inclined to plan a combined network on the assumption of business as usual. This assumption is a mistake. It creates the very real possibility that you will have an integrated voice and data network that will offer substandard quality as compared to the original network.

Ask two questions to determine if you are meeting current network objectives:

- Are the delay and throughput acceptable on the data network?
- Are you achieving your target GoS on the voice network?

If you conclude that your network performance is below objectives, add a factor to your current traffic analysis for excessive demand.

To understand how voice and data network demands relate to each other, first look at the relationship between the peak demands on each of the networks, as shown in Figure 5-20, if this information is available. It will give you some idea of what to expect later in this process, when you convert the number of voice trunks to bandwidth and add the voice bandwidth requirement to the data bandwidth requirement for the same period. Clearly, the peak bandwidth demand is less if the two network demands are out of phase with each other than if both peaks coincide.

Figure 5-20 *Network Demand*

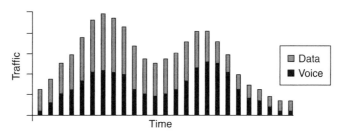

TIP   To best calculate the required bandwidth necessary to support demands, you need to understand peak usage times. Usually, networks exhibit peak demands early in the morning and just after the noon hour.

Traffic Theory

If you know the amount of traffic generated and the GoS required, you can calculate the number of trunks required to meet your needs. Use the following simple equation to calculate traffic flow:

$$A = C * T$$

In the equation, A is the offered traffic, C is the number of calls originating during a period of one hour, and T is the average holding time of a call.

It is important to note that C is the number of calls *originated*, not carried. Typically, the information received from the carrier or from the internal CDRs of the company is in terms of *carried* traffic. Information provided by PBXs is usually in terms of *offered* traffic.

The holding time of a call (T) must account for the average time a trunk is occupied and must factor in variables other than the length of a conversation. This includes the time required for dialing and ringing (call establishment), time to terminate the call, and a method of amortizing busy signals and noncompleted calls. Adding 10 to 16 percent to the length of an average call helps account for these miscellaneous time segments.

Hold times based on call billing records might have to be adjusted based on the increment of billing. Billing records based on one-minute increments are usually rounded up to the *next* minute, not rounded to the *nearest* minute. Consequently, billing records overstate calls by 30 seconds on average. For example, a bill showing 404 calls (C) totaling 1834 minutes of traffic (A) should be adjusted as follows:

> 404 calls * 0.5 minutes (overstated call length) = 202 excess call minutes
> Adjusted traffic (A): 1834 – 202 = 1632 actual call minutes

Another way to calculate this would be to use the formula A = C * T to derive the average holding time (T), reduce T by 0.5 minutes (the overstated amount), and recalculate the traffic offered (A).

Average holding time (T):
— T = 1834 minutes (A) / 404 calls (C)

— T = 4.54 minutes

Corrected holding time (T):
— T = 4.54 – 0.50

— T = 4.04 minutes

Adjusted traffic offered (A):
— A = 404 calls (C) * 4.04 minutes (T)

— A = 1632 call minutes

Busy Hour

It is important to look at call attempts during the busiest hour of the day, as shown in Figure 5-21. The most accurate method of finding the busiest hour is to take the ten busiest days in a year, sum the traffic on an hourly basis, find the busiest hour, and then derive the *busy hour traffic*.

As a shortcut, you can determine the amount of traffic that occurs in a day based on 22 business days in a month and then multiply that number by 15 to 17 percent. As a rule, the busy hour traffic represents 15 to 17 percent of the total traffic that occurs in one day. Assume that you have a trunk group that carries 66,000 minutes in one month or 3000 minutes per day on average (66,000/22). You might then estimate the busy hour traffic by calculating 15 percent of the average daily traffic, or 3000 * 15% = 450 minutes.

Figure 5-21 *Busy Hour*

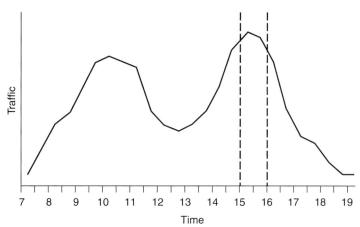

Erlangs

The traffic volume in telephone engineering is measured in units called *Erlangs*. An Erlang is the amount of traffic one trunk can handle in one hour. It is a nondimensional unit that has many functions. Other equivalent measurements that you might encounter include the following:

1 Erlang = 60 call minutes = 3600 call seconds = 36 centum call seconds (CCS)

Consider an example where, on average, each user in a branch makes 10 calls with an average duration of 5 minutes during the busy hour. If the branch has 25 employees, the total minutes of call time during the busy hour is 10 calls per busy hour multiplied by 5 minutes per call multiplied by 25 employees per branch. The result is 1250 total call minutes. To find the Erlangs, which is based on hours, divide 1250 by 60. This calculation yields 20.83 Erlangs.

Traffic Probability Assumptions

When you have determined the amount of traffic that occurs during the busy hour in Erlangs, you can determine the number of trunks required to meet a particular GoS. The number of trunks required differs, depending on these three traffic probability assumptions:

- **Number of potential sources**—There can be a major difference between planning for an infinite versus a small number of sources. As the number of sources increase, the probability of a wider distribution in the arrival times and holding times of calls increases. As the number of sources decrease, the ability to carry traffic increases.

- **Traffic arrival characteristics**—Usually, this assumption is based on a Poisson traffic distribution. This distribution was named after the mathematician who studied this concept extensively. Call arrivals follow a classic bell-shaped curve. You can commonly use Poisson distribution for infinite traffic sources. The arrival characteristics of traffic (calls) might be classified as random, smooth, or bursty.

- **Treatment of lost calls**—What do you do when the station you are calling does not answer or all trunks are busy? Traffic theory considers three possibilities:

  - **Lost calls cleared (LCC)**—LCC assumes that once a call is placed and the server (network) is busy or not available, the call disappears from the system. In essence, you give up and do something different.

  - **Lost calls held (LCH)**—LCH assumes that a call is in the system for the duration of the hold time, regardless of whether the call is placed. In essence, you continue to redial for as long as the hold time before giving up. Redialing is an important traffic consideration. Suppose 200 calls are attempted. Forty receive busy signals and attempt to redial. That results in 240 call attempts, a 20 percent increase. The trunk group is now providing an even poorer GoS than initially thought.

  - **Lost calls delayed (LCD)**—LCD means that when a call is placed, it remains in a queue until a server is ready to handle the call. Then it uses the server for the full holding time. This assumption is most commonly used for automatic call distribution (ACD) systems.

NOTE   LCC tends to understate the number of trunks that are required; on the other hand, LCH overstates the number of trunks that are required.

Random arrivals are common with a large or infinite source of users whose calls are independent of each other. Assuming random arrivals, the probability of calls arriving during any particular time interval, such as the busy hour, is modeled by a Poisson distribution. Given the average number of calls per busy hour and the distribution of call-holding times, the Poisson distribution predicts the probability of zero calls, one call, two calls, and so on, up to the probability of a large number of calls arriving during the hour.

The characteristic bell shape of the distribution suggests that the probability of few calls is low, as is the probability of a high number of calls. The peak probability represents the average. For example, if you calculated the average number of calls during the busy hour to be 250, the Poisson distribution estimates the probability that you will receive 0 calls (very low probability), 100 calls (modest probability), 250 calls (the average, which is peak probability), 900 calls (very low probability), or any other number of calls.

Smooth traffic arrivals are common in applications in which the traffic is dependent on other traffic, as in a telemarketing scenario. Due to their nonrandom nature, smooth traffic arrivals are not modeled on the Poisson distribution.

Bursty traffic arrivals are common in trunk overflow scenarios in which excess overflow tends to occur for a short time and then disappears for an extended period of time. Therefore, bursty traffic is not modeled on the Poisson distribution because of its nonrandom nature.

Traffic Calculations

The purpose of traffic calculations is to determine the number of physical trunks that are required. After you have determined the amount of offered traffic during the busy hour, established the target GoS, and recognized the three basic assumptions, you can calculate the number of trunks that are required by using formulas or tables.

Traffic theory consists of many queuing methods and associated formulas. Anyone who has taken a queuing theory class can testify to the complexity of the many queuing models that are derived for various situations. This is the reason why tables dealing with the most commonly encountered model are used.

The most commonly used model and table is Erlang B, as shown in Table 5-11. Erlang B is based on infinite sources, LCC, and a Poisson distribution that is appropriate for either exponential or constant holding times. In general, Erlang B understates the number of trunks because of the LCC assumption. However, Erlang B is the most commonly used algorithm.

A trunk group is a hunt group of parallel trunks. The following example determines the number of trunks in a trunk group carrying the following traffic:

- 352 hours of offered call traffic in a month
- 22 business days per month
- 10 percent call-processing overhead
- 15 percent of the traffic occurring in the busy hour
- GoS = P(.01)
- Busy hour = 352 / 22 * .15 * 1.10 (call-processing overhead) = 2.64 Erlangs

The traffic assumptions are:

- Infinite sources.
- Random or Poisson traffic distribution.
- Lost calls are cleared.

Table 5-11 *Erlang B Table*

Trunks	Probability of a Lost Call					
	0.003	0.005	0.01	0.02	0.03	0.05
1	0.003	0.005	0.011	0.021	0.031	0.053
2	0.081	0.106	0.153	0.224	0.282	0.382
3	0.289	0.349	0.456	0.603	0.716	0.900
4	0.602	0.702	0.870	1.093	1.259	1.525
5	0.995	1.132	1.361	1.658	1.876	2.219
6	1.447	1.622	1.909	2.276	2.543	2.961
7	1.947	2.158	2.501	2.936	3.250	3.738
8	2.484	2.730	3.128	3.627	3.987	4.543
9	3.053	3.333	3.783	4.345	4.748	5.371
10	3.648	3.961	4.462	5.084	5.530	6.216
11	4.267	4.611	5.160	5.842	6.328	7.077
12	4.904	5.279	5.876	6.615	7.141	7.950
13	5.559	5.964	6.608	7.402	7.967	8.835
14	6.229	6.664	7.352	8.201	8.804	9.730
15	6.913	7.376	8.108	9.010	9.650	10.630

Based on these assumptions, the appropriate algorithm to use is Erlang B. You can use Table 5-11 to determine the appropriate number of trunks for a GoS of P(.01).

Because a GoS of P(.01) is required, you use the column that is designated as P(.01) only. The calculations indicate a busy hour traffic amount of 2.64 Erlangs, which is between 2.501 and 3.128 in the P(.01) column. This corresponds to between seven and eight trunks. Because you cannot use a fractional trunk, you use the next larger value of eight trunks to carry the traffic.

Instead of using an Erlang B table, such as Table 5-11, you could alternatively use a web-based calculator, such as the one found at http://erlang.com/calculator/erlb. This calculator, as shown in Figure 5-22, allows you to enter your Erlang value in the BHT (that is, Busy Hour Traffic) field and your GoS value in the Blocking field.

Figure 5-22 *Erlang B Calculator – Inputting Busy Hour Traffic*

You can then click on the **Calc.** button, and the calculator displays the number of trunks needed to support the specified call volume, as shown in Figure 5-23. In this example, eight trunks are required for an Erlang value of 2.64 and a GoS value of 0.010, just as previously determined from the Erlang B table shown in Table 5-11.

Figure 5-23 *Erlang B Calculator – Calculating Lines*

Call Density Matrix

Unless your voice network is extremely small (two locations, for example), calculating the trunk requirements between any two points in a network is a tedious task. One way to manage this more effectively is to design a to/from traffic matrix.

As you determine the call minutes between any two points, you enter the amount into the matrix. If you do this on a spreadsheet, you can convert the minutes to busy hour minutes, to Erlangs, and then calculate the number of trunks from the Erlangs. The number of trunks represents the number of concurrent calls you should plan to support during the busy hour.

As an example of a call density matrix, Figure 5-24 shows a progression of spreadsheets for a network with one headquarters and three branches.

Figure 5-24 *Call Density*

Minutes (BH)	Headquarters	Branch 1	Branch 2
Branch 1	450		
Branch 2	396	268	
Branch 3	427	147	196

Erlangs	Headquarters	Branch 1	Branch 2
Branch 1	7.50		
Branch 2	6.60	4.47	
Branch 3	7.12	2.45	3.27

Trunks (P.01)	Headquarters	Branch 1	Branch 2
Branch 1	15		
Branch 2	13	10	
Branch 3	14	7	9

Bandwidth Calculations

If you are provisioning a circuit-switched voice network, you should estimate how much traffic each of your trunks is expected to carry. Then investigate the most cost-effective way to provision each of the trunks.

For this discussion, assume that all voice traffic is transported over the IP network. This approach will preclude the need to go through the rigors of choosing the most cost-effective solution for each individual trunk.

At this stage, the goal is to determine the IP bandwidth using the following steps:

Step 1.   Estimate the VoIP bandwidth required for different CODECs and over different data links. Also calculate the benefit of RTP header compression (Compressed Real-Time Transport Protocol [cRTP]). These estimates of bandwidth for VoIP are shown in Table 5-9, which was presented earlier in this chapter in the section "Calculating the Total Bandwidth for a VoIP Call."

Step 2.   Identify the number of concurrent calls that you expect during the busy hour between points in the network. Then, simply multiply the number of concurrent calls by the bandwidth per call.

You might want to consider some refinements to this simple multiplier. Consider the net benefits of bandwidth-reduction strategies, such as voice activity detection (VAD). VAD commonly reduces the bandwidth to between 60 and 70 percent of the original bandwidth. Just keep in mind that two animated talkers might not allow VAD to have any effect at all.

Finally, remember to combine the budget for data applications with the bandwidth budget for voice.

Now that you have the total bandwidth budget, you are ready to ensure that you do not overload the data links. However, on any network, as load approaches middle percentages, drops and delay exponentially increase. When designing networks to carry voice and data, peak bandwidth calculations should *not* equate to total bandwidth required for a given network link. For most business environments, you can use any of the following load levels as general rules for determining when a network is approaching excessive load:

- 20 percent of full capacity averaged over an 8-hour work day

- 30 percent averaged over the worst hour of the day

- 50 percent averaged over the worst 15 minutes of the day

Capacity planning should take these factors into account, and link speed should be chosen to accommodate the proper load factors. An ideal goal is to have demand equal to about 35 percent of the total link speed.

To put these rules into the context of the example, Figure 5-25 shows a demand for 416 kbps between headquarters and branch 1 during the busiest hour of the day. Using the rules, the average demand during the worst hour should represent only 30 percent of the link speed. If 30 percent of the link speed is 416 kbps, then the link speed must be 1387 kbps or greater.

Figure 5-25 *Bandwidth Example*

Voice Bandwidth (kbps)	Headquarters	Branch 1	Branch 2
Branch 1	168		
Branch 2	145.6	112	
Branch 3	156.8	78.4	100.8

+

Data Bandwidth (kbps)	Headquarters	Branch 1	Branch 2
Branch 1	248		
Branch 2	216	63	
Branch 3	187	28	46

=

Total Bandwidth (kbps)	Headquarters	Branch 1	Branch 2
Branch 1	416		
Branch 2	361.6	175	
Branch 3	343.8	106.4	146.8

Based on the traffic in your network, you might justify aiming for a higher utilization of the links, but expecting full utilization is unrealistic. Setting too high a value results in low throughput and high delay for data traffic. Although voice is prioritized so that it is not delayed, you need to determine, through experience, a utilization factor that balances throughput and delay with cost.

Practice Scenario 6: Calculating Bandwidth

Span Engineering LLC is assessing bandwidth requirements for the WAN connection between the Chicago Cicero campus and the Dallas campus, as shown in Figure 5-26. The traffic statistics and requirements for this topology are:

- 50 concurrent calls during busy hour
- G.729 using a 20-byte sample size
- Frame Relay with cRTP
- 10 percent call-processing overhead
- 30 percent bandwidth savings using VAD
- 2 Mbps requirement for data

Based on the Figure 5-26 and the preceding requirements, determine the bandwidth requirements for the Cicero-Dallas connection.

Figure 5-26 *Practice Item: Bandwidth Calculation*

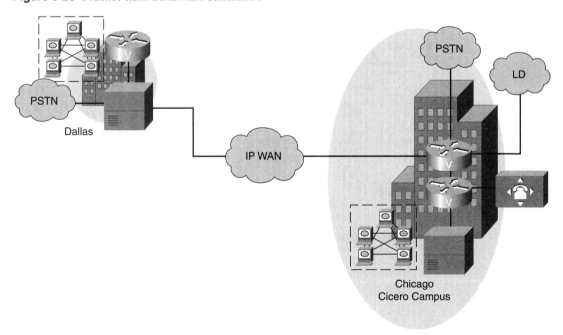

Call statistics obtained from the PBXs and the PSTN carrier show that traffic patterns during the busy hour require support for 50 concurrent calls between Cicero and Dallas.

Design specifications for the Cicero-Dallas connection are as follows:

- All calls traversing the WAN must be compressed to conserve bandwidth and keep connection costs to a minimum.
- Calls traversing the WAN should be configured to use the G.729 CODEC with a 20-byte sample size.
- Calls traversing the WAN should be configured to use VAD. It is estimated that the use of VAD will save 30 percent of calculated voice bandwidth.
- The connection will be Frame Relay between Cicero and Dallas.
- The connection must have RTP header compression enabled.
- It is estimated that there will be 10 percent overhead for call processing.
- The bandwidth requirement for data is 2 Mbps.

Table 5-12 provides per-call bandwidth requirement calculations for a selection of CODECs and connection types.

Table 5-12   *Per-Call Bandwidth Calculation Table*

CODEC	CODEC Speed (bps)	Sample Size (Bytes)	Frame Relay (bps)	Frame Relay with cRTP (bps)	Ethernet (bps)
G.711	64,000	240	76,267	66,133	79,467
G.711	64,000	160	82,400	67,200	87,200
G.726r32	32,000	120	44,267	34,133	47,467
G.726r32	32,000	80	50,400	35,200	55,200
G.726r24	24,000	80	37,800	26,400	41,400
G.726r24	24,000	60	42,400	27,200	47,200
G.726r16	16,000	80	25,200	17,600	27,600
G.726r16	16,000	40	34,400	19,200	39,200
G.728	16,000	80	25,200	17,600	27,600
G.728	16,000	40	34,400	19,200	39,200
G.729	8000	40	17,200	9600	19,600
G.729	8000	20	26,400	11,200	31,200
G.723r63	6300	48	12,338	7350	13,913
G.723r63	6300	24	18,375	8400	21,525
G.723r53	5300	40	11,395	6360	12,985
G.723r53	5300	20	17,490	7420	20,670

Use the information in Table 5-12 to calculate the following total bandwidth requirements:

1. Calculate the total bandwidth required for the expected concurrent call volume.

   _____

2. Calculate the total bandwidth required, including bandwidth needed for call-processing adjustment.

   _____

3. Calculate the total bandwidth required, reflecting VAD savings.

   _____

4. Calculate the total bandwidth required for both voice and data for the Frame Relay connection.

   _____

5. Calculate the total bandwidth required for both voice and data for the Frame Relay connection.

   _____

Practice Scenario 6: Solutions

1. Calculate the total bandwidth required for the expected concurrent call volume.

   For 50 concurrent calls, use G.729 for Frame Relay with cRTP: 50 * 11,200 = 560,000 (560 kbps)

2. Calculate the total bandwidth required, including bandwidth needed for call-processing adjustment.

   Add call-processing overhead of 10 percent: 560,000 * 1.1 = 616,000 (616 kbps)

3. Calculate the total bandwidth required, reflecting VAD savings.

   Adjust for VAD bandwidth savings of 30 percent: 616,000 – (.30 * 616,000) = 616,000 – 184,800 = 431,200 (431.2 kbps)

4. Calculate the total bandwidth required for both voice and data for the Frame Relay connection.

   Add data bandwidth requirements: 431,200 + 2,000,000 = 2,431,200 (2.43 Mbps)

Security Implications of VoIP Networks

Security is a top priority in most networks. Security solutions include router access lists, stateful firewalls, and VPNs. These solutions might be stand-alone or layered. Implementing voice in a secure network environment requires an understanding of potential issues and threats. It also requires an in-depth knowledge of existing security measures and how these measures affect the transit of voice through the network. This section describes the implications of implementing security measures in VoIP networks.

Security Policies for VoIP Networks

Numerous problems, from device failures to malicious attacks, affect the uptime of networks. With VoIP's reliance on the IP network, IP-based threats must be mitigated. Varying levels of security are available to suit individual corporate requirements. The requirements for secured IP telephony include the following:

- Provide ubiquitous IP telephony services to the locations and to the users that require them.

- Maintain as many of the characteristics of traditional telephony as possible without compromising security.

- Integrate with existing security architectures without interfering with existing functions.

The starting point for any security implementation is the development of a *security policy*. In a converged network, the security policy accounts for the impact of security measures on voice traffic. The security policy should address the following points that affect voice:

- **Transport security**—Traffic traversing public access and backbone networks must be properly secured. IP Security (IPSec) and VPNs provide transport security by ensuring data confidentiality (using encryption), data integrity, and data authentication between participating peers. Encryption adds to overhead and delays a voice packet. Therefore, you should factor in encryption when testing the delay budget and bandwidth calculations.

- **Network security**—Cisco firewalls provide stateful perimeter security that is critical to any public-facing network, such as a VPN. When deploying voice and video across VPNs, it is critical to statefully inspect all multiservice traffic traversing the firewall. Firewalls should be configured to allow known signal and payload ports to pass into the network. Designers should also understand where the VPN terminates. If the VPN terminates inside the firewall, then the traffic passing through the firewall is encrypted and is subject to stateful inspection. If the VPN terminates outside the firewall, then the firewall has access to RTP, UDP, TCP, or IP headers and is able to inspect the packet for call setup.

• **Intrusion detection**—The Cisco Security Agent (CSA) provides threat protection for server and desktop computing systems, also known as endpoints. CSA identifies and prevents malicious behavior. This eliminates known and unknown security risks and helps to reduce operational costs. CSA, by itself, aggregates and extends multiple endpoint security functions by providing host intrusion prevention, distributed firewall capabilities, malicious mobile code protection, operating system integrity assurance, and audit log consolidation. In addition, because CSA analyzes behavior rather than relying on signature matching, it reduces operational costs.

Figure 5-27 shows an example of network security, where the network between the branch office and the headquarters has a firewall. The firewall allows the users from the branch office to access only the headquarters network. A user without proper network identification will not be allowed to pass through the firewall. Network identification therefore protects voice networks from hackers.

Figure 5-27 *Network Security*

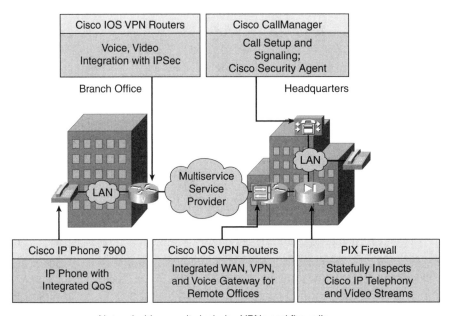

Networkwide security includes VPNs and firewalls.

Unfortunately, the security model chosen for VoIP networks today often mirrors the model chosen for legacy voice systems, which are generally wide open and require little or no authentication to gain access.

Threats to VoIP

Numerous threats to VoIP networks exist, and many of these are similar to threats facing traditional PBX systems. VoIP network threats include:

- **Theft and toll fraud**—Toll fraud is the theft of long-distance telephone service by unauthorized access to a PSTN trunk (that is, an "outside line") on a PBX or voice mail system. Toll fraud is a multibillion-dollar illegal industry, and all organizations are vulnerable. Theft can also be defined as the use of the telephony system, by both authorized and unauthorized users, using voice-network resources to access unauthorized numbers, such as 900 billable numbers.

- **Unauthorized access to voice resources**—Hackers can tamper with voice systems, user identities, and telephone configurations and also intercept voice mail messages. If hackers gain access to the voice mail system, they can change the voice mail greeting, which negatively impacts the image and reputation of the company. A hacker who gains access to the PBX or voice gateway could potentially shut down voice ports or change voice-routing parameters, affecting voice access into and through the network.

- **Compromise of network resources**—The goal of a secure network is to ensure that applications, processes, and users can reliably and securely interoperate using the shared network resources. Because the shared network infrastructure carries both voice and data, security and access to the network infrastructure is critical in securing voice functions. Because VoIP systems are installed on a data network, they are potential targets for hackers who previously targeted only PCs, servers, and data applications. Hackers are aided in their search for vulnerabilities in VoIP systems by the open and well-known standards and protocols used by IP networks.

- **Denial-of-service (DoS) attacks**—DoS attacks are defined as the malicious attacking or overloading of call-processing equipment to deny access to services by legitimate users. Most DoS attacks fall into one of the following categories:

  - **Network resource overload**—Overloading a network resource that is required for proper functioning of a service. The targeted network resource is most often bandwidth. The DoS attack uses up all available bandwidth, preventing authorized users from accessing the required services.

  - **Host resource starvation**—Using up critical host resources. When use of these resources is maximized by the DoS attack, the server can no longer respond to legitimate service requests.

  - **Out-of-bounds attack**—Using illegal packet structure and unexpected data, which can cause the operating system of the remote system to crash. One example of this type of attack might be to use illegal combinations of TCP flags. Most TCP/IP stacks are developed to respond to appropriate use. They are not developed for anomalies. When the stack receives illegal data, it might not know how to handle the packet and might cause a system crash.

- **Eavesdropping**—Eavesdropping involves the unauthorized interception of voice packets (that is, RTP media streams). Eavesdropping can expose confidential or proprietary information that is obtained by intercepting and reassembling packets in a voice stream. Numerous tools are used by hackers to eavesdrop.

Secure LAN Design

Many IP security solutions can be implemented only on Layer 3 (IP) devices. Because of protocol architecture, the MAC layer, Layer 2, offers very little or no inherent security. Understanding and establishing broadcast domains is one of the fundamental precepts in designing secure IP networks. Many simple yet dangerous attacks can be launched if the attacking device resides within the same broadcast domain as the target system.

IP phones, VoIP gateways, and network-management workstations should typically be on their own subnet, separate from the rest of the data network and from each other.

To ensure communications privacy and integrity, voice-media streams should be protected from eavesdropping and tampering. Data networking technologies, such as VLANs, can segment voice traffic from data traffic, preventing access to the voice VLAN from the data VLAN. Using separate VLANs for voice and data in a switched Ethernet infrastructure, as shown in Figure 5-28, prevents any attacker or attacking application from snooping or capturing traffic from other VLANs as it traverses the physical wire. By making sure that each device connects to the network using a switched infrastructure, you can render packet-sniffing tools less effective for capturing user traffic. Notice that an IEEE 802.1Q trunk is set up between the IP phone and the Catalyst switch. The 802.1Q trunk allows traffic from both the voice and data VLANs to flow over a single physical link.

Figure 5-28 *Secure LAN Design*

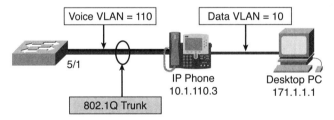

Assigning voice traffic to a specific VLAN, thereby logically segmenting voice and data traffic, is an industry-wide accepted best practice. As much as possible, devices identified as voice devices should be restricted to dedicated voice VLANs. This approach ensures that they can communicate only with other voice resources. More importantly, voice traffic is kept away from the general data network where it might more easily be intercepted or tampered with.

Communicating Through a Firewall

Firewalls inspect packets and match them against configured rules. It is difficult to specify ahead of time which ports will be used in a voice call because they are dynamically negotiated during call setup.

H.323 is a complex, dynamic protocol that consists of several interrelated subprotocols. The ports and addresses used with H.323 require detailed inspection as call setup progresses. As the dynamic ports are negotiated, the firewall must maintain a table of current ports associated with the H.323 protocol. As calls are torn down, the firewall must remove those ports from the table. The process of adding and removing ports from the table is called *stateful inspection of packets*. In addition to checking static ports and recognizing protocols that negotiate dynamic ports as in H.323, the firewall looks into the packets of that protocol to track the flows.

Any application might use a port in the range of 1024 to 65536. In Figure 5-29, the firewall initially blocks all packets destined for UDP port 16384. The firewall becomes H.323-aware when it is configured to look for TCP port 1720 for call setup and UDP port assignments.

Figure 5-29 *Firewall Access*

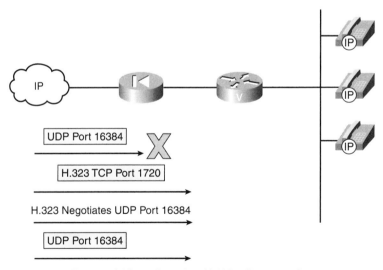

The stateful firewall watches H.323 call setup and
allows negotiated ports to pass.

Table 5-13 illustrates the dynamic access control process used by firewalls.

Table 5-13 *Dynamic Access Control*

Stage	What Happens
The firewall detects a new call setup destined for UDP port 16384.	The firewall places the port, the associated source, and the destination IP address into the table.
The firewall opens port 16384.	The firewall allows all packets with UDP port 16384 and the proper source/destination IP address through the firewall.
The firewall detects call teardown.	The firewall removes the port from the list, and the packets destined for the UDP port are blocked.

If the firewall does not support this dynamic access control based on inspection, an H.323 proxy can be used. An H.323 proxy passes all H.323 flows to the firewall with the appearance of a single static source IP address plus a TCP/UDP port number. The firewall can then be configured to allow that static address to pass through.

Firewalls can introduce variable delay into the path of the voice packet. Therefore, it is extremely important that you ensure that the firewall has the proper resources (that is, processor and memory resources) to handle the load.

Table 5-14 lists the ports used for various voice protocols.

Table 5-14 *Voice Protocol Ports*

Protocol	Ports	TCP/UDP	Description
H.323	1718	UDP	Gatekeeper discovery
H.323	1719	UDP	Gatekeeper registration
H.323 (H.225)	1720	TCP	Call setup
MGCP (Media Gateway Control Protocol)	2427, 2727	UDP	MGCP gateway, MGCP call agent
SIP (session initiation protocol)	5000	TCP or UDP	SIP call
Skinny	2000	TCP	Client
Skinny	2001	TCP	Digital gateway
Skinny	2002	TCP	Analog gateway
Skinny	2003	TCP	Conference bridge

Delivering VoIP over a VPN

VPNs, as depicted in Figure 5-30, are widely used to provide secure connections to the corporate network. The connections can originate from a branch office, a small office/home office (SOHO), a telecommuter, or a roaming user.

Figure 5-30 *Virtual Private Networks*

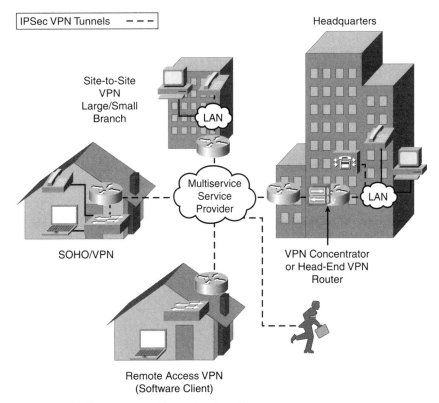

Frequently asked questions about voice over VPN generally deal with overhead and delay, which impact the quality of service (QoS) for the call.

NOTE   One important consideration to remember is the absence of QoS when deploying VPNs across the Internet or a public network. Where possible, QoS should be addressed with the provider through a service-level agreement (SLA). An SLA is a document that details the expected QoS parameters for packets transiting the provider's network.

Voice communications do not work well with latency, not even a modest amount of it. Because secure VPNs encrypt data, they might create a throughput bottleneck when they process packets through their encryption algorithm. The problem usually gets worse as security increases. For example, Triple Data Encryption Standard (3DES) uses a long, 168-bit key. 3DES requires that each packet be encrypted three times, effectively tripling the encryption overhead. Approaches to reduce the overhead and delay introduced by VPNs include:

- Optimize the encryption algorithm and data path.
- Handle all processing in a dedicated encryption processor.
- Ensure that the device uses hardware encryption instead of software encryption.
- Use proper QoS techniques.
- Use proper VPN technologies.

VoIP can be secure and free of perceptible latency on a VPN. The solution is to optimize the encryption algorithm and the data path and to handle all processing in a dedicated encryption processor. You should ensure that the device is utilizing hardware encryption instead of software encryption. Software encryption relies on CPU resources and could severely impact voice quality.

Delay can be further minimized through the use of proper QoS techniques. QoS and bandwidth management features allow a VPN to deliver high transmission quality for time-sensitive applications, such as voice or video. Each packet is tagged to identify the priority and time sensitivity of its payload, and traffic is sorted and routed based on its delivery priority. Cisco VPN solutions support a wide range of QoS features.

Designers need to understand that QoS cannot be completely controlled, independent of the underlying network. QoS is only as good as the network through which the voice travels. Users must confirm with a potential service provider that the network can support priority services over a VPN. Specifically, SLAs with carriers can guarantee expectations of network stability and QoS.

You can minimize overhead if you understand the proper use of VPN technologies. You can implement VPNs at Layer 2 through Point-to-Point Tunneling Protocol (PPTP) or Layer 2 Tunneling Protocol (L2TP), as well as at Layer 3 with IPSec. Often Layer 2 and Layer 3 technologies are combined to provide additional security. It is crucial that you understand the reasoning and requirements behind combining Layer 2 with Layer 3 security, because the combination adds overhead to the VoIP packet.

International Issues

VoIP and either Data Encryption Standard (DES) or 3DES encryptions are fully compatible with each other as long as the VPN delivers the necessary throughput. Internationally, corporations can run into other factors. The U.S. Department of Commerce places restrictions on the export of certain encryption technology. Usually, DES is exportable while 3DES is not, but that generality takes numerous forms, from total export exclusions applied to certain countries to allowing 3DES export to specific industries and users. Most corporations whose VPNs extend outside the United States should find out if their VPN provider has exportable products and how export regulations impact networks built with those products.

Bandwidth Overhead Associated with VPN

VPN implementations vary, and there are many options to explore. IPSec is the predominant VPN in use today. Figure 5-31 shows the IPSec header. Generally speaking, IPSec encrypts or authenticates the IP packet and adds additional headers to carry the VPN information. The VPN places the original IP packet into another IP packet so that the original information, including headers, is not easily seen or read.

Figure 5-31 *VPN Overhead: IPSec Example*

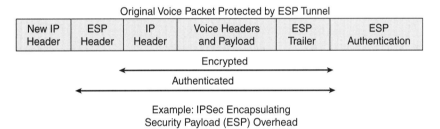

To properly calculate bandwidth overhead, the user must have a thorough understanding of the VPN technology by asking the following questions:

- Should the VPN be a Layer 2 tunnel running PPTP or L2TP?
- Should the VPN be a Layer 3 tunnel running IPSec?
- If the VPN is IPSec, is it using Authentication Header (AH) or Encapsulating Security Payload (ESP)?
- If the VPN is running AH or ESP, is it in transport mode or tunnel mode?

NOTE   Although the discussion of VPN technology is beyond the scope of this book, *Comparing, Designing, and Deploying VPNs* (ISBN 1587051796) from Cisco Press can help clarify these concepts.

Calculating VPN Bandwidth

The VPN adds a new IP header that is 20 bytes, plus the VPN header, which can add as much as 20 to 60 additional bytes, depending on which variation of VPN is installed. Table 5-15 shows what a complete VPN packet can look like.

Table 5-15 *VPN Packet Overhead*

Field	Subhead
Voice payload (G.729)	20 bytes
RTP header	12 bytes
UDP header	8 bytes
IP header	20 bytes
VPN header	20 to 60 bytes
New IP header	20 bytes

The total size of the packet will be 100 to 160 bytes.

To calculate the total bandwidth for a 160-byte G.729 packet, use the following calculations:

160 bytes * 8 = 1280 bits
Total bandwidth = 1280 bits / 20 ms
Total bandwidth = 64,000 bps

Practice Scenario 7: Span Engineering VoIP Network Security Components

Span Engineering LLC is defining its security infrastructure for the VoIP network. Figure 5-32 identifies various components that will provide networkwide security for Span Engineering voice transmissions.

Your task is to identify the benefits associated with each security component:

1. Separate voice and data VLANs:

_____

_____

_____

Figure 5-32 *Span Engineering VoIP Network Security Components*

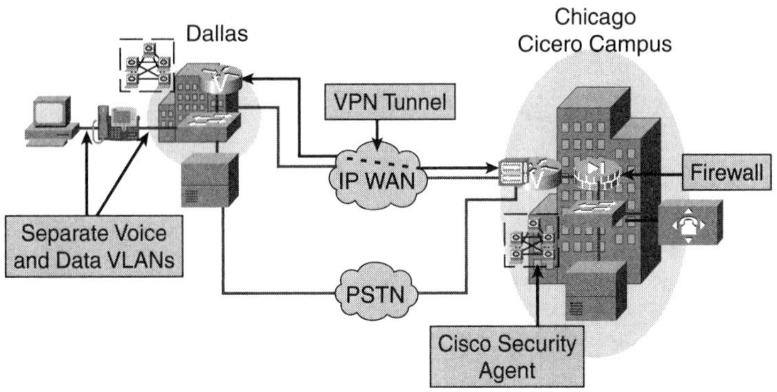

2. VPN connectivity between sites:

_____

3. Stateful firewall:

_____

_____

_____

4. Cisco Security Agent:

_____

_____

Practice Scenario 7: Solutions

1. Separate voice and data VLANs:

   Separate VLANs create separate broadcast domains.

   Separate VLANs protect against eavesdropping and tampering.

   Separate VLANs render packet-sniffing tools less effective.

2. VPN connectivity between sites:

   Voice packets are encrypted when they traverse the WAN.

3. Stateful firewalls:

   Stateful firewalls inspect packets and match them against a set of rules.

   Stateful firewalls watch call-setup packets and let negotiated ports pass through.

   Stateful firewalls tear down access to negotiated ports when the call is terminated.

4. Cisco Security Agent:

CSA provides intrusion detection for the network.

CSA identifies and prevents malicious behavior.

Summary

VoIP networks leverage multiple protocols, and this chapter introduced such protocols as H.323, MGCP, SIP, RTP, and RTCP. VoIP components can be deployed using one of several call-processing models, such as a centralized call-processing model, where a cluster of Cisco CallManager servers reside at a central location with remote IP phones registering with the CallManager cluster over the IP WAN. Conversely, a distributed call-processing model might have a Cisco CallManager cluster at each geographic location.

A VoIP network's scalability depends on a scalable dial plan design. This chapter examined various dial plan considerations and discussed how the North American Numbering Plan (NANP) might be adapted to a corporate environment.

When voice traffic is added to an existing IP WAN link, previously only being used for data, a designer must provision sufficient bandwidth to support anticipated call volumes. This chapter delved into the mathematics of calculating the amount of bandwidth required to support a voice call.

This chapter also covered the fundamentals of *traffic engineering*, the science of calculating the number of trunks required to support a certain percentage of calls during the busiest hour of the day for a phone system. In the VoIP world, traffic engineering goes a step further by equating a number of trunks with a bandwidth amount.

Finally, this chapter explored security issues surrounding VoIP networks. For example, existing firewalls might inadvertently block ports required for call setup. Also, while VPN networks enhance the security of VoIP sessions, VPN technologies add overhead to each packet. This chapter described how to account for this extra overhead and how to allow appropriate traffic through a firewall.

Chapter Review Questions

The following questions test your knowledge of topics explained in this chapter. You can find the answers to the questions in Appendix A, "Answers to Chapter Review Questions."

1. Which two functions does a gateway provide?

   a VLAN separation

   b Translation between the VoIP and PSTN network

   c Physical access for analog telephones and fax machines

d Power over Ethernet to the IP phone

e Database services

2. Which protocol provides out-of-band control information for RTP-based call flows?

a H.225 RAS

b RTP

c SNMP

d RTCP

3. A company has four sites and wants to implement VoIP at all of them. The requirements include implementing gateway devices with no call-processing intelligence at the remote sites, controlling all call traffic from the headquarters location, and having a single point of CAC. Which network architecture is appropriate to meet these requirements?

a Single-site architecture

b Distributed architecture

c Centralized architecture

d H.323 gateway architecture

4. In which of the following situations would a gateway be required?

a Cisco CallManager-to-IP network connection

b PBX-to-voice mail connection

c Key system-to-IP network connection

d PBX-to-PBX connection

5. Which function best describes a numbering plan?

a Determines routes between source and destination

b Defines a telephone number of a voice endpoint or application

c Performs digit manipulation when sending calls to the PSTN

d Performs least-cost routing for VoIP calls

6. Which worldwide prefix scheme was developed by the ITU to standardize numbering plans?

   a   G.114

   b   E.164

   c   G.164

   d   E.114

7. Which three factors must be considered when calculating the total bandwidth of a VoIP call?

   a   CODEC size

   b   CRC usage

   c   Network-link overhead

   d   Sample size

   e   Capacity of network links

8. What is the overhead for Frame Relay?

   a   3 bytes

   b   5 bytes

   c   6 bytes

   d   18 bytes

9. What is the equivalent of one Erlang?

   a   60 call seconds

   b   36 centum call seconds

   c   3600 centum call seconds

   d   1 minute

10. Which feature provides transport security for a VoIP network?

   a   Encryption and data authentication

   b   Inspection of traffic at the firewall

    c Proactive notification of an attempted attack

    d Intrusion detection

Lab Exercise: RTP Header Compression

In this lab, you will configure routers R1 and R2, which are shown in Figure 5-33, for RTP header compression (cRTP) and compare bandwidth usage before and after enabling cRTP.

Figure 5-33 *Lab Topology*

Task 1: Change the Load Interval on Router R2's Serial Interface

When you issue the **show interfaces** command for a router's interface, many of the statistics shown are, by default, five-minute average values. In this lab you will view the *input rate* on one of router R2's serial interfaces, and to avoid having to wait the default *load interval* of 5 minutes, in this task you will set the load interval to its minimum value of 30 seconds.

Complete these steps:

Step 1. Enter serial interface configuration mode on router R2, for your serial interface that connects router R2 to router R1. For example, in the sample topology shown in Figure 5-33, you would enter interface configuration mode for R2's Serial 0/0 interface.

Step 2. Configure a load interval of 30 seconds with the **load-interval 30** command.

Step 3. Exit to privileged mode with the **end** command.

Task 2: Take a Baseline Measurement

In this task, you will determine the amount of bandwidth being consumed by a VoIP phone call, without cRTP.

Complete these steps:

Step 1. Place a call from extension 2222 to extension 1111.

Step 2. After answering the call, wait at least 30 seconds in order for the load interval to elapse.

Step 3. On router R2, use the **show interfaces** command for your interface that connects router R2 to router R1 (for example, interface Serial 0/0 in the topology shown).

Step 4. Note the value of the **30 second input rate** value.

Task 3: Enable cRTP

In this task, you will enable cRTP on routers R2 and R1.

Complete these steps:

Step 1. Enter interface configuration mode for R2's serial interface that connects to router R1.

Step 2. Enable cRTP for this interface, such that this interface will begin sending compressed RTP headers after it receives compressed RTP headers, using the **ip rtp header-compression passive** command.

Step 3. Enter interface configuration mode for R1's serial interface that connects to router R2.

Step 4. Enable cRTP for this interface, such that this interface sends compressed RTP headers, even though it might not yet have received a compressed RTP header, using the **ip rtp header-compression** command.

Task 4: Verify cRTP

In this task, you will measure the 30 second input rate of router R2's serial interface that you configured for cRTP in Task 3.

Complete these steps:

Step 1. Wait at least 30 seconds from the time you enabled cRTP on router R1 to allow sufficient time for the load interval to elapse.

Step 2. On router R2, issue the **show interfaces** command for the interface on which you enabled cRTP.

Step 3. Note the **30 second input rate** value. This value should be significantly lower than the rate measured in Task 2. The bandwidth savings you are witnessing is a result of enabling RTP header compression.

Suggested Solution

Although your physical hardware might differ, Examples 5-1, 5-2, and 5-3 offer one solution to the preceding exercise. Note from these examples that the 30 second input rate prior to implementing cRTP was 26 kbps, and that rate dropped to 10 kbps after enabling cRTP, resulting in significant bandwidth savings.

Example 5-1 *Router R2's Configuration and Bandwidth Utilization Prior to cRTP*

```
R2#configure terminal
R2(config)#interface serial 0/0
R2(config-if)#load-interval 30
R2(config-if)#end
R2#show interfaces serial 0/0
Serial0/0 is up, line protocol is up
  Hardware is PowerQUICC Serial
  Internet address is 10.1.1.1/24
  MTU 1500 bytes, BW 128 Kbit, DLY 20000 usec,
     reliability 255/255, txload 51/255, rxload 51/255
  Encapsulation PPP, LCP Open
  Open: CDPCP, IPCP, loopback not set
  Last input 00:00:00, output 00:00:00, output hang never
  Last clearing of "show interface" counters 00:26:55
  Input queue: 0/75/0/0 (size/max/drops/flushes); Total output drops: 0
  Queueing strategy: weighted fair
  Output queue: 0/1000/64/0 (size/max total/threshold/drops)
    Conversations  0/2/32 (active/max active/max total)
    Reserved Conversations 2/2 (allocated/max allocated)
    Available Bandwidth 0 kilobits/sec
  30 second input rate 26000 bits/sec, 51 packets/sec
  30 second output rate 26000 bits/sec, 51 packets/sec
    8206 packets input, 524947 bytes, 0 no buffer
    Received 0 broadcasts, 0 runts, 0 giants, 0 throttles
    0 input errors, 0 CRC, 0 frame, 0 overrun, 0 ignored, 0 abort
    8146 packets output, 524470 bytes, 0 underruns
    0 output errors, 0 collisions, 2 interface resets
    0 output buffer failures, 0 output buffers swapped out
    21 carrier transitions
    DCD=up  DSR=up  DTR=up  RTS=up  CTS=up
R2#configure terminal
R2(config)#interface serial 0/0
R2(config-if)#ip rtp header-compression passive
R2(config-if)#end
```

Example 5-2 *Router R1's cRTP Configuration*

```
R1#configure terminal
R1(config)#interface serial 0
R1(config-if)#ip rtp header-compression
R1(config-if)#end
```

Example 5-3 *Router R2 Bandwidth Utilization after Enabling cRTP*

```
R2#show interfaces serial 0/0
Serial0/0 is up, line protocol is up
  Hardware is PowerQUICC Serial
  Internet address is 10.1.1.1/24
  MTU 1500 bytes, BW 128 Kbit, DLY 20000 usec,
     reliability 255/255, txload 23/255, rxload 19/255
  Encapsulation PPP, LCP Open
  Open: CDPCP, IPCP, loopback not set
  Last input 00:00:00, output 00:00:00, output hang never
  Last clearing of "show interface" counters 00:30:39
  Input queue: 0/75/0/0 (size/max/drops/flushes); Total output drops: 0
  Queueing strategy: weighted fair
  Output queue: 0/1000/64/0 (size/max total/threshold/drops)
     Conversations  0/3/32 (active/max active/max total)
     Reserved Conversations 2/2 (allocated/max allocated)
     Available Bandwidth 0 kilobits/sec
  30 second input rate 10000 bits/sec, 52 packets/sec
  30 second output rate 12000 bits/sec, 52 packets/sec
     19775 packets input, 1018699 bytes, 0 no buffer
     Received 0 broadcasts, 0 runts, 0 giants, 0 throttles
     0 input errors, 0 CRC, 0 frame, 0 overrun, 0 ignored, 0 abort
     19681 packets output, 1024385 bytes, 0 underruns
     0 output errors, 0 collisions, 2 interface resets
     0 output buffer failures, 0 output buffers swapped out
     21 carrier transitions
     DCD=up  DSR=up  DTR=up  RTS=up  CTS=up
```

After reading this chapter, you should be able to perform the following tasks:

- Identify the appropriate call control model for your network.
- Describe how H.323 gateways and gatekeepers are used in VoIP networks.
- Configure, monitor, and troubleshoot H.323 gateways and gatekeepers.
- Configure, monitor, and troubleshoot SIP on a Cisco router.
- Configure, monitor, and troubleshoot MGCP on a Cisco router.

CHAPTER 6

VoIP Signaling and Call Control Protocols

Real-Time Transport Protocol (RTP) sessions provide voice communication over an IP network. These sessions are dynamically created and facilitated by one of several call control procedures. Typically, these procedures also embody mechanisms for signaling events during voice calls and for managing and collecting statistics about the voice calls. This chapter focuses on three protocols that offer call control support for VoIP:

- H.323
- Session initiation protocol (SIP)
- Media Gateway Control Protocol (MGCP)

First, you learn more about the benefits of signaling and call control.

The Need for Signaling and Call Control

Signaling and call control are fundamental to the call establishment, management, and administration of voice communication in an IP network. This section discusses the benefits of using signaling and call control and offers an overview of what signaling and call control services provide.

VoIP Signaling

In the traditional telephony network, a voice call consists of two paths:

- An audio path carrying the voice
- A signaling path carrying administrative information such as call setup, teardown messages, call status, and call-progress signals.

ISDN D-channel signaling and Common Channel Signaling System 7 (CCSS7) or Signaling System 7 (SS7) are examples of signaling systems that are used in traditional telephony.

By introducing VoIP into the call path, the end-to-end path involves at least one call leg that uses an IP internetwork. As in a traditional voice call, support for this VoIP call leg requires two paths:

- A protocol stack that includes RTP, which provides the audio call leg
- One or more call control models that provide the signaling path

A VoIP signaling and call control environment model includes endpoints and optional common control components, as described in the following sections.

Endpoints

Endpoints are typically simple, single-user devices, such as terminals, that support either a voice process (for example, the Cisco IP phone application) or a gateway. In either case, the endpoint must be able to participate in signaling with other VoIP endpoints, directly or indirectly, through common control components. The endpoints must also be able to manipulate the audio that is in the audio path. This might involve performing analog-to-digital conversion or converting the format to digital voice so that it takes advantage of compression technology.

Gateways provide physical or logical interfaces to the traditional telephone network. A gateway that is connected digitally to a service provider central office (CO) switch is an example of a gateway providing a physical interface. A gateway providing access to an interactive response dialog application is an example of a gateway providing a logical interface.

Common Control

In some call control models, the common control component is not defined. In others, it is employed optionally. Common control components provide call administration and accounting. These components provide a variety of services to support call establishment, including the following:

- Call status
- Address registration and resolution
- Admission control

Typically, the services of the common control components are implemented as applications. These services are collocated in a single physical device or distributed over several physical devices with stand-alone endpoints and gateways.

Call Control Models

Cisco and other vendors support a variety of call control protocols. While this chapter focuses on H.323, SIP, and MGCP, some of the industry's most popular call control protocols include the following:

- **H.323**—ITU-T Recommendation H.323 describes the architecture to support multimedia communications over networks without quality of service (QoS) guarantees. Originally intended for LANs, H.323 has been adapted for any IP network.

- **Session initiation protocol (SIP)**—SIP is an Internet Engineering Task Force (IETF) RFC 3261 call control model for creating, modifying, and terminating multimedia sessions or calls.

- **Media Gateway Control Protocol (MGCP)**—MGCP (IETF RFC 2705) defines a call control model that controls VoIP gateways from an external call control element or *call agent.*

- **H.248/Megaco Protocol**—The Megaco protocol is used in environments in which a media gateway consists of distributed subcomponents, and communication is required between the gateway subcomponents. The Megaco protocol is a joint effort of IETF (RFC 3015) and the ITU-T (Recommendation H.248).

- **Session Announcement Protocol (SAP)**—SAP (IETF RFC 2974) describes a multicast mechanism for advertising the session characteristics of a multimedia session, including audio and video.

- **Real-Time Streaming Protocol (RTSP)**—RTSP (IETF RFC 2326) describes a model for controlled, on-demand delivery of real-time audio and video.

- **Cisco Unified CallManager ("Skinny")**—Cisco Unified CallManager is a proprietary Cisco implementation of a call control environment that provides basic call processing, signaling, and connection services to configured devices, such as IP phones, VoIP gateways, and software applications.

In the traditional telephone network, the individual call legs contributing to an end-to-end call often involve different signaling systems and procedures. The following section describes call control translation.

Call Control Translation

In Figure 6-1, an IP phone is communicating with its SIP proxy server using SIP. However, the IP phone is also attempting to reach an H.323 endpoint. Because the two VoIP protocols are different, a translation is necessary at the SIP proxy server (namely, an H.323 gateway) to allow the two telephony endpoints to establish a connection.

Figure 6-1 *Translation Between Signaling and Call Control Protocols*

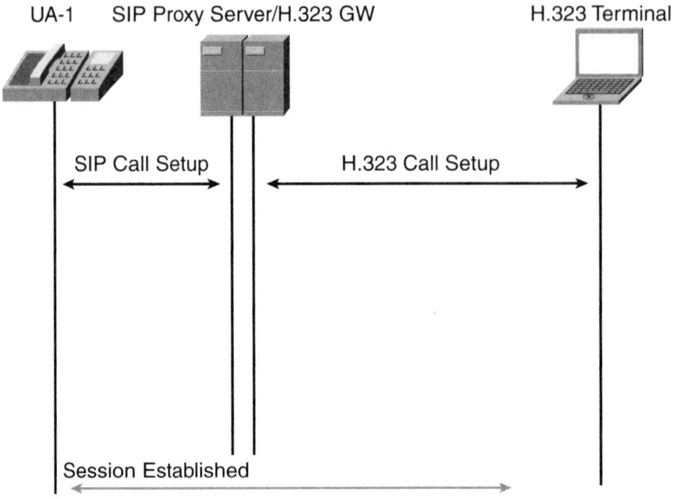

A call between a residential user and an office worker likely involves a signaling system that is unique to the various call legs that exist between the originator and the destination. In this scenario, the sequence of signaling systems includes the following:

- Analog signaling (Foreign Exchange Station [FXS] or Foreign Exchange Office [FXO] loop start) to the CO
- CCSS7 between the COs
- ISDN PRI signaling to the PBX
- Proprietary signaling to the desktop telephone

When part of the path is replaced with an IP internetwork, the audio path between the IP endpoints is provided by RTP, and the call control mechanism is based on a call control protocol, such as SIP, H.323, or MGCP.

But what if different call control models represent the endpoints? What if, for example, the originating endpoint uses H.323 and the destination is managed as an SIP endpoint? To complete calls across the IP internetwork, a call control gateway that recognizes the procedures of both call control models is required. Specifically, the translating gateway interprets the call setup procedure on the originating side and translates the request to the setup procedure on the destination side. Ideally, this translation is transparent to the endpoints that are involved and results in a single endpoint-to-endpoint audio relationship.

Call Setup

An audio path of a VoIP call leg is dependent on the creation of RTP sessions. These RTP sessions transport voice unidirectionally, so that bidirectional voice uses two RTP sessions. (In principle, if voice is needed in one direction only, as in the case of a recorded announcement or voice mail, only one RTP session is required.) Figure 6-2 shows RTP sessions being created during call setup.

Figure 6-2   *RTP Sessions*

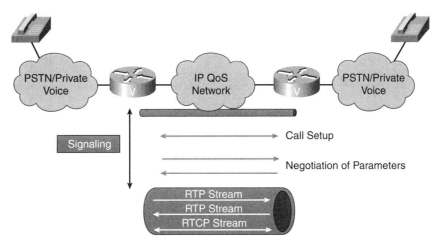

To create RTP sessions, each endpoint must recognize the IP address and User Datagram Protocol (UDP) port number of its peer. In a limited implementation of VoIP, these values are preprogrammed. However, to be truly scalable, the addresses and port numbers must be recognized dynamically and on demand.

NOTE   During call setup, call control procedures exchange the IP address and UDP port numbers for the RTP sessions.

Creating the RTP sessions is not the only task of call control during call setup. The endpoints need to establish a bilateral agreement in which the communicating parties discover acceptable call parameters and then agree on the operating parameters of the call, as depicted in Figure 6-3.

Figure 6-3 *Call Feature Negotiation*

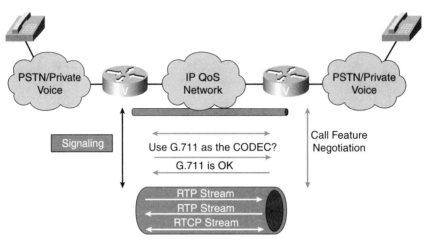

When agreement is not possible, the call is not completed and is dropped. Following are some examples of call parameters:

- **Coder-decoder (CODEC)**—Each endpoint must share a common format for the voice, or at least must recognize the opposite endpoint's choice for voice encoding. This is an example of a mandatory agreement. Not finding a common format is analogous to calling a foreign land and discovering that you are unable to carry on a conversation because the other party speaks a different language.

- **Receive/transmit**—Based on the application, the voice is one-way or two-way. Some endpoints do not meet the requirement for the session because they are designed to handle receive-only or transmit-only traffic when the call requests two-way communication.

- **Multipoint conferences**—Various types of multipoint conferences (for example, ad-hoc or meet-me) exist. The type of the multipoint conference, along with parameters (for example, the CODEC being used) required to participate in the conference, must be agreed upon.

- **Media type**—Potential media types include audio, video, or data.

- **Bit rate**—A session's bit rate defines its throughput requirements.

Call Administration and Accounting

Call administration and accounting functions provide optional services for the improved operation, administration, and maintenance of a VoIP environment.

Accounting makes use of the historical information that is usually formatted as call detail records (CDRs). CDRs are useful for cost allocation and for determining call distribution and service grade for capacity planning purposes.

Call administration includes the following capabilities:

- **Call status**—Monitoring calls in real time
- **Address management**—Supporting users with services such as address resolution
- **Admission control**—Ensuring that resources are being used effectively

The following sections describe each of these capabilities in more detail.

Call Status and CDRs

Several of the responsibilities assigned to call administration and accounting are dependent on access to current call status information or records of changes in the call status. Call status has both historical and instantaneous (real-time) benefits. Therefore, CDR functions include billing and capacity planning.

Call status provides an instantaneous view of the calls that are in progress. This view assists other processes (for example, bandwidth management) and can assist an administrator with troubleshooting or help provide user support.

CDRs, whose database is represented in Figure 6-4, include information about a call start time, duration, origin, destination, and other statistics that might be useful for a variety of purposes. This data is collected as a function of call status.

Figure 6-4 *Call Status*

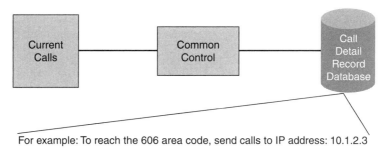

For example: To reach the 606 area code, send calls to IP address: 10.1.2.3

Address Management

When an endpoint registers with a call control component, it supplies its telephone address or addresses and, if it is a gateway, the addresses of the destinations it can reach. The endpoint provides other information relating to its capabilities. Multiple destinations that are reachable through a gateway are usually represented by a prefix. The use of a prefix allows call control to create a database that associates a telephony address, for example, with its corresponding IP address, as illustrated in Figure 6-5.

Figure 6-5 *Address Registration*

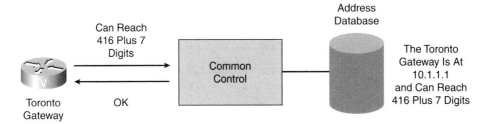

NOTE   In the traditional telephony network, the address of a station is limited to the keys available on a dual-tone multifrequency (DTMF) keypad. In VoIP, an address takes on one of several other formats as well. For example, the address can be a host name or a URL.

Figure 6-5 illustrates the Toronto gateway registering its accessibility information. In this example, the gateway informs the common control component that it can reach all telephone numbers in the 416 area. This information is deposited into a database for future reference.

After an address is registered, it can be discovered through address resolution, as depicted in Figure 6-6.

Figure 6-6 *Address Resolution*

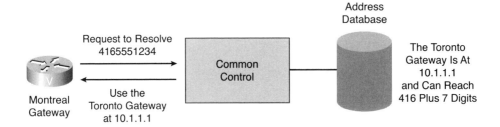

Address resolution translates a multimedia user address to an IP address so that the endpoints can communicate with each other to establish a control relationship and create an audio path.

Admission Control

Admission control has at least two aspects: authorization and bandwidth management. Access to a network should not imply permission to use the resources of the network. Common control limits access to the resources by checking the intentions and credentials of users before authorizing them to proceed.

Also, because bandwidth is a finite resource, appropriate bandwidth management is essential to maintaining voice quality. Allowing too many simultaneous voice calls over an IP internetwork results in a loss of quality for both new and existing voice calls.

To avoid degrading voice quality, a call control model establishes a bandwidth budget. By using data available from call status, the bandwidth management and Call Admission Control (CAC) functions monitor current bandwidth consumption. Calls might proceed up to the budgeted level, but are refused when the budget has reached its limit. This process is illustrated in Figure 6-7.

Figure 6-7   *Admission Control*

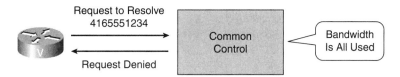

H.323 Concepts and Configuration

H.323 and its associated ITU-T recommendations represent a distributed environment for establishing voice, video, and data communication in a network without a quality of service (QoS) guarantee, which is typical of an IP internetwork. In addition to describing how to configure H.323, this section discusses the features and functions of the H.323 environment, including its components and how they interact. Scalability and survivability issues are also discussed.

H.323 and IP

Recommendation H.323 describes an infrastructure of terminals, common control components, services, and protocols that are used for multimedia (voice, video, and data) communications. Figure 6-8 illustrates the elements of an H.323 terminal and highlights the protocol infrastructure of an H.323 endpoint.

Figure 6-8 *H.323 and Associated Recommendations*

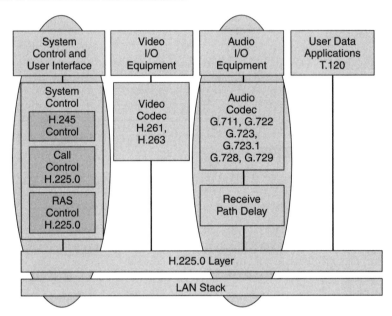

Registration, Admission, and Status (RAS)

H.323 was originally created to provide a mechanism for transporting multimedia applications over LANs. Although numerous vendors still use H.323 for videoconferencing applications, H.323 rapidly evolved to address the growing needs of VoIP networks. H.323 is currently the most widely used VoIP signaling and call control protocol, with international and domestic carriers relying on it to handle billions of minutes of use each year.

Considered an *umbrella protocol* because it defines all aspects of call transmission, from call establishment to capabilities exchange to network resource availability, H.323 defines the following protocols:

- H.245 for capabilities exchange
- H.225.0 for call setup
- H.225.0 for Registration, Admission, and Status (RAS) control for call routing

H.323 is based on the ISDN Q.931 protocol, which allows H.323 to interoperate easily with legacy voice networks, such as the public switched telephone network (PSTN) or SS7. In addition to providing support for call setup, H.225.0 provides a message transport mechanism for the H.245 control function and the RAS signaling function. These functions are described as follows:

- **Call-signaling function**—The call-signaling function uses a call-signaling channel that allows an endpoint to create connections with other endpoints. The call-signaling function defines call setup procedures based on the call setup procedures for ISDN (Recommendation Q.931). The call-signaling function uses messages formatted according to H.225.0.

- **H.245 control function**—The H.245 control function uses a control channel to transport control messages between endpoints or between an endpoint and a common control component, such as a gatekeeper or a multipoint controller (MC). The control channel used by the H.245 control function is separate from the call-signaling channel. The H.245 control function is responsible for the following:

  - **Logical channel signaling**—Opens and closes the channel that carries the media stream

  - **Capabilities exchange**—Negotiates audio, video, and coder-decoder (CODEC) capability between the endpoints

  - **Master or responder determination**—Determines which endpoint is master and which is responder; used to resolve conflicts during the call

  - **Mode request**—Requests a change in mode, or capability, of the media stream

  - **Timer and counter values**—Establishes values for timers and counters and agreement of those values by the endpoints

- **RAS signaling function**—The RAS signaling function uses a separate signaling channel (that is, the RAS channel) to perform registration, admissions, bandwidth changes, status, and disengage procedures between endpoints and a gatekeeper (GK). It uses messages formatted according to H.225.0.

In Figure 6-9, notice that the real-time aspects of H.323 rely on the User Datagram Protocol (UDP). However, both the session-oriented control procedures and the data media type of H.323 use TCP.

Figure 6-9 *H.323 Adapted to IP*

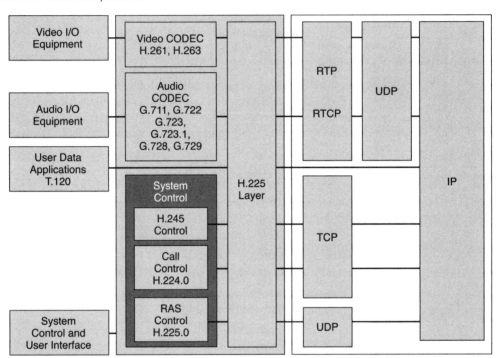

Functional Components of H.323

In addition to a suite of protocols, the H.323 standard also specifies numerous functional components, as illustrated in Figure 6-10. An *H.323 terminal* is an endpoint that provides real-time voice (and optionally, video and data) communications with another endpoint, such as an H.323 terminal, gateway (GW), or multipoint control unit (MCU).

An H.323 terminal must be capable of transmitting and receiving G.711 (α-Law and μ-Law), which uses 64 kbps pulse code modulation (PCM)–encoded voice, and might support other encoded voice formats, such as G.729 and G.723.1.

Figure 6-10 *H.323 Functional Components*

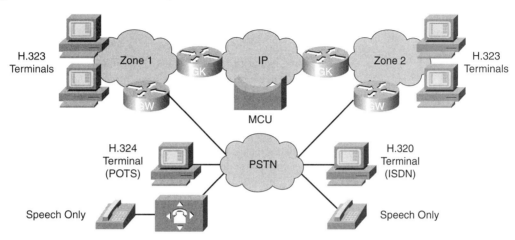

H.323 Gateways

An H.323 gateway is an optional type of endpoint that provides interoperability between H.323 endpoints and endpoints located on a switched-circuit network (SCN), such as the PSTN or an enterprise voice network, as depicted in Figure 6-11. Ideally, the gateway is transparent to both the H.323 endpoint and the SCN-based endpoint.

Figure 6-11 *H.323 Gateway*

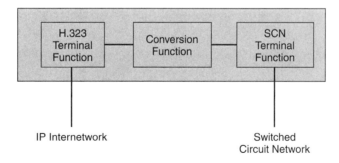

An H.323 gateway performs the following services:

- Translation between audio, video, and data formats
- Conversion between call setup signals and procedures
- Conversion between communication control signals and procedures

IP-to-IP Gateways

An IP-to-IP gateway facilitates easy and cost-effective connectivity between independent VoIP service provider networks. Some in the industry call IP-to-IP gateways *border elements* or *session border controllers.* The IP-to-IP gateway provides a network-to-network interface point for billing, security, Cisco Unified CallManager interconnectivity, call admission control, and signaling interworking. It performs most of the same functions of a PSTN-to-IP gateway, but joins two VoIP call legs. Media packets can either flow through the gateway and hide the networks from each other or flow around the IP-to-IP gateway if network security is not of primary importance.

Figure 6-12 illustrates a basic IP-to-IP gateway network. From the perspective of the private, or customer, networks, the IP-to-IP gateway appears as a single public address that must be routable on their private networks (in this case, a 12.*x.x.x* address routable on the 10.10.*x.x* and 192.168.*x.x* networks). Care must be taken at the IP-to-IP gateway to ensure that proper routing restrictions are in place to prevent communication directly between the private networks attached to it. Also note that this model works only if no overlapping address schemes are used on the customers' networks. Finally, to the hop-off gateways on the public network, all calls appear to originate from the 12.*x.x.x* address of the IP-to-IP gateway and not the private addresses on the customer networks. Also note that the gatekeepers shown in the diagram control each zone independently, with the 12.10.10.11 gatekeeper acting as the control point for the public network, and therefore the IP-to-IP gateway.

Figure 6-12 *IP-to-IP Gateway*

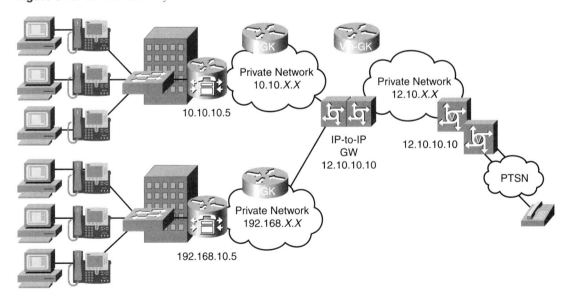

H.323 Gatekeepers

An H.323 gatekeeper is an optional component that provides call control support and services to H.323 endpoints, as shown in Figure 6-13. Although a gatekeeper is considered a distinct and optional component, it can be collocated with any other H.323 component.

Figure 6-13 *H.323 Gatekeeper*

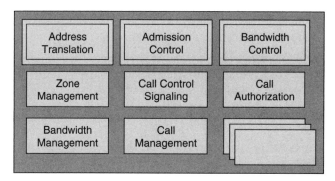

The scope of endpoints over which a gatekeeper exercises its authority is called a *zone*. H.323 defines a one-to-one relationship between a zone and a gatekeeper. When a gatekeeper is included, the gatekeeper must perform the following functions:

- **Address translation**—Converts an alias address to an IP address
- **Admission control**—Limits access to network resources based on call bandwidth restrictions
- **Bandwidth control**—Responds to bandwidth requests and modifications
- **Zone management**—Provides services to registered endpoints

A gatekeeper might also perform:

- **Call control signaling**—Performs call signaling on behalf of the endpoint (that is, *gatekeeper-routed call signaling*)
- **Call authorization**—Rejects calls based on authorization failure
- **Bandwidth management**—Limits the number of concurrent accesses to IP internetwork resources (that is, CAC)
- **Call management**—Maintains a record of ongoing calls

Multipoint Conferences

Support for multipoint conferences is provided by the following three functional components, as diagramed in Figure 6-14:

- **Multipoint controller (MC)**—An MC provides the functions that are necessary to support conferences involving three or more endpoints. The MC establishes an H.245 control channel with each of the conference participants. Through the control channel, the MC completes a capability exchange during which the MC indicates the mode of the conference (decentralized or centralized).

  An MC is not modeled as a stand-alone component. However, it might be located with an endpoint (for example, a terminal or a gateway), a gatekeeper, or a multipoint control unit.

- **Multipoint processor (MP)**—An MP adds functionality to multipoint conferences. An MP can receive multiple streams of multimedia input, process the streams by switching and mixing the streams, and then retransmit the result to all or some of the conference members.

  Similar to an MC, an MP is not modeled as a stand-alone component. Rather, an MP resides in an MCU.

- **Multipoint control unit (MCU)**—An MCU is modeled as an endpoint that provides support for multipoint conferences by incorporating one MC and zero or more MPs. An MCU is modeled as a stand-alone component.

Figure 6-14 *Multipoint Conference Components*

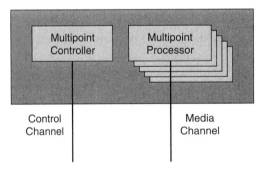

H.323 Call Establishment and Maintenance

Although H.323 is based on the concepts of a distributed call control model, it often embodies centralized call control model concepts.

Calls can be established between any of the following components:

- **Endpoint to endpoint**—The intelligence of H.323 endpoints allows them to operate autonomously. In this mode of operation, endpoints locate other endpoints through nonstandard mechanisms and initiate direct communication between the endpoints.

- **Endpoint to gatekeeper**—When a gatekeeper is added to the network, endpoints interoperate with the gatekeeper using the RAS channel.

- **Gatekeeper to gatekeeper**—In the presence of multiple gatekeepers, gatekeepers communicate with each other on the RAS channel.

RAS Messages

H.323 gatekeepers communicate with other H.323 devices (including other H.323 gatekeepers) through a series of RAS messages, as shown in Figure 6-15.

Figure 6-15 *RAS Messages*

Gatekeeper Discovery	Location Request
GatekeeperRequest (GRQ)	LocationRequest (LRQ)
GatekeeperConfirm (GCF)	LocationConfirm (LCF)
GatekeeperReject (GRJ)	LocationReject (LRJ)
Terminal/Gateway Registration	**Call Admission**
RegistrationRequest (RRQ)	AdmissionRequest (ARQ)
RegistrationConfirm (UCF)	AdmissionConfirm (ACF)
RegistrationReject (RRJ)	AdmissionReject (ARJ)
Terminal/Gateway Unregistration	**Disengage**
UnregistrationRequest (URQ)	DisengageRequest (DRQ)
UnregistrationConfirm (UCF)	DisengageConfirm (DCF)
UnregistrationReject (URJ)	DisengageReject (DRJ)

Bandwidth Change	Status Queries
Bandwidth Change Request (BRQ)	InfoRequest (IRQ)
Bandwidth Change Confirm (BCF)	InfoRequestResponse (IRR)
Bandwidth Change Reject (BRJ)	InfoRequestAck (IACK)
	InfoRequestNak (INAK)

Each of these RAS messages fall under one of the following categories:

- **Gatekeeper discovery**—An endpoint multicasts a gatekeeper discovery request (GRQ). A gatekeeper might confirm (gatekeeper confirmation [GCF]) or reject (gatekeeper rejection [GRJ]) an endpoint.

- **Terminal/gateway registration**—An endpoint sends a registration request (RRQ) to its gatekeeper to register and provide reachable prefixes. A gatekeeper confirms (registration confirmation [RCF]) or rejects (registration rejection [RRJ]) the registration.

- **Terminal/gateway unregistration**—An endpoint or gatekeeper sends an unregistration request (URQ) to cancel a registration. The responding device confirms (unregistration confirmation [UCF]) or rejects (unregistration rejection [URJ]) the request.

- **Bandwidth change**—An endpoint sends a bandwidth change request (BRQ) to its gatekeeper to request an adjustment in call bandwidth. A gatekeeper confirms (bandwidth confirmation [BCF]) or rejects (bandwidth rejection [BRJ]) the request.

- **Location request**—An endpoint or gatekeeper sends a location request (LRQ) to a gatekeeper. An LRQ is sent directly to a gatekeeper if one is known, or it is multicast to the gatekeeper discovery multicast address. An LRQ requests address translation of an E.164 address and solicits information about the responsible endpoint. The responding gatekeeper confirms (location confirmation [LCF]) with the IP address of the endpoint or rejects the request (location rejection [LRJ]) if the address is unknown.

- **Call admission**—An endpoint sends an admission request (ARQ) to its gatekeeper. The request identifies the terminating endpoint and the bandwidth required. The gatekeeper confirms (admission confirmation [ACF]) with the IP address of the terminating endpoint or rejects (admission rejection [ARJ]) if the endpoint is unknown or inadequate bandwidth is available.

- **Disengage**—When a call is disconnected, the endpoint sends a disengage request (DRQ) to the gatekeeper. The gatekeeper confirms (disengage confirmation [DCF]) or rejects (disengage rejection [DRJ]) the request.

- **Status queries**—A gatekeeper uses an information request (IRQ) to determine the status of an endpoint. In its response (IRR), the endpoint indicates whether it is online or offline. The endpoint might also reply that it understands the information request (information request acknowledged [IACK]) or that it does not understand the request (information request not acknowledged [INAK]).

Call Flows

While H.323-based networks scale better when a gatekeeper is used, a gatekeeper is not a required component in an H.323 network. H.323 networks containing a gatekeeper can scale even larger with multiple gatekeepers. This section discusses how H.323 calls are set up without a gatekeeper, with a single gatekeeper, and with more than one gatekeeper.

Figure 6-16 shows an H.323 basic call setup exchange between two gateways. The optional gatekeeper is not present in this example. Although gateways are shown, the same procedure is used when one or both endpoints are H.323 terminals.

Figure 6-16 *H.323 Basic Call Setup*

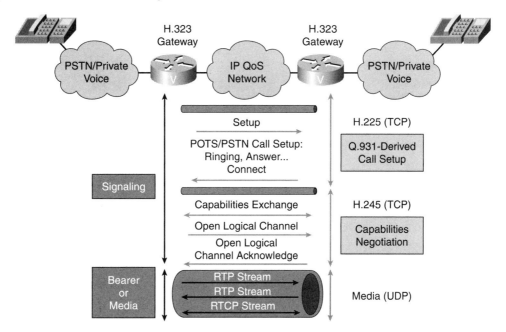

The call flow without a gatekeeper includes these steps:

1. The originating gateway initiates an H.225.0 session with the destination gateway on TCP port 1720. The gateway determines the IP address of the destination gateway internally. The gateway has the IP address of the destination endpoint in its configuration, or it knows a Domain Name System (DNS) resolvable domain name for the destination.

2. Call setup procedures based on Q.931 create a call-signaling channel between the endpoints.

3. The endpoints open another channel for the H.245 control function. The H.245 control function negotiates capabilities and exchanges logical channel descriptions.

4. The logical channel descriptions open RTP sessions.

5. The endpoints exchange multimedia over the RTP sessions, including exchanging call quality statistics using RTP Control Protocol (RTCP).

The basic setup procedure for an H.323 call requires multiple exchanges between the source and destination gateways. However, the *Fast Connect* procedure reduces the number of round-trip exchanges and achieves the capability exchange and logical channel assignments in one round trip, as illustrated in Figure 6-17.

Figure 6-17 *H.323 Fast Connect*

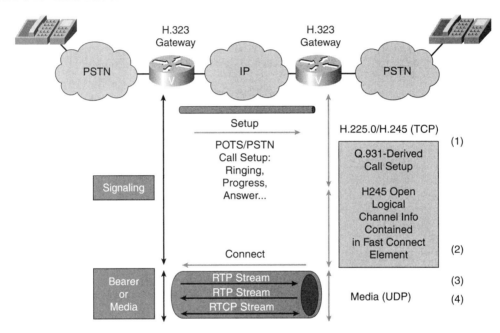

The Fast Connect procedure includes these steps:

1. The originating gateway initiates an H.225.0 session with the destination gateway on TCP port 1720.

2. Call setup procedures based on Q.931 create a combined call-signaling channel and control channel for H.245. Capabilities and logical channel descriptions are exchanged within the Q.931 call setup procedure.

3. Logical channel descriptions open RTP sessions.

4. The endpoints exchange multimedia over the RTP sessions.

NOTE   Cisco H.323 voice equipment supports up to version 4 of H.323 and is backward compatible to earlier versions.

Call Flows with a Gatekeeper

Figure 6-18 shows how an endpoint locates and registers with a gatekeeper. A *gatekeeper* adds scalability to H.323. Without a gatekeeper, an endpoint must recognize or have the ability to resolve the IP address of the destination endpoint.

Figure 6-18 *Finding and Registering with a Gatekeeper*

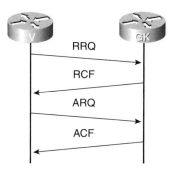

Before an endpoint can use a gatekeeper, it must register with the gatekeeper. To register, an endpoint must recognize the IP address of the gatekeeper. One of these two methods are used to determine the address of the gatekeeper:

* An endpoint can be preconfigured to recognize the domain name or IP address of its gatekeeper. If configured to recognize the name, an endpoint must have a means to resolve the name to an IP address. A common address resolution technique is the DNS.

* An endpoint can issue a multicast GRQ to the gatekeeper discovery address (224.0.1.41) to discover the IP address of its gatekeeper. If the endpoint receives a GCF to the request, it uses the IP address to proceed with registration.

To initiate registration, an endpoint sends an RRQ to the gatekeeper. In the register request, the endpoint identifies itself with its ID and provides its IP address. Optionally, the endpoint lists the prefixes (for example, telephone numbers) that it supports. These prefixes are gleaned from the plain old telephone service (POTS) dial peer destination patterns associated with any FXS port.

To illustrate the steps involved in a call setup using an H.323 gatekeeper, consider the example depicted in Figure 6-19. In this example, both endpoints have registered with the same gatekeeper.

Figure 6-19 *Call Flow with an H.323 Gatekeeper*

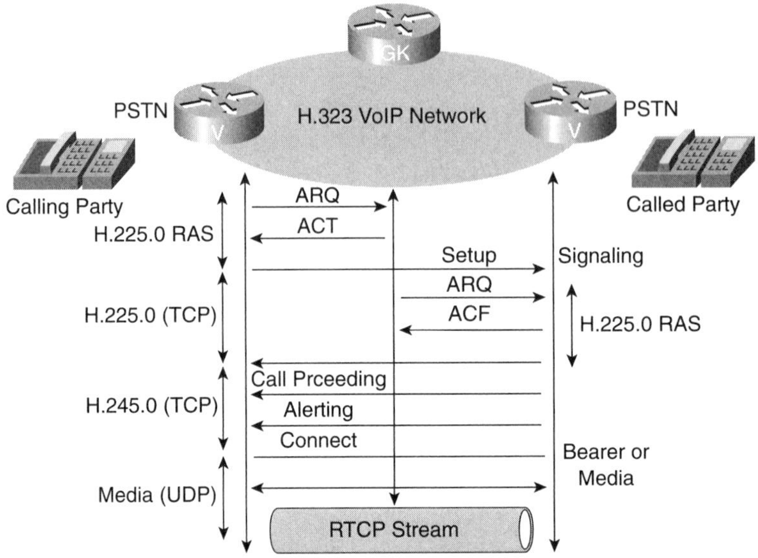

Call flow with a gatekeeper proceeds as follows:

1. The gateway sends an ARQ to the gatekeeper to initiate the procedure. The gateway is configured with the domain name or address of the gatekeeper.

2. The gatekeeper responds to the admission request with an ACF. In the confirmation, the gatekeeper provides the IP address of the remote endpoint.

3. When the originating endpoint identifies the terminating endpoint, it initiates a basic call setup.

4. Before the terminating endpoint accepts the incoming call, it sends an ARQ to the gatekeeper to gain permission.

5. The gatekeeper responds affirmatively, and the terminating endpoint proceeds with the call setup procedure.

During this procedure, if the gatekeeper responds to either endpoint with an ARJ to the admission request, the endpoint that receives the rejection terminates the procedure.

In the previous examples, the call-signaling channel is created from endpoint to endpoint. However, in some cases, it is desirable to have the gatekeeper represent the other endpoint for signaling purposes. This method is called *gatekeeper-routed call signaling,* which is shown in Figure 6-20.

Figure 6-20 *Gatekeeper-Routed Call Signaling*

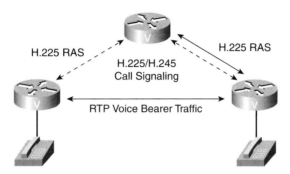

The process for gatekeeper-routed call signaling is as follows:

1. The gatekeeper responds to an admission request and advises the endpoint to perform the call setup procedure with the gatekeeper, not with the terminating endpoint.

2. The endpoint initiates the setup request with the gatekeeper.

3. The gatekeeper sends its own request to the terminating endpoint and incorporates some of the details acquired from the originating request.

4. When a connect message is received from the terminating endpoint, the gatekeeper sends a connect message to the originating endpoint.

5. The two endpoints establish an H.245 control channel between them. The call procedure continues normally from this point.

Call Flows with Multiple Gatekeepers

By simplifying configuration of the endpoints, gatekeepers aid in building large-scale VoIP networks. As the VoIP network grows, incorporating additional gatekeepers enhances the network scalability, as shown in Figure 6-21.

Without a gatekeeper, endpoints must find each other by any means available. This limits the growth potential of the VoIP network. Through the registration and address resolution services of a gatekeeper, growth potential improves significantly.

A single gatekeeper design might not be appropriate for several reasons. A single gatekeeper can become overloaded, or it can have an inconvenient network location, necessitating a long and expensive round trip to and from the gatekeeper. Deploying multiple gatekeepers offers a more scalable and robust environment.

Figure 6-21   *Scalability with Multiple H.323 Gatekeepers*

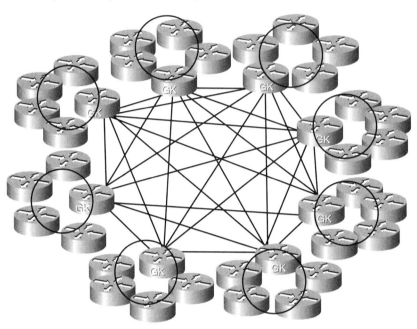

In Figure 6-22, each endpoint is registered with a different gatekeeper.

Notice the changes in the following call setup procedure:

1. The originating endpoint sends an admission request to its gatekeeper requesting permission to proceed and asks for the session parameters for the terminating endpoint.

2. The gatekeeper for the originating endpoint (Gatekeeper 1) determines from its configuration or from a directory resource that the terminating endpoint is potentially associated with Gatekeeper 2. Gatekeeper 1 sends an LRQ to Gatekeeper 2.

3. Gatekeeper 2 recognizes the address and sends back an LCF. In the confirmation, Gatekeeper 2 provides the IP address of the terminating endpoint.

4. If Gatekeeper 1 considers the call acceptable in terms of security and bandwidth, it maps the LCF to an ARQ and sends the confirmation back to the originating endpoint.

5. The endpoint initiates a call setup to the remote endpoint.

6. Before accepting the incoming call, the remote endpoint sends an ARQ to Gatekeeper 2 requesting permission to accept the incoming call.

7. Gatekeeper 2 performs admission control on the request and responds with a confirmation.

Figure 6-22 *Call Flows with Multiple H.323 Gatekeepers*

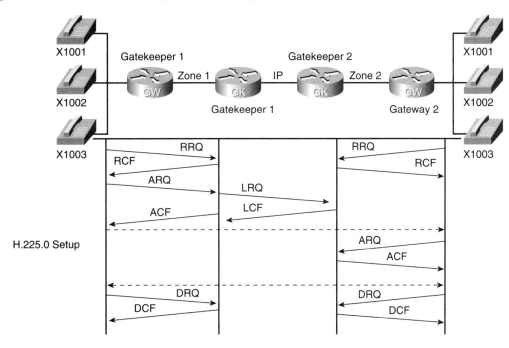

H.225.0 Connect with H.245 Capabilities

Active Call

8. The endpoint responds to the call setup request.

9. The call setup progresses through the H.225.0 call function and H.245 control function procedures until the RTP sessions are initiated.

10. At the conclusion of the call, each endpoint sends a disconnect request to its gatekeeper to advise its gatekeeper that the call is complete.

11. Each gatekeeper responds with a confirmation.

Types of Multipoint Conferences

All types of multipoint conferences rely on a single MC to coordinate the membership of a conference. Each endpoint has an H.245 control channel connection to the MC.

Either the MC or the endpoint initiates the control channel setup. H.323 defines the following three types of conferences, as shown in Figure 6-23:

- **Centralized multipoint conference**—The endpoints must have their audio, video, or data channels connected to an MP. The MP performs mixing and switching of the audio, video, and data, and if the MP supports the capability, each endpoint can operate in a different mode.

- **Decentralized multipoint conference**—The endpoints do not have a connection to an MP. Instead, endpoints multicast their audio, video, and data streams to all participants in the conference. Because an MP is not available for switching and mixing, any mixing of the conference streams is a function of the endpoint, and all endpoints must use the same communication parameters.

  To accommodate situations in which two streams (audio and video) would be handled by the different multipoint conference models, H.323 defines a hybrid. A *hybrid* describes a situation in which the audio and video streams are managed by a single H.245 control channel with the MC, but where one stream relies on multicast (according to the distributed model) and the other uses the MP (as in the centralized model).

- **Ad-hoc multipoint conference**—Any two endpoints in a call can convert their relationship into a point-to-point conference. If neither of the endpoints has a collocated MC, then the services of a gatekeeper are used. When the point-to-point conference is created, other endpoints become part of the conference by accepting an invitation from a current participant, or the endpoint can request to join the conference.

Figure 6-23 *Multipoint Conferences*

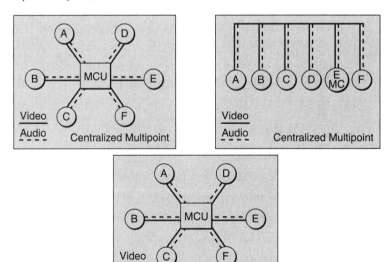

Deploying and Configuring H.323

Gateways and gatekeepers each provide specific features and functionality to the VoIP network. This section discusses the configuration of each device type to enable the use of these features and to enable the appropriate communication between device types. Reliability is critical for success in a voice network. This section also discusses strategies that are used to provide fault tolerance in the voice network. Finally, this section discusses the steps necessary to monitor and troubleshoot the VoIP network as required.

Survivability Strategies

In any environment that depends on common control components, the vulnerability of the environment is directly proportional to the probability of common control component failure. In a classical telephony application, fault tolerance is accommodated by incorporating extra common control technology. One strategy replicates all critical components. This expensive approach is often replaced with the more cost-effective solution of "n out of $n + 1$" redundancy. Specifically, a single spare component is available to step in when any one of the active n components fails. The essential part of either strategy is the replication of key components.

The key components of an H.323 network include the gateways and the gatekeeper. H.323 can employ any of the following survivability strategies:

- **Hot Standby Router Protocol (HSRP)**—HSRP allows two gatekeepers to share both an IP address and access to a common LAN. However, at any time, only one gatekeeper is active. Endpoints are configured with the name of the gatekeeper, which they can resolve using DNS or the IP address of the gatekeeper.

- **Virtual Router Redundancy Protocol (VRRP)**—VRRP allows a group of gatekeepers on a multiaccess link to use the same virtual IP address, with one device acting as the master virtual router and one or more devices configured to be available as backup virtual routers. Endpoints are configured with the name or virtual IP address of the gatekeeper. VRRP is defined by the IETF as RFC 3768.

- **Multiple gatekeepers with gatekeeper discovery**—Deployment of multiple gatekeepers reduces the probability of total loss of gatekeeper access. However, adding new gatekeepers presents a new challenge. Each gatekeeper creates a unique H.323 zone. Because an H.323 endpoint is associated with only one gatekeeper at a time (in only one zone at a time), endpoints are configured to find only one of several working gatekeepers. Fortunately, a gateway can be configured with an ordered list of gatekeepers, or the gateway can be configured to use IP multicast to locate a gatekeeper.

- **Multiple gatekeepers configured for the same prefix**—Gatekeepers send location request messages to other gatekeepers when locating an endpoint. By supporting the same prefix on multiple gatekeepers, the location request can be resolved by multiple gatekeepers. This strategy makes the loss of one gatekeeper less significant.

- **Multiple gateways configured for the same prefix**—Survivability is enhanced at the gateway with multiple gateways that are configured to reach the same SCN destination. By configuring the same prefix of destinations in multiple gateways, the gatekeeper sees the same prefix more than once as each gateway registers with its gatekeeper.

H.323 Proxy Server

An H.323 proxy server can circumvent the shortcomings of a direct path in cases where the direct path between two H.323 endpoints is not the most appropriate (for example, when the direct path has poor throughput and delay characteristics, when it is not easily available because of a firewall, or when zones are configured as inaccessible on the gatekeepers in order to isolate addressing information in different zones).

When a proxy server is involved, two sessions are typically established as follows:

- Originating endpoint to the proxy server
- Proxy server to the terminating endpoint

However, when a proxy server also represents the terminating endpoint, a third session is required, as follows:

- Originating endpoint to proxy server 1
- Proxy server 1 to proxy server 2
- Proxy server 2 to terminating endpoint

Figure 6-24 illustrates an example with three sessions.

The objective in this scenario is for Terminal 1 and Terminal 3 to establish an end-to-end relationship for multimedia communications. The following sequence of events occurs:

1. Terminal 1 asks Gatekeeper 1 for permission to call Terminal 3.

2. Gatekeeper 1 locates Gatekeeper 3 as the Terminal 3 gatekeeper. Gatekeeper 1 asks Gatekeeper 3 for the address of Terminal 3.

3. Gatekeeper 3 responds with the address of Proxy 3 (instead of the address of Terminal 3) to hide the identity of Terminal 3.

4. Gatekeeper 1 is configured to get to Proxy 3 by way of Proxy 1. So, Gatekeeper 1 returns the address of Proxy 1 to Terminal 1.

5. Terminal 1 calls Proxy 1.

6. Proxy 1 consults Gatekeeper 1 to discover the true destination of the call, which is Terminal 3 in this example.

7. Gatekeeper 1 instructs Proxy 1 to call Proxy 3.

Figure 6-24 *H.323 Proxy Server*

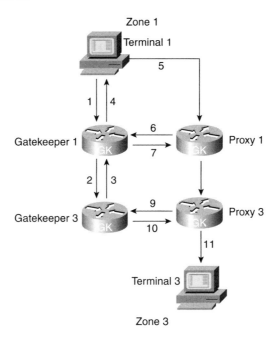

8. Proxy 1 calls Proxy 3.

9. Proxy 3 consults Gatekeeper 3 for the true destination, which is Terminal 3.

10. Gatekeeper 3 gives the address of Terminal 3 to Proxy 3.

11. Proxy 3 completes the call to Terminal 3.

Notice that the resulting path between Terminal 1 and Terminal 3 involves three separate legs: one between Terminal 1 and Proxy 1, one between Proxy 1 and Proxy 3, and one between Proxy 3 and Terminal 3. Both the media and any signaling are carried over these three legs.

Cisco's Implementation of H.323

Cisco provides support for a variety of H.323 components, as depicted in Figure 6-25.

Figure 6-25   *Cisco's Implementation of H.323*

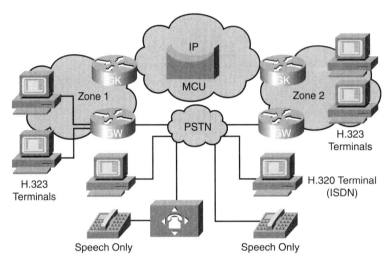

Cisco-supported H.323 components include the following:

- **H.323 terminals**—Cisco provides support for H.323 terminals in Cisco IP phones.
- **Gateways**—Cisco implements H.323 gateway support in:
  - — Cisco voice-enabled routers (first available in Cisco IOS Release 11.3)
  - — Cisco SC2200 Signaling Controllers
  - — Cisco PGW 2200 Public Switched Telephone Network (PSTN) Gateways
  - — Voice-enabled Cisco AS5*xx*0 access servers
  - — Cisco BTS 10200 Softswitch
- **Gatekeepers**—Cisco implements gatekeeper support in:
  - — Cisco Multimedia Conference Manager
  - — Cisco Unified CallManager
  - — Routers (first available in Cisco IOS Release 11.3)
- **Multipoint Control Unit (MCU)**—The multipoint controller (MC) and multipoint processor (MP) of the Cisco IP/VC 3500 Series MCU support all H.323 conference types. The IP/VC 3500 also incorporates a gatekeeper.
- **Other support**—Cisco PIX 500 Series firewalls and Context-Based Access Control (CBAC) support in the Cisco Secure Integrated Software monitor the logical channel handshaking of the H.245 control function and dynamically open conduits for the Real-Time Transport Protocol (RTP) sessions.

Configuring H.323 Gateways and Gatekeepers

Figure 6-26 offers a sample topology, which contains two H.323 gateways and two H.323 gatekeepers. This figure will be used to illustrate the configuration of both an H.323 gateway and an H.323 gatekeeper.

Figure 6-26 *H.323 Gateway and Gatekeeper Sample Topology*

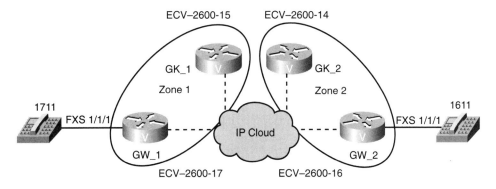

First, consider the configuration of the GW_1 gateway, as presented in Example 6-1.

Example 6-1 *Gateway GW_1's Configuration*

```
GW_1(config)#hostname ECV-2610-17
GW_1(config)#interface Ethernet 0/0
GW_1(config-if)#ip address 10.52.218.49 255.255.255.0
GW_1(config-if)#h323-gateway voip interface
GW_1(config-if)#h323-gateway voip id gk-zone1.test.com ipaddr 10.52.218.47 1718
GW_1(config-if)#h323-gateway voip h323-id gw_1
GW_1(config-if)#h323-gateway voip bind srcaddr 10.52.218.49
GW_1(config-if)#h323-gateway voip tech-prefix 1#
GW_1(config-if)#exit
GW_1(config)#dial-peer voice 1 voip
GW_1(config-dial-peer)#destination-pattern 16..
GW_1(config-dial-peer)#session target ras
GW_1(config-dial-peer)#exit
GW_1(config)#dial-peer voice 2 pots
GW_1(config-dial-peer)#destination-pattern 911
GW_1(config-dial-peer)#port 1/1/1
GW_1(config-dial-peer)#no register e164
GW_2(config-dial-peer)#exit
GW_2(config)#gateway
```

To use a gatekeeper, an administrator must complete the following three tasks on the gateway:

Step 1. Enable the gateway with the **gateway** command.

Step 2. Configure the relationship with the gatekeeper. This requires the following three interface subcommands:

— **h323-gateway voip interface**—Tells the router that this interface should be enabled for H.323 packet processing.

— **h323-gateway voip id**—Identifies the ID of the gatekeeper.

— **h323-gateway voip h323-id**—Configures the ID of this router. When the router registers with the gatekeeper, the gatekeeper recognizes the gateway by this ID.

Step 3. Configure a dial peer to use the gatekeeper with the **ras** parameter on the **dial peer** subcommand session target.

Example 6-2 shows the configuration of gateway GW_2. As you examine the configuration, notice that it is a mirror of GW_1's configuration.

Example 6-2 *Gateway GW_2's Configuration*

```
GW_2(config)#hostname ECV-2610-16
GW_2(config)#interface Ethernet 0/0
GW_2(config-if)#ip address 10.52.218.48 255.255.255.0
GW_2(config-if)#h323-gateway voip interface
GW_2(config-if)#h323-gateway voip id gk-zone2.test.com ipaddr 10.52.218.46 1718
GW_2(config-if)#h323-gateway voip h323-id gw_2
GW_2(config-if)#h323-gateway voip bind srcaddr 10.52.218.48
GW_2(config-if)#h323-gateway voip tech-prefix 1#
GW_2(config-if)#exit
GW_2(config)#dial-peer voice 1 voip
GW_2(config-dial-peer)#destination-pattern 17..
GW_2(config-dial-peer)#session target ras
GW_2(config-dial-peer)#exit
GW_2(config)#dial-peer voice 2 pots
GW_2(config-dial-peer)#destination-pattern 911
GW_2(config-dial-peer)#port 1/1/1
GW_2(config-dial-peer)#no register e164
!
gateway
```

Also, notice a couple of optional gateway commands presented in these examples:

- **h323-gateway voip tech-prefix 1#**—Registers a technology prefix
- **h323-gateway voip bind srcaddr 10.52.218.48**—Sets the source address of H.323 packets

A technology prefix advises the gatekeeper that this gateway can handle type 1# destinations. For routing purposes, a technology prefix might be assigned to a multimedia type, such as video. By registering type 1# support, the gateway supports the video applications.

In the dial peer, the **no register e164** subcommand causes the gateway not to register the destination pattern when communicating with the gatekeeper. When the dial peer does not register its prefix, it requires an alternative mechanism for the gatekeeper to acquire this information.

Now that you have examined the configuration for the H.323 gateways, turn your attention to the configuration of the H.323 gatekeepers. Example 6-3 presents a sample configuration for the GK_1 gatekeeper.

Example 6-3   *Gatekeeper GK_1's Configuration*

```
GK_1(config)#hostname ECV-2610-15
GK_1(config)#interface Ethernet 0/0
GK_1(config-if)#ip address 10.52.218.47 255.255.255.0
GK_1(config-if)#exit
GK_1(config)#gatekeeper
GK_1(config-gk)#zone local gk-zone1.test.com test.com 10.52.218.47
GK_1(config-gk)#zone remote gk-zone2.test.com test.com 10.52.218.46 1719
GK_1(config-gk)#zone prefix gk-zone2.test.com 16..
GK_1(config-gk)#zone prefix gk-zone1.test.com 17..
GK_1(config-gk)#gw-type-prefix 1#* default-technology
GK_1(config-gk)#no shutdown
```

The gatekeeper application is enabled with the **gatekeeper** command. For Example 6-3, the gateways are configured to withhold their E.164 addresses, so the gatekeepers must define the addresses locally. This is done with **zone prefix** commands. In the example, each gatekeeper has two **zone prefix** commands: the first pointing to the other gatekeeper and the second pointing to the local zone (meaning the prefix is in the local zone). The **zone prefix** command that points to itself is configured with the name of the gateway used to direct traffic to the destination. The address of the gateway is not required because it is determined automatically when the gateway registers. The commands in the example perform the following functions:

- **zone local gk-zone1.test.com test.com 10.52.218.47**—Defines the ID of the local gatekeeper

- **zone remote gk-zone2.test.com test.com 10.52.218.46 1719**—Defines the identity and IP address of a neighboring gatekeeper

For completion, Example 6-4 illustrates the configuration of the GK_2 gatekeeper. Again, notice that the GK_2 configuration is a mirror of GK_1's configuration.

Example 6-4 *Gatekeeper GK_2's Configuration*

```
GK_2(config)#hostname ECV-2610-14
GK_2(config)#interface Ethernet 0/0
GK_2(config-if)#ip address 10.52.218.46
GK_2(config-if)#exit
GK_2(config-if)#gatekeeper
GK_2(config-gk)#zone local gk-zone2.test.com test.com 10.52.218.46
GK_2(config-gk)#zone remote gk-zone1.test.com test.com 10.52.218.47 1719
GK_2(config-gk)#zone prefix gk-zone2.test.com 16..
GK_2(config-gk)#zone prefix gk-zone1.test.com 17..
GK_2(config-gk)#gw-type-prefix 1#* default-technology
GK_2(config-gk)#no shutdown
```

Because the gateways register their technology prefixes, the gatekeeper does not need to be configured. If a technology prefix is required, the **gw-type-prefix** defines a technology prefix and can manually update technology prefix knowledge in the gatekeeper. In Example 6-4, the gatekeeper attempts to define a technology prefix as the default with the command **gw-type-prefix 1#* default-technology.** Any unknown destination is assumed to be of the default technology type, and calls are forwarded to any gateway that registered the default technology type.

Monitoring and Troubleshooting H.323

Cisco offers a variety of **show** and **debug** commands for examining the status of the H.323 components and for troubleshooting H.323-related issues.

Following are **show** commands used for H.323:

- **show call active voice [brief]**—Displays the status, statistics, and parameters for all active voice calls
- **show call history voice [last *n*|record|brief]**—Displays call records from the history buffer
- **show gateway**—Displays the current status of the H.323 gateway configured in the router
- **show gatekeeper calls**—Displays the active calls for which the gatekeeper is responsible
- **show gatekeeper endpoints**—Lists the registered endpoints with H.323 IDs and supported prefixes
- **show gatekeeper gw-type-prefix**—Displays the current technology prefix table
- **show gatekeeper status**—Displays the current status of the gatekeeper
- **show gatekeeper zone prefix**—Displays the gateways and their associated E.164 prefixes
- **show gatekeeper zone status**—Displays the status of the connections to gateways in the local zone and the status of connections to gatekeepers in other zones

Example 6-5 shows output from the **show gatekeeper calls** command.

Example 6-5   *The* **show gatekeeper calls** *Output*

```
Router#show gatekeeper calls
Total number of active calls = 1.
                         GATEKEEPER CALL INFO
                         ====================
LocalCallID                         Age(secs)   BW
1-19342                             101         16(Kbps)
 Endpt(s): Alias                    E.164Addr
   src EP: R3                       2222
           CallSignalAddr  Port  RASSignalAddr   Port
           10.7.7.2        1720  10.7.7.2        56763
 Endpt(s): Alias                    E.164Addr
   dst EP: R1                       1111
           CallSignalAddr  Port  RASSignalAddr   Port
   10.1.1.2        1720  10.1.1.2        52888
```

While troubleshooting, **show** commands do not always provide the level of detail needed to diagnose an issue. The following **debug** commands can aid in troubleshooting by providing a more granular and real-time view of H.323 activity:

- **debug voip ccapi inout**—Shows every interaction with the call control application programming interface (CCAPI) on the telephone interface and the VoIP side. Monitoring the **debug voip ccapi inout** command output allows administrators to follow the progress of a call from the inbound interface or VoIP peer to the outbound side of the call. Because this debug is processor-intensive, use it sparingly in a live network.

- **debug cch323 h225**—Traces the transitions in the H.225.0 state machine during the establishment of the call control channel. The first step in establishing a relationship between any two components is to bring up the call control channel. Monitoring the output of the **debug cch323 h225** command allows administrators to follow the call setup progress and determine if the channel is established correctly.

- **debug cch323 h245**—Traces the state transitions in the H.245 state machine during the establishment of the H.245 control channel. Monitoring the output of the **debug cch323 h245** command allows administrators to see if the channel is established correctly.

- **debug cch323 ras**—Traces the state transition in the establishment of the Registration, Admission, and Status (RAS) control channel. Monitoring the output of the **debug cch323 ras** command allows administrators to determine if the channel is established correctly.

- **debug h225 asn1**—Displays an expansion of the ASN.1-encoded H.225.0 messages. When investigating VoIP peer association problems, this **debug** command helps administrators monitor the activity of the call-signaling channel. Because H.225.0 encapsulates H.245, this is a useful approach for monitoring both H.225.0 and H.245.

- **debug h225 events**—Similar to the Abstract Syntax Notation One (ASN.1) version of the command, but does not expand the ASN.1. This **debug** command only debugs events, which usually imposes a lighter load on the router.

- **debug h245 [asn1 | events]**—Similar to the H.225.0 variant except that it displays only the H.245 messages.

To turn off a **debug** command, issue the **no debug** or **undebug all** command. Leaving a **debug** command running can cause excessive processor overhead on the router.

SIP Concepts and Configuration

An understanding of the features and functions of SIP components, and the relationships the components establish with each other, is important in implementing a scalable, resilient, and secure SIP environment.

This section describes how to configure the session initiation protocol (SIP) and explores the features and functions of a SIP environment, including SIP components, how these components interact, and how to accommodate scalability and survivability in a SIP network.

SIP and Associated Standards

SIP is a signaling and control protocol for the establishment, maintenance, and termination of multimedia sessions with one or more participants. Examples of SIP multimedia sessions include Internet telephone calls, multimedia conferences, and multimedia distribution. Session communications might be based on multicast, unicast, or both.

SIP operates on the principle of session invitations. Through invitations, SIP initiates sessions or invites participants into established sessions. Descriptions of these sessions are advertised by any one of several means, including the Session Announcement Protocol (SAP), defined in RFC 2974, which incorporates a session description according to the Session Description Protocol (SDP), defined in RFC 2327.

SIP uses other IETF protocols to define other aspects of VoIP and multimedia sessions. For example, SIP can use URLs for addressing, DNS for service location, and Telephony Routing over IP (TRIP) for call routing.

SIP supports personal mobility and other intelligent ietwork (IN) telephony subscriber services through name mapping and redirection services. Personal mobility allows a potential participant in a session to be identified by a unique personal number or name.

IN provides carriers with the ability to rapidly deploy new user services on platforms that are external to the switching fabric. Access to the external platforms is by way of an independent vendor and standard user interface. Calling-card services, 1-800 services, and local number portability are just three of these services.

Multimedia sessions are established and terminated by the following services:

- **User location services**—Locate an end system
- **User capabilities services**—Select the media type and parameters
- **User availability services**—Determine the availability and desire for a party to participate
- **Call setup services**—Establish a session relationship between parties and manage call progress
- **Call handling services**—Transfer and terminate calls

Although the IETF has made great progress in defining extensions that allow SIP to work with legacy voice networks, the primary motivation behind SIP is to create an environment that supports next-generation communication models that use the Internet and Internet applications. SIP is described in IETF RFC 3261 (June 2002), which renders obsolete RFC 2543 (March 1999).

Cisco SIP Support

The Cisco SIP-enabled product portfolio encompasses multiple components of a SIP network infrastructure, from IP phones and access devices to call control and PSTN interworking. Examples of Cisco SIP products include the following:

- **Cisco IP phones**—The Cisco IP phone series, including the 7970, 7960, and 7940 Cisco IP phones, support SIP user-agent functionality. These IP phones deliver functionality such as inline-power support and dual-Ethernet ports, and deliver traditional desktop functionality such as call hold, transfer, conferencing, caller ID, call waiting, and a lighted message-waiting indicator.
- **Cisco ATA 186 Analog Telephone Adaptor**—The Cisco ATA 186 supports SIP user-agent functionality. With two FXS ports and a single Ethernet port, the ATA 186 provides a low-cost means to connect analog phones to a SIP network. The ATA 186 also delivers traditional desktop functionality such as call hold, transfer, conferencing, caller ID, and lighted call-waiting and message-waiting indicators.

- **Cisco packet voice gateways**—The Cisco 1700 modular access routers that are voice capable—Cisco 2600 Series multiservice platforms, Cisco 3800 Series multiservice platforms, 3700 Series multiservice platforms, Cisco AS5000 universal gateways, and Cisco 7200 Series voice gateways—all support SIP user-agent functionality. These devices provide a means of connecting SIP networks to traditional time-division multiplexing (TDM) networks via T1, E1, Digital Service 3 (DS3), channel associated signaling (CAS), PRI/BRI, R2 signaling, FXS, Foreign Exchange Office (FXO), or ear-and-mouth (E&M) interfaces. Cisco packet voice gateways are used to build the largest IP telephony networks in the world.

- **Cisco SIP Proxy Server**—The Cisco SIP Proxy Server provides the functionality of a SIP proxy, SIP redirect, SIP registrar, and SIP location services server. The Cisco SIP Proxy Server provides the foundation for call routing within SIP networks and can work with traditional SIP location services such as DNS or telephone number mapping (ENUM), with feature servers via a SIP redirect message and with H.323 location services using standard location request (LRQ) messages. The Cisco SIP Proxy Server runs on either Solaris or Linux operating systems.

- **Cisco BTS 10200 Softswitch**—The Cisco BTS 10200 provides softswitch functionality to Class 4 and Class 5 networks and provides SIP-to-Signaling System 7 (SIP-to-SS7) gateway functionality for American National Standards Institute (ANSI) standardized networks. The BTS 10200 supports SIP user-agent functionality in conjunction with a Cisco voice media gateway such as a Cisco AS5000 Universal Gateway or a Cisco MGX 8000 Series Voice Gateway.

- **Cisco PGW 2200 PSTN Gateway**—The Cisco PGW 2200 provides softswitch functionality for Class 4 networks, as well as Internet offload and SIP-to-SS7 gateway functionality for international networks. The PGW 2200 supports ISDN User Part (ISUP) certification in over 130 countries. The PGW 2200 supports SIP user-agent functionality in conjunction with a Cisco packet voice media gateway such as an AS5000 Universal Gateway or an MGX 8000 Series Voice Gateway.

- **Cisco PIX and ASA Security Appliances**—The Cisco PIX and the ASA Security Appliances are SIP-aware networking devices that provide firewall and Network Address Translation (NAT) functionality. Because they are SIP-aware, these appliances are able to dynamically allow SIP signaling to traverse network and addressing boundaries without compromising overall network security. The Cisco PIX and the ASA Security Appliances functioning in this capacity are called application layer gateways (ALGs).

SIP Components

SIP is a peer-to-peer protocol. The peers in a session are called user agents (UAs), as illustrated in Figure 6-27.

Figure 6-27 *SIP Functional Components*

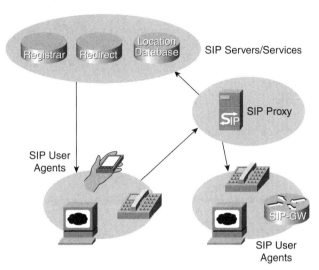

A UA consists of two functional components:

- **User agent client (UAC)**—A client application that initiates a SIP request

- **User agent server (UAS)**—A server application that contacts the user when a SIP invitation is received and then returns a response on behalf of the user to the invitation originator

Typically, a SIP UA can function as a UAC or a UAS during a session, but not both in the same session. Whether the endpoint functions as a UAC or a UAS depends on the UA that initiated the request. Specifically, the initiating UA uses a UAC and the terminating UA uses a UAS.

From an architectural standpoint, the physical components of a SIP network are grouped into the following two categories:

- **User agents**—SIP user agents include the following devices:

   — **IP phone**—Acts as a UAS or UAC on a session-by-session basis. Software phones and Cisco SIP IP phones initiate SIP requests and respond to requests.

   — **Gateway**—Acts as a UAS or UAC and provides call control support. Gateways provide many services, the most common being a translation function between SIP user agents and other terminal types. This function includes translation between transmission formats and between communications procedures. A gateway translates between audio and video signals and performs call setup and clearing on both the IP side and the SCN side.

- **SIP servers**—SIP servers include the following types:

    — **Proxy server**—Acts as an intermediate component that receives SIP requests from a client, and then forwards the requests on behalf of the client to the next SIP server in the network. The next server can be another proxy server or a UAS. Proxy servers can provide functions such as authentication, authorization, network access control, routing, reliable request transmissions, and security.

    — **Redirect server**—Provides a UA with information about the next server that the UA should contact. The server can be another network server or a UA. The UA redirects the invitation to the server identified by the redirect server.

    — **Registrar server**—Requests from UACs for registration of their current location. Registrar servers are often located near or even collocated with other network servers, most often a location server.

    — **Location server**—Acts as a service providing address resolution services to SIP proxy or redirect servers. A location server embodies mechanisms to resolve addresses. These mechanisms can include a database of registrations or access to commonly used resolution tools such as finger, rwhois, Lightweight Directory Access Protocol (LDAP), or operating system–dependent mechanisms. A registrar server can be modeled as one subcomponent of a location server. The registrar server is partly responsible for populating a database associated with the location server.

SIP Applications

Leaders in the communications industry are developing new products and services that rely on SIP, and they are offering attractive new communications services to their customers. Microsoft added support for SIP clients in core product offerings (for example, Windows XP), a step that will proliferate SIP clients on personal computers worldwide. SIP is gaining momentum in every market, and many interexchange carriers have deployed SIP in their networks.

Cisco is enabling the advance of new communications services with a complete SIP-enabled portfolio, including proxy servers, packet voice gateways, call control and signaling, IP phones, and firewalls. These products are available today. Also, Cisco introduced support for SIP trunks in Cisco Unified CallManager 4.0. A SIP trunk can connect a Unified CallManager environment to a SIP proxy server, allowing these diverse network types to communicate.

SIP Messages

Communication between SIP components uses a request and response message model. Example 6-6 provides a sample of a SIP request message.

Example 6-6   *SIP Request Message*

```
INVITE: sip:bob@biloxi.com SIP/2.0
Via: SIP/2.0/UDP
pc33.atlanta.com;branch=z9hG4bK776asdhds
Max-Forwards: 70
To: Bob <sip:bob@biloxi.com>
From: Alice <sip:alice@atlanta.com>;tag=1928301774
Call-ID: a84b4c76e66710@pc33.atlanta.com
CSeq: 314159 INVITE
Contact: <sip:alice@pc33.atlanta.com>
Content-Type: application/sdp
Content-Length: 142
```

SIP communication involves the following two message types:

* **Request from a client to a server**—Consists of a request line, header lines, and a message body

* **Response from a server to a client**—Consists of a status line, header lines, and a message body

All SIP messages are text based and modeled on RFC 822, "Standard for ARPA Internet Text Messages," and RFC 2068, "Hypertext Transfer Protocol — HTTP/1.1."

SIP defines four types of headers:

* General header

* Entity header

* Request header

* Response header

The first two appear on both message types. The latter two are specific to request and response messages, respectively.

In the request line, SIP uses a *method* to indicate the action to be taken by the responding component (usually a server). The following request methods indicate the action that the responding component should take:

* **INVITE**—A client originates the INVITE method to indicate that the server is invited to participate in a session. An invitation includes a description of the session parameters.

* **ACK**—A client originates the ACK method to indicate that the client has received a response to its earlier invitation.

- **BYE**—A client or server originates the BYE method to initiate call termination.
- **CANCEL**—A client or server originates the CANCEL method to interrupt any request currently in progress. CANCEL is not used to terminate active sessions.
- **OPTIONS**—A client uses the OPTIONS method to solicit capabilities information from a server. This method is used to confirm cached information about a UA or to check the ability of a UA to accept an incoming call.
- **REGISTER**—A UA uses the REGISTER method to provide information to a network server. Registrations have a finite life and must be renewed periodically. This prevents the use of stale information when a UA moves.

SIP response messages are sent in response to a request and indicate the outcome of request interpretation and execution. Responses take one of three basic positions: success, failure, or provisional. A status code reflects the outcome of the request.

Status Codes

The following response messages indicate the status of a request:

- **1xx—Informational**—Provisional response. Indicates that the request is still being processed.
- **2xx—Successful**—Indicates that the requested action is complete and successful.
- **3xx—Redirection**—Indicates that the requestor requires further action. For example, a redirect server responds with a "moved" message to advise the client to redirect its invitation.
- **4xx—Client error**—Fatal response. Indicates that the client request is flawed or impossible to complete.
- **5xx—Server error**—Fatal response. Indicates that the request is valid but the server failed to complete it.
- **6xx—Global failure**—Fatal response. Indicates that the request cannot be fulfilled by any server.

SIP Addressing

An address in SIP is defined in the syntax for a URL with **sip:** or **sips:** (for secure SIP connections) as the URL type. SIP URLs are used in SIP messages to identify the originator, the current destination, the final recipient, and any contact party. When two UAs communicate directly with each other, the current destination and final recipient URLs are the same. However, the current destination and the final recipient are different if a proxy or redirect server is used.

An address consists of an optional user ID, a host description, and optional parameters to qualify the address more precisely. The host description might be a domain name or an IP address. A password can be associated with the user ID, and a port number can be associated with the host description.

Consider the SIP address examples presented in Example 6-7.

Example 6-7   *SIP Address Examples*

```
Fully Qualified Domain Names: sip:joe@cisco.com
E.164 Addresses:              sip:14085551234@gateway.com;user=phone
Mixed Addresses:              sip:14085551234;password=changeme@10.1.1.1
                              sip:joe@10.1.1.1
```

In Example 6-7, the **user=phone** parameter of **sip:14085551234@gateway.com; user=phone** is required to indicate that the user part of the address is a telephone number. Without the **user=phone** parameter, the user ID is taken literally as a numeric string. The **14085551234** in the URL **sip:14085551234@10.1.1.1** is an example of a numeric user ID. In the same example, the password **changeme** is defined for the user.

A SIP address can be acquired in several ways, including interacting with a user, caching information from an earlier session, or interacting with a network server. For a network server to assist, it must recognize the endpoints in the network. This knowledge is dynamically acquired by a location server, which queries its registrar server.

To contribute to this dynamic knowledge, an endpoint registers its user addresses with a registrar server. Figure 6-28 illustrates a REGISTER mode request to a registrar server.

Figure 6-28   *SIP Address Registration*

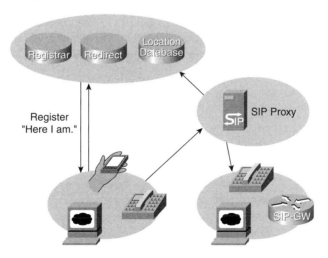

To resolve an address, a UA uses a variety of internal mechanisms such as a local host table, DNS lookup, finger, rwhois, or LDAP, or it leaves that responsibility to a network server. A network server uses any of the tools available to a UA or interacts through a nonstandard interface with a location server. Figure 6-29 illustrates a SIP proxy server resolving the address by using the services of a location server.

Figure 6-29 *SIP Address Resolution*

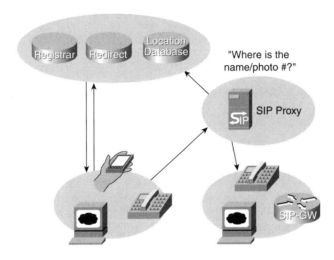

SIP Call Setup Models

If a UAC recognizes the destination UAS, the client communicates directly with the server. In situations in which the client is unable to establish a direct relationship, the client solicits the assistance of either a proxy server or a redirect server.

Direct Call Setup

When a UA recognizes the address of a terminating endpoint from cached information, or has the capacity to resolve it by some internal mechanism, the UAC might initiate direct (UAC-to-UAS) call setup procedures.

As illustrated in Figure 6-30, direct setup is the fastest and most efficient of the call setup procedures. However, direct setup has some disadvantages. It relies on cached information or internal mechanisms to resolve addresses, which can become outdated if the destination is mobile. In addition, if the UA must keep information on a large number of destinations, management of the data can become prohibitive. This makes the direct method nonscalable.

Figure 6-30 *Direct Call Setup*

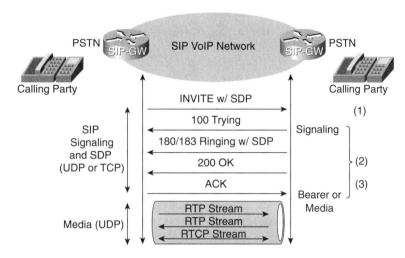

Direct call setup proceeds as follows:

1. The originating UAC sends an invitation (INVITE) to the UAS of the recipient. The message includes an endpoint description of the UAC and SDP.

2. If the UAS of the recipient determines that the call parameters are acceptable, it responds positively to the originator UAC.

3. The originating UAC issues an ACK.

At this point, the UAC and UAS have all the information required to establish RTP sessions between them.

Call Setup Using a Proxy Server

The proxy server procedure is transparent to a UA. The proxy server intercepts and forwards an invitation to the destination UA on behalf of the originator, as depicted in Figure 6-31.

A proxy server responds to the issues of the direct method by centralizing control and management of call setup and providing a more dynamic and up-to-date address resolution capability. The benefit to the UA is that it does not need to learn the coordinates of the destination UA, yet can still communicate with the destination UA. The disadvantages of this method are that using a proxy server requires more messaging and creates a dependency on the proxy server. If the proxy server fails, the UA is incapable of establishing its own sessions.

Figure 6-31 *Call Setup Using a Proxy Server*

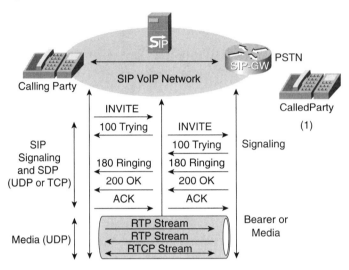

NOTE Although the proxy server acts on behalf of a UA for call setup, the UAs establish RTP sessions directly with each other.

When a proxy server is used, the call setup procedure is as follows:

1. The originating UAC sends an invitation (INVITE) to the proxy server.

2. The proxy server, if required, consults the location server to determine the path to the recipient and its IP address.

3. The proxy server sends the invitation to the UAS of the recipient.

4. If the UAS of the recipient determines that the call parameters are acceptable, it responds positively to the proxy server.

5. The proxy server responds to the originating UAC.

6. The originating UAC issues an ACK.

7. The proxy server forwards the ACK to the recipient UAS.

The UAC and UAS now have all the information required to establish RTP sessions.

Call Setup Using a Redirect Server

A redirect server is programmed to discover a path to the destination. Instead of forwarding the invitation to the destination, the redirect server reports back to a UA with the destination coordinates that the UA should try next, as shown in Figure 6-32.

Figure 6-32 *Call Setup Using a Redirect Server*

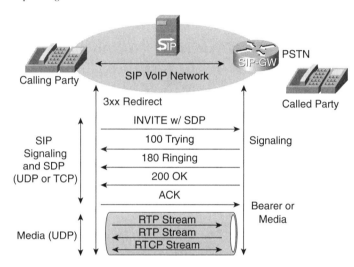

A redirect server offers many of the advantages of the proxy server. However, the number of messages involved in redirection is fewer than with the proxy server procedure. The UA has a heavier workload because it must initiate the subsequent invitation. When a redirect server is used, the call setup procedure is as follows:

1. The originating UAC sends an invitation (INVITE) to the redirect server.

2. The redirect server, if required, consults a location server to determine the path to the recipient and its IP address.

3. The redirect server returns a "moved" response to the originating UAC, which contains the IP address obtained from the location server.

4. The originating UAC acknowledges the redirection.

5. The originating UAC sends an invitation to the remote UAS.

6. If the UAS of the recipient determines that the call parameters are acceptable, it responds positively to the UAC.

7. The originating UAC issues an acknowledgment.

The UAC and UAS now have all the information required to establish RTP sessions between them.

Robust SIP Design

In a SIP environment, the failure of a network server cripples UAs that are dependent on that server. The network servers in a SIP network are the proxy server, the redirect server, the registrar server, and the location server. The most obvious way to preserve access to the critical components is to implement multiple instances of access.

For replication of a proxy or redirect server to be effective, a UA must have the ability to locate an active server dynamically. You can achieve this in any of the following ways:

- Preconfigure a UA with the address of at least two of the servers. If access to its first choice fails, the UA shifts to he second.

- If all servers are configured with the same name, you can configure a UA to look up the name using DNS. The DNS query returns the addresses of all the servers matching the name, and the UA proceeds down the list until it finds one that works.

Figure 6-33 illustrates replication of SIP servers for survivability.

Figure 6-33 *Survivability Strategies*

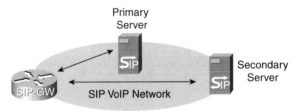

Cisco's Implementation of SIP

Cisco provides support for the following SIP components:

- **SIP user agents**—Cisco provides support for SIP UAs in Cisco IP phones. Cisco also implements SIP UA (gateway) support in the following devices:
  - Cisco voice-enabled routers (first available in Cisco IOS Release 12.1)
  - Cisco PGW 2200 PSTN gateways
  - Voice-enabled AS5xx0 access servers
  - Cisco BTS 10200 Softswitch

- **Network servers**—Cisco implements SIP proxy and redirect server support in the Cisco SIP Proxy Server. The server is an application designed for a Linux (Redhat 7.3) or Solaris 8 operating environment.

- **Other support**—Cisco PIX and ASA Security Appliances monitor the SIP handshaking to dynamically open conduits for the RTP sessions.

Configuring SIP on a Cisco Router

A SIP configuration consists of two parts: the SIP UA and the VoIP dial peers that select SIP as the session protocol.

User Agent

A Cisco voice-enabled router can be configured as a SIP UA. Example 6-8 shows a sample SIP UA configuration.

Example 6-8   *SIP User Agent*

```
Router(config)#sip-ua
Router(config-sip-ua)#retry invite 2
Router(config-sip-ua)#retry response 2
Router(config-sip-ua)#retry bye 2
Router(config-sip-ua)#retry cancel 2
Router(config-sip-ua)#sip-server dns:ACME_SERVER
```

The UA is enabled with the **sip-ua** command. Subcommands are optional. Example 6-8 also shows how you can change the value of four retry counters, which optionally adjust SIP signaling timers. The configuration also specifies the name of a SIP proxy or redirect server with the **sip-server** command.

Dial Peer

SIP is selected as the call control protocol from inside a dial peer. Specifically, SIP is requested by the **session protocol sipv2** dial peer subcommand. Example 6-9 illustrates two dial peer variations.

Example 6-9   *SIP Dial Peers*

```
Router(config)#dial-peer voice 444 voip
Router(config-dial-peer)#destination-pattern 2339000
Router(config-dial-peer)#session protocol sipv2
Router(config-dial-peer)#session target ipv4:172.18.192.205
Router(config-dial-peer)#exit
Router(config)#dial-peer voice 111 voip
Router(config-dial-peer)#destination-pattern 111
Router(config-dial-peer)#session protocol sipv2
Router(config-dial-peer)#session target sip-server
```

Notice that in Example 6-9, both dial peers include **session protocol sipv2,** and SIP is used when the destination pattern matches either dial peer. However, in **dial-peer 444,** the IP address of the server is provided as the session target. The address can be the address of a UA, proxy server, or redirect server.

In **dial peer 111,** the session target is **sip-server**. When **sip-server** is the target, the IP address of the actual server is taken from the **sip-server** subcommand in the SIP UA configuration. This means that from global configuration mode, the network administrator has entered the **sip-ua** command and the **sip-server dns:***server_name* subcommand. The address represents the location of a proxy server or redirect server. In Example 6-8, the name of the SIP server is ACME_SERVER.

Monitoring and Troubleshooting SIP

The Cisco IOS provides a series of **show** and **debug** commands to provide support for monitoring and troubleshooting SIP. Example 6-10 demonstrates sample output from the **show sip-us status** command, and Example 6-11 shows sample output from the **show sip-us timers** command.

Example 6-10   *The* **show sip-us status** *Command*

```
Router# show sip-ua status
SIP User Agent Status
SIP User Agent for UDP :ENABLED
SIP User Agent for TCP :ENABLED
SIP max-forwards :6
```

Example 6-11   *The* **show sip-us timers** *Command*

```
Router# show sip-ua timers
SIP UA Timer Values (millisecs)
Trying 500, expires 180000, connect 500, disconnect 500
```

The following **show** commands are valuable when examining the status of SIP components and troubleshooting:

- **show call active voice [brief]**—Displays the status, statistics, and parameters for all active voice calls
- **show call history voice [last *n* | record | brief]**—Displays call records from the history buffer
- **show sip-ua retry**—Displays the SIP protocol retry counts
- **show sip-ua statistics**—Displays the SIP UA response, traffic, and retry statistics
- **show sip-ua status**—Displays the SIP UA listener status, which should be enabled
- **show sip-ua timers**—Displays the current value of the SIP UA timers

The following **debug** commands are valuable when examining the status of SIP components and troubleshooting:

- **debug voip ccapi inout**—Shows every interaction with the CCAPI on both the telephone interface and on the VoIP side. By monitoring the output, you can follow the progress of a call from the inbound interface or VoIP peer to the outbound side of the call. Because this debug is very active, you should use it sparingly in a live network.

- **debug ccsip all**—Enables general SIP debugging. This debug is very active; you must use it sparingly in a live network.

- **debug ccsip calls**—Displays all SIP call details as they are updated in the SIP call control block. You must use this debug to monitor call records for suspicious clearing causes.

- **debug ccsip errors**—Traces all errors encountered by the SIP subsystem.

- **debug ccsip events**—Traces events, such as call setups, connections, and disconnections. An **events** version of a debug is often the best place to start because detailed debugs provide a great deal of useful information.

- **debug ccsip messages**—Shows the headers of SIP messages that are exchanged between a SIP client and a server.

- **debug ccsip states**—Displays the SIP states and state changes for sessions within the SIP subsystem.

MGCP Concepts and Configuration

An understanding of the features and functions of the Media Gateway Control Protocol (MGCP), its components, and the relationships that the components establish with each other is important when implementing a scalable, resilient, and secure MGCP environment. The MGCP environment is an example of a centralized call control model. This section describes how to configure MGCP on a gateway, as well as the features and functions of the MGCP environment.

MGCP and Its Associated Standards

MGCP defines an environment for controlling telephony gateways from a centralized call control component known as a *call agent*. MGCP gateways handle the translation of audio between the telephone SCN and the packet-switched network of the Internet. These gateways interact with a call agent that performs signaling and call processing.

IETF RFC 2705 defines MGCP. Additionally, RFC 2805 defines an architecture for MGCP. These IETF standards describe MGCP as a centralized device control protocol with simple endpoints. The MGCP protocol allows a central control component, or call agent, to remotely control various devices. This protocol is referred to as a *stimulus protocol,* because the endpoints and gateways cannot function alone. MGCP incorporates SDP to describe the type of session to initiate.

Basic MGCP Components

MGCP defines a number of components and concepts. An *MGCP component* is a physical piece of an MGCP network, whereas an MGCP concept is a logical piece of an MGCP network.

Figure 6-34 illustrates the following three MGCP components:

- **Endpoints**—Represent the point of interconnection between the packet network and the traditional telephony network.

- **Gateways**—Handle the translation of audio between the SCN and a packet network. A Cisco voice gateway can act as an MGCP gateway.

- **Call agent**—Exercises control over the operation of a gateway. Cisco Unified CallManager can act as an MGCP call agent.

Figure 6-34 *MGCP Components*

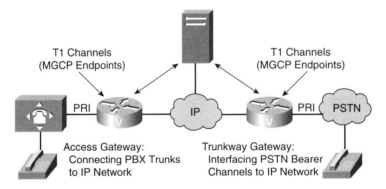

MGCP Endpoints

Endpoints represent the point of interconnection between the packet network and the traditional telephony network. Endpoints can be physical, representing an FXS port or a channel in a T1 or E1, or they can be logical, representing an attachment point to an announcement server.

To manage an endpoint, the call agent must recognize the characteristics of an endpoint. To aid in this process, endpoints are categorized into several types. The intent is to configure a call agent to manage a type of endpoint rather than to manage each endpoint individually.

RFC 2705 defines eight types of endpoints, as follows:

- **Digital Service Level Zero (DS0)**—Represents a single channel (DS0) in the digital hierarchy. A digital channel endpoint supports more than one connection.

- **Analog line**—Represents the client-side interface, such as FXS; or switch-side interface, such as FXO; to the traditional telephony network. An analog line endpoint supports more than one connection.

- **Announcement server access point**—Represents access to an announcement server (for example, to play recorded messages). An announcement server endpoint might have only one connection. Multiple users of the announcement server are modeled to use different logical endpoints.

- **Interactive voice response (IVR) access point**—Represents access to an IVR service. An IVR endpoint has one connection. Multiple users of the IVR system use different logical endpoints.

- **Conference bridge access point**—Represents access to a specific conference. Each conference is modeled as a distinct endpoint. A conference bridge endpoint supports more than one connection.

- **Packet relay**—Represents access that bridges two connections for interconnecting incompatible gateways or relaying them through a firewall environment. A packet relay endpoint has two connections.

- **Wiretap access point**—Represents access for recording or playing back a connection. A wiretap access point endpoint has one connection.

- **ATM trunk side interface**—Represents a single instance of an audio channel in the context of an ATM network. An ATM interface supports more than one connection.

When interacting with a gateway, the call agent directs its commands to the gateway for the express purpose of managing an endpoint or a group of endpoints. An endpoint identifier, as its name suggests, provides a name for an endpoint.

Endpoint identifiers consist of two parts: a local name of the endpoint in the context of the gateway and the domain name of the gateway itself. The two parts are separated by an at sign (@). If the local part represents a hierarchy, the subparts of the hierarchy are separated by a slash. In Figure 6-35, the local ID might be representative of a particular gateway/circuit #, and the circuit # might in turn be representative of a circuit ID/channel #. In Figure 6-35, **mgcp.gateway.cisco.com** is the domain name, and **t1toSJ/17** refers to channel 17 in the T1 to San Jose.

Figure 6-35 *MGCP Endpoint Identifier*

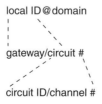

local ID@domain

gateway/circuit #

circuit ID/channel #

t1toSJ/17@mgcp.gateway.cisco.com

MGCP Gateways

Gateways are clustering points for endpoints. These gateways handle the translation of audio between the SCN and the packet network.

Although gateways are implemented in real systems, from a modeling point of view, gateways are logical components. In this context, gateways represent a clustering of a single type and profile of endpoints.

NOTE   A gateway interacts with one call agent only. Therefore, a gateway associates with one call agent at a time.

RFC 2705 identifies the following seven types of gateways:

- **Trunk gateway Signaling System 7 (SS7) ISDN User Part (ISUP)**—Supports digital circuit endpoints subject to ISDN signaling

- **Trunk gateway multifrequency (MF)**—Typically supports digital or analog circuit endpoints that are connected to a service provider of an enterprise switch that is subject to MF signaling

- **Network access server (NAS)**—Supports an interconnect to endpoints over which data (for example, modem) applications are provided

- **Combined NAS/VoIP gateway**—Supports an interconnect to endpoints over which a combination of voice and data access is provided

- **Access gateway**—Supports analog and digital endpoints connected to a PBX

- **Residential gateway**—Supports endpoints connected to traditional analog interfaces

- **Announcement servers**—Supports endpoints that represent access to announcement services

Multiple gateway types, and multiple instances of the same type, can be incorporated into a single physical gateway implementation.

MGCP Call Agents

A call agent, or Media Gateway Controller (MGC), represents the central controller in an MGCP environment, as depicted in Figure 6-36.

A call agent exercises control over the operation of a gateway and its associated endpoints by requesting that a gateway observe and report events. In response to the events, the call agent instructs the endpoint what signal, if any, the endpoint should send to the attached telephone equipment. This requires a call agent to recognize each endpoint type that it supports and the signaling characteristics of each physical and logical interface attached to a gateway.

Figure 6-36 *MGCP Call Agent*

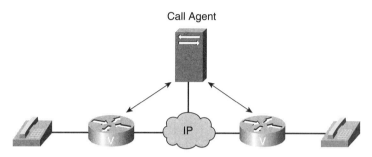

Call Agent

IP

A call agent uses its directory of endpoints and the relationship that each endpoint has with the dial plan to determine call routing patterns. These call agents also have the responsibility of initiating all VoIP call legs.

Basic MGCP Concepts

The following are MGCP's basic concepts:

- **Calls and connections**—Allow end-to-end calls to be established by connecting two or more endpoints
- **Events and signals**—Allow a call agent to provide instructions for the gateway
- **Packages and digit maps**—Allow a gateway to determine the call destination

MGCP Sessions

End-to-end calls are established by connecting two or more endpoints, as illustrated in Figure 6-37. To establish a call, the call agent instructs the gateway associated with each endpoint to make a connection with a specific endpoint or an endpoint of a particular type. The gateway returns the session parameters of its connection to the call agent, which in turn sends these session parameters to the other gateway. With this method, each gateway acquires the necessary session parameters to establish RTP sessions between the endpoints. All connections associated with the same call share a common call ID and the same media stream. At the conclusion of a call, the call agent sends a delete connection request to each gateway.

To create a multipoint call, the call agent instructs an endpoint to create multiple connections. The endpoint bears the responsibility for mixing audio signals.

Figure 6-37 *MGCP Calls and Connections*

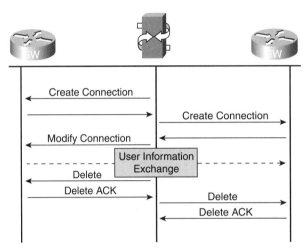

MGCP Control Commands

A call agent uses control commands or messages to direct its gateways and their operational behavior. Gateways use the following control commands in responding to requests from a call agent and notifying the call agent of events and abnormal behavior:

- **EndpointConfiguration (EPCF)**—Identifies the coding characteristics of the endpoint interface on the line side of the gateway. The call agent issues the command.

- **NotificationRequest (RQNT)**—Instructs the gateway to watch for events on an endpoint and specifies the action to take when the events occur. The call agent issues the command.

- **Notify (NTFY)**—Informs the call agent of an event for which notification was requested. The gateway issues the command.

- **CreateConnection (CRCX)**—Instructs the gateway to establish a connection with an endpoint. The call agent issues the command.

- **ModifyConnection (MDCX)**—Instructs the gateway to update its connection parameters for a previously established connection. The call agent issues the command.

- **DeleteConnection (DLCX)**—Informs the recipient to delete a connection. The call agent or the gateway can issue the command. The gateway or the call agent issues the command to advise that it no longer has the resources to sustain the call.

- **AuditEndpoint (AUEP)**—Requests the status of an endpoint. The call agent issues the command.

- **AuditConnection (AUCX)**—Requests the status of a connection. The call agent issues the command.

- **RestartInProgress (RSIP)**—Notifies the call agent that the gateway and its endpoints are removed from service or are being placed back in service. The gateway issues the command.

MGCP Call Flows

Figure 6-38 illustrates a dialog between a call agent and two gateways.

Figure 6-38 *MGCP Call Flows*

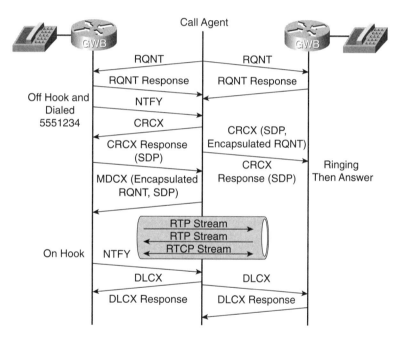

Although the gateways in this example are both residential gateways, the following principles of operation are the same for other gateway types:

1. The call agent sends a notification request (RQNT) to each gateway. Because the gateways are residential gateways, the request instructs the gateways to wait for an off-hook transition (event). When the off-hook transition event occurs, the call agent instructs the gateways to supply dial tone (signal). The call agent asks the gateway to monitor for other events as well. By providing a digit map in the request, the call agent can have the gateway collect digits before it notifies the call agent.

2. The gateways respond to the request. At this point, the gateways and the call agent wait for a triggering event.

3. A user on Gateway A goes off hook. As instructed by the call agent in its earlier request, the gateway provides dial tone. Because the gateway is provided with a digit map, it begins to collect digits (as they are dialed) until either a match is made or no match is possible. For the remainder of this example, assume that the digits match a digit map entry.

4. Gateway A sends a notify (NTFY) to the call agent to advise the call agent that a requested event was observed. The notify message identifies the endpoint, the event, and, in this case, the dialed digits.

5. After confirming that a call is possible based on the dialed digits, the call agent instructs Gateway A to create a connection (CRCX) with its endpoint.

6. The gateway responds with a session description if it is able to accommodate the connection. The session description identifies at least the IP address and UDP port for use in a subsequent RTP session. The gateway does not have a session description for the remote side of the call, and the connection enters a *wait state.*

7. The call agent prepares and sends a connection request to Gateway B. In the request, the call agent provides the session description obtained from Gateway A. The connection request is targeted to a single endpoint if only one endpoint is capable of handling the call, or to any one of a set of endpoints. The call agent also embeds a notification request that instructs the gateway about the signals and events that it should now consider relevant. In this example, where the gateway is residential, the signal requests ringing, and the event is an off-hook transition.

8. Gateway B responds to the request with its session description. Notice that Gateway B has both session descriptions and recognizes how to establish its RTP sessions.

9. The call agent relays the session description to Gateway A in a modify connection request (MDCX). This request might contain an encapsulated notify request that describes the relevant signals and events at this stage of the call setup. Now Gateway A and Gateway B have the required session descriptions to establish the RTP sessions over which the audio travels.

10. At the conclusion of the call, one of the endpoints recognizes an on-hook transition. In the example, the user on Gateway A hangs up. Because the call agent requested a notification of such an event, Gateway A notifies the call agent.

11. The call agent sends a delete connection (DLCX) request to each gateway.

12. The gateways delete the connections and respond.

Robust MGCP Design

In the MGCP environment, the call agent controls all call setup processing on the IP and the telephony sides of a gateway. Because a gateway is associated with only one call agent at a time, if that call agent fails or is inaccessible for any reason, the gateway and its endpoints are left uncontrolled and, for all practical purposes, useless. Cisco developed two methods to handle lost communication between a call agent and its gateways: *MGCP switchover and switchback* and *MGCP gateway fallback*. The following sections describe how these features operate.

MGCP Switchover and Switchback

MGCP switchover permits the use of redundant MGCP call agents. This feature requires two or more Cisco Unified CallManager servers to operate as MGCP call agents. One Cisco Unified CallManager server becomes the primary server and functions as the MGCP call agent. The other Cisco Unified CallManager servers remain available as backup servers.

The MGCP gateway monitors MGCP messages sent by the Cisco Unified CallManager server. If traffic is undetected, the gateway transmits keepalive packets to which the Cisco Unified CallManager server responds. If the gateway does not detect packets from the Cisco Unified CallManager for a specified period, the gateway tries to establish a new connection with a backup Cisco Unified CallManager server.

You can configure a Cisco voice gateway to reestablish connection with the primary Cisco Unified CallManager server when it becomes available again. This is the *switchback* function.

MGCP Gateway Fallback

MGCP gateway fallback is a feature that improves the reliability of MGCP branch networks. A WAN link connects the MGCP gateway at the remote site to the Cisco Unified CallManager at the central sites (that is, the MGCP call agent). If the WAN link fails, the fallback feature keeps the gateway working as an H.323 gateway, as depicted in Figure 6-39.

MGCP gateway fallback works in conjunction with the Survivable Remote Site Telephony (SRST) feature. SRST allows Cisco gateways and routers to manage connections temporarily for Cisco IP phones when a connection to a Cisco Unified CallManager is unavailable.

Figure 6-39 *Survivable Remote Site Telephony*

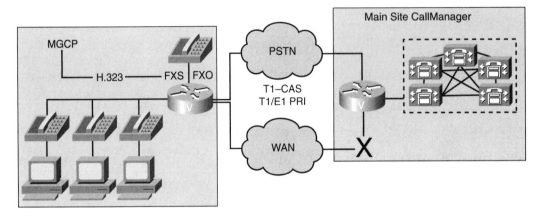

Cisco's Implementation of MGCP

Cisco provides support for MGCP gateways and the call agent in the following ways:

- **Gateways**—Cisco implements MGCP trunk gateway and residential gateway support in the following devices:
  - Cisco voice-enabled routers (first available in Cisco IOS Release 12.1)
  - Cisco PGW 2200 PSTN gateways
  - Cisco Voice Gateway 224 (VG224)
  - Voice-enabled AS5*xx*0 access servers
  - BTS 10200 Softswitch
- **Call agent**—Cisco implements call agent support in the following applications:
  - Cisco Unified CallManager
  - BTS 10200 Softswitch

Configuring MGCP

Example 6-12 highlights the commands required to configure an MGCP residential gateway.

Example 6-12 *Configuring an MGCP Residential Gateway*

```
Router(config)#ccm-manager mgcp
Router(config)#mgcp
Router(config)#mgcp call-agent 172.20.5.20
Router(config)#voice-port 1/0/0
Router(config-voiceport)#voice-port 1/0/1
Router(config-voiceport)#exit
Router(config)#dial-peer voice 1 pots
Router(config-dial-peer)#application MGCPAPP
Router(config-dial-peer)#port 1/0/0
Router(config-dial-peer)#exit
Router(config)#dial-peer voice 2 pots
Router(config-dial-peer)#application MGCPAPP
Router(config-dial-peer)#port 1/0/1
```

MGCP is invoked with the **mgcp c**ommand. If the call agent expects the gateway to use its default port (UDP 2427), the **mgcp** command is used without any parameters. If the call agent requires a different port, then the port must be configured as a parameter in the **mgcp** command. For example, **mgcp 5036** tells the gateway to use port 5036 instead of the default port.

At least one **mgcp call-agent** command is required below the **mgcp** command. This command indicates the location of the call agent. The command identifies the call agent by an IP address or a host name. Using a host name adds a measure of fault tolerance in a network that has multiple call agents. When the gateway asks the DNS for the IP address of the call agent, the DNS can provide more than one address, in which case the gateway can use either one. If multiple instances of the **mgcp call-agent** command are configured, the gateway uses the first call agent to respond.

When the parameters of the MGCP gateway are configured, the active voice ports (endpoints) are associated with the MGCP. Dial peer 1 illustrates an **application MGCPAPP** subcommand. This command binds the voice port (**1/0/0** in this case) to MGCP. Also, notice that the dial peer does not have a destination pattern. A destination pattern is not used because the relationship between the dial number and the port is maintained by the call agent.

NOTE   The **ccm-manager-mgcp** command is required only if the call agent is a Cisco Unified CallManager. Also, in some recent versions of the Cisco IOS, the **application MGCPAPP** subcommand has been replaced with the **service mgcp** command.

Example 6-13 illustrates the configuration of a trunk gateway.

Example 6-13 *Configuring an MGCP Trunk Gateway*

```
Router(config)#ccm-manager mgcp
Router(config)#mgcp 4000
Router(config)#mgcp call-agent 209.165.202.129 4000
Router(config)#controller t1 1/0
Router(config-controller)#framing esf
Router(config-controller)#clock source internal
Router(config-controller)#ds0-group 1 timeslots 1-24 type none service mgcp
Router(config-controller)#exit
Router(config)#controller t1 1/1
Router(config-controller)#framing esf
Router(config-controller)#clock source internal
Router(config-controller)#ds0-group 1 timeslots 1-24 type none service mgcp
Router(config-controller)#exit
```

Configuring trunk gateways requires the address or the name of the call agent, which is a requirement common to a residential gateway (RGW). The trunk package is the default for a trunk gateway and does not need to be configured. Again, other parameters are optional.

Example 6-13 illustrates commands for configuring a trunk gateway. Instead of using the **application mgcpapp** command in a dial peer, a trunk endpoint identifies its association with MGCP using the **service mgcp** parameter in the **ds0-group controller** subcommand. As always in MGCP, the call agent maintains the relationship between the endpoint (in this case a digital trunk) and its address.

Cisco Unified CallManager MGCP Configuration

Cisco Unified CallManager acts as a call agent in an MGCP environment. Therefore, a complete MGCP setup requires Unified CallManager configuration in addition to IOS configuration on the voice-enabled gateway.

NOTE The following steps apply to Cisco Unified CallManager version 4.1. Menu options might vary in other releases. Also, in releases prior to 4.1, the URL used to access the CCM administrative interface uses http, as opposed to https.

The following set of steps describes how to configure Cisco Unified CallManager as an MGCP call agent for an IOS MGCP gateway:

Step 1. Access Cisco Unified CallManager's administrative interface, shown in Figure 6-40, by pointing a browser to the following URL:

https://*CCM_IP_Address_or_Name*/ccmadmin

Figure 6-40 *Cisco Unified CallManager Administrative Interface*

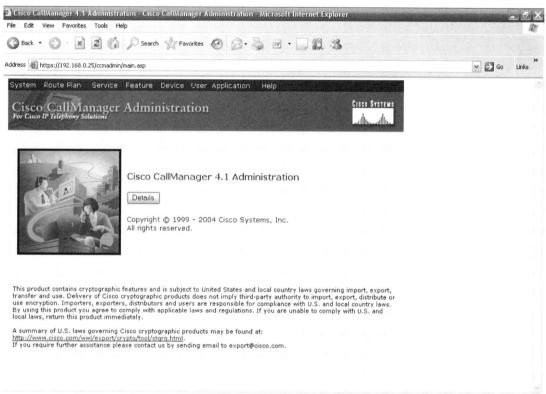

Step 2. After logging in with the appropriate credentials, select the **Device** menu and then select the **Gateway** option.

Step 3. Click the **Add a New Gateway** link, shown in Figure 6-41.

Figure 6-41 *Add a New Gateway*

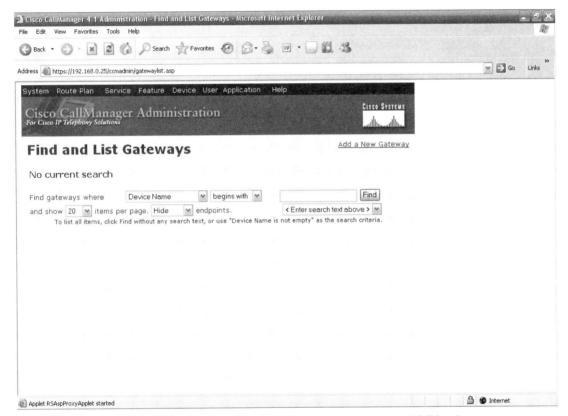

Step 4. From the Gateway Type drop-down menu, select the IOS hardware platform you have configured as an MGCP gateway (for example, 26XX), as shown in Figure 6-42, and click the **Next** button.

Step 5. In the Domain Name field, enter the DNS name of the IOS gateway if the gateway's domain name is resolvable. Otherwise, use the host name as defined on the MGCP gateway (for example, R4).

Step 6. Select an appropriate Unified CallManager group (for example, Default) from the Unified CallManager Group drop-down menu.

Step 7. Identify the module(s) (for example, NM-1V) installed in the gateway's slots, as illustrated in Figure 6-43, and click the **Insert** button.

Figure 6-42 *Selecting a Gateway*

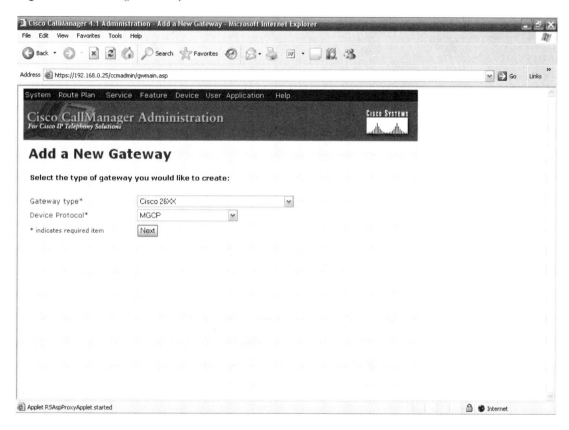

Figure 6-43 *Identifying Network Modules*

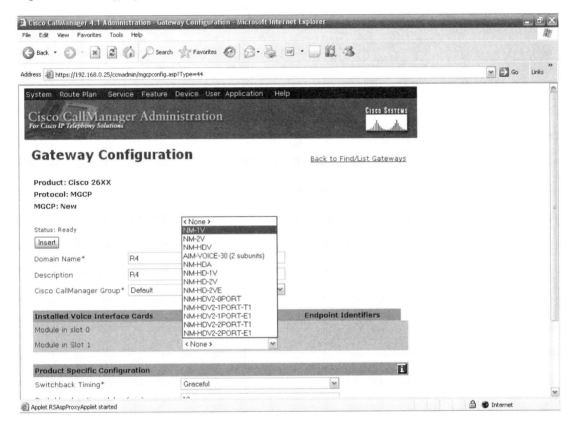

Step 8. Once the screen refreshes, you are prompted for the subunits (for example, specific voice interface cards) installed in the module(s) you specified in Step 7. Select the appropriate subunit(s), as shown in Figure 6-44, and click the **Update** button.

Figure 6-44 *Identifying Voice Interface Cards*

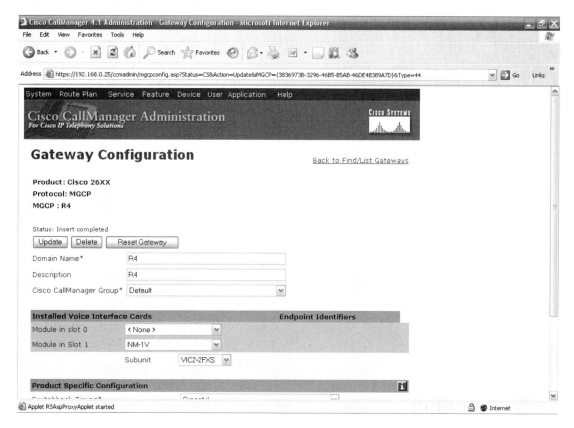

Step 9. Once the screen refreshes, you see links for the endpoint identifiers for the voice ports in the voice interface card(s) you specified in Step 8, as depicted in Figure 6-45. To configure an endpoint, click the appropriate endpoint identifier (for example, 1/0/0).

Figure 6-45 *Selecting an Endpoint Identifier*

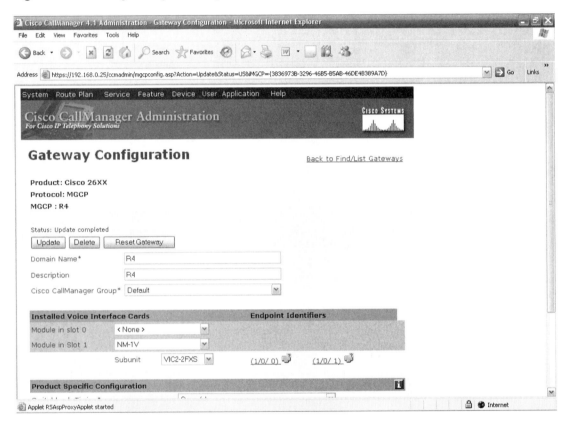

Step 10. After the screen refreshes, select an appropriate device pool (for
example, Default) from the Device Pool drop-down menu, as illustrated
in Figure 6-46, and click the **Insert** button.

Figure 6-46 *Specifying a Device Pool*

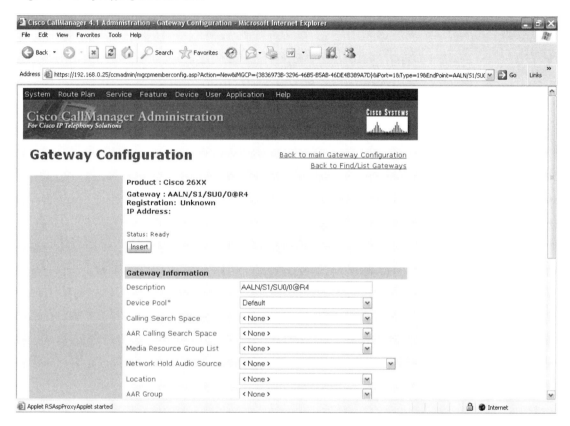

Step 11. After the screen refreshes, you have the option to add a directory number (that is, a DN) to the endpoint. Click the **Add DN** link in the left pane of the screen, as shown in Figure 6-47.

Figure 6-47   *Adding a Directory Number*

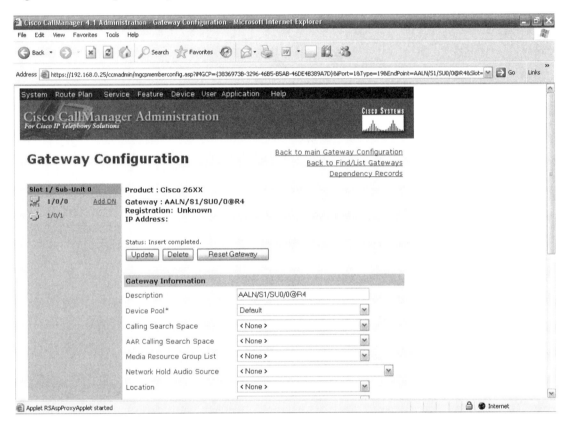

Step 12.   After the screen refreshes, enter the endpoint's directory number (for example, 3333) in the Directory Number field, as illustrated in Figure 6-48, and click the **Add** button.

Figure 6-48 *Specifying a Directory Number*

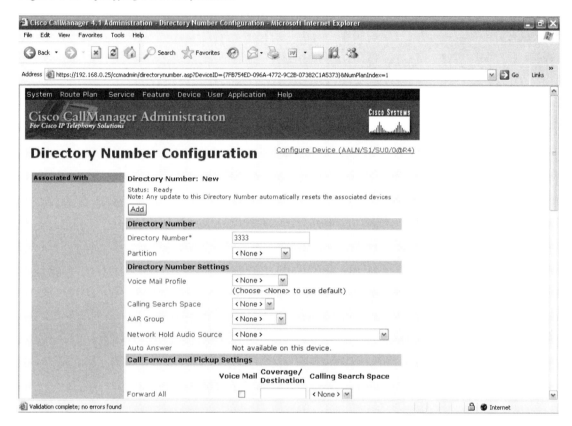

Step 13. After the gateway has registered with the call agent (that is, Cisco Unified CallManager), the Gateway Configuration screen confirms the registration and shows the IP address of the MGCP gateway, as shown in Figure 6-49.

Figure 6-49 *Verifying Gateway Registration*

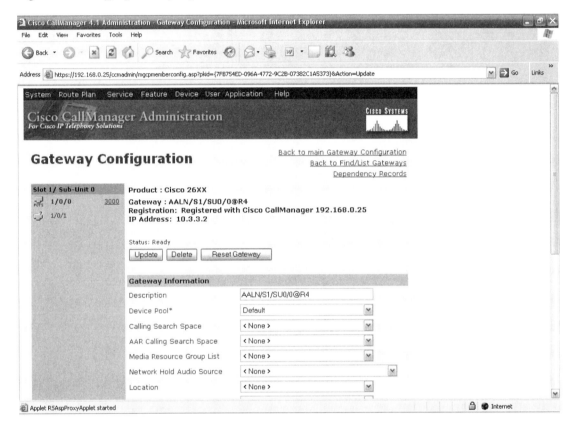

Monitoring and Troubleshooting MGCP

Several **show** and **debug** commands provide support for monitoring and troubleshooting MGCP. These commands are valuable for examining the current status of the MGCP components and for troubleshooting. You should be familiar with the information provided from each command and how this information can help you.

The following **show** commands are useful for monitoring and troubleshooting MGCP:

- **show call active voice [brief]**—Displays the status, statistics, and parameters for all active voice calls. When the call is disconnected, this information is transferred to the history records.

- **show call history voice [last *n* | record | brief]**—Displays call records from the history buffer.

- **show mgcp**—Displays basic configuration information about the gateway.

- **show mgcp connection**—Displays details of the current connections.

- **show mgcp endpoint**—Displays a list of the voice ports that are configured for MGCP.

- **show mgcp statistics**—Displays a count of the successful and unsuccessful control commands (shown in Example 6-14). You should investigate a high unsuccessful count.

Example 6-14 *The* **show mgcp statistics** *Output*

```
Router# show mgcp statistics
UDP pkts rx 8, tx 9
Unrecognized rx pkts 0, MGCP message parsing errors 0
Duplicate MGCP ack tx 0, Invalid versions count 0
CreateConn rx 4, successful 0, failed 0
DeleteConn rx 2, successful 2, failed 0
ModifyConn rx 4, successful 4, failed 0
DeleteConn tx 0, successful 0, failed 0
NotifyRequest rx 0, successful 4, failed 0
AuditConnection rx 0, successful 0, failed 0
AuditEndpoint rx 0, successful 0, failed 0
RestartInProgress tx 1, successful 1, failed 0
Notify tx 0, successful 0, failed 0
ACK tx 8, NACK tx 0
ACK rx 0, NACK rx 0
IP address based Call Agents statistics:
IP address 10.24.167.3, Total msg rx 8, successful 8,
failed 0
```

In addition to **show** commands, the Cisco IOS also provides the following **debug** commands, which are useful for monitoring and troubleshooting MGCP:

- **debug voip ccapi inout**—Shows every interaction with the call control API on the telephone interface and the VoIP side. Watching the output allows users to follow the progress of a call from the inbound interface or VoIP peer to the outbound side of the call. This debug is very active. You must use it sparingly in a live network.

- **debug mgcp [all | errors | events | packets | parser]**—Reports all MGCP command activity. You must use this debug to trace the MGCP request and responses.

Comparing Call Control Models

Understanding the capabilities of the H.323, SIP, and MGCP models helps you decide which call control model best meets your requirements. This section compares the features and functions of the three call control models. This section also highlights the environments for which each call control model is best suited.

Call Control Model Feature Comparison

In a generic model, the components of signaling and call control are identified as common control components and endpoints. Common control components provide a set of optional services: call administration and accounting, call status, address management, and admission control. Table 6-1 identifies how the basic components of the generic model are configured in H.323, SIP, and MGCP, and, if applicable, where optional services are provided.

Table 6-1 *Components and Services*

	H.323	**SIP**	**MGCP**
Common Control Components	Gatekeeper	Proxy server, redirect server, location server, registrar server	Call agent
Endpoints	Gateway, terminal	Client (IP phone gateway)	Media gateway
Call Administration and Accounting	Gateway, gatekeeper	Gateway	Call agent
Call Status	Gateway, gatekeeper	Gateway	Call agent
Address Management	Gatekeeper	Location server, registrar server	Call agent
Admission Control	Gatekeeper	Not directly supported	Call agent

As a design aid, Table 6-2 compares several factors that can influence your decision to select H.323, SIP, or MGCP.

Table 6-2 *Call Control Model Characteristics*

	H.323	**SIP**	**MGCP**
Standards Body	ITU-T	IETF	IETF
Architecture	Distributed	Distributed	Centralized
Current Version	H.323v4	SIP 2.0 (RFC 3261)	MGCP 1.0 (RFC 2705)
Signaling Transport	TCP (call signaling channel, H.245 control channel) or UDP (RAS channel)	TCP or UDP	UDP

Table 6-2   *Call Control Model Characteristics (Continued)*

	H.323	**SIP**	**MGCP**
Call Control Encoding	Abstract Syntax Notation One (ASN.1) basic encoding rules (BER)	Text	Text
Supplementary Services	Provided by endpoints or call control	Provided by endpoints or call control	Provided by call control

NOTE   As of version 3 of H.323, the call signaling channel and the H.245 control channel can operate over UDP.

The following sections describe the call control protocol characteristics identified in Table 6-2.

Standards Body: ITU-T or IETF

The two originating authorities for the model might seem to have little relevance. However, the ITU-T and the IETF work under different conditions, a fact which impacts the results and the speed of their work.

Although the ITU-T is older than the IETF, its associated publishing cycle and consensus process is often blamed for delay. However, its rigorous procedures result in mature recommendations with consistent use of language and terminology. The consensus process requires a high level of agreement and is generally accepted as the preferred way to proceed internationally.

Without being subject to the rigors of the ITU-T's procedures and policies, the IETF can respond quickly to user demands, although the solutions can be less mature than those created by the ITU-T.

Knowing which standards body is involved provides a sense of the standards development process, the pace of work, and the quality of results.

Architecture: Centralized or Distributed

The distinction between the centralized architecture and the distributed architecture can influence which model you choose. For example, a design that had call routing intelligence located at a central location might benefit from the centralized architecture.

Current Version

The current version of a specification or recommendation is an indication of the specification's maturity. For example, H.323 is currently in version 4, which provides some indication as to its level of maturity, as compared to other protocols. For example, SIP is currently at version 2.0, and MGCP is at version 1.0.

Signaling Transport: TCP or UDP

Understanding the underlying transport of the signaling channels helps to explain the relationship among H.323, SIP, or MGCP components. Connectionless, UDP-based relationships must shift reliability and sequencing into the application, making them more complex. Both reliability and sequencing are built into TCP. However, UDP-based applications are designed to respond more quickly than TCP-based applications. This speed is significant, for example, during call setup.

Call Control Encoding: ASN.1 or Text

Traditionally, the ITU-T and the IETF have proposed different methods of encoding information that travels between endpoints. It is generally accepted that applications using text-based encoding are easier to encode, decode, and troubleshoot, compared to ASN.1-based encoding, which is more compact and efficient.

Supplementary Services: Endpoint or Call Control

Where and how you introduce supplementary services (for example, hold, transfer, and conferencing services) can be important considerations in a comparison of H.323, SIP, or MGCP.

Services deployed throughout the network are easily implemented centrally in a call control component. Services with regional relevance can be implemented effectively in the endpoints.

Strengths of H.323, SIP, and MGCP

Because there are several different telecommunication environments, more than one choice for signaling and call control is necessary. This section describes some of the strengths of the call control models discussed in this chapter.

H.323

H.323, which was the only viable option in VoIP signaling and call control solutions for a long period of time, is mature and attracts supporters. Consequently, H.323 products are widely available and deployed extensively.

When properly designed, H.323 is both *scalable* (accommodates the implementation of large distributed networks) and *adaptable* (allows for the introduction of new features). The H.323 call control model works well for large enterprises because gatekeeper-centralized call control provides some capability for Operation, Administration, and Maintenance (OA&M).

SIP

SIP is a multimedia protocol that uses the architecture and messages found in popular Internet applications. By using a distributed architecture, with URLs for naming, and text-based messaging, SIP takes advantage of the Internet model for building VoIP networks and applications.

SIP is used in a distributed architecture and allows companies to build large-scale networks that are scalable, resilient, and redundant. SIP provides mechanisms for interconnecting with other VoIP networks and for adding intelligence and new features on the endpoints, SIP proxy, or redirect servers.

Although the IETF is progressive in defining extensions that allow SIP to work with legacy voice networks, the primary motivation behind SIP is to create an environment supporting next-generation communication models that utilize the Internet and Internet applications. In addition, the lack of centralized management support makes SIP more suitable for growing, dynamic organizations and Internet telephony service providers.

MGCP

MGCP describes an architecture in which call control and services such as OA&M are centrally added to a VoIP network. As a result, MGCP architecture closely resembles the existing PSTN architecture and services.

In a centralized architecture, MGCP allows companies to build large-scale networks that are scalable, resilient, and redundant. MGCP provides mechanisms for interconnecting with other VoIP networks and adding intelligence and features to the call agent.

MGCP works well for organizations that are comfortable with centralized management and control. For example, service providers are well suited for MGCP.

Selecting Appropriate Call Control

Call control selection takes into account corporate policy and business requirements. Consider some of the major design requirements for MGCP, H.323, and SIP.

H.323 Call Control Model

The H.323 call control model is used where there is a strong requirement for mature standards with distributed call-logic functionality. Figure 6-50 illustrates a topology using the H.323 call control model.

Figure 6-50 *H.323 Call Control Solution*

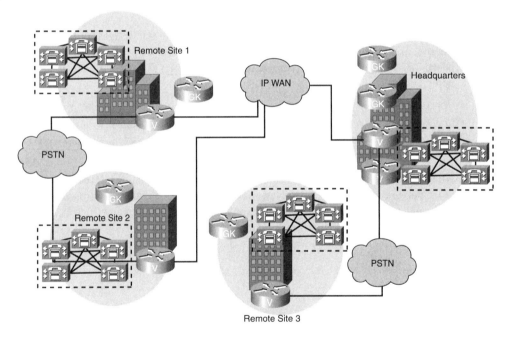

The H.323 call control model has the following design characteristics:

- **Distributed call control intelligence**—H.323 gateways contain the intelligence to perform all required functions for call routing, call completion, and call termination. External call control servers are not required.

- **Mature call control protocol**—H.323 was designed for multimedia transport across a LAN environment. It was first approved in 1996. H.323 is widely deployed because it was the first comprehensive voice-signaling protocol available for VoIP deployment.

- **Local call control functionality**—The ability to add applications locally allows individual sites to implement and control applications independently of the head office. This ability enables locations to quickly implement new services when they are required.

- **Scalability**—As H.323 networks grow, gatekeepers provide scalability by dividing the growing network into zones and distributing call control configuration to one gatekeeper per zone. When the number of zones grows, hierarchical scalability provides for the use of directory gatekeepers (DGKs) to provide summarization for multiple zone gatekeepers.

- **Dial plan administered at gatekeeper level**—When the VoIP network expands, configuring dial plans in individual gateways becomes cumbersome and inefficient. H.323 specifies the ability for a gatekeeper to dynamically learn dial plan assignments from gateways, thereby simplifying dial plan configuration in large networks.

SIP Call Control Model

The SIP call control model is used where there is a strong requirement for innovative services and application deployment with distributed call-logic functionality. Figure 6-51 illustrates a topology using the SIP call control model.

The SIP call control model has the following design characteristics:

- **Distributed call control intelligence**—SIP gateways contain the intelligence to perform all required functions for call routing, call completion, and call termination. External call control servers are not required.

- **Easy development of new services and applications**—The use of widely deployed Internet standards such as HTTP and Simple Mail Transfer Protocol (SMTP) as part of the SIP standard translates into a large base of developers with the ability to create SIP-enabled applications.

- **Access to a wide variety of endpoints**—SIP-enabled endpoints include IP phones, PCs, laptops, personal digital assistants (PDAs), and cell phones.

- **Scalability**—SIP operates in a stateless manner so that servers need not maintain state information and can handle more concurrent sessions. The use of proxy servers, redirect servers, location servers, and registrar servers enables large groups of users to communicate efficiently.

Figure 6-51 *SIP Call Control Solution*

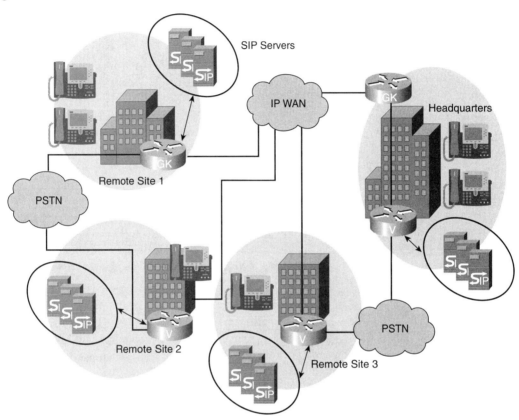

MGCP Call Control Model

The MGCP call control model is used where there is a strong requirement for centralized control. Figure 6-52 illustrates a topology using the MGCP call control model.

The MGCP call control model has the following design characteristics:

- **Centralized management, provisioning, and call control**—All intelligence resides in the MGCP call agent. This approach presents a central site for configuration management, provisioning of new devices and endpoints, and call control configuration.

- **Centralized application servers**—Although centralized application servers are not required in an MGCP environment, typically when there is a strong requirement to centralize call control, the same requirement is applied to application servers.

Figure 6-52 *MGCP Call Control Solution*

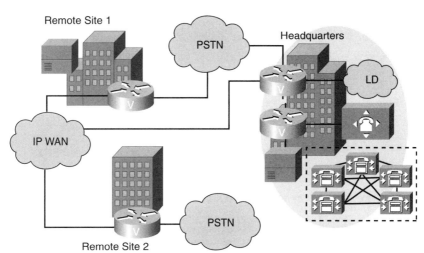

- **Centralized dial plan management**—MGCP enables a centralized approach to dial plan management. All configuration for access to endpoints resides in the central call agent.

- **Easy implementation of new services**—When new services are implemented in a centralized call control model, only the call agent needs to be updated. Individual gateways across the enterprise can remain untouched, speeding the implementation of upgrades and new services and simplifying fallback procedures.

- **Scalability**—Cisco Unified CallManager clusters, acting as MGCP call agents, can support up to 30,000 devices per cluster.

Summary

IP telephony networks use call control protocols to make call routing decisions. This chapter detailed three call control protocols: H.323, SIP, and MGCP. H.323 represents the most mature of the call control standards. However, in a Cisco Unified CallManager environment, designers might prefer to use MGCP, which leverages Cisco Unified CallManager's centralized call control capability. SIP is an emerging standard suitable for environments where development and deployment of new services and applications in a distributed call control environment is required.

Chapter Review Questions

The following questions test your knowledge of topics explained in this chapter. You can find the answers to the questions in Appendix A, "Answers to Chapter Review Questions."

1. Which three of the following are examples of VoIP call control protocols?

   a SIP

   b RSVP

   c Megaco

   d SAP

   e SGBP

2. Which two functions are associated with CDRs?

   a Bandwidth management

   b Troubleshooting

   c Billing

   d User support

   e Capacity planning

3. In H.323 call establishment, which channel do endpoints use to communicate with the gatekeeper?

   a B-channel

   b RAS channel

   c Forward channel

   d In-band control channel

4. The following command is configured on a gatekeeper:

   zone remote gk-zone2.test.com test.com 10.52.218.46 1719

   What is the function of this command?

   a Defines a technology prefix

   b Defines the identity and IP address of a neighboring gatekeeper c Defines the identity and IP address of the local gatekeeper

d Defines the IP address of the gateway to which default calls will be forwarded

5. Which four of the following are SIP servers?

a Registrar

b Gateway

c Redirect

d Location

e Proxy

6. What does the **session target sip-server** dial peer subcommand do?

a It tells the router to use DNS to resolve **sip-server**.

b It tells the router to use the server identified in the SIP UA configuration.

c It tells the router to use SIP as the session protocol.

d This is invalid syntax, and an error will be generated.

7. Which call control model is used by MGCP?

a Distributed

b Centralized

c Ad-hoc

d Hybrid

8. How do you configure a router to use MGCP on a digital port?

a Add the **application mgcpapp** subcommand to the dial peer.

b Add the **service mgcp** subcommand to the dial peer.

c Add the parameter **application mgcpapp** to the **ds0-group controller** subcommand.

d Add the **service mgcp** parameter to the **ds0-group controller** subcommand.

9. Which call control model's encoding is more compact but harder to decode and troubleshoot?

   a H.323

   b SGCP

   c SIP

   d MGCP

10. MGCP supports which of these requirements?

    a Integration with instant messaging

    b Distributed call processing

    c Scalability through the use of proxy servers, redirect servers, registrar servers, and location servers

    d Call processing controlled from a central server with no intelligence at the end-points

Lab Exercise: H.323 Gatekeeper

In this lab, you will configure two routers to act as H.323 gateways and one router to act as an H.323 gatekeeper. Routers R1 and R3, which are illustrated in Figure 6-53, will each act as H.323 gateways in different zones. Router R2 will serve as an H.323 gatekeeper and restrict call bandwidth usage between these zones to a total of 64 and limit per-call bandwidth to 16 kbps.

Figure 6-53 *Lab Topology*

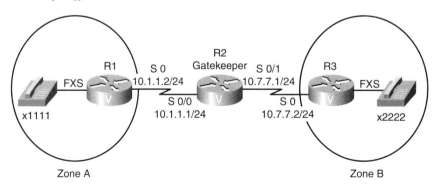

The per-call bandwidth limit of 16 kbps accommodates a single G.729 call. The gatekeeper does not measure the actual bandwidth used per call. Rather, the gatekeeper assumes the required bandwidth for a call is double the bandwidth required for the payload of the call. In this example, a call using the G.729 CODEC requires 8 kbps of bandwidth for the voice payload, not including overhead. Therefore, the H.323 gatekeeper assumes the required bandwidth for the call is double that amount (that is, 16 kbps).

Task 1: Configure the H.323 Gatekeeper

In this task, you will configure router R2 as an H.323 gatekeeper.

Complete these steps:

Step 1. Enable gatekeeper services on router R2 with the **gatekeeper** command.

Step 2. In gatekeeper configuration mode, with the following commands, identify two local zones that are part of the **acme.com** domain:

```
zone local ZoneA acme.com 10.7.7.1
zone local ZoneB acme.com
```

Note the IP address of **10.7.7.1** in the first **zone local** command. This optional parameter specifies the RAS address used when endpoints in local zones register with the gatekeeper. The IOS accepts only a single IP address for the local zone's RAS address, which is why the **zone local** command for **ZoneB** does not contain an IP address.

Step 3. One of the responsibilities of a gatekeeper is phone number resolution. Therefore, use the following **zone prefix** commands to indicate which zones can reach which phone numbers:

```
zone prefix ZoneA 1...
zone prefix ZoneB 2...
```

Step 4. H.323 gateways can register with specific technology prefixes. These technology prefixes can indicate to the gatekeeper what type of calls a gateway can handle. However, if a dial string does not contain a technology prefix, the gateway can use a gateway that has registered with a *default technology* prefix. In this lab, the H.323 gateways register with a technology prefix of 1#. Therefore, configure the gateway to recognize 1# as a default technology prefix with the **gw-type-prefix 1#* default-technology** command.

NOTE	Notice the * appended to the technology prefix of **1#**. While the H.323 gateways register with a technology prefix of **1#**, the H.323 gatekeeper is configured to recognize this technology prefix as **1#***. Think of the * as a wildcard representing the dial string following the technology prefix of **1#**.

Step 5. An H.323 gatekeeper can perform Call Admission Control (CAC) by permitting or rejecting call attempts between zones. In this lab, configure the total amount of voice bandwidth permitted between Zone A and Zone B to 64 kbps, using the **bandwidth interzone default 64** command. Next, restrict the bandwidth allowed for a single call to 16 kbps, using the **bandwidth session default 16** command.

Step 6. A gatekeeper can be administratively shut down, much like you can administratively shut down an interface. Verify that the gatekeeper is administratively up using the **no shutdown** command.

Task 2: Configure H.323 Gateways

In this task, you will configure routers R1 and R2 as H.323 gateways that register with the gatekeeper you configured in Task 1.

Complete these steps:

Step 1. Enable H.323 gateway processing on router R1 with the **gateway** command in global configuration mode.

Step 2. Go into interface configuration mode for the R1 interface that connects R1 to R2 and indicate that the interface is an H.323 interface using the **h323-gateway voip interface** command.

Step 3. Still in interface configuration mode, tell router R1 to register with the gatekeeper you created in Task 1 using the **h323-gateway voip id ZoneA ipaddr 10.7.7.1 1719** command. This command causes router R1 to register as an H.323 gateway in Zone A using the gatekeeper's RAS address of 10.7.7.1 and using the default port number of 1719.

Step 4. Using the **h323-gateway voip h323-id R1** command, specify the name router R1 will use when registering with the gatekeeper.

Step 5. Enter the command **h323-gateway voip tech-prefix 1#** to tell router R1 to register with the gatekeeper using the gatekeeper's default technology prefix of **1#**.

Step 6. In the lab at the end of Chapter 4, "Voice Dial Peer Configuration," you configured a VoIP dial peer on router R1 that pointed to a phone number of 2222 by sending VoIP packets to an IP address of 10.7.7.2. Enter dial peer configuration mode for this dial peer and remove the previous session target with the **no session target ipv4:10.7.7.2** command. Then add a new session target pointing this dial peer to the gatekeeper, using the **session target ras** command. This command instructs this H.323 gateway to use the RAS channel to send a call setup request to the interface's gatekeeper when attempting to place a call to a dial string of 2222.

Step 7. Now that you have successfully configured router R1, next create a mirrored configuration for router R3. Adapt the commands given in Steps 1–6 for router R3, such as specifying a zone name of Zone B and an H.323 ID of **R3.** Also, the VoIP dial peer you modify on router R3 will be the VoIP dial peer that points to a dial string of 1111.

Task 3: Verify the Configuration

In this task, you will verify the configuration of the H.323 gatekeeper and the two H.323 gateways.

Complete these steps:

Step 1. The first indication that your configuration is correct is the ability to successfully place a phone call between extensions 1111 and 2222. Therefore, from extension 1111, attempt to place a phone call to extension 2222. If the call is successful, leave the handsets off-hook while performing the following steps. If, however, the call does not complete successfully, work back through each step of the lab, carefully examining the configurations of the routers.

Step 2. With a call successfully in progress, issue the **show gateway** command on routers R1 and R3 to verify that these gateways have registered with the gatekeeper.

Step 3. You can also see what H.323 gateways have registered with the gatekeeper by issuing the **show gatekeeper endpoints** command from router R2.

Step 4. To see the types of RAS messages (for example, admission request [ARQ] and admission confirmation [ACF] messages) sent and received by a gateway, you can issue the **show h323 gateway ras** command. Issue this command on router R1 and notice the ARQ and the ACF representing the call you were permitted to make.

Suggested Solution

Although your physical hardware might differ, and your selection of dial peer tags might vary, Examples 6-15 through 6-20 offer possible solutions to the preceding exercise.

Example 6-15 shows the configuration for R2's H.323 gatekeeper.

Example 6-15 *Router R2's H.323 Gatekeeper Configuration*

```
gatekeeper
 zone local ZoneA acme.com 10.7.7.1
 zone local ZoneB acme.com
 zone prefix ZoneA 1...
 zone prefix ZoneB 2...
 gw-type-prefix 1#* default-technology
 arq reject-unknown-prefix
 bandwidth interzone default 64
 bandwidth session default 16
 no shutdown
```

Example 6-16 shows the configuration for R1's H.323 gateway.

Example 6-16 *Router R1's H.323 Gateway Configuration*

```
interface Serial0
 bandwidth 128
 ip address 10.1.1.2 255.255.255.0
 encapsulation ppp
 h323-gateway voip interface
 h323-gateway voip id ZoneA ipaddr 10.7.7.1 1719
 h323-gateway voip h323-id R1
 h323-gateway voip tech-prefix 1#
 !
gateway
 !
dial-peer voice 2222 voip
 destination-pattern 2222
 session target ras
```

Example 6-17 shows the configuration for R3's H.323 gateway.

Example 6-17 *Router R3's H.323 Gateway Configuration*

```
interface Serial0
 bandwidth 2000
 ip address 10.7.7.2 255.255.255.0
 encapsulation ppp
 clock rate 2000000
 h323-gateway voip interface
 h323-gateway voip id ZoneB ipaddr 10.7.7.1 1719
 h323-gateway voip h323-id R3
```

Example 6-17   *Router R3's H.323 Gateway Configuration (Continued)*

```
interface Serial0
 h323-gateway voip tech-prefix 1#
!
gateway
!
dial-peer voice 1111 voip
 destination-pattern 1111
 session target ras
```

Example 6-18 shows the output of the **show gateway** command on R1.

Example 6-18   *Router R1's* **show gateway** *Output*

```
R1#show gateway
H.323 ITU-T Version: 4.0   H323 Stack Version: 0.1

 H.323 service is up
 Gateway  R1  is registered to Gatekeeper ZoneA

Alias list (CLI configured)
 E164-ID 1111
 H323-ID R1
Alias list (last RCF)
 E164-ID 1111
 H323-ID R1


 H323 resource thresholding is Disabled
```

Example 6-19 shows the output of the **show gateway** command on R3.

Example 6-19   *Router R3's* **show gateway** *Output*

```
R3#show gateway
H.323 ITU-T Version: 4.0   H323 Stack Version: 0.1

 H.323 service is up
 Gateway  R3  is registered to Gatekeeper ZoneB

Alias list (CLI configured)
 E164-ID 2222
 H323-ID R3
Alias list (last RCF)
 E164-ID 2222
 H323-ID R3


 H323 resource thresholding is Disabled
```

Example 6-20 shows the output of the **show gatekeeper endpoints** command on R2.

Example 6-20 *Router R2's* **show gatekeeper endpoints** *Output*

```
R2#show gatekeeper endpoints
                GATEKEEPER ENDPOINT REGISTRATION
                ================================
CallSignalAddr  Port  RASSignalAddr   Port  Zone Name      Type      Flags
--------------- ----- --------------- ----- ---------      ----      -----
10.1.1.2        1720  10.1.1.2        52605 ZoneA          VOIP-GW
    E164-ID: 1111
    H323-ID: R1
    Voice Capacity Max.= Avail.= Current.= 1
10.7.7.2        1720  10.7.7.2        52354 ZoneB          VOIP-GW
    E164-ID: 2222
    H323-ID: R3
    Voice Capacity Max.= Avail.= Current.= 1
Total number of active registrations = 2
```

Example 6-21 shows the output of the **show h323 gateway ras** command on R1.

Example 6-21 *Router R1's* **show h323 gateway ras** *Output*

```
R1#show h323 gateway ras
RAS STATISTICS AT 00:25:56
  RAS MESSAGE      REQUESTS SENT      CONFIRMS RCVD      REJECTS RCVD
  GK Discovery     grq       5        gcf       1        grj       0
  Registration     rrq      34        rcf      34        rrj       0
  Admission        arq       1        acf       1        arj       0
  Bandwidth        brq       0        bcf       0        brj       0
  Disengage        drq       0        dcf       0        drj       0
  Unregister       urq       0        ucf       0        urj       0
  Resource Avail   rai       0        rac       0
  Req In Progress  rip       0
```

After reading this chapter, you should be able to perform the following tasks:

- Identify problems presented by IP networks that affect voice and describe the QoS mechanisms used to address those problems.

- Set up basic QoS configurations, on both Cisco IOS-based Catalyst switches and routers, using Cisco's AutoQoS feature.

- Implement call control on the network using CAC tools and mechanisms.

CHAPTER 7

Improving and Maintaining Voice Quality

When human speech is converted to analog electrical signals and then digitized and compressed, some of the qualitative components are lost. This chapter explores the components of voice quality that you must maintain, the methods that you can use to measure voice quality, and quality of service (QoS) tools that you can implement in a network to improve voice quality.

Optimizing Voice Quality

Because of the inherent characteristics of a converged voice and data IP network, administrators face certain challenges in delivering voice traffic correctly. This section describes these challenges and offers solutions for avoiding and overcoming them when designing a VoIP network for optimal voice quality.

Factors that Affect Voice Quality

Because of the nature of IP networking, voice packets sent via IP are subject to certain transmission problems. Conditions present in the network might introduce problems such as echo, jitter, or delay. These problems must be addressed with QoS mechanisms.

The clarity, or cleanliness and crispness, of the audio signal is of utmost importance. The listener must be able to recognize the speaker's identity and sense the mood of the speaker. These factors can affect clarity:

- **Fidelity**—The degree to which a system, or a portion of a system, accurately reproduces, at its output, the essential characteristics of the signal impressed upon its input or the result of a prescribed operation on the signal impressed upon its input (definition from the Alliance for Telecommunications Industry Solutions [ATIS]). The bandwidth of the transmission medium almost always limits the total bandwidth of the spoken voice. Human speech typically requires a bandwidth from 100 to 10,000 Hz, although 90 percent of speech intelligence is contained between 100 and 3000 Hz.

- **Echo**—A result of electrical impedance mismatches in the transmission path. Echo is always present, even in traditional telephony networks, but at a level that cannot be detected by the human ear. The two components that affect echo are amplitude (that is, loudness of the echo) and delay (that is, the time between the spoken voice and the echoed sound). You can control echo using echo suppressors or echo cancellers.

- **Jitter**—Variation in the arrival of coded speech packets at the far end of a VoIP network. The varying arrival time of the packets can cause gaps in the re-creation and playback of the voice signal. These gaps are undesirable and annoy the listener. Delay is induced in the network by variation in the routes of individual packets, contention, or congestion. You can often resolve variable delay by using dejitter buffers.

- **Packet drops**—The discarding of voice packets. Typically, when a VoIP packet is dropped from a network, 20 ms of audio is lost.

- **Delay**—The time between the spoken voice and the arrival of the electronically delivered voice at the far end. Delay results from multiple factors, including distance (that is, propagation delay), coding, compression, serialization, and buffering.

- **Sidetone**—The purposeful design of the telephone that allows the speaker to hear the spoken audio in the earpiece. Without sidetone, the speaker is left with the impression that the telephone instrument is not working.

- **Background noise**—The low-volume audio that is heard from the far-end connection. Certain bandwidth-saving technologies can eliminate background noise altogether, such as voice activity detection (VAD). When this technology is implemented, the speaker audio path is open to the listener, while the listener audio path is closed to the speaker. The effect of VAD is often that speakers think that the connection is broken, because they hear nothing from the other end.

Although each of the preceding factors affects audio clarity, factors that present the greatest challenges to VoIP networks include jitter, delay, and packet drops. A lack of network bandwidth is usually the underlying cause for these issues, which are addressed in the following sections.

Jitter

Jitter is defined as a variation in the delay of received packets, as illustrated in Figure 7-1. On the sending side, packets are sent in a continuous stream with the packets spaced evenly. Because of network congestion, improper queuing, or configuration errors, this steady stream can become uneven, because the delay between each packet varies instead of remaining constant.

When a router receives a VoIP audio stream, it must compensate for the jitter that is encountered. The mechanism that handles this function is the *playout delay buffer,* or *dejitter buffer.* The playout delay buffer must buffer these packets and then play them out in a steady stream to the digital signal processors (DSPs) to be converted back to an analog audio stream. The playout delay buffer, however, affects the overall absolute delay.

When a conversation is subjected to jitter, the results can be clearly heard. If the talker says, "Watson, come here. I want you," the listener might hear "Wat....s...on.......come here, I......wa......nt........y......ou." The variable arrival of the packets at the receiving end causes the speech to be delayed and garbled.

Figure 7-1 *Jitter in IP Networks*

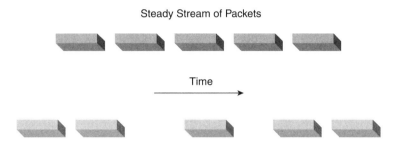

Steady Stream of Packets

Time

Same Packet Stream After Congestion or Improper Queuing

Delay

Overall or absolute delay can affect VoIP. You might have experienced delay in a telephone conversation with someone on a different continent. The delays can cause entire words in the conversation to be cut off, and can therefore be very frustrating.

When you design a network that transports voice over packet, frame, or cell infrastructures, it is important to understand and account for the predictable delay components in the network. You must also correctly account for all potential delays to ensure that overall network performance is acceptable. Overall voice quality is a function of many factors, including the compression algorithm, errors and frame loss, echo cancellation, and delay.

Figure 7-2 shows various sources and types of delay. Notice that there are two distinct types of delay:

- **Fixed delay** components are predictable and add directly to overall delay on the connection. Fixed delay components include the following:
    - **Coding**—The time it takes to translate the audio signal into a digital signal
    - **Packetization**—The time it takes to put digital voice information into packets and remove the information from packets
    - **Serialization**—The insertion of bits onto a link
    - **Propagation**—The time it takes a packet to traverse a link
- **Variable delays** arise from queuing delays in the egress trunk buffers that are located on the serial port connected to the WAN. These buffers create variable delays (that is, jitter) across the network.

Figure 7-2 *Sources of Delay*

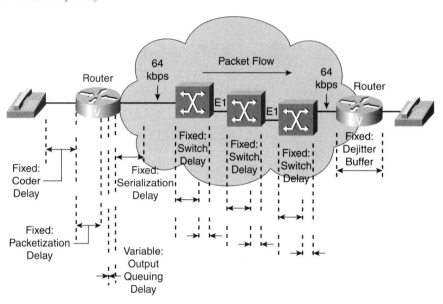

Acceptable Delay

The ITU specifies network delay for voice applications in Recommendation G.114. This recommendation defines three bands of one-way delay, as shown in Table 7-1.

Table 7-1 *Components and Services*

Range in Milliseconds	Description
0 to 150	Acceptable for most user applications.
150 to 400	Acceptable, provided that administrators are aware of the transmission time and its impact on the transmission quality of user applications.
Above 400	Unacceptable for general network planning purposes; however it is recognized that in some exceptional cases, this limit will be exceeded.

NOTE This recommendation is for connections where echo is adequately controlled, implying that echo cancellers are used. Echo cancellers are required when one-way delay exceeds 25 ms (G.131).

This G.114 recommendation is oriented toward national telecommunications administrations and therefore is more stringent than recommendations that would normally be applied in private voice networks. When the location and business needs of end users are well known to a network designer, more delay might prove acceptable. For private networks, a 200 ms delay is a reasonable goal and a 250 ms delay is a limit. This goal is what Cisco proposes as reasonable, as long as excessive jitter does not impact voice quality. However, all networks must be engineered so that the maximum expected voice connection delay is known and minimized.

The G.114 recommendation is for one-way delay only and does not account for round-trip delay. Network design engineers must consider both variable and fixed delays in their design. Variable delays include queuing and network delays, while fixed delays include coding, packetization, serialization, and dejitter buffer delays. Table 7-2 provides an example of a delay budget calculation.

Table 7-2 *Sample Delay Budget*

Delay Type	Fixed (ms)	Variable (ms)
Coder delay	18	N/A
Packetization delay	30	N/A
Queuing and buffering	N/A	8
Serialization (64 kbps)	5	N/A
Network delay (through public network)	40	25
Dejitter buffer	45	N/A
Totals	138	33

Packet Loss

Lost data packets, as depicted in Figure 7-3 are recoverable if the endpoints can request retransmission. However, lost voice packets are *not* recoverable, because the audio must be played out in real time and retransmission is not an option.

Figure 7-3 *Packet Loss*

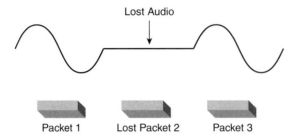

Voice packets might be dropped under the following conditions:

- The network is unstable (flapping links).
- The network is congested.
- There is too much variable delay in the network.

Packet loss causes voice clipping and skips. As a result, the listener hears gaps in the conversation. The industry-standard coder-decoder (CODEC) algorithms used in Cisco DSPs correct for 20–50 ms of lost voice through the use of Packet Loss Concealment (PLC) algorithms. PLC intelligently analyzes missing packets and generates a reasonable replacement packet to improve the voice quality. Cisco VoIP technology uses 20 ms samples of voice payload per VoIP packet by default. Effective CODEC correction algorithms require that only a single packet can be lost at any given time. If more packets are lost, the listener experiences gaps.

If a conversation experiences packet loss, the effect is immediately heard. If the talker says, "Watson, come here. I want you," the listener might hear, "Wat...., come here, ...you."

Quality Metrics

Quality must be measurable in order to be manageable. Three quality metrics include the Mean Opinion Score (MOS), the Perceptual Speech Quality Measurement (PSQM), and the Perceptual Evaluation of Speech Quality (PESQ).

MOS

MOS is a scoring system for voice quality. An MOS score is generated when listeners evaluate prerecorded sentences that are subject to varying conditions, such as compression algorithms. Listeners then assign the sentences values, based on a scale from 1 to 5, where 1 is the worst and 5 is the best. The sentence used for English language MOS testing is, "Nowadays, a chicken leg is a rare dish." This sentence is used because it contains a wide range of sounds found in human speech, such as long vowels, short vowels, hard sounds, and soft sounds.

The test scores are then averaged to a composite score. The test results are subjective because they are based on the opinions of the listeners. The tests are also relative, because a score of 3.8 from one test cannot be directly compared to a score of 3.8 from another test. Therefore, a baseline needs to be established for all tests, such as G.711, so that the scores can be normalized and compared directly.

PSQM

PSQM is an automated method of measuring speech quality "in service," or as the speech happens. PSQM software usually resides with IP call-management systems, which are sometimes integrated into Simple Network Management Protocol (SNMP) systems.

Equipment and software that can measure PSQM is available through third-party vendors but is not implemented in Cisco devices. The PSQM measurement is made by comparing the original transmitted speech to the resulting speech at the far end of the transmission channel. PSQM systems are deployed as in-service components. The PSQM measurements are made during real conversation on the network. This automated testing algorithm has over 90 percent accuracy compared to subjective listening tests, such as MOS. Scoring is based on a scale from 0 to 6.5, where 0 is the best and 6.5 is the worst. Because it was originally designed for circuit-switched voice, PSQM does not take into account the jitter or delay problems that are experienced in packet-switched voice systems.

PESQ

MOS and PSQM are not recommended for present-day VoIP networks. Both were originally designed before the emergence of VoIP technologies and do not measure typical VoIP problems such as jitter and delay. For example, it is possible to obtain an MOS score of 3.8 on a VoIP network when the one-way delay exceeds 500 ms, because the MOS evaluator has no concept of a two-way conversation and listens only to audio quality. The one-way delay is not evaluated.

PESQ, whose operation is illustrated in Figure 7-4, was originally developed by British Telecom, Psytechnics, and KPN Research of the Netherlands. It has evolved into ITU Standard P.862, which is considered the current standard for voice quality measurement. PESQ can take into account CODEC errors, filtering errors, jitter problems, and delay problems that are typical in a VoIP network. PESQ combines the best of the PSQM method along with a method called Perceptual Analysis Measurement System (PAMS). PESQ scores range from 1 (worst) to 4.5 (best), with 3.8 considered "toll quality" (that is, acceptable quality in a traditional telephony network). PESQ is meant to measure only one aspect of voice quality. The effects of two-way communication, such as loudness loss, delay, echo, and sidetone, are not reflected in PESQ scores.

Figure 7-4   *PESQ*

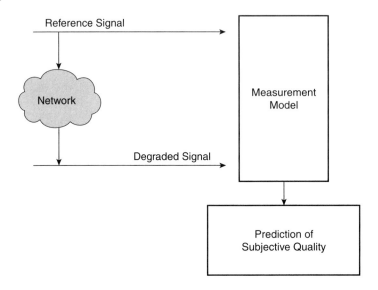

Many equipment vendors offer PESQ measurement systems. Such systems are either stand-alone or they plug into existing network management systems. PESQ was designed to mirror the MOS measurement system. So, if a score of 3.2 is measured by PESQ, a score of 3.2 should be achieved using MOS methods.

Quality Measurement Comparison

Early quality measurement methods, such as MOS and PSQM, were designed before widespread acceptance of VoIP technology. PESQ was designed to address the shortcomings of MOS and PSQM.

MOS uses subjective testing where the average opinion of a group of test users is calculated to create the MOS score. This method is both time-consuming and expensive, and might not provide consistent results between groups of testers.

PSQM and PESQ use objective testing where an original reference file sent into the system is compared with the impaired signal that came out. This testing method provides an automated test mechanism that does not rely on human interpretation for result calculations. However, PSQM was originally designed for circuit-switched networks and does not take into account the effects of jitter and packet loss.

PESQ measures the effect of end-to-end network conditions, including CODEC processing, jitter, and packet loss. Therefore, PESQ is the preferred method of testing voice quality in an IP network. Table 7-3 offers a comparison of the various quality metrics.

Table 7-3 *Voice Quality Measurement Comparison*

Feature	MOS	PSQM	PESQ
Test method	Subjective	Objective	Objective
End-to-end packet test	Inconsistent	No	Yes
End-to-end jitter test	Inconsistent	No	Yes

Objectives of QoS

To ensure that VoIP is an acceptable replacement for standard public switched telephone network (PSTN) telephony services, customers must receive the same consistently high quality of voice transmission that they receive with basic telephone services.

Like other real-time applications, VoIP is extremely sensitive to issues related to bandwidth and delay. To ensure that VoIP transmissions are intelligible to the receiver, voice packets cannot be dropped, excessively delayed, or subjected to variations in delay (that is, jitter).

VoIP guarantees high-quality voice transmission only if the signaling and audio channel packets have priority over other kinds of network traffic. A successful VoIP deployment must provide an acceptable level of voice quality by meeting VoIP traffic requirements for issues related to bandwidth, latency, and jitter. QoS provides better, more predictable network service by performing the following:

- **Supporting dedicated bandwidth**—Designing the network such that the necessary bandwidth is always available to support voice and data traffic

- **Improving loss characteristics**—Designing a Frame Relay network such that discard eligibility is not a factor for frames containing voice, keeping voice below the committed information rate (CIR)

- **Avoiding and managing network congestion**—Ensuring that the LAN and WAN infrastructure can support the volume of data traffic and voice calls

- **Shaping network traffic**—Using Cisco traffic-shaping tools to ensure smooth and consistent delivery of frames to the WAN

- **Setting traffic priorities across the network**—Marking the voice traffic as priority traffic and queuing it first

Cisco routers support multiple QoS mechanisms that can be leveraged to accomplish the objectives listed in the preceding bullet points. The following sections detail specific QoS mechanisms and caution against poor design characteristics.

Using QoS to Improve Voice Quality

Voice features that provide QoS are deployed at different points in the network and are designed for use with other QoS features to achieve specific goals, such as minimization of jitter and delay. Cisco IOS includes a complete set of features for delivering QoS throughout the network. Following are a few examples of Cisco IOS features that address the voice packet delivery requirements of end-to-end QoS and service differentiation:

- The output queue of the router can use the following QoS mechanisms:
  - **Class-based weighted fair queuing (CBWFQ)**—Extends the standard Weighted Fair Queuing (WFQ) functionality by providing support for user-defined traffic classes. You can create a specific class for voice traffic by using CBWFQ.
  - **Low latency queuing (LLQ)**—Provides strict priority queuing in conjunction with CBWFQ. LLQ configures the priority status for a class within CBWFQ, in which voice packets receive priority over all other traffic. LLQ is considered a "best practice" by the Cisco Enterprise Solutions Engineering (ESE) group for delivering voice QoS services over a WAN.
  - **Weighted fair queuing (WFQ)**—Segregates traffic into flows and then schedules traffic to meet specified bandwidth allocation or delay bounds.
  - **Weighted random early detection (WRED)**—Provides differentiated performance characteristics for different classes of service. Specifically, WRED drops lower-priority traffic more aggressively than higher-priority traffic, as an interface's output queue begins to become congested.
- The WAN or WAN protocol can use the following QoS mechanisms:
  - **Class-based policing** —Provides a rate-limiting feature for allocating bandwidth commitments and bandwidth limitations to traffic sources and destinations. At the same time, it specifies policies for handling the traffic that might exceed bandwidth allocation.

NOTE   Class-based policing typically replaces the rate-limiting feature previously provided by the committed access rate (CAR) feature.

  - **Traffic shaping**—Delays excess traffic by using a buffer or queuing mechanism to hold packets and shape the flow when the data rate of the source is higher than expected.

    — **Frame Relay Forum 12 (FRF.12)**—Ensures predictability for voice traffic by providing better throughput on low-speed Frame Relay links (that is, link speeds less than 768 kbps). FRF.12 interleaves delay-sensitive voice traffic with fragments of a long frame.

    — **Multilink PPP (MLP)**—Allows large packets to be multilink encapsulated, fragmented, and interleaved so that they are small enough to satisfy the delay requirements of real-time traffic.

VoIP traffic can use the following QoS mechanisms:

    — **Compressed Real-Time Transport Protocol (cRTP)**—The Real-Time Transport Protocol (RTP) is a protocol for the transport of real-time traffic, including voice. RTP uses extensive headers that incorporate time stamps for individual packets. The cRTP feature compresses the extensive RTP header. The result is decreased consumption of available bandwidth for voice traffic and a corresponding reduction in delay.

    — **Resource Reservation Protocol (RSVP)**—RSVP supports the reservation of resources across an IP network, allowing end systems to request QoS guarantees from the network. For networks that support VoIP, RSVP—in conjunction with features that provide queuing, traffic shaping, and voice call signaling—provides Call Admission Control (CAC) for voice traffic.

Recognizing Common Design Faults

Successful implementations of delay-sensitive applications such as VoIP require a network that is carefully engineered with QoS from end to end. Fine-tuning the network to adequately support VoIP involves a series of protocols and features geared toward improving voice quality.

QoS is the ability of a network to provide better service levels to selected network traffic over various underlying technologies. However, QoS is not inherent in a network infrastructure. Instead, QoS is implemented by strategically enabling appropriate QoS features throughout the network.

Poor design is characterized by the following issues:

- **Ignoring Layer 2 QoS requirements**—QoS technologies such as priority Layer 2 congestion management, FRF.12, Link Fragmentation and Interleaving (LFI), and traffic shaping must be correctly configured.

- **Ignoring other QoS requirements**—QoS technologies such as LLQ, RTP, congestion management, and congestion avoidance must be enabled.

- **Ignoring bandwidth considerations**—Planning for the total number of calls and their effect on data bandwidth is critical to all users of the network.

- **Simply adding VoIP to an existing IP network**—When considering VoIP, network administrators might need to insist on a complete network redesign for a comprehensive end-to-end solution.

Many people believe that the fastest way to fix network performance is simply to add a lot of bandwidth. That approach might work well in certain situations like campus networks, in which upgrading from 10 Mbps to 100 Mbps or even 1 GB links might be possible. However, it is not always feasible to add bandwidth in a WAN. Upgrading a WAN circuit from 56 kbps to T1 might be cost prohibitive and might not be possible for certain locations on the network. To provide effective performance in a voice network, you should configure QoS throughout the network, not just on the devices running VoIP. Not all QoS techniques are appropriate for all network routers. Edge routers and backbone routers in a network do not necessarily perform the same operations. The QoS tasks these routers perform might differ as well. To configure an IP network for real-time voice traffic, you should consider the functions of both edge and backbone routers and select the appropriate QoS tools accordingly.

AutoQoS

Cisco AutoQoS minimizes the complexity, time, and operating cost of QoS deployment. Cisco AutoQoS incorporates value-added intelligence into Cisco IOS software and Cisco Catalyst Operating System software to provision and manage large-scale QoS deployments. This section focuses on the Cisco IOS implementation of AutoQoS, on both router and Catalyst switch platforms.

AutoQoS Features

To expedite QoS deployment, the user interface must be simplified. Cisco AutoQoS addresses this issue by automating the following five main aspects of QoS deployment while maintaining a tunable solution:

- **Application classification**—Cisco AutoQoS identifies VoIP control and bearer traffic. Cisco AutoQoS uses Cisco Discovery Protocol (CDP) to ensure that the device attached to the LAN is really an IP phone.

- **Policy generation**—Cisco AutoQoS evaluates the network environment and automatically generates an initial policy on a given interface, port, or permanent virtual circuit (PVC).

- **Configuration**—With one command, Cisco AutoQoS configures a port to prioritize voice traffic without affecting other network traffic, while still offering the flexibility to adjust QoS settings for unique network environments. QoS settings are automatically disabled when a Cisco IP phone is relocated or moved.

- **Monitoring and reporting**—Cisco AutoQoS provides visibility into the classes of service deployed via system logging and SNMP traps.

- **Consistency**—Cisco AutoQoS policies are designed to work in harmony with each other across Cisco devices, ensuring consistent end-to-end QoS.

The increased deployment of delay-sensitive applications in networks (for example, voice, video, and other multimedia applications) requires proper QoS configuration to ensure application performance.

Before the availability of Cisco AutoQoS, proper QoS configuration of a network required a deep understanding of various QoS features (that is, queuing, dropping, traffic conditioning, queue depth, drop thresholds, burst parameters, LFI, and RTP). The use of Cisco AutoQoS helps minimize the complexity of configuring a network correctly for QoS by automatically configuring a device with the correct QoS parameters. Cisco AutoQoS automates consistent deployment of QoS features across Cisco routers and switches. It enables various Cisco QoS components based on the network environment and Cisco best-practice recommendations.

Users can subsequently tune parameters generated by Cisco AutoQoS to suit their particular application needs.

Cisco AutoQoS can perform the following functions on WAN interfaces:

- Automatically classifies RTP payload and VoIP control packets (H.323, H.225 Unicast, Skinny Client Control Protocol [SCCP], session initiation protocol [SIP], and Media Gateway Control Protocol [MGCP])

- Builds service policies for VoIP traffic that are based on Cisco's Modular QoS Command-Line Interface (MQC) configuration approach

- Provisions LLQ priority queuing for VoIP bearer and bandwidth guarantees for control traffic

- Enables WAN traffic shaping that adheres to Cisco best practices, where required

- Enables link efficiency mechanisms, such as LFI and RTP header compression (cRTP), where required

- Provides SNMP and syslog alerts for VoIP packet drops

Cisco AutoQoS can perform the following functions on LAN interfaces:

- Enforce the trust boundary on Cisco Catalyst switch access ports, uplinks, and downlinks

- Enable Cisco Catalyst strict priority queuing (also known as *expedite queuing*) with weighted round-robin (WRR) scheduling for voice and data traffic, where appropriate

- Configure queue admission criteria (that is, maps Layer 2 CoS priority markings in incoming packets to the appropriate queues)

- Modify queue sizes and weights where required

NOTE   Cisco AutoQoS is available in the following Cisco IOS software releases—Cisco IOS
Software Release 12.1E or later for the Cisco Catalyst 2950 and 3550 Series switches;
Cisco IOS Software Release 12.2T or later for the Cisco 2600, 2600XM, 3600, 3700, and
7200 Series routers; Cisco IOS Software Release 12.1E or later for the Cisco Catalyst 4500
Series switches; and Cisco Catalyst Operating System 7.5.1 or later for the Cisco Catalyst
6500 Series switches. For current information concerning AutoQoS platform support,
check Cisco's Feature Navigator at http://www.cisco.com/go/fn.

Configuring AutoQoS on a Router

On a router platform, the following command enables AutoQoS from either interface
configuration mode or from DLCI configuration mode (for a Frame Relay circuit):

```
Router(config-if)#auto qos voip [trust] [fr-atm]
```

The **trust** option indicates that AutoQos should classify voice traffic based on Layer 3
Differentiated Services Code Point (DSCP) priority markings, instead of using Network-
Based Application Recognition (NBAR). The **fr-atm** option enables the AutoQoS feature
for Frame Relay-to-ATM links and is issued from DLCI configuration mode.

Before enabling AutoQoS on a router interface, consider the following prerequisites:

- Cisco Express Forwarding (CEF) must be enabled, because AutoQoS uses NBAR,
  which requires the CEF feature.

- A QoS policy must not be currently attached to the interface.

- The correct bandwidth should be configured on the interface, using the **bandwidth**
  command.

- An IP address must be configured on an interface if its speed is less than 768 kbps.

- The interface must not be administratively shut down.

Note that the interface's bandwidth determines which AutoQoS features are enabled. If an
interface's bandwidth is less than 768 kbps, it is considered a low-speed interface. On a low-
speed interface, AutoQoS configures Multilink PPP (MLP), which requires an IP address
on the physical interface. AutoQoS takes the IP address from the physical interface and uses
it for the virtual multilink interface that it creates.

To verify that AutoQoS is configured for a router interface, use the following command:

```
Router#show auto qos [interface interface-identifier]
```

To illustrate some of the configuration changes that AutoQoS can perform, consider the
configuration of a serial interface shown in Example 7-1, without AutoQoS enabled.

Example 7-1 *Router Configuration Without AutoQoS*

```
interface Serial0/0
 bandwidth 128
 ip address 10.1.1.1 255.255.255.0
 encapsulation ppp
```

Example 7-2 illustrates the configuration changes after entering the **auto qos voip** command for interface Serial 0/0.

Example 7-2 *Router Configuration with AutoQoS*

```
class-map match-any AutoQoS-VoIP-Remark
class-map match-any AutoQoS-VoIP-Remark
  match ip dscp ef
  match ip dscp cs3
  match ip dscp af31
class-map match-any AutoQoS-VoIP-Control-UnTrust
  match access-group name AutoQoS-VoIP-Control
class-map match-any AutoQoS-VoIP-RTP-UnTrust
  match protocol rtp audio
  match access-group name AutoQoS-VoIP-RTCP
!
policy-map AutoQoS-Policy-UnTrust
  class AutoQoS-VoIP-RTP-UnTrust
   priority percent 70
   set dscp ef
  class AutoQoS-VoIP-Control-UnTrust
   bandwidth percent 5
   set dscp af31
  class AutoQoS-VoIP-Remark
   set dscp default
  class class-default
   fair-queue
!
interface Multilink2001100114
 bandwidth 128
 ip address 10.1.1.1 255.255.255.0
 service-policy output AutoQoS-Policy-UnTrust
 ip tcp header-compression iphc-format
 ppp multilink
 ppp multilink fragment delay 10
 ppp multilink interleave
 ppp multilink group 2001100114
 ip rtp header-compression iphc-format
!
interface Serial0/0
 bandwidth 128
 no ip address
 encapsulation ppp
 auto qos voip
 clockrate 128000
```

continues

Example 7-2   *Router Configuration with AutoQoS (Continued)*

```
no fair-queue
ppp multilink
ppp multilink group 2001100114
!
ip access-list extended AutoQoS-VoIP-Control
 permit tcp any any eq 1720
 permit tcp any any range 11000 11999
 permit udp any any eq 2427
 permit tcp any any eq 2428
 permit tcp any any range 2000 2002
 permit udp any any eq 1719
 permit udp any any eq 5060
ip access-list extended AutoQoS-VoIP-RTCP
 permit udp any any range 16384 32767
!
rmon event 33333 log trap AutoQoS description "AutoQoS SNMP traps for Voice Drops"
owner AutoQoS
rmon alarm 33333 cbQosCMDropBitRate.1081.1083 30 absolute rising-threshold 1 33333
falling-threshold 0 owner AutoQoS
```

The bandwidth configured for interface Serial 0/0 was set to 128 kbps. Therefore, AutoQoS determined that certain link efficiency mechanisms (for example, Multilink PPP, RTP Header Compression, and TCP Header Compression) were appropriate. AutoQoS, therefore, automatically configured these link efficiency mechanisms in addition to multiple other QoS mechanisms, including classification, marking, LLQ, and Remote Monitoring (RMON) traps to alert administrators if packet drops are excessive.

AutoQoS for Enterprise

Introduced in Cisco IOS Software Release 12.3(7)T, *AutoQoS for Enterprise* extends the capabilities of AutoQoS on a Cisco router platform. Specifically, AutoQoS for Enterprise allows a router to recognize multiple protocols traversing an interface and recommends a customized policy, based on learned traffic patterns.

To configure a router's interface to begin learning traffic patterns, enter the following command in interface configuration mode:

```
Router(config-if)#auto discovery qos
```

After entering the previous command, wait for a period of time for the router to learn the traffic patterns crossing the interface. The ability to dynamically learn these patterns is made possible by the Cisco IOS software's NBAR feature.

After waiting a period of time (for example, 30 minutes to an hour in a time period representative of peak network usage) during which the router is learning the traffic patterns of the network, enter the following command to view the router's findings and to see the recommended policy for the interface:

```
Router#show auto discovery qos
```

Example 7-3 offers an example of the output received after issuing the **show auto discovery qos** command.

Example 7-3   *Output from the* **show auto discovery qos** *Command*

```
R4#show auto discovery qos
Serial0/0
 AutoQoS Discovery enabled for applications
 Discovery up time—46 seconds
 AutoQoS Class information:
 Class Voice—
  Recommended Minimum Bandwidth—40 Kbps/31% (PeakRate)
  Detected applications and data:
  Application/      AverageRate       PeakRate          Total
  Protocol          (kbps/%)          (kbps/%)          (bytes)
  ----------        -----------       --------          -----------
   rtp audio        28/21             40/31             161160
 Class Interactive Video—
  No data found.
 Class Signaling—
  Recommended Minimum Bandwidth—0 Kbps/0% (AverageRate)
  Detected applications and data:
  Application/      AverageRate       PeakRate          Total
  Protocol          (kbps/%)          (kbps/%)          (bytes)
  ----------        -----------       --------          -----------
   skinny           0/0               0/0               3648
 Class Streaming Video—
  No data found.
 Class Transactional—
  No data found.
 Class Bulk—
  No data found.
 Class Scavenger—
  No data found.
 Class Management—
  No data found.
 Class Routing—
  Recommended Minimum Bandwidth—0 Kbps/0% (AverageRate)
  Detected applications and data:
  Application/      AverageRate       PeakRate          Total
  Protocol          (kbps/%)          (kbps/%)          (bytes)
  ----------        -----------       --------          -----------
   eigrp            0/0               0/0               640
   icmp             0/0               0/0               120
 Class Best Effort—
  Current Bandwidth Estimation—77 Kbps/60% (AverageRate)
  Detected applications and data:
  Application/      AverageRate       PeakRate          Total
  Protocol          (kbps/%)          (kbps/%)          (bytes)
  ----------        -----------       --------          -----------
   http             77/60             110/85            446413
   unknowns         0/0               0/0               104

 Suggested AutoQoS Policy for the current uptime:
  !
```

continues

Example 7-3 *Output from the* **show auto discovery qos** *Command (Continued)*

```
R4#show auto discovery qos
 class-map match-any AutoQoS-Voice-Se0/0
  match protocol rtp audio
  !
 policy-map AutoQoS-Policy-Se0/0
  class AutoQoS-Voice-Se0/0
   priority percent 31
   set dscp ef
  class class-default
fair-queue
```

If you find the suggested policy acceptable and wish to apply the dynamically created policy, go into interface configuration mode for the monitored interface and enter the following command:

```
Router(config-if)#auto qos
```

This **auto qos** command applies the recommended policy to the router.

Configuring AutoQoS on a Catalyst Switch

The QoS mechanisms on a Catalyst switch differ from those QoS mechanisms found on a router. For example, while a router uses LLQ as a priority queuing strategy, a Catalyst switch might use weighted round-robin (WRR) as a priority queuing strategy. Fortunately, the AutoQoS feature available on some Catalyst switch models (for example, the Cisco Catalyst 2950(EI) and 3550 Series) apply voice-specific QoS features globally to a Catalyst switch and also at the port level.

To configure AutoQoS on supported Catalyst switch platforms (running the Native IOS), issue the following command from interface configuration mode:

```
Switch(config-if)#auto qos voip [trust | cisco-phone]
```

If the **trust** option is used in the previous command, the Catalyst switch makes queuing decisions based on Layer 2 Class of Service (CoS) markings. However, if the **cisco-phone** option is used, the Catalyst switch makes queuing decisions based on CoS markings originating from a Cisco IP phone. The switch detects the presence of a Cisco IP phone via the CDP.

To illustrate the configuration changes made by a Catalyst switch's AutoQoS feature, consider Example 7-4, which shows the initial configuration of interface Gigabit 0/1 on a Catalyst 3550 switch.

Example 7-4 *Catalyst Switch Configuration Without AutoQoS*

```
interface GigabitEthernet0/1
 no ip address
```

Example 7-5 illustrates the configuration changes after entering the **auto qos voip cisco-phone** command for interface Gigabit 0/1.

Example 7-5   *Catalyst Configuration with AutoQoS*

```
mls qos map cos-dscp 0 8 16 26 32 46 48 56
mls qos
!
interface GigabitEthernet0/1
 no ip address
 mls qos trust device cisco-phone
 mls qos trust cos
 auto qos voip cisco-phone
 wrr-queue bandwidth 20 1 80 1
 wrr-queue queue-limit 80 1 20 1
 wrr-queue cos-map 1 0 1 2 4
 wrr-queue cos-map 3 3 6 7
 wrr-queue cos-map 4 5
 priority-queue out
```

Example 7-5 demonstrates that the AutoQoS feature configured the Catalyst switch to enable QoS globally (with the **mls qos** command) and remark Layer 2 CoS markings to Layer 3 Differentiated Services Code Point (DSCP) markings (with the **mls qos map cos-dscp** command). Also, AutoQoS configured WRR for interface Gigabit 0/1 and placed traffic with a CoS value of 5 (that is, voice traffic) in a priority queue, which is emptied ahead of other queues.

Implementing Call Admission Control

To prevent oversubscription of VoIP networks, the number of voice calls allowed on the network must be limited. This section describes the configuration parameters for implementing CAC, which can prevent oversubscription of WAN resources.

Effects of Bandwidth Oversubscription

QoS tools such as queuing ensure that voice traffic receives priority over data traffic. However, if a network link is oversubscribed with too much voice traffic, data packets are dropped, and the remaining voice calls suffer because they must compete for bandwidth available to the low-latency queue.

Figure 7-5 illustrates the effect of voice oversubscription. Using LLQ, voice traffic is directed into a priority queue (PQ) while all other traffic is directed into various CBWFQ queues. Note that the priority queue forwards packets while the data packets, destined for the CBWFQ queues, are denied entry to the queue and are dropped. In the case shown in Figure 7-5, even the priority queue buffer is full. Therefore, the voice packets are competing with other voice packets for access to the network link. This situation results in a degradation of all voice calls on this link.

Figure 7-5 *Effect of Oversubscription*

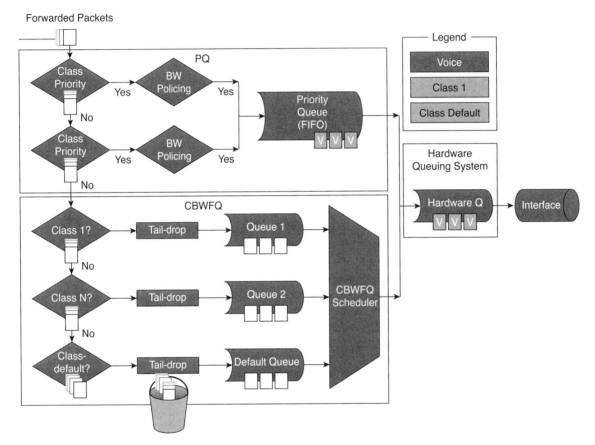

CAC Operation

CAC can function on the outgoing gateway and base its decision on nodal information, such as the state of the outgoing LAN or WAN link. For example, if the local IP network link is down, there is no point in executing complex decision logic based on the state of the rest of the network, because the network is unreachable.

As another example, if the network designer already knows that bandwidth limitations allow no more than two calls across the outgoing WAN link, as illustrated in Figure 7-6, then the local node can be configured to allow no more than two calls. You can configure this type of CAC on outgoing dial peers.

Figure 7-6   *The Need for CAC*

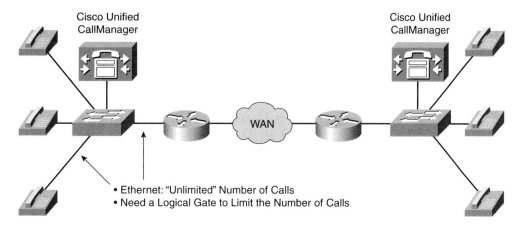

- Ethernet: "Unlimited" Number of Calls
- Need a Logical Gate to Limit the Number of Calls

RSVP

RSVP is the only CAC mechanism that makes actual bandwidth reservations for calls. RSVP offers the unique advantage of not only providing CAC for voice but also guarantees the QoS against changing network conditions for the duration of the call. The RSVP reservation is made in both directions because a voice call requires a two-way speech path. Therefore, bandwidth is reserved in both directions, as depicted in Figure 7-7.

Figure 7-7   *RSVP*

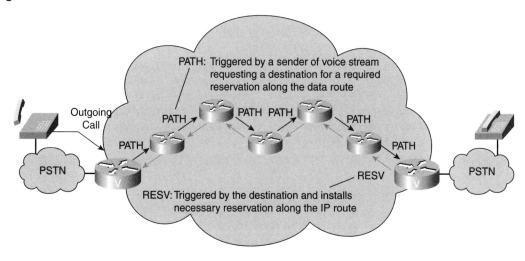

The terminating gateway ultimately makes the CAC decision based on whether both reservations succeed. At that point, H.323 continues with either an H.225 Alerting/Connect (the call is allowed and proceeds), or with an H.225 Reject/Release (the call is denied). The RSVP reservation is in place by the time the destination phone starts ringing and the caller hears ringback.

RSVP has the following important differences from other CAC methods discussed in this section:

- RSVP can maintain QoS for the duration of the call.

- RSVP is aware of topology. In theory, the RSVP reservation is installed on every interface that the call passes through as it traverses the network. RSVP ensures bandwidth over every segment without any requirement to know the actual bandwidth provisioning on each interface or the path on which the routing protocols direct the packets. RSVP, therefore, adjusts automatically to network configuration changes, and no manual calculations are necessary to keep different aspects of the configuration synchronized.

- To function correctly, RSVP is dependent on the correct configuration of all devices in the network. However, RSVP might introduce a scaling issue depending on how the network is designed.

- RSVP provides end-to-end reservations per call and has visibility for that call only. RSVP is unaware of how many other calls are active from a site or across an interface, or the source or destination of any other call.

Configuring RSVP in Cisco routers allows the administrator to limit the amount of bandwidth requested per call and the total amount of bandwidth allowed for all calls. This configuration is entered directly against the interface that will permit or deny the calls. The configuration also requires RSVP to be configured on the dial peers for the calls that will be managed by RSVP.

CAC Tools

As the various aspects of CAC on IP networks have been considered, several different solutions have come into prominence. None of them solves the entire problem, but they all are useful to address a particular aspect of CAC. Unlike circuit-based networks, which reserve a free digital service level zero (DS0) time slot on every leg of the path that the call will take, determining whether an IP network has the resources to carry a voice call is not a simple undertaking.

There are four areas in which CAC can be implemented:

- H.323 CAC
- Session initiation protocol (SIP) CAC
- Media Gateway Control Protocol (MGCP) CAC
- Cisco Unified CallManager CAC

H.323 CAC

The CAC for the H.323 VoIP gateways feature allows you to configure thresholds for local resources, memory, and CPU resources. With the **call threshold** command, you can configure two thresholds, high and low, for each resource. Call treatment is triggered when the current value of a resource exceeds the configured high. The call treatment remains in effect until the current resource value falls below the configured low. Having high and low thresholds prevents call admission flapping and provides hysteresis in call admission decision making. Hysteresis is a phenomenon in which the response of a physical system to an external influence depends not only on the present magnitude of that influence but also on the previous history of the system.

With the **call spike** command, you can configure the limit for incoming calls during a specified time period. A call spike occurs when a large number of incoming calls arrive from the public switched telephone network (PSTN) in a very short period of time (for example, 100 incoming calls in 10 ms).

With the **call treatment** command, you can select how the call should be treated when local resources are not available to handle the call. For example, when the current resource value for any one of the configured triggers for call threshold has exceeded the configured threshold, the call treatment choices are as follows:

- **Time-division multiplexing (TDM) hairpinning**—Hairpins the calls through the plain old telephone service (POTS) dial peer
- **Reject**—Disconnects the call
- **Play message or tone**—Plays a configured message or tone to the user

To enable the global resources of this gateway, use the **call threshold** command in global configuration mode. To disable this command, use the **no** form of this command.

```
call threshold {global trigger-name | interface interface-name interface-number int-
calls} low value high value [busyout | treatment]
no call threshold {global trigger-name | interface interface-name int-calls}
```

Table 7-4 shows the **call threshold** command options.

Table 7-4   **call threshold** *Commands*

Command	Description
global *trigger-name*	Specifies the global resources on the gateway.
	The *trigger-name* arguments are as follows:
	• **cpu-5sec**—CPU utilization in the last 5 seconds.
	• **cpu-avg**—Average CPU utilization.
	• **io-mem**—I/O memory utilization.
	• **proc-mem**—Processor memory utilization.
	• **total-calls**—Total number of calls. The valid range is from 1 to 10,000.
	• **total-mem**—Total memory utilization.
interface *interface-name* *interface-number*	Specifies the gateway. The types of interfaces and their numbers depend on the configured interfaces.
int-calls	Number of calls through the interface. The valid range is from 1 to 10,000 calls.
low *value*	Value of low threshold. The valid range is from 1 to 100 percent for the utilization triggers.
high *value*	Value of high threshold. The valid range is from 1 to 100 percent for the utilization triggers.
busyout	(Optional: global only) Automatically busies out the T1/E1 channels if the resource is not available.
treatment	(Optional: global only) Applies call treatment from session application if the resource is not available.

To configure the limit of incoming calls in a short period of time, use the **call spike** command in global configuration mode. To disable this command, use the **no** form of this command. The **call spike** command uses a sliding window to determine the period in which the spike is limited. The sliding window period is defined using the **size** command, with valid ranges from 100 to 250 ms. If a longer spike period is desired, the **steps** command is used as a multiplier for the **size** command. For example, if the **steps** were set to 2 and the **size** was set to 250, the spike period would be 500 ms.

```
call spike call-number [steps number-of-steps size milliseconds]
no call spike
```

Table 7-5 details the **call spike** command options.

Table 7-5   **call spike** *Commands*

Command	Description
call-number	Incoming call numbers for spiking threshold; valid range is from 1 to 2,147,483,647
steps *number-of-steps*	(Optional) Number of steps; valid range is from 3 to 10
size *milliseconds*	(Optional) Step size in milliseconds; valid range is from 100 to 2000

To configure how calls should be processed when local resources are unavailable, use the **call treatment** global configuration mode command. To disable the call treatment triggers, use the **no** form of this command.

```
call treatment {on | action action [value] | cause-code cause-code | isdn-reject
value}
no call treatment {on | action action [value] | cause-code cause-code | isdn-reject
value}
```

Table 7-6 shows the **call treatment** command options.

Table 7-6   **call treatment** *Commands*

Command	Description
on	Enables call treatment from the default session application.
action *action*	Action to take when call treatment is triggered.
	The action argument has the following possible values:
	• **hairpin**—Hairpin
	• **playmsg**—Specifies the URL of the audio file to play
	• **reject**—Disconnects the call and pass down cause code
cause-code *cause-code*	Specifies reason for disconnect to caller.
	The cause-code argument can have the following values:
	• **busy**—Indicates that gateway is busy
	• **no-QoS**—Indicates that the gateway cannot provide QoS
	• **no-resource**—Indicates that the gateway has no resources available
isdn-reject *value*	Selects the ISDN rejection cause code.

ISDN cause codes that can be used in the **isdn-reject** *value* command are presented in Table 7-7.

Table 7-7   *ISDN Cause Codes*

Cause No.	Description	Function
34	No circuit available (circuit/channel congestion)	Indicates that there is no channel available to handle the call
38	Net out of order	Indicates that the network is not functioning properly and the malfunction is likely to last a long time. Re-attempting the call is not likely to be successful
41	Net problem, redial (temporary failure)	Indicates that the network is not functioning properly and the malfunction is not going to last a long time. Re-attempting the call is likely to be successful
42	Net busy, redial (switching equipment congestion)	Indicates that the switching equipment is experiencing high traffic load
43	Access/user information discarded	Indicates that the network is unable to deliver user information to the remote users as was requested
44	No channel available (requested circuit/channel not available)	Indicates that the circuit or channel indicated by the requesting side cannot be used by the other side of the interface
47	Resource unavailable/new destination	Indicates a resource unavailable event only when no other cause in the resource unavailable class applies

Consider a few examples of H.323 CAC commands:

- The following example busies out the total-calls resource if 5 (low) or 5000 (high) is reached:

  ```
  call threshold global total-calls low 5 high 5000 busyout
  ```

- The following example enables thresholds of 5 (low) and 2500 (high) for interface calls on interface Ethernet 0:

  ```
  call threshold interface Ethernet 0 int-calls low 5 high 2500
  ```

- The following example busies out the average CPU utilization if 5 percent (low) or 65 percent (high) is reached:

  ```
  call threshold global cpu-avg low 5 high 65 busyout
  ```

- The following configuration of the **call spike** command has a call number of 30, 10 steps, and a step size of 2000 ms:

```
call spike 30 steps 10 size 2000
```

- The following example enables the call treatment feature with a hairpin action:

```
call treatment on
```

```
call treatment action hairpin
```

- The following example displays the proper formatting of the **playmsg** action keyword:

```
call treatment action playmsg tftp://keyer/prompts/conjestion.au
```

NOTE   The **congestion.au** file plays when local resources are not available to handle the call.

- The following example configures a call treatment cause code to display "no QoS" when local resources are unavailable to process a call:

```
call treatment cause-code no-qos
```

SIP CAC

Measurement-based CAC for SIP can monitor IP network capacity and reject or redirect calls based on congestion detection. This feature does the following:

- Verifies that adequate resources are available to carry a successful VoIP session

- Implements a mechanism to prevent calls arriving from the IP network from entering the gateway when required resources are not available to process the call

- Supports measurement-based CAC processes

The following sections illustrate the configuration of CAC for a SIP environment. Specifically, configurations for the following CAC mechanisms are addressed: SAA RTR Responder, PSTN Fallback, and Resource Availability Check.

Configuring SAA RTR Responder

Service Assurance Agent (SAA) is a generic network management feature that provides a mechanism for network congestion analysis. SAA determines latency, delay, and jitter and provides real-time ITU Calculated Planning Impairment Factor (ICPIF) calculations before establishing a call across an IP infrastructure. The SAA Responder feature uses SAA probes to traverse the network to a given IP destination and measure the loss and delay characteristics of the network along the path traveled. These values are returned to the outgoing gateway to use in making a decision on the condition of the network and its ability to carry a call. Threshold values for rejecting a call are configured at the outgoing gateway.

Each probe consists of multiple packets, a configurable parameter of this feature. SAA packets can emulate voice packets and therefore receive the same priority as voice throughout the entire network. The delay, loss, and ICPIF values entered into the cache for the IP destination are averaged from all the responses. If the call uses G.729 and G.711 coder-decoders (CODECs), the probe packet sizes mimic those of a voice packet for that CODEC. Other CODECs use G.711-like probes. In Cisco IOS software releases later than Release 12.1(3)T, other CODEC choices might also be supported with their own specific probes.

The IP Precedence (that is, a Layer 3 priority marking) of the probe packets can also be configured to simulate the priority of a voice packet more closely. This parameter should be set equal to the IP Precedence used for other voice media packets in the network. Typically, voice packets have an IP Precedence value of 5.

SAA probes used for CAC go out randomly on ports selected from within the top end of the audio User Datagram Protocol (UDP), defined port range (16,384 through 32,767). Probes use a packet size based on the CODEC that the call will use. IP Precedence can be set if desired, and full RTP, UDP, and IP headers are used, just as a real voice packet would carry. The SAA Responder feature was called Response Time Reporter (RTR) in earlier releases of Cisco IOS software. You can use the **rtr responder** command to enable SAA Responder functionality on the destination node.

Configuring PSTN Fallback

The measurement-based CAC for SIP feature supports *PSTN Fallback*, which monitors congestion in the IP network and either redirects calls to the PSTN or rejects calls based on network congestion. Calls can be rerouted to an alternate IP destination or to the PSTN if the IP network is found unsuitable for voice traffic at that time. You can define congestion thresholds based on the configured network. This functionality allows the service provider to give a reasonable guarantee about the quality of the conversation to VoIP users at the time of call admission.

NOTE   PSTN Fallback does not provide assurances that a VoIP call that proceeds over the IP network is protected from the effects of congestion. This is the function of the other QoS mechanisms, such as LLQ.

PSTN Fallback includes the following capabilities:

- Provides the ability to define the congestion thresholds based on the network.
  - — Defines a threshold based on ICPIF, which is derived as part of ITU G.113
  - — Defines a threshold based solely on packet delay and loss measurements
- Uses SAA probes to provide packet delay, jitter, and loss information for the relevant IP addresses. Based on the packet loss, delay, and jitter encountered by these probes, an ICPIF or delay or loss value is calculated. Typically, an ICPIF value of 10 or lower is considered acceptable.
- Supports calls of any CODEC. Only G.729 and G.711 have accurately simulated probes. Calls of all other CODECs are emulated by a G.711 probe.

The call fallback subsystem has a network traffic cache that maintains the ICPIF or delay or loss values for various destinations. This capability helps performance because each new call to a well-known destination need not wait for a probe to be admitted, as the value is usually cached from a previous call.

Once the ICPIF or delay or loss value is calculated, it is stored in a fallback cache where it remains until the cache ages out or overflows. Until an entry ages out, probes are sent periodically for that particular destination. This time interval is configurable.

To configure PSTN Fallback, use the following global configuration mode command:

```
call fallback active
```

This command enables a call request to fallback to alternate dial peers in case of network congestion. The **active** keyword enables a call request to fall back to alternate dial peers in case of network congestion.

Configuring Resource Availability Check

User-selected thresholds allow you to configure call admission thresholds for local resources and end-to-end memory and CPU resources. You can configure two thresholds, high and low, for each global or interface-related resource. The specified call treatment is triggered when the current value of a resource goes beyond the configured high and remains in effect until the current resource value falls below the configured low.

You can select how the call should be treated when local resources are not available to handle the call. For example, when the current resource value for any one of the configured triggers for call threshold exceeds the configured threshold, you have the following call treatment choices:

- **TDM hairpinning**—Hairpins (that is, redirects) the calls through the POTS dial peer
- **Reject**—Disconnects the call
- **Play message or tone**—Plays a configured message or tone to the user

To configure resource availability checking, use the following global configuration mode command:

```
call threshold global trigger-name low value high value [busyout][treatment]
```

This command enables a trigger and defines associated parameters to allow or disallow new calls on the router. Action is enabled when the trigger value exceeds the value specified by the **high** keyword and is disabled when the trigger value drops below the value specified by the **low** keyword.

Table 7-8 shows the **call threshold** command options.

Table 7-8   **call threshold** *Commands*

Command	Description
trigger-name	Can be one of the following: • **cpu-5sec**—CPU utilization in the last 5 seconds • **cpu-avg**—Average CPU utilization • **io-mem**—I/O memory utilization • **proc-mem**—Processor memory utilization • **total-calls**—Total number of calls • **total-mem**—Total memory utilization
low *value*	Value of low threshold; range is from 1 to 100 percent for utilization triggers and from 1 to 10,000 for total calls
high *value*	Value of high threshold; range is from 1 to 100 percent for utilization triggers and from 1 to 10,000 for total calls
busyout	(Optional) Busies out the T1 or E1 channels if the resource is not available
treatment	(Optional) Applies call treatment from the session application if the resource is not available

To configure call treatment, use the following global configuration mode command:

```
call treatment {on ¦ action action [value]¦ cause-code cause-code ¦ isdn-reject
value}
```

This command configures how calls should be processed when local resources are unavailable.

Table 7-9 shows the **call treatment** command options.

To configure resource availability checking for interface resources, enter the following global configuration mode command:

```
call threshold interface interface-name interface number int-calls low value high
value
```

This command allows threshold values to be configured for total numbers of voice calls placed through a particular interface. This command is used to allow or disallow admission for new calls on the router.

Table 7-10 shows the **call threshold interface** command options.

Table 7-9 **call treatment** *Commands*

Command	Description
on	Enables call treatment from the default session application.
action *action*	Specifies the action to be taken when call treatment is triggered. The action argument can be one of the following: • **hairpin**—Specifies the hairpinning action. • **playmsg**—Specifies that the gateway play the selected message. The optional value argument specifies the audio file to play, in URL format. • **reject**—Specifies whether the call should be disconnected and the ISDN cause code passed.
cause-code *cause-code*	Specifies the reason for disconnection to the caller. The cause-code argument can be one of the following: • **busy**—Indicates that the gateway is busy. • **no-qos**—Indicates that the gateway cannot provide QoS. • **no-resource**—Indicates that the gateway has no resources available.
isdn-reject *value*	Applies to ISDN interfaces only and specifies the ISDN reject cause code. The *value* argument ranges from 34 through 47 (ISDN cause code for rejection).

Table 7-10 **call threshold interface** *Commands*

Command	Description
interface-name	Specifies the interface used in making call admission decisions. Types of interfaces and their numbers depend on the configured interfaces.
interface-number	Specifies the number of calls through the interface that triggers a call admission decision.
int-calls	Configures the gateway to use the number of calls through the interface as a threshold.
low *value*	Enables the specified call treatment until the number of calls through the interface drops below the configured low value. The *value* argument specifies the number of calls used to make call admission decisions. The range is from 1 to 10,000 calls.
high *value*	Enables the specified call treatment until the number of calls through the interface exceeds the configured high value. The *value* argument specifies the number of calls used to make call admission decisions. The range is from 1 to 10,000 calls.

Consider the following examples of the SIP CAC commands:

- SAA RTR Responder:

  ```
  Router(config)#rtr responder
  ```

- PSTN Fallback

  ```
  Router(config)#call fallback active
  ```

- Resource availability checking

  ```
  Router(config)#call threshold global total-calls low 5 high 1000 busyout
  Router(config)#call treatment action cause-code 17
  Router(config)#call threshold interface ethernet 0 int-calls low 5 high 2500
  ```

MGCP CAC

The MGCP VoIP CAC feature enables certain Cisco CAC capabilities on VoIP networks that are managed by MGCP call agents. These capabilities permit a gateway to identify and gracefully refuse calls that are susceptible to poor voice quality.

Poor voice quality on an MGCP voice network can result from transmission artifacts such as echo, from the use of low-quality CODECs, from network congestion and delay, or from overloaded gateways. You can overcome the first two causes of echo by using echo cancellation and better CODEC selection. You can address network congestion, delay, and overloaded gateways by using MGCP VoIP CAC.

Before the release of MGCP VoIP CAC, MGCP voice calls were often established regardless of the availability of resources for those calls in the gateway and the network. MGCP VoIP CAC ensures resource availability by disallowing calls when gateway and network resources are below configured thresholds and by reserving guaranteed bandwidth throughout the network for each completed call.

MGCP VoIP CAC has three components for improving voice quality and reliability:

- System Resource Check (SRC) CAC evaluates memory and call resources local to the gateway. It is supported in MGCP 1.0 and MGCP 0.1.
- RSVP CAC allocates bandwidth on the network. RSVP is supported in MGCP 1.0 and MGCP 0.1.
- Cisco SAA CAC appraises network congestion conditions on the network. It is supported only in MGCP 1.0.

To set thresholds and enable MGCP SRC CAC, use the following command in global configuration mode:

```
call threshold global trigger-name low value high value treatment
```

This command enables a resource and defines its parameters. Treatment of attempted calls is enabled when the resource cost goes beyond the high value. Treatment is not disabled until the resource cost drops below the low value. The arguments and keywords are shown in Table 7-11.

Table 7-11   **call threshold global** *Commands*

Command	Description
trigger-name	Can be one of the following: • **cpu-5sec**—CPU utilization in the last 5 seconds • **cpu-avg**—Average CPU utilization • **io-mem**—I/O memory utilization • **proc-mem**—Processor memory utilization • **total-calls**—Total number of calls • **total-mem**—Total memory utilization
low *value*	Value of low threshold; range is from 1 to 100 percent for utilization triggers and from 1 to 10,000 for total calls
high *value*	Value of high threshold; range is from 1 to 100 percent for utilization triggers and from 1 to 10,000 for total calls
treatment	(Optional) Applies call treatment from the session application if the resource is not available

If network conditions rise above the high threshold value, SRC rejects the call by sending the call agent an MGCP error message with the return code 403. The call agent applies a treatment to the rejected call.

The following sections illustrate the configuration of CAC for an MGCP environment. Specifically, configurations for the following CAC mechanisms are addressed: RSVP CAC, Cisco SAA CAC, and Cisco Unified CallManager CAC.

Configuring RSVP CAC

To configure MGCP RSVP CAC on a media gateway, use the following command in global configuration mode:

```
ip rsvp bandwidth (interface-kbps [single-flow-kbps])
```

This command enables RSVP for IP on an interface. RSVP is disabled by default. It should be noted that, in order for RSVP to operate correctly end to end, it must be configured on all routers in the network. The arguments are shown in Table 7-12.

Table 7-12 **ip rsvp** *Bandwidth Commands*

Command	Description
interface-kbps	(Optional) Maximum amount of bandwidth, in kilobits per second, that might be allocated by RSVP flows. The range is from 1 to 10,000,000. This parameter should be configured for the maximum amount of voice bandwidth that this interface is limited to for all calls.
single-flow-kbps	(Optional) Maximum amount of bandwidth, in kilobits per second, that might be allocated to a single flow. The range is from 1 to 10,000,000. This parameter should be configured for the amount of bandwidth for one call.

Configuring Cisco SAA CAC

Cisco SAA is an application-aware synthetic operation agent that monitors network performance by measuring response time, network resource availability, application performance, jitter (interpacket delay variance), connect time, throughput, and packet loss. Performance can be measured between any Cisco device that supports this feature and any remote IP host (server), Cisco routing device, or mainframe host. Performance measurement statistics provided by this feature can be used for troubleshooting, problem analysis, and designing network topologies.

The SAA Responder, enabled using the **rtr responder** command, is a component embedded in the target Cisco routing device that allows the system to anticipate and respond to SAA request packets. The SAA Responder can listen on any user-defined port for UDP and TCP protocol messages. In client/server terminology, the SAA Responder is a *concurrent multiservice server.*

The global configuration mode commands to configure Cisco SAA CAC are as follows:

- **call fallback active**—Enables a call request to fall back to alternate dial peers in case of network congestion
- **mgcp rtrcac**—Enables MGCP SAA CAC
- **rtr responder**—Enables the SAA Responder functionality on a Cisco device

The configuration shown in Example 7-6 enables all three types of MGCP VoIP CAC: SRC, RSVP, and SAA. Notice that CAC configuration commands are highlighted in the output. Comments are provided in the example in the lines preceding the CAC commands to help you identify the commands needed for a particular CAC type.

Example 7-6   *MGCP CAC Configuration (Continued)*

```
version 12.2
!
! Output omitted for brevity
!

! The following command is used in MGCP SA Agent CAC.
call fallback active
! The following command is used in MGCP RSVP CAC.
call rsvp-sync
! The following six commands are used in MGCP SRC CAC.
call threshold global cpu-5sec low 55 high 70 treatment
call threshold global cpu-avg low 70 high 80 treatment
call threshold global total-mem low 70 high 80 treatment
call threshold global io-mem low 70 high 80 treatment
call threshold global proc-mem low 70 high 80 treatment
call threshold global total-calls low 10 high 12 treatment
!
! Output omitted for brevity


!
interface FastEthernet0/0
ip address 192.168.1.61 255.255.255.0
duplex auto
speed auto
! The following command is used in MGCP RSVP CAC to configure the bandwidth alloca
ted.
! for VoIP calls through the interface.
ip rsvp bandwidth 512 512
!

! Output omitted for brevity
!
mgcp
mgcp call-agent 10.13.57.88 service-type mgcp version 1.0
mgcp modem passthrough voip mode nse
mgcp modem passthrough voaal2 mode
mgcp package-capability trunk-package
! The following command is used for MGCP SA Agent CAC.
mgcp rtrcac
! The following command is used in MGCP SRC CAC.
mgcp src-cac
no mgcp timer receive-rtcp
!
mgcp profile default
!
dial-peer voice 1 pots
application mgcpapp
port 3/0:1
!
dial-peer voice 2 pots
application mgcpapp
```

continues

Example 7-6 *MGCP CAC Configuration (Continued)*

```
port 3/0:2
!
dial-peer voice 3 pots
application mgcpapp
port 3/1:1
!
dial-peer voice 4 pots
application mgcpapp
port 3/1:2
!
! The following command is used in MGCP SA Agent CAC.
rtr responder
!
! Output omitted for brevity
!
end
```

Cisco Unified CallManager CAC

While Cisco supports a variety of CAC mechanisms, most of these mechanisms are router-centric. However, in environments containing multiple Cisco Unified CallManager (CCM) clusters, other CAC approaches might be more appropriate. With CCMs, two types of call admission are possible:

- **Locations CAC**—The locations feature provides CAC for centralized call-processing systems. A centralized system uses a single CCM cluster to control all of the locations. CCM's locations feature allows you to specify the maximum amount of bandwidth available for calls *to* and *from* each location, thereby limiting the number of active calls and preventing oversubscription of the bandwidth on the IP WAN links.

- **Gatekeeper zone CAC**—A gatekeeper device provides CAC for distributed call-processing systems. In a distributed system, each site contains its own call-processing capability. Calls are limited between zones in this configuration.

Summary

This chapter introduced the need for quality of service (QoS) in a converged network environment (that is, a network that simultaneously transports voice, data, and/or video). In the absence of QoS mechanisms, voice packets might suffer from packet loss, packet delay, and variable delay (that is, jitter). QoS mechanisms help mitigate such challenges through tools such as classification, marking, low latency queuing (LLQ), RTP Header Compression (cRTP), and Link Fragmentation and Interleaving (LFI).

Even with its relatively high-speed connectivity, local area networks (LANs) also need QoS. For example, an interface speed mismatch for traffic entering (for example, on a 1 Gbps link) and exiting (for example, on a 100 Mbps link) a switch could cause a switch interface queue to fill to capacity and overflow. On the LAN, many Cisco Catalyst switches can use QoS mechanisms, such as weighted round-robin (WRR) and CoS to DSCP remarking.

While the study of how to configure the various aspects of QoS mechanisms is beyond the scope of this book, this chapter did introduce a way to configure QoS on both IOS router platforms and IOS-based Catalyst switch platforms, through a feature called AutoQoS.

In the voice arena, most QoS mechanisms are aimed at protecting voice from data. However, too many simultaneous voice calls can also oversubscribe available WAN bandwidth. Therefore, Call Admission Control (CAC) mechanisms help protect voice from voice. This chapter discussed the configuration of H.323, SIP, MGCP, and Cisco Unified CallManager CAC approaches.

Chapter Review Questions

The following questions test your knowledge of topics explained in this chapter. You can find the answers to the questions in Appendix A, "Answers to Chapter Review Questions."

1. Which two factors affect voice clarity?

   a   Fidelity

   b   Echo

   c   Sidetone

   d   Background noise

   e   Distance

2. Identify two broad categories of delay under which more specific types of delay are categorized?

   a   Variable delay

   b   Serialization delayfixed delay

   c   FIFO delay

   d   Processing delay

3. According to ITU-T Recommendation G.114, how much delay is acceptable for most user applications?

   a   0 to 150 ms

   b   200 to 250 ms

    c 150 to 400 ms

    d Above 400 ms

4. Which of the following QoS mechanisms does the AutoQoS feature enable on a Catalyst switch port?

    a LFI

    b cRTP

    c WRR

    d LLQ

5. What Cisco IOS software feature allows AutoQoS for Enterprise to dynamically discover an interface's traffic patterns?

    a NBAR

    b ACLs

    c CEF

    d CBAC

6. Which of the following interface configuration mode commands enables AutoQoS on an interface and instructs the interface to trust Layer 2 CoS priority markings only if those CoS markings came from a Cisco IP phone?

    a **auto qos voip device cisco-phone**

    b **auto qos voip cisco-phone**

    c **auto qos voip trust cos**

    d **auto qos voip trust cisco-phone**

7. If CAC and LLQ are enabled on a link, which traffic will be transmitted first?

    a Small data packets

    b Large data packets

    c Voice packets

    d Packets that arrived first

8. At what location in the network are CAC call control services configured?

    a Incoming gateway

    b Outgoing gateway

    c Incoming gatekeeper

    d Outgoing gatekeeper

    e Entire network

9. With the _____ command, you can configure two thresholds, high and low, for each resource.

    a **call spike**

    b **call threshold**

    c **call treatment**

    d **rtr responder**

10. Which feature of Cisco Unified CallManager allows you to specify the maximum bandwidth available for calls to and from each location?

    a Set bandwidth

    b Locations

    c Gatekeeper zone

    d Active calls

Lab Exercise: Router AutoQoS

In this lab, you will configure AutoQoS on two different router interfaces. One interface runs at a speed of 128 kbps, and the other interface runs at a speed of 2 Mbps. You will see that AutoQoS treats these interfaces differently, based on their available bandwidth.

Specifically, you will configure router R2, as shown in Figure 7-8. The interface speeds were configured in the "Initial Configuration" task of the lab exercise in Chapter 2, "Analog and Digital Voice Connections."

Figure 7-8 *Lab Topology*

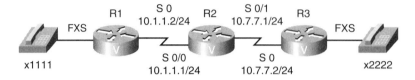

Task 1: Configure AutoQoS on the Slower Interface

In this task, you will configure AutoQoS on router R2's slower serial interface.

Complete these steps:

Step 1. Enter interface configuration mode on router R2 for the interface that connects R2 to router R1 (for example, interface Serial 0/0 in Figure 7-8).

Step 2. Enable AutoQoS for this interface with the **auto qos voip** command.

Task 2: Configure AutoQoS on the Faster Interface

In this task, you will configure AutoQoS on router R2's faster serial interface.

Complete these steps:

Step 1. Enter interface configuration mode on router R2 for the interface that connects R2 to router R3 (for example, interface Serial 0/1 in Figure 7-8).

Step 2. Enable AutoQoS for this interface with the **auto qos voip** command.

Task 3: Exercise Verification

In this task, you will verify the configuration of AutoQoS on router R2's serial interfaces.

Complete these steps:

Step 1. From router R2's privileged mode, enter the **show auto qos** command to view the commands entered by AutoQoS globally, for the slower serial interface, and for the faster serial interface.

Step 2. Notice that for the slower serial interface, AutoQoS configured Multilink PPP (MLP) and enabled RTP Header Compression (cRTP) because these are *link efficiency* mechanisms designed to optimize bandwidth usage on slower-speed serial interfaces (that is, interfaces with interface speeds less than 768 kbps).

NOTE   The purpose of this lab is to illustrate how AutoQoS intelligently applies appropriate QoS mechanisms to interfaces, based on interface characteristics. In order to be able to place a phone call across the lab topology after completing this lab, you should also configure AutoQoS on router R1's serial interface that connects back to router R2, because MLP must be configured on both ends of a link.

Suggested Solution

Although your physical hardware might differ, Example 7-7 shows the output of the **show auto qos** command on R2 after entering the **auto qos voip** command for interfaces Serial 0/0 and Serial 0/1. Notice that cRTP and MLP are enabled only for interface Serial 0/0 since these link efficiency mechanisms are appropriate for slower link speeds (that is, link speeds less than 768 kbps), such as Serial 0/0's link speed of 128 kbps. However, these link efficiency mechanisms are not appropriate for higher-speed links (that is, link speeds equal to or greater than 768 kbps), such as Serial 0/1's link speed of 2 Mbps.

Example 7-7   *Output from the* **show auto qos** *Command on R2*

```
R2#show auto qos
 !
  ip access-list extended AutoQoS-VoIP-RTCP
   permit udp any any range 16384 32767
 !
  ip access-list extended AutoQoS-VoIP-Control
   permit tcp any any eq 1720
   permit tcp any any range 11000 11999
   permit udp any any eq 2427
   permit tcp any any eq 2428
   permit tcp any any range 2000 2002
   permit udp any any eq 1719
   permit udp any any eq 5060
 !
  class-map match-any AutoQoS-VoIP-RTP-UnTrust
    match protocol rtp audio
    match access-group name AutoQoS-VoIP-RTCP
 !
  class-map match-any AutoQoS-VoIP-Control-UnTrust
    match access-group name AutoQoS-VoIP-Control
 !
  class-map match-any AutoQoS-VoIP-Remark
    match ip dscp ef
    match ip dscp cs3
    match ip dscp af31
 !
   policy-map AutoQoS-Policy-UnTrust
    class AutoQoS-VoIP-RTP-UnTrust
     priority percent 70
     set dscp ef
```

continues

Example 7-7 *Output from the* **show auto qos** *Command on R2*

```
     class AutoQoS-VoIP-Control-UnTrust
      bandwidth percent 5
      set dscp af31
     class AutoQoS-VoIP-Remark
      set dscp default
     class class-default
      fair-queue

Serial0/0 -
 !
 interface Serial0/0
  no ip address
  encapsulation ppp
  no fair-queue
  ppp multilink
  ppp multilink group 2001100114
 !
 interface Multilink2001100114
  bandwidth 128
  ip address 10.1.1.1 255.255.255.0
  service-policy output AutoQoS-Policy-UnTrust
  ppp multilink
  ppp multilink fragment delay 10
  ppp multilink interleave
  ppp multilink group 2001100114
  ip rtp header-compression iphc-format

Serial0/1 -
 !
 interface Serial0/1
   service-policy output AutoQoS-Policy-UnTrust
 !
 rmon event 33333 log trap AutoQoS description "AutoQoS SNMP traps for Voice Dr
ops" owner AutoQoS
  rmon alarm 33333 cbQosCMDropBitRate.1081.1083 30 absolute rising-threshold 1 3
3333 falling-threshold 0 owner AutoQoS
  rmon alarm 33334 cbQosCMDropBitRate.1137.1139 30 absolute rising-threshold 1 3
3333 falling-threshold 0 owner AutoQoS
```

NOTE   LLQ is appropriate for all interface speeds and is configured for both interfaces.

Answers to Chapter Review Questions

Chapter 1

1. c
2. b
3. a
4. a
5. d
6. b, c
7. c
8. b
9. b
10. c

Chapter 2

1. a, d, f
2. b
3. b
4. c
5. d
6. c, d
7. d
8. c
9. d
10. b

Chapter 3

1. e
2. a
3. d, f
4. a, b
5. c
6. b
7. c
8. b, c
9. b
10. b

Chapter 4

1. b
2. a, d
3. c
4. d
5. b
6. c
7. b
8. c
9. a
10. c

Chapter 5

1. b, c
2. d
3. c
4. c

5. b

6. b

7. a, c, d

8. c

9. b

10. a

Chapter 6

1. a, c, d

2. c, e

3. b

4. b

5. a, c, d, e

6. b

7. b

8. d

9. a

10. d

Chapter 7

1. a, b

2. a, c

3. a

4. c

5. a

6. b

7. c

8. b

9. b

10. b

Cisco VoIP Applications

Implementation of creative and cost-saving applications is the cornerstone of Voice over IP (VoIP) networks. Network administrators who have knowledge of various VoIP applications and who can successfully cut corporate costs bring added value to a company. This appendix describes various implementations and applications of VoIP networks.

Hoot and Holler

A hoot and holler network, as illustrated in Figure B-1 (also known as a junkyard circuit, squawk box system, holler down circuit, or shout down circuit), provides always-on multiuser conferences without requiring users to dial in to a conference bridge. This type of network was devised more than 50 years ago when local concentrations of small, specialized businesses needed to communicate common, time-critical information. Junkyard operators up and down the East Coast of the United States were among the first users of these networks. They began to install their own telephone wires, speakers (called *squawk boxes*), and microphones to share information with other locations about parts that their customers needed. These networks functioned as crude, do-it-yourself, business-to-business intercom systems.

Hoot and holler broadcast audio network systems have evolved into the specialized leased-line networks of today. Financial and brokerage firms use these networks to trade stocks and currency futures and provide time-critical information, such as market updates and morning reports. In addition to financial and brokerage firms, users of various forms of hoot and holler networks include news agencies, publishers, government and municipal emergency response agencies, weather bureaus, transportation providers, utility operators, manufacturers, collectibles dealers, talent agencies, airlines, and nationwide salvage yard organizations.

Hoot and holler over IP transports hoot and holler voice traffic over traditional data networking equipment on an existing enterprise multiservice network. Hoot and holler enables businesses to eliminate expensive, dedicated leased lines while protecting investments in existing hoot and holler equipment such as turrets, bridges, and four-wire telephones. In addition to eliminating leased lines, running hoot and holler traffic over an IP network allows businesses to utilize bandwidth more efficiently. When bandwidth is not being used for hoot and holler traffic, it can be made available for data.

Figure B-1 *Hoot and Holler*

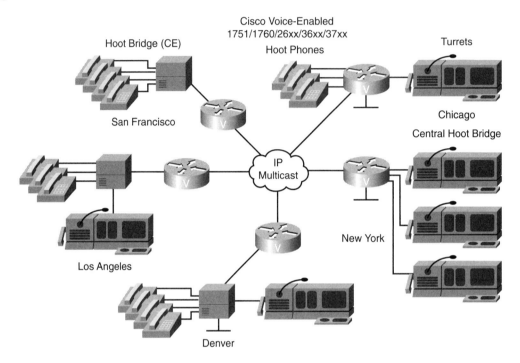

Hoot and holler requires that IP multicast be active on the routers that support the hoot and holler circuit. The connections are configured using special dial peers configured with **session protocol multicast**.

Cisco Unified CallManager

Cisco's IP Communications product line, including IP telephony, unified communication, audio/video conferencing, and customer contact applications, helps organizations realize business gains by improving operational efficiencies. These improved operational efficiencies result in increased organizational productivity and enhanced customer satisfaction. Cisco Unified CallManager, an integral component of the Cisco IP Communications system, is the software-based call-processing component of the Cisco enterprise IP telephony product line. It is enabled by Cisco Architecture for Voice, Video and Integrated Data (AVVID). Figure B-2 offers a sample Cisco Unified CallManager topology.

Figure B-2 *Cisco Unified CallManager Topology*

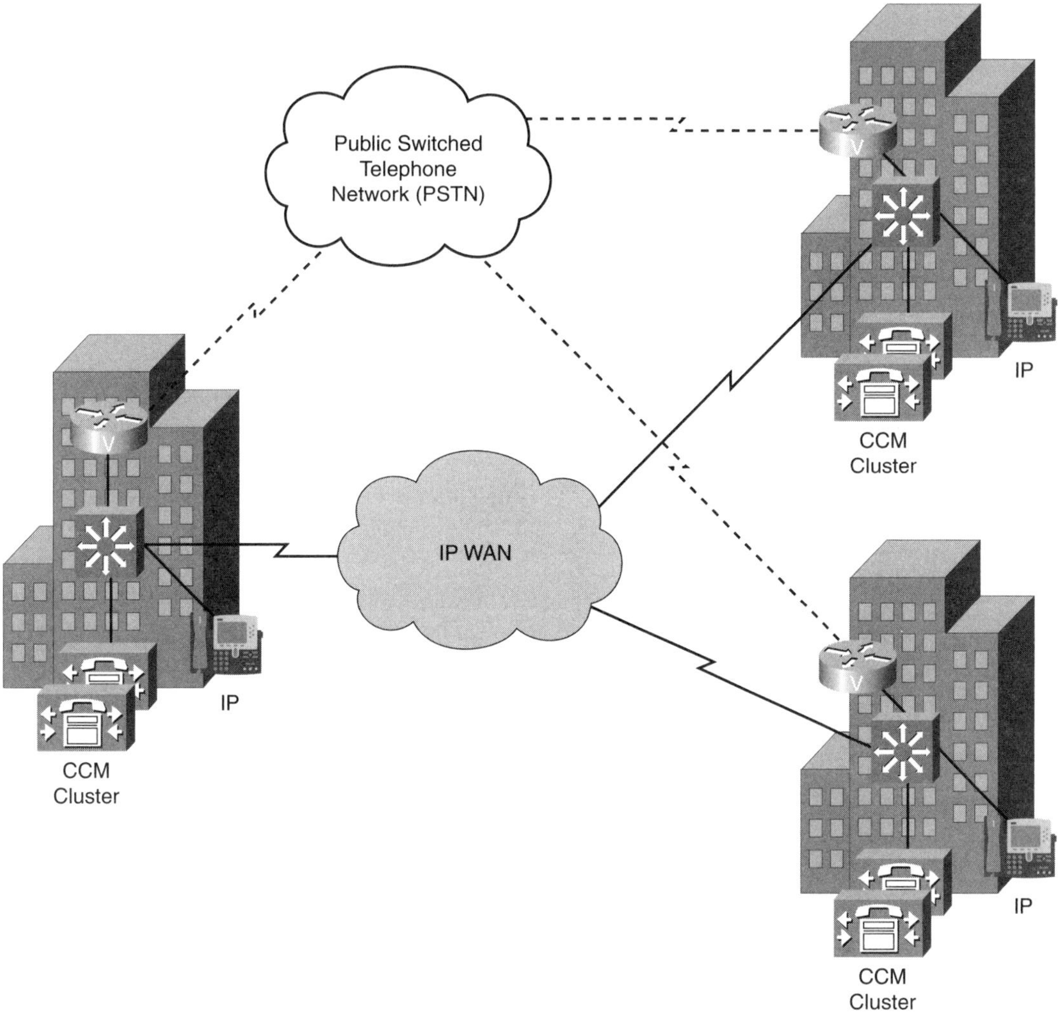

Cisco Unified CallManager software extends enterprise telephony features and capabilities to IP telephony network devices such as IP phones, media processing devices, VoIP gateways, and multimedia applications. Additional data, voice, and video services such as unified messaging, multimedia conferencing, collaborative contact centers, and interactive multimedia response systems interact with the IP telephony environment through Cisco Unified CallManager open telephony application programming interfaces (APIs).

Cisco Unified CallManager is installed on the Cisco Media Convergence Servers (MCSs) and selected third-party servers. Cisco Unified CallManager software is shipped with a suite of integrated voice applications and utilities, including the Cisco Unified CallManager Attendant Console (a software-only manual attendant console), a software-only ad-hoc conferencing application; the Bulk Administration Tool (BAT); the CDR Analysis and Reporting (CAR) tool, the Admin Serviceability Tool (AST), a simple Cisco Unified CallManager Auto Attendant (CM-AA); the Tool for Auto-Registered Phones Support (TAPS), and the IP Manager Assistant (IPMA) application.

Cisco Unified CallManager provides a scalable, distributable, and highly available enterprise IP telephony call-processing solution. Multiple Cisco Unified CallManager servers are clustered and managed as a single entity. Clustering multiple call-processing servers on an IP network is a unique capability in the industry and highlights the leading architecture provided by Cisco AVVID. Cisco Unified CallManager clustering yields scalability from 1 to 30,000 IP phones per cluster, load balancing, and call-processing service redundancy. By interlinking multiple clusters, system capacity can be increased up to one million users in a system of 100 or more sites. Clustering aggregates the power of multiple, distributed Cisco Unified CallManagers, enhancing the scalability and accessibility of the servers to phones, gateways, and applications. Also, triple call-processing server redundancy improves overall system availability.

The benefit of this distributed architecture is improved system availability, load balancing, and scalability. Connection admission control (CAC) ensures that voice quality of service (QoS) is maintained across constricted WAN links and automatically diverts calls to alternate public switched telephone network (PSTN) routes when WAN bandwidth is not available. A web-based interface to the configuration database enables remote configuration. Additionally, HTML-based online help is available for users and administrators.

Toll Bypass

Toll bypass allows customers to bypass the PSTN. The PSTN consists of the tandem time-division multiplexing (TDM)–based switches used for long-distance (or toll) voice calls. Enterprise customers who typically depend on the PSTN for their interoffice voice traffic avoid toll charges by using an IP network with the Cisco routers that serve as the edge voice gateways. Toll bypass allows some Internet service providers (ISPs) to offer residential customers free, or very low-cost, long-distance voice calls by routing the calls over an IP network.

As an example, in Figure B-3, traffic from the enterprise PBX enters the Cisco routers that serve as edge voice gateways. The edge voice gateways, in turn, route the call over the IP network using the H.323 protocol. As shown, the enterprise customers avoid the TDM-based toll switches for their interoffice voice traffic and rely on an IP network.

Figure B-3 *Toll Bypass*

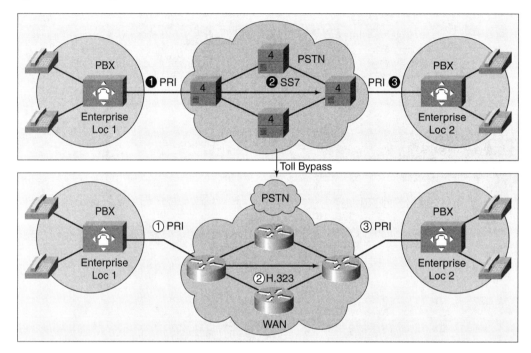

Hospitality Network

Hospitality enterprises (for example, hotels, airports, and convention centers) host guests who demand high-speed connections to the Internet and access to telephony services. Enterprises that are used by a large number of travelers spend money to support LAN-like performance and extend high-speed telecommuting to corporate users.

Hospitality providers build networks that offer high-speed Internet services in a flexible, affordable, and transparent manner. Figure B-4 illustrates a sample hospitality network.

Applications include fast Internet access and high-volume VoIP solutions. In hotels, one building or the entire hotel campus is wired with a single broadband access line to supply voice, video, and Internet applications to guest rooms. The hotel can take advantage of high-volume, long-distance discounts from its provider while realizing revenue from direct long-distance dialing by hotel guests. A hospitality environment can deploy the following components:

- **Cisco Building Broadband Service Manager (BBSM)**—This service-creation platform enables hotel property owners to create, market, and operate broadband access services. BBSM provides plug-and-play access; customizable portals to restaurants, wineries, and retail shops; and support for multiple authentication and billing options.

Figure B-4 *Hospitality Network*

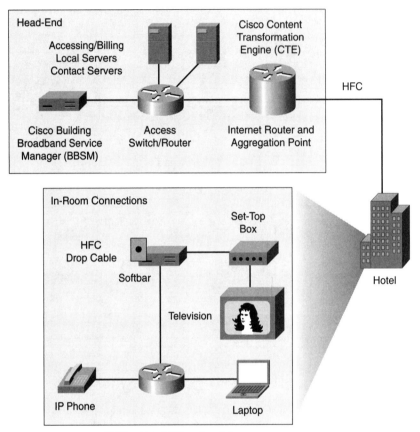

HFC = Hybrid Fiber-Coaxial

- **Cisco IP phone**—This device provides hotel guests with added conveniences, such as telephone-based applications that might include concierge services, linked directories to local attractions, and automatic speed-dial setup. For groups taking advantage of meeting services, the Cisco IP phones can provide personalized group directories, meeting agenda and room locations, and broadcast alert capabilities.

- **Cisco Content Transformation Engine (CTE)**—The CTE is an appliance-based product that optimizes the delivery of web content to a variety of wireless and wired devices, such as cell phones, personal digital assistants (PDAs), and IP phones. Using the CTE with Cisco IP telephones in every room, guests have quick and easy access to hotel information (room service, in-house events) and third-party information (airline schedules, stock quotes, and weather information).

IP Centrex

Centrex service is regarded as an "outsourcing" of telephony call services. Centrex does not maintain a PBX on customer premises. Instead, Centrex service removes the PBX function from the customer premises, provides a Centrex trunk to the customer, and provides the telephony services over the trunk. Typically, the Centrex trunk is arranged as a TDM channel associated signaling (CAS) circuit or as an ISDN Q.931 connection. Customer billing for this service is similar to the billing for outsourcing services.

IP Centrex performs the same job as a PBX but delivers the service over an IP network instead of a circuit-switched network. Service is accessed via an IP network and delivered to customers in a private or multitenant installation. The call control functions that Centrex delivers include:

- Dial tone
- Interpretation of dialed digits
- Determination of called party status
- Call status return to caller, such as busy and ringback
- Call to voice mail reroute, if applicable
- Billing services

Cisco delivers IP Centrex through the use of a call agent, such as the Cisco BTS 10200 Softswitch. Figure B-5 illustrates the use of a call agent for the Centrex services that are delivered to telephones with the trunking gateway serving as a path to the PSTN. Notice that Media Gateway Control Protocol (MGCP) acts as the gateway control protocol because the call routing intelligence resides in the call agent, which is maintained by the service provider.

Figure B-5   *IP Centrex*

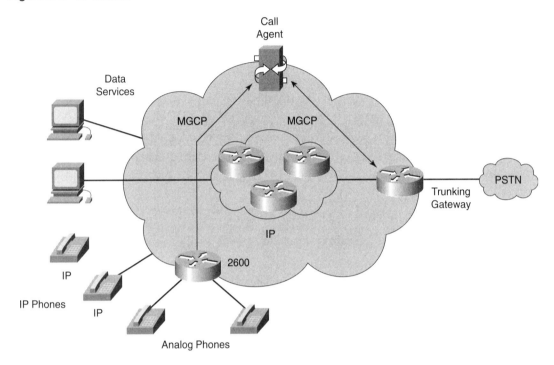

Multitenant

Multitenant applications, as depicted in Figure B-6, allow building owners to deploy low-cost services such as VoIP, cable television, and IP data services to tenants in a common campus or building.

Candidates for multitenant applications include the following:

- **Multidwelling units (MDUs)**—MDUs consist of high-rise and garden-style apartments, townhouses, and condominiums. Apartment renters and owners are now demanding high-speed Internet connections to home offices. Owners or MDU associations can attract new buyers or renters when they build an advanced cable IP infrastructure offering secure, high-speed Internet access, cable television service, and VoIP access services.

- **Multitenant units (MTUs)**—MTUs are commercial properties that house a number of small or medium-sized offices. These users can leverage the existence of a cable IP infrastructure to:

    — Use a high-speed cable broadband medium for improved internal communications, which includes LAN services

Figure B-6 *Multitenant Applications*

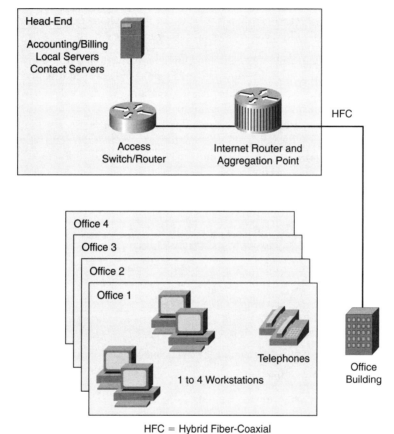

HFC = Hybrid Fiber-Coaxial

— Develop businesses, attract new opportunities, and increase revenue streams through infrastructure advancements and services that support IP data and VoIP

Prepaid Calling Card

Prepaid and postpaid calling-card services represent one of the fastest-growing types of enhanced voice services. A variety of consumer segments have propelled the growth of these services, including students, business and leisure travelers, and immigrants. They are especially popular among mobile telephone users as an alternative to the costly international rates of mobile operators. For carriers who want to realize more profit from a global long-distance network, prepaid and postpaid calling-card services represent an opportunity to improve margins, direct minutes to the network, and increase customer retention. For service providers that currently offer prepaid and postpaid calling-card services over a switched-circuit network, Cisco IP telephony networks provide a more cost-effective alternative for network expansions or upgrades.

Packet voice technology offers a compelling alternative to the traditional TDM switched-circuit network. Packet telephony networks reduce the cost and time-to-market requirements associated with launching or expanding voice services, such as national and international transport, voice mail and unified communications, text-to-speech, speech recognition, and calling-card services. TDM-based services use a leased line and typically require a long-term financial commitment to that specific link. A TDM switch also represents a significant initial cash outlay and lengthy time period to achieve investment payback. The need to accelerate investment payback leads some providers to add fees for calling-card activation or connection, diminishing the service marketability in the process.

Cisco offers a feature-rich product called Cisco Voice Infrastructure and Applications (VIA) for prepaid and postpaid calling-card services that is deployed via VoIP technology. Cisco VIA includes key features and attributes such as:

- A telephony user interface similar to PSTN card services applications
- Cost-efficiency in equipment and bandwidth
- Card recharging
- Balance transfer
- Personal identification number (PIN) change
- Support for multiple languages

Cisco VIA offers the following benefits:

- Lower infrastructure and operating costs compared to other industry offerings
- Industry-leading voice quality, built-in reliability, and scalability
- Architectural and protocol flexibility
- Ability for service providers of any size and location to compete in the calling-card services market

In Figure B-7, Cisco AS5xxx Access Servers allow calling-card customers into the network from the PSTN. The authentication, authorization, and accounting (AAA) server verifies the customer account status. When the account status is authorized, the gatekeeper directs the call across the IP core network to the remote router or gateway, and connects to the PSTN. The service provider receives revenue for routing the call across the IP core.

Figure B-7 *Prepaid Calling Card*

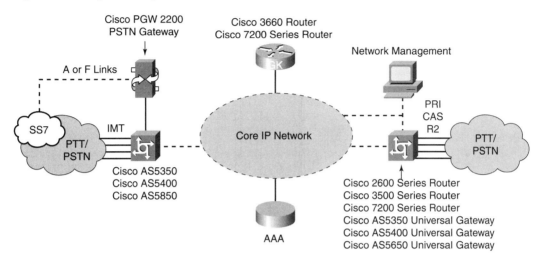

Computer Telephony Integration

Computer telephony integration (CTI) enables access to computer-processing functions while making, receiving, and managing telephone calls. CTI applications allow users to perform tasks such as retrieving customer information from a database provided by the caller ID. CTI applications also enable users to use the information captured by an interactive voice response (IVR) system to route a call to an appropriate customer service representative or to provide information to the individual receiving the call.

The following is a partial list of Cisco CTI applications:

- **Cisco IP SoftPhone**—Cisco IP SoftPhone, a desktop application, turns your computer into a full-feature telephone with the added advantages of call tracking, desktop collaboration, and one-click dialing from online directories. You can also use Cisco IP SoftPhone in tandem with a Cisco IP phone to place, receive, and control calls from your desktop PC. All features function in both modes of operation.

- **Cisco IP Auto Attendant**—The Cisco IP Auto Attendant application works with Cisco Unified CallManager to receive calls on specific telephone extensions and allows callers to select extensions.

- **Cisco WebAttendant**—Cisco WebAttendant provides a GUI for controlling a Cisco IP phone to perform attendant console functions.

- **Cisco Personal Assistant**—Cisco Personal Assistant or a virtual secretary can selectively handle incoming calls and help users place outgoing calls.

To illustrate how CTI works, consider a customer inquiry to a banking institution, as shown in Figure B-8. The customer dials a toll-free telephone number from a home telephone. The agent who answers the call is in a pool of agents whose calls are delivered via an automatic call distributor (ACD). Figure B-8 follows these steps:

1. The customer dials the toll-free number.

2. A Network Voice Response (NVR) system plays a script that collects caller-entered digits (CEDs), such as an account number.

3. The network sends a route request through an optical carrier (OC) interface to access the customer-profile database.

4. The CED, dialed number (DN), and calling line ID (CLID) are referenced in the customer profile database.

5. A route destination is returned to the network applications management/service control point (NAM/SCP) and the DN, CLID, CED, and account information are forwarded to the automatic call distribution (ACD) system and peripheral gateway/CTI server.

6. The CTI server matches the selected agent from the ACD.

7. The CTI server sends a preroute indication across the CTI server interface to the TCP/IP network for pop-up delivery to the selected agent.

8. The TCP/IP network delivers the caller account information and CED information to the selected agent desktop.

NOTE   The sample call data flow outlined in this section depicts an IVR in the carrier network. Alternatively, prompting may occur through an IVR at the premises or through a combination of network and premises-based IVRs.

Figure B-8 *Computer Telephony Integration*

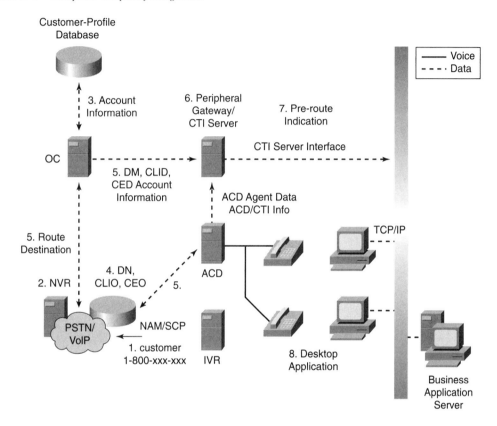

Collaborative Computing

Collaborative computing allows team members on a shared project to share resources and applications in real time, regardless of their physical location. Figure B-9 illustrates a simple VoIP internetwork that allows collaborative computing. The PSTN serves as a gateway to non-enterprise-connected participants.

At the heart of the collaborative computing solution is the IP internetwork. Participants connect to each other via a private IP network or the public Internet. Servers and applications are deployed across the network, including the client software on the participant desktops. Collaborative computing applications include the following:

• Telephony and meeting applications, such as Microsoft NetMeeting

• Scheduling and collaboration software, such as IBM Lotus Notes

Figure B-9 *Collaborative Computing*

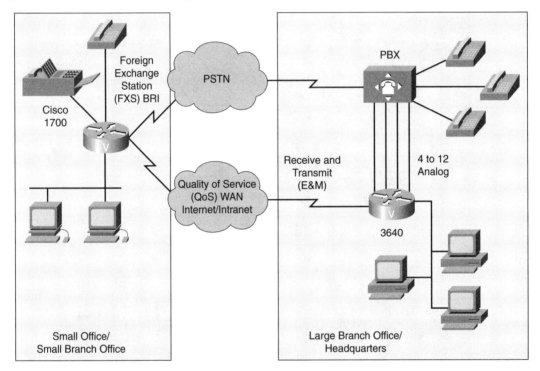

- Video streaming software
- FTP, TFTP, and peer-to-peer file-sharing applications
- IP phones
- Shared whiteboarding software

The goals of collaborative computing include:

- Reduced travel expenses
- Network transparency
- Shared calendar
- Real-time document sharing
- Real-time communication, such as telephony or videoconferencing

Voice-Enabled Web Applications

Cisco AS5400 Series Universal Gateways can interpret Voice Extensible Markup Language (VoiceXML) documents. VoiceXML is an open-standard markup language that creates voice-enabled web browsers and IVR applications. While HTML enables users to retrieve data with a PC, VoiceXML enables subscribers to retrieve data with a telephone. The universal accessibility of the telephone and its ease of use make VoiceXML applications a powerful alternative to HTML for Internet access.

To illustrate a voice-enabled web application in action, consider the following scenario:

1. A baseball fan dials a number from the PSTN and is connected to a Cisco voice gateway configured as a VoiceXML-enabled gateway.

2. The Cisco voice gateway uses the caller ID information and associates it with the appropriate VoiceXML document residing on a web server. This document provides baseball scores for the caller.

3. The voice gateway runs the VoiceXML document and responds to the caller by playing the appropriate audio content. The application might play a recorded prompt that asks the caller to press a specific dual-tone multifrequency key to hear a sports score, such as "Press 2 to hear the results of the playoff game between Baltimore and New York."

4. Cisco IOS VoiceXML can transfer the caller to another party, such as customer service. For example, after playing the score, the application might prompt the caller with the message, "If you sign up for a one-year subscription to this service now, you will be entered into a drawing for two tickets to the next World Series. Press 5 to speak to one of our agents."

Contact Centers

Contact centers are the hubs of the customer service efforts of many growing businesses. Forward-thinking companies are integrating this key function with Internet technology to transform customer care into a powerful business-building force.

Firms such as catalog sellers, telemarketers, and computer helpdesks use traditional contact centers to manage large volumes of telephone calls and customer contacts. Contact center applications route incoming calls to sales and service agents who can respond to customer needs. Integrating this contact center activity with an Internet-based customer-relationship management (CRM) solution gives agents immediate access to customer purchase histories, order tracking capabilities, and other key information and tools. This enhanced information flow enables contact center staff to use customer interaction to build customer loyalty and retention.

Traditional contact center technology, as illustrated in Figure B-10, recognizes incoming contact requests (for example, calls, e-mails, faxes, and web requests) and routes them to available agents. These contact center technologies include recognition of customer telephone numbers, account numbers, or IDs. Customer data appears on the agent computer screen, ensuring that the agent can access the customer orders, account balance, and other crucial data. However, real-time collaboration between the customer and the agent is limited to the spoken word. Services and product offerings are limited to verbal description, usually a script read by the agent.

Figure B-10 *Contact Center Technology*

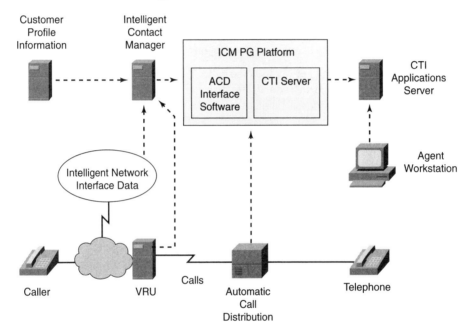

Cisco IP Contact Center (IPCC) with Internet access allows contact center agents to respond to customer queries over a variety of channels, such as telephone, e-mail, web, and fax.

As an example, consider a situation where a customer calls a contact center with questions about a new product and an agent can immediately send an e-mail message that includes product specifications and a link to a downloadable interactive demo. This scenario allows customer-service agents to take on sales and marketing roles, which helps the company roll out new initiatives and promotions quickly to targeted customers. Other ways to enhance real-time customer collaboration include fax-back services and web-page collaboration, where the customer and agent interact on the same web page to ensure, for example, that the color of a sweater is correct.

Contact centers use a range of telephone, computer, and network technologies, including VoIP. In Figure B-10, Cisco Intelligent Call Management (ICM) software is at the heart of the contact center application. The ICM uses CTI technology to deliver caller account information to the agent desktop while the agent receives the VoIP call. The location independence of the agents adds another benefit to this model. "Follow-the-sun" customer support programs allow around-the-clock customer service, regardless of the agent location.

Unified Messaging

Cisco Unity is designed for an IP environment and complements the full range of IP communications solutions (for example, Cisco Unified CallManager, Cisco Personal Assistant, and Cisco IP Contact Center). Cisco Unity provides advanced capabilities that unify data and voice. Cisco AVVID enables Cisco Unity to provide a solid foundation to roll out future convergence-based communications services. IP is less expensive to use for a comprehensive communications solution deployment because it is a single network for both voice and data. Figure B-11 shows an example of this type of unified messaging system.

Cisco Unity leverages existing communications infrastructure investments by integrating with leading legacy PBXs and interoperating with existing voice mail systems. Cisco Unity supports legacy PBX systems and Cisco Unified CallManager, paving the way for a cost-effective migration to full IP telephony. Cisco Unity has an optional Audio Messaging Interchange Specification analog (AMIS-a) networking module that allows message interchange between disparate voice messaging systems that support this industry-standard messaging protocol. Cisco Unity Bridge enables advanced message interchange functionality with Avaya and Octel voice messaging systems. With AMIS-a and Cisco Unity Bridge, customers who deploy Cisco Unity can continue to use their existing messaging systems to ensure a smooth transition.

Because Cisco Unity shares the same directory as the Microsoft Exchange network3, users can make subscriber moves, adds, and changes from one place, eliminating redundant tasks. Studies show that the average cost of a typical system move, addition, or change to a user account is between $75 and $100. Eliminating duplicate administration for separate voice and e-mail systems can quickly pay for the entire system. In addition, because all messages are housed in the same message store, backup costs are reduced.

Figure B-11 *Unified Messaging*

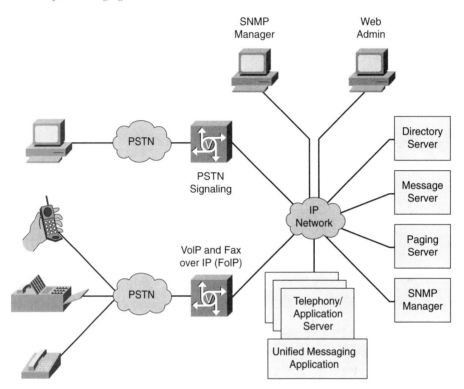

3DES (Triple Data Encryption Standard). A stronger form of the Data Encryption Standard (DES), 3DES follows a pattern of encryption/decryption/encryption. 3DES has many different variations.

AAL1 (ATM adaptation layer 1). One of four AALs recommended by the ITU-T. AAL1 is used for connection-oriented, delay-sensitive services requiring constant bit rates, such as uncompressed video and other isochronous traffic.

ABR (available bit rate). A QoS class defined by the ATM Forum for ATM networks. ABR is used for connections that do not require timing relationships between source and destination. ABR provides no guarantees in terms of cell loss or delay, providing only best-effort service. Traffic sources adjust their transmission rate in response to information they receive describing the status of the network and its capability to successfully deliver data.

ad-hoc conference. A conference call feature where a conference is started by an initiator and only the initiator of the conference can add people into the conference.

ADPCM (adaptive differential pulse code modulation). A waveform process by which analog voice samples are encoded into digital signals.

AF (assured forwarding). A means of providing different levels of forwarding assurances for IP packets. This method is used by providers who offer differentiated services to their customers.

AIM (advanced integration module). A module in some Cisco routers that provides enhanced processing capabilities to the routers.

AMI (alternate mark inversion). A line-code modulation type used on T1 and E1 circuits. In AMI, marks (or 1s) cause a pulse in alternating positive and negative directions, while 0s never pulse. Two pulses of the same polarity are not allowed. AMI requires that the sending device maintain ones density. Ones density is not maintained independently of the data stream. Sometimes called *binary coded alternate mark inversion.*

ANI (automatic number identification). An SS7 feature in which a series of digits, either analog or digital, are included in the call, identifying the telephone number of the calling device. In other words, ANI identifies the number of the calling party. See also CLID.

ANSI (American National Standards Institute). A voluntary organization composed of corporate, government, and other members that coordinates standards-related activities, approves U.S. national standards, and develops positions for the United States in international standards organizations. ANSI helps develop international and U.S. standards relating to, among other things, communications and networking. ANSI is a member of the International Electrotechnical Commission (IEC) and the International Organization for Standardization (ISO).

APC (adaptive predictive coding). A narrowband analog-to-digital conversion technique employing a one-level or multilevel sampling system in which the value of the signal at each sample time is adaptively predicted to be a linear function of the past values of the quantized signals. APC is related to LPC in that both use adaptive predictors. However, APC uses fewer prediction coefficients, thus requiring a higher bit rate than LPC.

API (application programming interface). The means by which an application program talks to communications software. Standardized APIs allow application programs to be developed independently of the underlying method of communication. An API is a set of standard software interrupts, calls, and data formats that computer application programs use to initiate contact with other devices (for example, network services, mainframe communications programs, or other program-to-program communications devices). Typically, APIs make it easier for software developers to create the links that an application needs to communicate with the operating system or with the network.

AR (access rate). A Frame Relay term that addresses the maximum transmission rate supported by the access link into the network and the port speed of the device (switch or router) at the edge of the carrier network. The AR defines the maximum rate for data transmission or receipt. See also CIR.

ARPA (Advanced Research Projects Agency). A research and development organization that is part of the Department of Defense (DoD). ARPA is responsible for numerous technological advances in communications and networking. It evolved into the Defense Advanced Research Projects Agency (DARPA), and then back into ARPA again (in 1994).

ARQ (admission request). An RAS (Registration, Admission, and Status) admission message defined as an attempt by an endpoint to initiate a call.

AS5300. A series of Cisco gateways that provide reliable, scalable, and feature-rich data and voice gateway functionality. The Cisco AS5300 Series Universal Gateways include the Cisco AS5300 Access Server/Voice Gateway and the Cisco AS5350 Universal Gateway.

ATM (Asynchronous Transfer Mode). The international standard for cell relay in which multiple service types (such as voice, video, or data) are conveyed in fixed-length (53-byte) cells. Fixed-length cells allow cell processing to occur in hardware, thereby reducing transit delays. ATM is designed to take advantage of high-speed transmission media, such as E3, SONET, and T3.

B8ZS (binary 8-zero substitution). A line-code modulation type used on T1 circuits. In B8ZS, marks (that is, binary ones) cause a pulse in alternating positive and negative directions, while zeros never pulse. Two pulses of the same polarity are not allowed, except when inserting a code to represent eight zeros. B8ZS maintains ones density by inserting a special code in place of eight consecutive zeros. The special code contains intentional violations of the bipolar pattern.

BC (basic call). A call between two users that does not require Advanced Intelligent Network Release 1 features (for example, a POTS call).

Bc (committed burst). A negotiated tariff metric in Frame Relay internetworks. The maximum amount of data (in bits) that a Frame Relay internetwork is committed to transmit in a timing interval. See also Be and CIR.

Be (excess burst). A negotiated tariff metric in Frame Relay internetworks. The number of bits that a Frame Relay internetwork attempts to transmit after Bc is accommodated. Be data, in general, is delivered with a lower probability than Bc data because Be data can be marked as discard eligible (DE) by the network. See also Bc.

BHCA (busy hour call attempts). A traffic engineering term that refers to the number of call attempts made during the busiest hour of the day.

BLF (busy lampfield). A visual display of the status of all or some of your phones. Your BLF tells you if a phone is busy or on hold. A BLF is typically attached to or part of an operator phone.

BOC (Bell operating company). BOC is a term for any of the 22 original companies (or their successors) that were created when AT&T was broken up in 1983 and given the right to provide local telephone service in a given geographic area. The companies previously existed as subsidiaries of AT&T and were called the "Bell System."

BRQ (bandwidth change request). A RAS bandwidth control message sent from endpoint to gatekeeper requesting an increase or decrease in call bandwidth.

BVM (BRI voice module). An optional device for Cisco modular routers providing ISDN BRI ports for connection to ISDN PBXs or PINXs.

call agent. The central repository of call routing information in an MGCP-based centralized call processing environment.

CAS (channel associated signaling). The transmission of signaling information in association with the voice channel. In T1 networks, CAS signaling is often referred to as *robbed-bit signaling* because the network is robbing framing bits for signaling purposes.

CBR (constant bit rate). QoS class defined by the ATM Forum for ATM networks. CBR is used for connections that depend on precise clocking to ensure undistorted delivery.

CBWFQ (class-based weighted fair queuing). A congestion management mechanism that extends the standard WFQ functionality to provide support for user-defined traffic classes.

CCIS (common channel interoffice signaling). A technology that uses a common link to carry signaling information for a number of trunks. CCIS is similar to the ITU-T SS6 protocol that operated at low bit rates (that is, 2.4, 4.8, and 9.6 kbps) and transmitted messages that were only 28 bits in length.

CCITT (Consultative Committee for International Telegraph and Telephone). The former name for the international organization responsible for the development of communications standards. It is now called the ITU-T. See also ITU-T.

CCS (common channel signaling). A signaling system used in telephone networks that utilizes a statistical multiplexing protocol for signaling. A specified channel is exclusively designated to carry signaling information for all channels in the system. An example is ISDN or SS7. See also SS7.

CDVT (cell delay variation tolerance). In ATM, a QoS parameter for managing traffic that is specified when a connection is set up. In CBR transmissions, CDVT determines the level of jitter that is tolerable for the data samples taken by the peak cell rate (PCR). See also CBR.

CELP (code excited linear prediction). A compression algorithm used in low bit-rate voice encoding. CELP is used in ITU-T Recommendations G.728, G.729, G.723.1.

centum call seconds. Units used to measure traffic load. A centum call second is 1/36th of an Erlang and its formula is the number of calls per hour multiplied by their average duration in seconds, all divided by 100.

CES (circuit emulation service). A service that enables users to multiplex or to concentrate multiple circuit emulation streams for voice and video with packet data on a single high-speed ATM link without a separate ATM access multiplexer.

CID (channel ID). A value that designates the Frame Relay subchannel ID for Voice over Frame Relay.

CIR (committed information rate). The rate at which a Frame Relay network agrees to transfer information under normal conditions, averaged over a minimum increment of time. CIR, measured in bits per second, is one of the key negotiated tariff metrics. See also Bc.

Cisco AVVID (Cisco Architecture for Voice, Video and Integrated Data).
Cisco AVVID includes three components: infrastructure, such as switches and routers; clients, such as IP phones, H.323 videoconferencing equipment, and PCs; and applications, such as call control, that use a common IP network.

Cisco ICM software (Cisco Intelligent Call Management software). Software that delivers an integrated suite of contact center capabilities. Cisco ICM software provides intelligent queue management in a contact center environment. It enables improved queue management across a variety of ACD (automatic call Distribution) systems from different vendors and integrates IVR (interactive voice response) systems, database and desktop applications, and CTI (computer telephony integration) solutions.

Cisco IOS software. Cisco software that provides common functionality, scalability, and security for many Cisco platforms. Cisco IOS software allows centralized, integrated, and automated installation and management of internetworks while ensuring support for a wide variety of protocols, media, services, and platforms.

Cisco IP phone. The Cisco family of IP phones provides a complete range of intelligent communication systems that use the data network while providing the convenience and ease of use of a business telephone.

Cisco IP SoftPhone. A Windows-based application for the PC. Used as a stand-alone end station or in conjunction with a Cisco IP phone, Cisco IP SoftPhone provides mobility, directory integration, user interface, and a virtual conference room.

Cisco IPCC (Cisco IP Contact Center). An integrated suite of products that enables contact center agents using Cisco IP phones to receive both TDM and VoIP calls. IPCC provides ACD (automatic call distribution) and IVR (interactive voice response) capabilities in a single-vendor IP suite. The IPCC can be implemented in a single-site environment or integrated into an enterprise-wide multisite contact center.

Cisco Unified CallManager. A software-based call-processing agent. It is a component of the Cisco IP telephony solution, part of Cisco AVVID. The software extends enterprise telephony features and functions to IP telephony network devices such as IP phones, media processing devices, VoIP gateways, and multimedia applications.

CLEC (competitive local exchange carrier). A company that builds and operates communication networks in metropolitan areas and provides its customers with an alternative to the local telephone company.

CLI (command-line interface). An interface that allows the user to interact with the operating system by entering commands and optional arguments.

CLID (calling line ID). Information about the billing telephone number from which a call originated. The CLID value might be the entire telephone number, the area code, or the area code plus the local exchange. CLID is also known as *Caller ID*.

CNG (comfort noise generation). While using VAD, the emulation of background noise from the source side by the DSP at the destination to prevent the perception that a call is disconnected.

CO (central office). The local telephone company office to which all local loops in a given area connect and in which circuit switching of subscriber lines occurs.

committed burst. See Bc.

CPE (customer premises equipment). Terminating equipment, such as terminals, telephones, and modems, installed at customer sites and connected to the telephone company's network.

CRC (cyclic redundancy check). An error-checking technique in which the frame recipient calculates a remainder by dividing frame contents by a prime binary divisor and compares the calculated remainder to a value stored in the frame by the sending node.

cross-connect. A connection scheme between cabling runs, subsystems, and equipment, using patch cords or jumpers that attach to connecting hardware on each end. Cross-connection is the attachment of one wire to another, usually by anchoring each wire to a connecting block and then placing a third wire between them so that an electrical connection is made.

cRTP (Compressed Real-Time Transport Protocol). A type of header compression designed to reduce the IP/UDP/RTP headers to two bytes for most packets in the case where no UDP checksums are being sent, or four bytes with UDP checksums.

CS-ACELP (conjugate structure algebraic code excited linear prediction). A CELP voice compression algorithm providing 8 kbps, or 8:1 compression, standardized in ITU-T Recommendations G.729 and G.729A.

CTI (computer telephony integration). The name given to the merger of traditional telecommunications (PBX) equipment with computers and computer applications. The use of caller ID to retrieve customer information automatically from a database is an example of a CTI application.

DACS (digital access and crossconnect system). A digital cross-connect system that provides switching and aggregation.

dB (decibel). A unit for measuring relative power ratios in terms of gain or loss. The rule of thumb to remember is that 10 dB indicates an increase (or a loss) by a factor of 10; 20 dB indicates an increase (or a loss) by a factor of 100; 30 dB indicates an increase (or a loss) by a factor of 1000.

DCD (data carrier detect). A signal from the DCE (for example, a modem or printer) to the DTE (typically a PC), indicating that the modem is receiving a carrier signal from the DCE (modem) at the other end of the telephone circuit.

DCE (data communications equipment - EIA expansion) (data circuit-terminating equipment - ITU-T expansion). Devices and connections of a communications network that comprise the network end of the user-to-network interface. The DCE provides a physical connection to the network, forwards traffic, and typically provides a clocking signal used to synchronize data transmission between DCE and DTE devices. Modems and interface cards are examples of DCE.

DDS (digital data service). A class of service offered by telecommunications companies to transport data rather than voice. DDS was originally called *Dataphone Digital Service* by AT&T in the late 1970s.

DE bits (discard eligible bits). Bits that are used to tag Frame Relay frames eligible to be discarded if the network becomes congested.

delay budget. The maximum amount of delay in data, voice, and video applications. The total end-to-end delay when engineering a VoIP implementation should not exceed the 150 ms to 200 ms delay budget.

delay dial. A signaling method in which the terminating side remains off hook until it is ready to receive address information. The off-hook interval is the delay dial signal.

DHCP (Dynamic Host Configuration Protocol). A protocol that provides a mechanism for allocating IP addresses dynamically so that they can be reused when hosts no longer need them.

dial plan mapper. Technology that provides the mapping of IP addresses to telephone numbers. After enough digits are accumulated to match a configured destination pattern, the dial plan mapper maps the IP host to a telephone number.

dial-up. Modem access to a data network. The use of a dial or push-button telephone to create a telephone or data call. Dial-up calls are usually billed by time of day, duration of call, and distance traveled. Dial-up is a connection to the Internet, or any network, where a modem and a standard telephone are used to make a connection between computers.

dial-up remote access server. Computer hardware that resides on a corporate LAN and into which employees dial on the PSTN to get access to their e-mail, software, and data on the corporate LAN (for example, status on customer orders). Remote access servers are also used by commercial service providers, such as ISPs, to allow their customers access into their networks. Remote access servers are typically measured by how many simultaneous dial-in users (on analog or digital lines) they can handle and whether they can work with cheaper digital circuits, such as T1 and E1 connections.

Digital T1/E1 Packet Voice Trunk Network Module. A flexible and scalable T1/E1 voice solution for Cisco 2600 and 3600 Series Modular Access routers that supports up to 60 voice channels in a single network module.

Digital T1/E1 Voice Port Adapter. A single-width port adapter that incorporates one or two universal ports configurable for either T1 or E1 connection with high-performance DSP support for up to 24 to 120 channels of compressed voice.

DLCI (data-link connection identifier). A value that specifies a PVC (permanent virtual circuit) or an SVC (switched virtual circuit) in a Frame Relay network. In the basic Frame Relay specification, DLCIs are locally significant. (Connected devices might use different values to specify the same connection at different ends of the network.)

DNIS (dialed number identification service). A feature of trunk lines where the called number is identified. This called number information is used to route the call to the appropriate service. DNIS is a service used with toll-free dedicated services whereby calls placed to specific toll-free numbers are routed to the appropriate area within the company.

DP (dial pulse). A means of signaling that consists of regular momentary interruptions of a current at the sending end in which the number of interruptions corresponds to the value of the digit or character—in short, the old style of rotary dialing. For example, dial the number 5, and you will hear five clicks.

DPNSS (Digital Private Network Signaling System). A common-channel, message-oriented signaling protocol commonly used by PBXs.

drop and insert. A function that allows DS-0 channels from one T1 or E1 facility to be cross-connected digitally to DS-0 channels on another T1 or E1. By using this method, channel traffic is sent between a PBX and a CO PSTN switch or other telephony device so that some PBX channels are directed for long-distance service through the PSTN while the router compresses others for interoffice VoIP calls. In addition, drop and insert can cross-connect a telephony switch (from the CO or PSTN) to a channel bank for external analog connectivity. Also called *TDM cross-connect.* See also DACS.

DRQ (disengage request). An RAS message sent by the gateway to the gatekeeper during the process of a call. The gateway waits for the DCF message before it sends the setup message to the new destination gatekeeper.

DS0 (digital service level zero). A single timeslot on a DS1 (also known as *T1*) digital-interface (that is, 64 kbps), synchronous, full-duplex data channel, typically used for a single voice connection on a PBX. It can also be a single timeslot on an E1.

DSI (digital speech interpolation). An algorithm that analyzes voice channels for silence. It suppresses the voice bits to conserve packet-line bandwidth and inserts a code to indicate to the far end that these bits have been removed. Also referred to as VAD (voice activity detection).

DSL (digital subscriber line). A public network technology that delivers high bandwidth over conventional copper wiring at limited distances. Because most DSL technologies do not use the whole bandwidth of the twisted pair, there is room remaining for a voice channel.

DSP (digital signal processor). An electronic circuit that compresses voice signals, generates tones, and decodes received compressions. DSPs can also emulate modems for purposes of fax relay.

DTE (data terminal equipment). A device at the user end of a user-network interface that serves as a data source, a destination, or both. DTE connects to a data network through a DCE device (for example, a modem) and typically uses clocking signals generated by the DCE. DTE includes such devices as computers, protocol translators, and multiplexers.

DTMF (dual-tone multifrequency). Tones generated when a button is pressed on a telephone to convey address signaling.

DTR (data terminal ready). An EIA/TIA-232 circuit that is activated to let the DCE know when the DTE is powered up and not in test mode.

E1. A wide-area digital transmission scheme used throughout the world that carries data at a rate of 2.048 Mbps. E1 lines can be leased for private use from common carriers.

E&M (ear and mouth, Earth and Magneto, recEive and transMit). A trunking arrangement generally used for two-way switch-to-switch or switch-to-network connections. Cisco's analog E&M interface is an 8-pin modular connector that allows connections to PBX trunk lines (tie-lines). E&M also is emulated on E1 and T1 digital interfaces.

ECMA (European Computer Manufacturers Association). A group of European computer vendors that have done substantial OSI standardization work.

E-lead. The wiring arrangement on an E&M circuit in which the signal side sends its signaling information.

ESF (Extended Superframe). A framing type used on T1 circuits that consists of 24 frames, 193 bits each, with the 193rd bit providing framing information. ESF is an enhanced version of SF. See also SF.

ETSI (European Telecommunication Standards Institute). A nonprofit organization that produces voluntary telecommunications standards used throughout Europe.

excess burst. See Be.

FDM (frequency-division multiplexing). A technique whereby information from multiple channels can be allocated bandwidth on a single wire based on frequency. An example is DSL.

FIFO (first-in/first-out). A buffering scheme where the first byte of data entering the buffer is the first byte retrieved by the CPU. In telephony, FIFO refers to a queuing scheme where the first calls received are the first calls processed.

flash memory. A special type of EEPROM (electrically erasable programmable read-only memory) that can be erased and reprogrammed in blocks instead of one byte at a time. Many modern PCs have their BIOS (basic input/output system) stored on a flash memory chip so that it can be updated easily if necessary. Such a BIOS is sometimes called a flash BIOS. Flash memory is also popular in modems because it enables the modem manufacturer to support new protocols as they become standardized.

four-wire. One of two distinct types of audio interfaces (two-wire and four-wire). The four-wire implementation provides separate paths for receiving and sending audio signals, consisting of T, R, T1, and R1 leads.

frame forwarding. A mechanism by which frame-based traffic, such as HDLC and SDLC, traverses an ATM network.

FRTS (Frame Relay traffic shaping). A queuing method that uses queues on a Frame Relay network to limit surges that can cause congestion. Data is buffered and sent into the network in regulated amounts to ensure that the traffic can fit within the promised traffic envelope for the particular connection.

FXO (Foreign Exchange Office). An interface that connects to the PSTN central office. Cisco's FXO interface is an RJ-11 connector that allows an analog connection at the PSTN's central office or to a station interface on a PBX.

FXS (Foreign Exchange Station). An FXS interface connects directly to a standard telephone and supplies ring, voltage, and dial tone. Cisco's FXS interface is an RJ-11 connector that allows connections to basic telephone service equipment, key sets, and PBXs.

gatekeeper. In telecommunications, an H.323 entity on a LAN that provides address translation and control access to the LAN for H.323 terminals and gateways. The gatekeeper can provide other services to the H.323 terminals and gateways, such as bandwidth management and locating gateways. It maintains a registry of devices in the multimedia network. The devices register with the gatekeeper at startup and request admission for a call from the gatekeeper.

gateway. An H.323 term that describes the component of a H.323 telephony network that translates between one technology and another, typically between a traditional telephony network and an IP network.

generic traffic shaping. A way of shaping traffic by reducing outbound traffic flow to avoid congestion by constraining traffic to a particular bit rate using the token bucket mechanism.

GRQ (gatekeeper discovery request). An RAS gatekeeper discovery message sent from endpoint to gatekeeper.

HDB3 (high-density binary 3). A line coding method used to maintain synchronization by ensuring a sufficient number of binary ones. HDB3 is used on E1 circuits.

HDLC (High-Level Data Link Control). A bit-oriented synchronous data-link-layer protocol developed by the International Organization for Standardization (ISO). See also SDLC.

hoot and holler. A broadcast audio network used extensively by the brokerage industry for market updates and trading. Similar networks are used in publishing, transportation, power plants, and manufacturing.

HSRP (Hot Standby Router Protocol). A protocol that provides high network availability and transparent network topology changes. HSRP creates a hot standby router group with a lead router that services all packets sent to the hot standby address. Other routers in the group monitor the active router, and if it fails, one of the standby routers inherits the lead position and the hot standby group address.

HTTP (Hypertext Transfer Protocol). The protocol used by web browsers and web servers to transfer files, such as text and graphic files.

HyperTerminal software. Terminal emulation software.

IETF (Internet Engineering Task Force). A task force consisting of over 80 working groups responsible for developing Internet standards.

ILEC (incumbent local exchange carrier). A telephone company in the United States that was providing local service when the Telecommunications Act of 1996 was enacted. ILECs include the former Bell operating companies (BOCs), which were grouped into holding companies known collectively as the regional Bell operating companies (RBOCs) when the Bell System was broken up by a 1983 consent decree.

IMAP (Internet Message Access Protocol). A method of accessing e-mail or bulletin board messages kept on a mail server that can be shared. IMAP permits client e-mail applications to access remote message stores as if they were local without actually transferring the message.

IMT (Inter-Machine Trunk). A means for giving service providers access to more favorable tariffs and rates. In SS7 environments, IMTs terminate bearer traffic on the voice gateways.

IN (intelligent network). A network that provides IP routing, QoS, network access and control, and network management services.

IP (Internet Protocol). A network layer protocol in the TCP/IP stack offering a connectionless internetwork service. IP provides features for addressing, type-of-service specification, fragmentation and reassembly, and security. Defined in RFC 791.

IP cloud. The area in which data travels through an IP network. It is illustrated in diagrams as a cloud.

IP precedence. A 3-bit value in an IP version 4 type of service (ToS) byte used to assign priority to IP packets.

ISDN (Integrated Services Digital Network). Communication architecture offered by telephone companies that permits customers to access digital networks to carry data, voice, and other source traffic.

ISUP (ISDN User Part). An SS7 protocol layer that defines the protocol used to prepare, manage, and release trunks that carry voice and data between calling and called parties under the auspice of ISDN.

ITU (International Telecommunication Union). An organization established by the United Nations to set international telecommunications standards and to allocate frequencies for specific uses.

ITU-T (International Telecommunication Union Telecommunication Standardization Sector). An international body that develops worldwide standards for telecommunications technologies. The ITU-T carries out the functions of the former CCITT. See also CCITT.

IVR (interactive voice response). A term used to describe systems that provide information in the form of recorded messages over telephone lines in response to user input in the form of spoken words, or, more commonly, DTMF signaling. Examples include banks that allow you to check your balance from any telephone and automated stock quote systems.

IXC (inter-exchange carrier). A common carrier providing long-distance connectivity between local access and transport areas (LATAs). The three major IXCs are AT&T, MCI, and Sprint, but several hundred IXCs offer long-distance service in the United States.

JTAPI (Java Telephony Application Programming Interface). A Java API for call control developed by Sun Microsystems.

LDAP (Lightweight Directory Access Protocol). A protocol that provides read/write interactive access to X.500 directories for uniform application security and access levels.

LDCELP (low-celay CELP). A CELP voice compression algorithm requiring 16 kbps of bandwidth (that is, 4:1 compression). Standardized in ITU-T Recommendation G.728.

LEC (local exchange carrier). A public telephone company in the United States that provides local service. Some of the largest LECs are the Bell operating companies (BOCs), which were grouped into holding companies known collectively as the regional Bell operating companies (RBOCs) when the Bell System was broken up by a 1983 consent decree. In addition to the Bell companies, there are a number of independent LECs, such as Alltel. LEC companies are also sometimes referred to as *telcos*. A local exchange is the local "central office" of a LEC. Lines from homes and businesses terminate at a local exchange. Local exchanges connect to other local exchanges within a local access and transport area (LATA) or to inter-exchange carriers (IXCs) such as long-distance carriers AT&T, MCI, and Sprint.

LFI (Link Fragmentation and Interleaving). A Cisco IOS feature that reduces delay on slower-speed links by breaking up large datagrams and interleaving delay-sensitive traffic packets, with the smaller packets resulting from the fragmented datagram.

line code. An electrical modulation scheme used by digital carrier systems. In North America, T1 uses AMI or B8ZS line coding. In other countries, E1 uses AMI or HDB3 line coding.

LLQ (low latency queuing). A queuing scheme that enables use of a single priority queue in conjunction with CBWFQ. The priority queue typically carries VoIP traffic, while other traffic is carried in the user-defined queues of CBWFQ.

LPC (linear predictive coding). Voice coding that uses a special algorithm that models the way human speech works. Because LPC can take advantage of an understanding of the speech process, it can be efficient without sacrificing voice quality.

LRQ (location request). An RAS location request message sent from one gatekeeper to another gatekeeper to request contact information for one or more E.164 addresses.

LSB (least significant bit). The bit of a binary expression having the least value.

MC (multipoint controller). A required part of an MCU. The MC is the conference controller. It handles negotiation between all terminals to determine common capabilities and controls conference resources such as multicasting. The MC does not deal directly with any of the media streams.

MCS (Media Convergence Server). An integral component of the Cisco IP Communications system. A high availability server platform for Cisco AVVID.

MCU (multipoint control unit). A component that manages videoconferences of three or more participants.

MDF (main distribution frame). The point where all network-related external services, IP equipment, and wiring converge within a building.

meet-me conference. A conference feature where everyone who dials the same meet-me number will join the conference.

MEL CAS (Mercury Exchange Limited Channel Associated Signaling). A voice signaling protocol used primarily in the United Kingdom.

MGCP (Media Gateway Control Protocol). A protocol that helps bridge the gap between circuit-switched and IP networks. A combination of IPDC (Internet Protocol Device Control) and SGCP (Simple Gateway Control Protocol), MGCP allows external control and management of data communications devices, or "media gateways" at the edge of multiservice IP networks.

MICA (Modem ISDN Channel Aggregation). A modem module and card used in the Cisco AS5300 universal access servers. A MICA modem provides an interface between an incoming or outgoing digital call and an ISDN telephone line. The call does not have to be converted to analog as it does with a conventional modem and an analog telephone line. Each line can accommodate, or aggregate, up to 24 (T1) or 30 (E1) calls.

Microsoft NetMeeting. A complete H.323 desktop Internet multimedia solution for all Windows users with multipoint data conferencing, text chat, whiteboard, and file transfer, as well as point-to-point audio and video.

M-lead. The wiring arrangement on an E&M circuit in which the trunking side sends its signaling information.

MLP (Multilink Point-to-Point Protocol). A method of splitting, recombining, and sequencing datagrams across one or more data links under the PPP protocol.

MOS (Mean Opinion Score). A common benchmark used to determine the perceived quality of sound produced by specific CODECs.

MP (multipoint processor). The part of an MCU that processes the media streams. It receives audio, video, or data bits from the endpoints for which it does the required mixing, switching, and other processing before distributing the stream to the videoconference participants.

MTP (media termination point). A device that allows the Cisco Unified CallManager or hardware containing digital signal processors to extend supplementary services, such as hold and transfer, to calls routed through an H.323 endpoint or an H.323 gateway.

multicast backbone (MBONE). The multicast backbone of the Internet. The MBONE is a virtual multicast network composed of multicast LANs and the point-to-point tunnels that interconnect them.

NSAP (network service access point). A network address, as specified by ISO. An NSAP is the point at which OSI network service is made available to a transport layer (Layer 4) entity.

ODBC (Open DataBase Connectivity). A specification that abstracts data using applications from database management systems. It is the standard API for accessing data in both relational and nonrelational database management systems. Using this API, common database applications can be written to access data stored in a variety of database management systems on a variety of computers regardless of the DBMS or programming interface.

off hook. A call condition, also known as *busy,* in which transmission facilities are already in use.

OMAP (operations, maintenance, administration, and provisioning). A set of services that provides telephony operation functions including monitoring and discovery of problems before they negatively impact service. The telephony maintenance function is similar to the data networking processes of fault isolation and correction. Administration deals with billing, department cross-charges, accounting, and capacity management. The final element, provisioning, is used to define services for individual subscribers.

on hook. A condition that exists when a receiver or a handset is resting on the switch hook or is not in use.

OOS (out-of-service). A state of the call or trunk.

OPX (Off-Premises eXtension). A telephone line from a telephone system that is terminated in a different building than the one in which the telephone system resides.

OSI (Open System Interconnection). An international standardization program created by ISO and ITU-T to develop standards for data networking that facilitate multivendor equipment interoperability.

PAM (pulse amplitude modulation). A modulation scheme where samples of a waveform are represented as amplitudes of a higher-frequency waveform, known as the *carrier frequency.*

PBX (private branch exchange). Digital or analog telephone switches located on the customer premises and used to connect private and public telephone networks.

PCI (protocol control information). Control information added to user data to construct an OSI packet. It is the OSI equivalent of the term *header.*

PCM (pulse code modulation). The technique of encoding analog voice into a 64 kbps data stream by sampling with 8-bit resolution at a rate of 8000 samples per second.

PCMCIA (Personal Computer Memory Card Industry Association). A standard interface that connects a device to a portable computer.

PINX (private integrated services network exchange). A PBX or key system, in which a BRI voice application uses QSIG (Q Signaling).

PLAR (private line, automatic ringdown). A voice circuit that connects two single endpoints together. When a telephone handset is taken off hook, the remote telephone automatically rings.

PLAR-OPX (PLAR Off-Premises eXtension). A PLAR Off-Premises eXtension connection. Using this option, the local voice port provides a local response before the remote voice port receives an answer. On FXO interfaces, the voice port will not answer until the remote side answers.

PLL (phase-lock loop). A circuit on a T1 or E1 module that provides clocking information.

POP (point of presence). In an OSS (Operations Support System), a physical location where an inter-exchange carrier installed equipment to interconnect with a LEC.

POTS (plain old telephone service). Basic telephone service supplying standard single-line telephones, telephone lines, and access to the PSTN. See also PSTN.

PQ (priority queuing). A queuing scheme that ensures "important" traffic gets the fastest handling at each point where it is used. Priority queuing was designed to give strict priority to important traffic. PQ is a legacy queuing method, which is typically replaced by LLQ in modern configurations.

PSQM (Perceptual Speech Quality Measurement). A technique used for measuring voice quality. It compares the received audio with the transmitted audio.

PSTN (public switched telephone network). A general term referring to the variety of telephone networks and services in place worldwide.

PTT (Post, Telephone, and Telegraph). A government agency that provides telephone services. PTTs exist in most areas outside North America and provide both local and long-distance telephone services.

PVC (permanent virtual circuit). A virtual circuit that is permanently established. PVCs save bandwidth associated with circuit establishment and teardown in situations where certain virtual circuits must exist all the time. In ATM terminology, a PVC is called a *permanent virtual connection.*

PVDM (packet voice digital signal processor module). A product that provides the ability to increase the voice processing capabilities within a single network module.

QoS (quality of service). A set of tools used in networking devices to ensure best-of-class transmission quality and service availability.

QSIG (Q Signaling). An inter-PBX signaling protocol for networking PBX supplementary services in a multivendor or single-vendor environment.

RAS (Registration, Admission, and Status). A protocol used between endpoints and the gatekeeper to perform management functions. The RAS signaling function performs registration, admissions, bandwidth changes, status, and disengage procedures between the VoIP gateway and the gatekeeper.

RBOCs (regional Bell operating companies). Seven regional telephone companies formed by the breakup of AT&T. RBOCs differ from regional Bell holding companies (RBHCs) in that RBOCs do not cross boundaries that were set out by the consent decree.

RBS (robbed-bit signaling). A technique by which a single bit in every DS0 bearer channel is "stolen" from every sixth frame. The stolen bit is then used to carry signaling information.

redirect server. A server that accepts a SIP request, maps the address into zero or more new addresses, and returns these addresses to the client. A redirect server does not initiate its own SIP request nor does it accept calls.

RFC (Request For Comments). A document series generated by the IETF and used as the primary means for communicating information about the Internet. Some RFCs are designated by the Internet Architecture Board (IAB) as Internet standards. Most RFCs document protocol specifications, such as Telnet and FTP, but some are humorous or historical. RFCs are available online from numerous sources.

RISC (reduced instruction set computing). A microprocessor design that provides fewer and simpler instructions burned into the silicon than other processors. Fewer instructions let a processor perform at a higher speed. The difference is made up by requiring more work to be done by compilers and greater memory usage.

round-robin. An algorithm used to schedule processes in a fixed cyclic order. Simply put, it means to "take turns."

RQNT (request notification). An RAS message that instructs a gateway to watch for specific events.

RRQ (registration request). An RAS message sent as a registration request.

RSVP (Resource Reservation Protocol). A protocol that supports the reservation of resources across an IP network. Applications running on IP end systems can use RSVP to indicate to other nodes the nature (for example, bandwidth, jitter, and maximum burst) of the packet streams they want to receive. It is also known as the *Resource Reservation Setup Protocol.*

RTCP (RTP Control Protocol). A protocol that monitors the QoS of an IP RTP connection and conveys information about the ongoing session.

RTP (Real-Time Transport Protocol). A protocol commonly used with IP networks. RTP is designed to provide end-to-end network transport functions for applications transmitting real-time data (for example, audio, video, or simulation data over multicast or unicast network services). RTP provides such services as payload type identification, sequence numbering, time stamping, and delivery monitoring to real-time applications.

RTSP (Real Time Streaming Protocol). A protocol that enables the controlled delivery of real-time data, such as audio and video. Sources of data can include both live data feeds (such as live audio and video) and stored content (such as prerecorded events). RTSP is designed to work with established protocols, such as RTP and HTTP.

SAP (Session Announcement Protocol). A protocol used to assist in the advertisement of multicast multimedia conferences and other multicast sessions, and to communicate relevant session setup information to prospective participants.

SCCP (Skinny Client Control Protocol). The Cisco standard for real-time calls and conferencing over IP.

SCP (service control point). An element of an SS7-based intelligent network that performs various service functions, such as number translation and call setup and teardown.

SDLC (Synchronous Data Link Control). An IBM Systems Network Architecture (SNA) data-link-layer communications protocol. SDLC is a bit-oriented, full-duplex serial protocol that has spawned numerous similar protocols, including HDLC. See also HDLC.

SDP (Session Description Protocol). A protocol used to describe multimedia sessions in order to enable session announcement, session invitation, and other forms of multimedia session initiation.

SF (Super Frame). A framing type used on T1 circuits. SF consists of 12 frames of 193 bits each, with the 193rd bit providing frame synchronization. SF is superseded by ESF but is still widely used. It is also called D4 framing. See also ESF.

signal ground. The common electrical reference point of a circuit.

SIMM (single in-line memory module). A small circuit board that holds a number of memory chips.

SIP (session initiation protocol). A protocol developed by the IETF MMUSIC Working Group as an alternative to H.323. SIP features are compliant with IETF RFC 2543, published in March 1999. SIP equips platforms to signal the setup of voice and multimedia calls over IP networks.

SLA (service-level agreement). An agreement between the ISP and the client that guarantees a certain level of data transmission over the network.

SMDS (Switched Multimegabit Data Service). A high-speed, packet-switched, datagram-based WAN networking technology offered by telephone companies.

SMTP (Simple Mail Transfer Protocol). The standard Internet protocol providing e-mail services.

SNR (signal-to-noise ratio). A measure of transmission quality. The ratio of good or usable data (signal) to bad or undesired data (noise) on a line, expressed in decibels (dB).

SOHO (small office/home office). Networking solutions and access technologies for offices that are not directly connected to large corporate networks.

spanning-tree. A loop-free subset of a network topology.

SQL (Structured Query Language). An international standard language for defining and accessing relational databases.

SRST (Survivable Remote Site Telephony). A feature on some Cisco routers that uses the Skinny protocol (SCCP) to provide call-handling support for the local IP phones if the WAN connection to the Cisco Unified Communications CallManager fails.

SS7 (Signaling System 7). A standard CCS system used with BISDN and ISDN. Developed by Bellcore. See also CCS.

SSP (service switching point). An element of an SS7-based intelligent network that performs call origination, termination, and tandem switching.

STP (signal transfer point). An element of an SS7-based intelligent network that performs routing of SS7 signaling.

STUN (serial tunnel). A router feature allowing two SDLC-compliant or HDLC-compliant devices to connect to one another through an arbitrary multiprotocol topology (using Cisco routers) rather than through a direct serial link.

SVC (switched virtual circuit). A virtual circuit that is dynamically established on demand and is torn down when transmission is complete. SVCs are used in situations where data transmission is sporadic.

T1. The standard digital multiplexed 24-channel voice/data digital span line. T1 is used predominantly in North America. It operates at a data rate of 1.544 Mbps. T1 is a digital WAN carrier facility. T1 transmits DS-1 formatted data through the telephone-switching network using AMI or B8ZS coding. See also AMI and B8ZS.

tabletop phone. A conference telephone used on a conference room table.

TAPI (Telephony Application Programming Interface). A call control model developed by Microsoft and Intel.

TCAP (transaction capabilities application part). An SS7 protocol layer that helps exchange noncircuit-related data between applications.

T-CCS (Transparent Common Channel Signaling). A feature that allows the connection of two PBXs with digital interfaces that use a proprietary or unsupported CCS protocol without the need for interpretation of CCS signaling for call processing. T1/E1 traffic is transported transparently through the data network, and the feature preserves proprietary signaling. From the PBX standpoint, this is accomplished through a point-to-point connection. Calls from the PBXs are not routed but follow a preconfigured route to the destination.

TDM (time-division multiplexing). A technique in which information from multiple channels can be allocated bandwidth on a single wire based on preassigned timeslots. Bandwidth is allocated to each channel regardless of whether the station has data to transmit.

time-stamp. A field in certain FastPacket formats that indicates the amount of time the packet has spent waiting in queues during the transmission between its source and destination nodes. It is used to control the delay experienced by the packet.

two-wire. One of two distinct types of audio interfaces (two-wire and four-wire). With the two-wire implementation, full-duplex audio signals are transmitted over a single pair, which consists of tip (T) and ring (R) leads.

U interface. The ISDN interface between the telco and the user, also known as the local loop.

UAC (user agent client). A client application that initiates the SIP request.

UAS (user agent server). A server application that contacts the user when a SIP request is received and then returns a response on behalf of the user. The response accepts, rejects, or redirects the request.

UDP (User Datagram Protocol). A connectionless transport layer protocol in the TCP/IP protocol stack. UDP is a simple protocol that exchanges datagrams without acknowledgments or guaranteed delivery, requiring that error processing and retransmission be handled by other protocols. UDP is defined in RFC 768.

V card. An electronic business card. V cards carry information such as names, telephone numbers, mail addresses, e-mail addresses, and URLs.

VAD (voice activity detection). A feature used to statistically save bandwidth by not sending packets in the absence of speech. When enabled on a voice port or a dial peer, silence is not transmitted over the network, only audible speech. When VAD is enabled, the sound quality is slightly degraded but the connection uses much less bandwidth.

VBR (variable bit rate). A QoS class defined by the ATM Forum for ATM networks. VBR is subdivided into an RT class and an NRT class.

VBR-NRT (variable bit rate-nonreal time). A subclass of VBR used for connections in which there is no fixed timing relationship between samples but which still need a guaranteed QoS.

VBR-RT (variable bit rate-real time). A subclass of VBR. Used for connections in which there is a fixed timing relationship between samples.

VIC (voice interface card). A Cisco interface card used to connect the system to either the PSTN or to a PBX. See also PBX and PSTN.

videoconference. A meeting between people in different locations, using audio and video. The simplest type of videoconference can involve transmission of static images between two locations. The most complex videoconferences can use full-motion video and high-quality audio between multiple locations.

VoATM (Voice over ATM). A technology that enables a router to carry voice traffic (for example, telephone calls and faxes) over an ATM network. When sending voice traffic over ATM, the voice traffic is encapsulated using a special AAL5 encapsulation for multiplexed voice. VoATM dial peers point to local PVCs, as compared to remote IP addresses used by VoIP dial peers.

VoD (video on demand). A system using video compression to supply video programs to viewers when requested via ISDN or cable.

VoFR (Voice over Frame Relay). A technology that enables a router to carry voice traffic (for example, telephone calls and faxes) over a Frame Relay network. When sending voice traffic over Frame Relay, the voice traffic is segmented and encapsulated for transit across the Frame Relay network. VoFR dial peers point to local DLCIs, as compared to remote IP addresses used by VoIP dial peers.

VoIP (Voice over IP). The capability to carry normal telephony-style voice over an IP-based internetwork with POTS-like functionality, reliability, and voice quality. VoIP enables a router to carry voice traffic (for example, telephone calls and faxes) over an IP network. In VoIP, DSPs segment the voice signal into frames, which are then coupled in groups of two and stored in voice packets. These voice packets are transported using a variety of signaling protocols.

VoIPovFR (VoIP over Frame Relay). The capability to provide VoIP application interworking over an existing Frame Relay network. VoIPovFR can be used over point-to-point leased lines or over a Frame Relay circuit. It does not require a full-fledged Frame Relay network or service.

VPN (virtual private network). Technology that enables IP traffic to travel securely over a public TCP/IP network by encrypting all traffic from one network to another. A VPN can use a "tunneling" protocol to encrypt all information at the IP level.

WFQ (weighted fair queuing). A congestion management algorithm that identifies conversations (in the form of traffic streams), separates packets that belong to each conversation, and ensures that capacity is shared fairly between these individual conversations. WFQ is an automatic way of stabilizing network behavior during congestion and results in increased performance and reduced retransmission.

WIC (WAN interface card). A Cisco interface card that connects a system to a WAN link service provider.

wink-start. A method of E&M signaling. When the signaling leads indicate a change to an off-hook state, the other side must send a momentary wink (on-hook to off-hook to on-hook transition) on the correct signaling lead before the call signaling information can be sent by the sending side. After the call signaling information is received, the side that sent the wink goes off hook again when the subscriber answers and stays that way for the duration of the call.

Numerics

A

B

C

T

W-X-Y-Z

CISCO SYSTEMS

Cisco Press

3 STEPS TO LEARNING

STEP 1　　　　　**STEP 2**　　　　　**STEP 3**

First-Step　　　　　**Fundamentals**　　　　　**Networking Technology Guides**

STEP 1　**First-Step**—Benefit from easy-to-grasp explanations. No experience required!

STEP 2　**Fundamentals**—Understand the purpose, application, and management of technology.

STEP 3　**Networking Technology Guides**—Gain the knowledge to master the challenge of the network.

NETWORK BUSINESS SERIES

The Network Business series helps professionals tackle the business issues surrounding the network. Whether you are a seasoned IT professional or a business manager with minimal technical expertise, this series will help you understand the business case for technologies.

Justify Your Network Investment.

Look for Cisco Press titles at your favorite bookseller today.

Visit **www.ciscopress.com/series** for details on each of these book series.

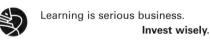

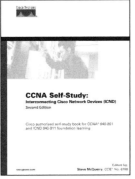
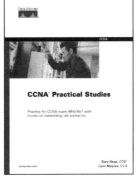

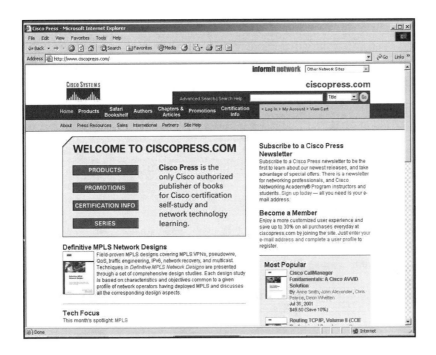

SEARCH THOUSANDS OF BOOKS FROM LEADING PUBLISHERS

Safari® Bookshelf is a searchable electronic reference library for IT professionals that features more than 2,000 titles from technical publishers, including Cisco Press.

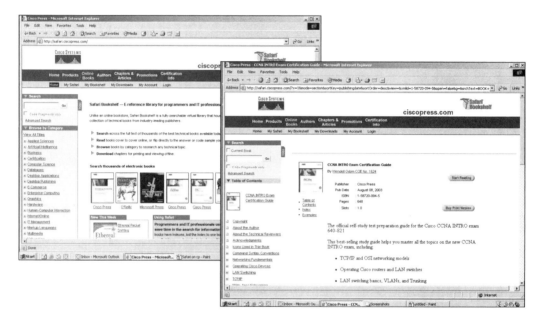

With Safari Bookshelf you can

- **Search** the full text of thousands of technical books, including more than 70 Cisco Press titles from authors such as Wendell Odom, Jeff Doyle, Bill Parkhurst, Sam Halabi, and Karl Solie.

- **Read** the books on My Bookshelf from cover to cover, or just flip to the information you need.

- **Browse** books by category to research any technical topic.

- **Download** chapters for printing and viewing offline.

With a customized library, you'll have access to your books when and where you need them—and all you need is a user name and password.

TRY SAFARI BOOKSHELF FREE FOR 14 DAYS!

You can sign up to get a 10-slot Bookshelf free for the first 14 days.
Visit **http://safari.ciscopress.com** to register.